FORTRAN 77
LANGUAGE AND STYLE

FORTRAN 77

LANGUAGE AND STYLE
A Structured Guide to Fortran 77

MICHAEL J. MERCHANT

Wadsworth Publishing Company
Belmont, California

A Division of Wadsworth, Inc.

Computer Science Editor: Jon Thompson
Editorial production services: Cobb/Dunlop Publisher
Services, Inc.

Printed in the United States of America

       7 8 9 10   85 84 83

ISBN 0-534-00920-4

Library of Congress Cataloging in Publication Data

Merchant, Michael J.
  FORTRAN 77: language and style.

  Includes index.
  1. FORTRAN (Computer program language) 2. Structured
programming. I. Title.
QA76.73.F25M463   001.64'24   80-39551
ISBN 0-534-00920-4

ABOUT THE ART

The publisher acknowledges with great appreciation the generosity of the persons and institutions named below for providing the computer-generated images that appear at the beginning of each chapter and on the cover of this book. In addition to their visual appeal, these images illustrate an important application of FORTRAN, the original high-level, scientific language.

The images that precede Chapters 1 and 7 are the result of computer graphics research into the problem of depicting three-dimensional objects. The "ball of yarn" image was produced in part by "random walk" commands. Reprinted by permission of Ken Knowlton, Bell Laboratories.

Chapters 2, 8, and 9, as well as the text's cover, are illustrated by simulation experiments involving stress, contour, and other factors. These studies were conducted at the University of Utah, and the graphics are reprinted by permission of Hank Christiansen, Brigham Young University.

Three images were produced with the aid of a massive graphics program running on one of the largest computer installations in the world. The dual magnets (Chapter 3) and the nose cone impact simulation (Chapter 10) are reprinted by permission of Bruce Brown, and the portion of the DNA molecule (Chapter 4) is reprinted by permission of Nelson Max, Lawrence Livermore National Laboratory.

The illustration of pawns on a chessboard (Chapter 6) is one example of many synthetically generated images of complex scenes produced at the University of Utah under a research contract with DARPA, and it is reprinted by permission of Martin Newell, Xerox Palo Alto Research Center.

"L Space," the work opening Chapter 5, is an artistic exercise in balancing random parameters and control parameters created at Syracuse University. It is reprinted by permission of Judson Rosebush, Digital Effects Incorporated.

PREFACE

This book was written with two questions in mind: What is the best way to teach the new FORTRAN language, and what is the best way to teach structured programming using FORTRAN?

In answering the first question, choices about the selection of topics and the order of presentation often were dictated by features of the 1968 FORTRAN language standard. Character data, for example, has been placed on an equal footing with numerical data and has been covered early in the text. The addition of a CHAR-ACTER data type not only extends the capability of the language, but also makes it easier to teach, since it opens a broad range of applications to the student which illustrate important programming concepts without requiring advanced mathematics. The addition of list-directed input and output allows students to write programs without having to master the rather complicated technical details of FORMAT statements.

Teaching structured programming with FORTRAN was difficult before the new standard because the language lacked the necessary control statements. The addition of the IF-THEN-ELSE structure has made it possible to teach students to write clearly structured programs.

Throughout the book, programming language concepts are integrated with concepts of programming style. Style modules in each chapter give practical advice on how to write a program and how to apply the FORTRAN language. Top-down design and structured programming are continually emphasized.

In the firm belief that programming is a subject best learned by practice, Chapters 1 and 2 are organized to get the student running programs right from the start. In Chapter 1, students see a complete program developed from top-down design to finished code. Chapter 2 guides students through the details of running the program on a computer.

The entire text can be covered in a one-semester introduction to programming with FORTRAN. Students who are already familiar with another programming language could omit Chapters 1 and 2, or cover them rapidly. By omitting the sections labeled as optional, Chapters 1 through 7 can serve as a short course in FORTRAN or as a supplement to a course in introductory data processing.

Although the responsibility for any deficiencies in this text is my own, I would like to express my sincere thanks to the many people who read the manuscript and made valuable suggestions for its improvement: John H. Crenshaw, Western Kentucky University; Henry A. Etlinger, Rochester Institute of Technology; Krzysztof Frankowski, University of Minnesota; Robert Frye, Central Michigan University; Kenneth Geller, Drexel University; Mark Luker, University of Minnesota—Duluth; Franz Oppacher, Concordia University; and Frank G. Walters, University of Missouri—Rolla.

Michael Merchant

CONTENTS

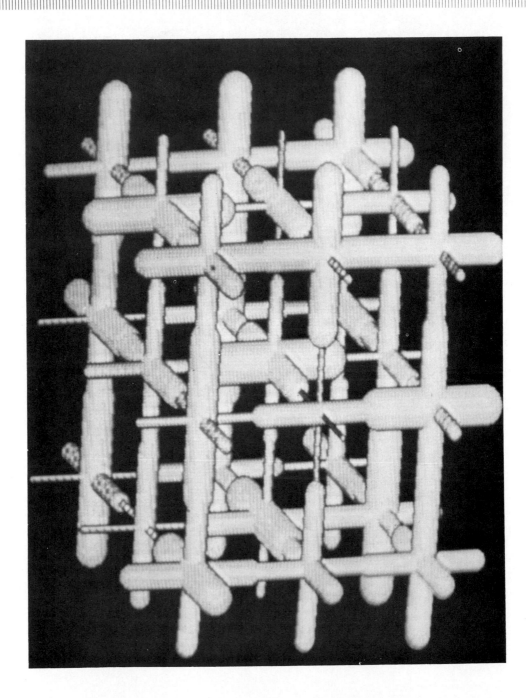

COMPUTERS, ALGORITHMS, AND PROGRAM DESIGN

INTRODUCTION   In science fiction novels, in movies, and in cartoons, computers are often represented as being much like superintelligent human beings. In such works of fiction, computers converse fluently in the English language, exercise independent judgment in solving problems, and are able to retrieve from their memory banks all pertinent data for any problem at a moment's notice. It is an exciting dream. And one of the exciting aspects of studying computing is that the dream may someday come true—perhaps within your lifetime.

But the day of the genuinely intelligent computer is still in the future. The computers of today are incredibly fast, and they can follow extremely complex sets of instructions, but they are just machines—in some ways, rather simple machines at that. All a computer can really do is to follow very simple orders which have been carefully thought out by a programmer and written in a programming language like FORTRAN.

In this book you will learn two things. The first thing is how to solve problems with a computer—that is, how to make up instructions to the computer to get your job done. Specifically, you will learn to design and write an **algorithm**, which is a procedure that a computer can carry out.

In this chapter we explain what an algorithm is, how you can represent an algorithm by a kind of diagram called a **flowchart**, and how you can use the method of **top-down design** to invent an algorithm.

After you design an algorithm to solve your problem, you must express the algorithm in a language that the computer can understand. A **computer program** is an algorithm written in a programming language like FORTRAN. So the second thing you will learn, which goes hand in hand with the first, is how to write a FORTRAN program.

1

Chapter 1 will give you an introduction to the FORTRAN language. In Chapter 2, you will see how to run a FORTRAN program on the computer.

ALGORITHMS

People are often imprecise when giving instructions to each other. A simple instruction such as "Go to the store for a loaf of bread." requires hundreds of decisions to carry out: Should you go out the front door or the back? Should you turn left or right? Which way is the store? Where is the bread? Do you want whole-wheat, sourdough, or carraway rye? People, having intelligence and reasoning ability, can figure out the real meaning of general, ambiguous instructions. Computers, on the other hand, have no common sense. When you write a procedure for a computer to carry out, every instruction must be explicit.

Suppose you want to solve a math problem using a calculator. You do not have a calculator, but you have a friend who does, so you call her on the phone to ask for help. She is not at home, but her young brother, who knows very little math, offers to work the calculator if you will tell him exactly what to do. Now you must specify how to solve your problem using instructions that are so precise and unambiguous that he cannot possibly misinterpret them. You might say, "Enter the number 56.2, press the plus key, enter the number 475.3, press the plus key, enter the number 11.63, press the equals key, and read me the number in lights at the top." This is an *algorithm*, expressed in English.

An **algorithm*** is a step-by-step procedure for solving a problem. A correct algorithm must meet three conditions:

1. Each step in the algorithm must be an instruction that can be carried out.
2. The order of the steps must be precisely determined.
3. The algorithm must eventually terminate.

An algorithm does not necessarily have to be written for a computer. You could carry out the instructions with a paper and pencil, for example. A cookbook might give an "algorithm" for baking chocolate chip cookies. The instruction "Bake until done." might be meaningful for a human cook, so it satisfies the first condition for an algorithm.

It would be convenient if you could just tell a computer "Solve the following problem . . ." and make the machine obey. A computer, however, has an **instruction set** consisting of only a hundred or so basic commands that it can carry out electronically. These commands are similar to the commands you can give to a calculator by pressing the keys. For example, you can tell a computer to add two numbers. The first condition for a correct algorithm means that when writing an algorithm for a computer, each step must be something that a computer can carry out by executing these basic instructions.

In carrying out the instructions in an algorithm, the machine performs one

---

*The word *algorithm* comes from the name of the Persian mathematician al-Khowarizmi (c. 825).

instruction at a time. The second condition for a correct algorithm means that the algorithm must precisely specify the order in which the instructions are performed.

The third condition means that an algorithm must not go on forever. The following procedure, then, is *not* an algorithm.

Procedure to Count
Step 1   Let N equal zero.
Step 2   Add 1 to N.
Step 3   Go to Step 2.

If you tried to have a computer carry out this procedure, the machine would, in theory, run forever. The following procedure, on the other hand, *is* an algorithm, because it will eventually terminate.

Algorithm to Count to One Million
Step 1   Let N equal zero.
Step 2   Add 1 to N.
Step 3   If N is less than 1,000,000, then go to Step 2; otherwise, halt.

TOP-DOWN DESIGN

When working on an algorithm for a simple problem, a solution may suddenly occur to you after just thinking about the problem for a while. Practical computer applications, however, are seldom so simple. Professional programmers commonly write programs consisting of thousands of computer instructions. Designing such a program can be as complicated as designing a machine with thousands of parts. In order for it to work, all the pieces must fit together in an organized framework.

Top-down design is an approach to the problem of designing an algorithm. It is a method you can use to organize your work and also to organize your algorithm.

In some ways, designing an algorithm is similar to writing an essay. When writing an essay, you begin with a general idea of what you want to say. You then proceed to organize your thoughts and choose words to convey your meaning to the reader. When designing an algorithm, you begin with a general idea of what you want it to do. You must then organize your ideas and choose the right sequence of instructions to the computer that make it carry out the desired actions. But in programming, as in writing, it is often difficult to know where to begin.

A good way to begin writing an essay is to make an outline. First, you set forth the main topics to be covered, as in the following example:

Gettysburg Speech
  I. Conception of the nation
 II. The current civil war
III. Our purpose here today
IV. Our resolve for the future

This bare outline provides a framework for the essay, into which all the paragraphs and sentences will fit. The overall structure is determined, and what remains is to elaborate the topics in more detail. You can do that by adding subheadings under each topic, as in the following example:

Gettysburg Speech
   I. Conception of the nation
      A. The nation was founded 87 years ago.
      B. It was conceived in liberty.
      C. It was dedicated to the proposition that all men (persons?) are created equal.
  II. The current civil war
      A. We are now engaged in civil war.
      B. The war tests the ability of this nation, as conceived by its founders, to endure.
 III. Our purpose here today
      A. We are meeting on a battlefield of the civil war.
      B. We dedicate a portion of this field as a cemetery.
      C. The soldiers who fought here have consecrated this ground with their brave struggle.
 IV. Our resolve for the future
      A. We must dedicate ourselves to the unfinished work before us.
      B. We must devote ourselves to the cause for which the dead have fought.
      C. We must preserve the ideals of freedom in which the nation was conceived.

Of course, even with the best of outlines to work from, one cannot hope always to emulate Lincoln's deathless prose; but good writing is always well organized, and making an outline is a very useful way to begin.

In programming, as in writing, good organization is vital. Before beginning to fill in the details, it is best to have a clear overall plan. The method of top-down design is like making an outline of an algorithm. The first step is to formulate a general plan—like writing the main topics in an outline. Next, you fill in more detail, like making subheads in an outline, to specify how to carry out each major step. By successively refining this plan, adding more detail at each stage in the development, you arrive at your ultimate goal: a precise algorithm that can be expressed in terms of the basic types of instructions that a computer can follow.

As an illustration, suppose you want to write an algorithm (we'll call it Algorithm X), to solve some homework problem for your algebra class. As you begin, you have a rough idea of what the algorithm should do, but little idea of the specific instructions. At this point, you conceive of Algorithm X as a single entity (Figure 1.1).

As you think about the problem some more, you realize that there are really three parts to the solution, and you say to yourself, "If I could do Part 1, and then Part 2, and Part 3, that would solve the problem." This is your **top-level design**, as shown in Figure 1.2.

FIGURE 1.1

As you begin to write an algorithm you conceive of it as a single entry.

FIGURE 1.2

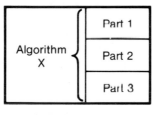

In the method of top-down design, you first specify the general organization of the algorithm.

You may not have a detailed algorithm yet, but you have made some progress; instead of one big problem, you have three smaller ones to solve. Continuing your analysis, you might find that Part 1 can be broken down into two subproblems—Part 1A and Part 1B—and that Parts 2 and 3 can be similarly subdivided. This is your second-level design, as shown in Figure 1.3. If the algorithm is complicated, you may need to carry this process to yet another level of refinement. Eventually, you arrive at a detailed plan that you can write in computer language.

In summary, the basic principle of top-down design is this:

> Concentrate first on the overall design of the algorithm. Write it as a sequence of general steps to be carried out. Then, using the same method, fill in the details for each step.

An important principle in top-down design is **validation**, which means analyzing your algorithm to make sure that it is correct. Even though your first draft of an algorithm may be an outline, it must be a valid solution to the problem you are trying to solve. The question you should ask yourself is this: If you could carry out each step in your proposed algorithm, would that really solve the problem? Thus, a second principle of top-down design is this:

> At each stage of the top-down design process, validate your algorithm by analyzing it for correctness. Do not expand on the details until you are sure that the overall plan is sound.

FIGURE 1.3

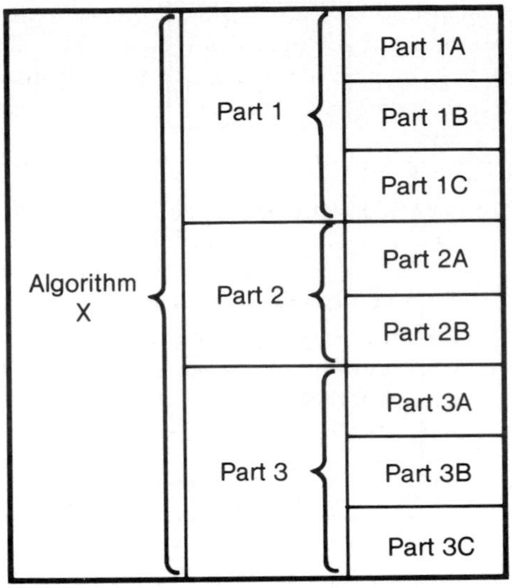

You refine the top-level design by adding more detail.

EXAMPLE 1.1 Averaging Numbers

Suppose you were given the task of finding the average of the numbers 5.2, 11.35, 4.0, 6.7, and 5.9. How would you do it? Using a calculator, you would probably enter the first number, add the second number to it, add the third number to the sum, add the fourth number to that sum, then add the fifth number. Mentally observing that there are five numbers, you would divide by 5 to find the average. What you would really be doing is carrying out the steps in a familiar *algorithm* for averaging numbers.

Now suppose you want to write a general algorithm that could be used to instruct a computer to find the average of a set of numbers and print out the result. To begin very simply, there are two main steps in the algorithm.

Algorithm for Averaging Numbers (Version 1)
 I. Compute the average.
 II. Print the average.

This is your top-level design.

To fill in more detail, you need to describe the procedure to compute the average as you would do it with a calculator. Here is a revised version.

Algorithm for Averaging Numbers (Version 2)
 I. Compute the average.
   A. Read each number. As you go through the list, compute the sum of the numbers and count them.
   B. Compute the average, using the sum and the count from Step IA.
 II. Print the average.

This is your second-level design.

Next you should validate the algorithm to check your work. You should ask yourself: Is it really possible to carry out Step IA? Is it really possible to carry out Step IB? Do these two steps together really compute the average required in Step II? Theoretically, you can use this type of reasoning to construct a mathematical proof that an algorithm is correct. For most practical purposes it is sufficient to go through an informal mental proof to convince yourself that you haven't made any mistakes.

In validating Step IB, there is one small "catch" to consider. To compute the average you must divide the sum of the numbers by the count. What would happen if the count were zero? Dividing a number by zero is mathematically undefined, and will cause problems if you try to do it on a computer. If you were averaging numbers with a calculator, the question would not arise, since you, as a human, have the common sense not to divide by zero. When writing an algorithm for a computer, however, it is wise to consider exceptional cases, like carrying out the algorithm with no input data. Such exceptional cases are called **boundary conditions**. With a little extra effort, you can design algorithms that work even for the boundary conditions. This practice will simplify the job of checking the algorithm on a computer, as you will soon appreciate when you begin running your own programs.

You can now refine the algorithm to fill in the details of the computation.

Algorithm for Averaging Numbers (Version 3)
I. Compute the average.
   A. Count the numbers and find their sum.
      1. Let SUM and COUNT be zero.
      2. For each number to be averaged, do the following.
         a. Read the number.
         b. Add its value to SUM.
         c. Add 1 to COUNT.
   B. Compute the average.
      1. If COUNT is not zero, then
         a. Let AVERAGE equal SUM divided by COUNT.
           Otherwise,
         b. Let AVERAGE equal zero.
II. Print the value of AVERAGE.

This is a complete algorithm which gives enough detail to tell you exactly how to carry out the computation. As before, you should validate this algorithm to convince yourself that Steps IA1 and IA2 really do count the numbers and find their sum and that Step IB really does compute the average (and that it computes an average of zero for the exceptional case when COUNT is zero).

This algorithm illustrates several common programming techniques. The words COUNT, SUM, and AVERAGE are **variables** which represent numbers used in the computation. In programming, as in algebra, you use variables to stand for numbers whose specific values are not known.

Step IA1 says to start with SUM and COUNT equal to zero. This practice is called **initializing** the variables—that is, giving them an initial value. This is somewhat like pressing the CLEAR key on a calculator before starting a new computation.

Step IA2 is an example of a **loop**, a procedure that is repeated over and over. Each execution of the instructions in this step is called an **iteration** of the loop (to *iterate* means to do again). The loop is controlled by a **condition**. In this case the condition is whether or not there are any more numbers to be averaged. When the condition is false, after all the numbers have been read, the algorithm **breaks out** or **exits** the loop and proceeds to Step IB.

The variable COUNT is used to count the number of values read. Any variable used in this way is called a **counter**. The process of adding 1 to COUNT is called **incrementing** the counter. The algorithm increments the counter on each iteration of the loop.

Step IB1 in the algorithm is a **conditional instruction** (often called an **if-then-else instruction**) which says to carry out either Step IB1a or IB1b depending on the *condition* "COUNT is not equal to zero."

STRUCTURED FLOWCHARTS

A **flowchart** is an easy-to-read diagram of an algorithm. You write each step inside a box and assemble the boxes to show the order in which the instructions are to be carried out. The kind of flowcharts in this book are called **structured flowcharts**.* These flowcharts facilitate the technique of structured programming explained in Chapter 4.

You diagram a simple instruction, like initializing a variable, inside a rectangular box (Figure 1.4).

FIGURE 1.4

(A simple instruction can be written inside a box.)

To indicate a loop in an algorithm, you use an L-shaped box that surrounds the instructions in the loop (Figure 1.5). The condition in the outer box is the condition that controls the loop. This indicates that the instructions in the loop are to be performed while the condition is true. You can test the condition either at the beginning of the loop [Figure 1.5(a)] or at the end [Figure 1.5(b)]. For example, Step IA2 of the algorithm for averaging numbers is a loop which you can diagram as in Figure 1.6.

To indicate a conditional instruction you use a triangular shape (Figure 1.7). If the condition in the triangle is true, the algorithm carries out the instructions underneath the word "then." If the condition is false, the algorithm carries out the instruction underneath the word "else." For example, Step IB1 of the algorithm for averaging numbers can be diagrammed as in Figure 1.8.

Thus, you can represent the entire algorithm to average numbers by the structured flowchart in Figure 1.9.

---

*Also called Nassi-Schneiderman diagrams, they are based on a method invented by I. Nassi and B. Schneiderman [ACM SIGPLAN Notices, Vol. 8, No. 8, August 1973].

FIGURE 1.5
TWO WAYS OF SHOWING A LOOP

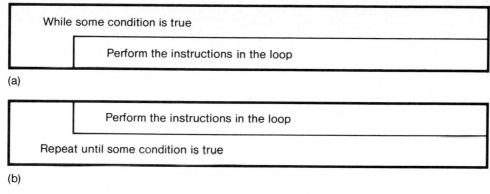

(a)

(b)

In (a) the condition is tested at the beginning of the loop, while in (b) the condition is tested at the end.

FIGURE 1.6

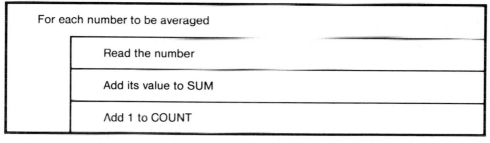

FIGURE 1.7

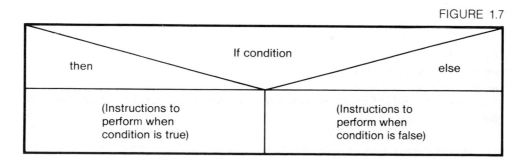

FIGURE 1.8

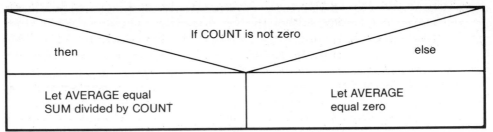

FIGURE 1.9

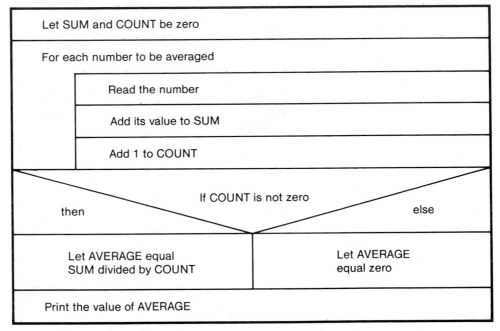

THE FORTRAN LANGUAGE

Inventing an algorithm is the first step in solving a problem with a computer. You can write the algorithm in outline form,* as on page 7, or you can diagram the algorithm with a structured flowchart. The principles of top-down design apply in either case.

The next step is to write a program. A **program** is an algorithm written in a

---

*Another name for this "outline form" is **pseudocode**—so called because it resembles a real "code" (that is, a FORTRAN program) but is not a complete program.

computer language. In this book, you will learn the FORTRAN language.* Compared to ordinary English, FORTRAN is a simple language. The vocabulary consists of only a few dozen words (plus any variable names you make up yourself), and you can get by if you know fewer than a dozen types of sentences. The sentences in FORTRAN are called **statements**. A program consists of a series of statements, each one written on a separate line.

Though FORTRAN is simple, it is precise. If you write an English sentence that is grammatically incorrect, the chances are that your reader will understand you anyway. Not so in FORTRAN. Every statement has a certain required form. Leave out a comma where one is required in FORTRAN and the computer will fail to recognize the statement or else will misinterpret it.

Because FORTRAN is precise and unambiguous, the computer can read your program, translate it into commands in its instruction set, and carry out the steps in your algorithm. In fact, the name FORTRAN stands for FORmula TRANslation. What we now call "statements" were originally called "formulas." Thus, FORTRAN is a language for translating the statements in your program into instructions that the machine can carry out.

The following sections introduce some basic concepts of FORTRAN and some simple FORTRAN statements so that you can begin running programs right away. For the moment, we will skip over many details. Just as you first learned English by listening to people speak, you can learn something about FORTRAN by seeing some complete programs. We will cover the exact rules in later chapters.

WHAT COMPUTERS DO

To understand the instructions that make up a FORTRAN program, you need a basic knowledge of what a computer is and what it does.

Figure 1.10 is a simplified block diagram of a typical computer system. It is called a *system* since it consists of several components. The **central processor** is the actual computer. This is the machine that carries out the instructions in your program. The **memory unit** is where instructions and data are stored. The other components are **peripheral devices** used for input and output.

The computer, although very fast, is really a very simple machine. There are only four basic types of instructions that it can carry out:

1. storing and recalling from memory
2. computation
3. input and output
4. program control

All programs, no matter how complex, are made up of instructions of these types, along with declarative statements that help the computer interpret the instructions.

---

*To be specific, you will learn FORTRAN 77 (see the Preface).

FIGURE 1.10
A SCHEMATIC DIAGRAM OF A COMPUTER SYSTEM

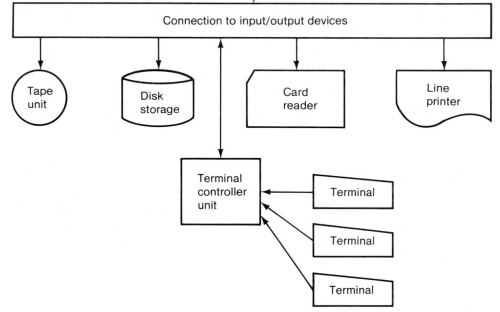

Storing and Recalling from Memory

A computer memory is nothing like a human memory. It is just a device for storing data electronically. Many hand calculators have a memory key that lets you save a number in the calculator. For instance, in a constant percentage problem, you might store a percent figure in memory. Each time you need to use the figure, you can recall it from memory rather than reenter it on the keyboard. This is exactly how a computer memory works. The difference is that instead of a single number, the computer memory can store thousands of numbers.

Each memory location has a unique **address**, a number used to distinguish it from other memory locations. Think of computer memory as a sequence of mailboxes with a different address on each one as in Figure 1.11. Each mailbox can contain one item of data. A program instruction might say, "Store the number 5.2 in address 1001." Later in the same program, an instruction might say, "Recall the contents of address 1001."

FIGURE 1.11

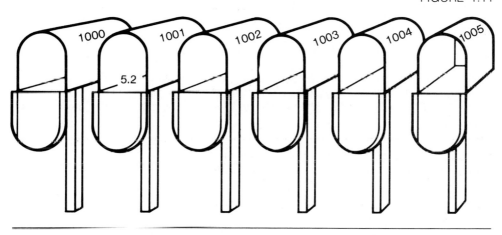

Think of computer memory as a sequence of mailboxes, each with its own address. The instruction "Store 5.2 at address 1001" stores the data 5.2 as the contents of mailbox number 1001.

The actual structure of memory varies slightly among different computers, but you can assume that memory locations are numbered consecutively, and that each location can contain one number or symbol. We often represent memory locations by boxes, as in Figure 1.12. The numbers 1001, 1002, . . . are the addresses, and the numbers inside the boxes are the contents of the memory. Thus, the contents of address 1003 is the number 762.333.

FIGURE 1.12

1001	11
1002	0
1003	762.333
1004	2
1005	0.666667

Each memory location stores a value. The addresses distinguish different memory locations from one another.

In the FORTRAN language, you don't use the actual addresses to refer to memory locations; you use **variables** instead. As in algebra, you can denote a variable by a letter such as *X* or *Y*. In FORTRAN a variable name can be a word such as WEIGHT or TAX. To be exact, a FORTRAN variable name consists of one to six letters and digits and must begin with a letter. You can use variables in FORTRAN in much the same way as you use them in algebra, but there is a difference which you should remember:

A FORTRAN variable is just a name for a memory location.

Figure 1.13 depicts a portion of computer memory assigned to five variables: A, B, X, COUNT, and SUM. The **value** of a variable is the number stored in the memory location that the variable represents. Thus in Figure 1.13, the value of the variable X is 0.666667, and the value of SUM is 704.2. To use the mailbox analogy again, a variable is a name for a box, and the value of the variable is the number inside the box.

The FORTRAN instruction to store a value in a variable is the **assignment statement**. An assignment statement looks like an algebraic equation, but the meaning is slightly different. You write a variable to the *left* of an equal sign, and you write a number (or an expression) to the *right* of the equal sign. For example:

COUNT = 0

This statement tells the computer to store the value 0 in the variable COUNT.

When you assign a value to a variable, the previous value is destroyed. The new value remains in the variable until you replace it with another.

FIGURE 1.13

A	11
B	0
X	762.333
COUNT	2
SUM	0.666667

You generally use variables, instead of addresses, to refer to memory locations. The *value* of a variable is the contents of the memory location.

Values are recalled from memory when they are used on the right of an equal sign. The FORTRAN statement

    X = A

means to fetch the value of the variable A and store it in the variable X. The value of A is unchanged.

Here are four FORTRAN assignment statements that could be part of a program.

    A = 1.2
    B = 3.0
    A = B
    B = A

If these four instructions were carried out in order, what do you think the result would be? At first glance, you might think that they set A equal to 3.0 and B equal to 1.2; but that is not the case. They set *both* A and B equal to 3.0, because the instruction

    A = B

destroys the previous value of A (Figure 1.14). To interchange the value of two variables, you would need a third variable for temporary storage, as in the following instructions.

    A = 1.2
    B = 3.0
    C = A
    A = B
    B = C

The effect of these five statements is shown in Figure 1.15.

As you will see, FORTRAN has several kinds of variables. You use **integer variables** to store integer numbers and **real variables** to store real numbers (numbers that are not necessarily whole numbers). You can specify the types of the variables in your program with **type declaration statements** at the beginning of the program. If a program is going to use an integer variable COUNT and three real variables VALUE, SUM, and AVERAG, the program can begin with the statements

    INTEGER COUNT
    REAL VALUE, SUM, AVERAG

Computation

Computers can perform arithmetic with numbers stored in memory. Like a calculator, a computer has electronic circuits that perform the operations of addition, multiplication, and so forth.

In FORTRAN, you can specify computation with an assignment statement, like the ones you just saw. Instead of writing a number or a variable to the right of the equal sign, you write an **expression**. For example, the statement

X = A + B

means to fetch the values of the variables A and B from memory, add them, and store the result as the new value of the variable X. The **expression** A + B indicates the desired computation.

Addition and subtraction are indicated by plus (+) and minus (−), as usual. In FORTRAN, you use an asterisk (∗) to indicate multiplication and a slash (/) to indicate division. Thus, the instruction "Let X equal 2 times TOTAL" is written as

X = 2 ∗ TOTAL

FIGURE 1.14

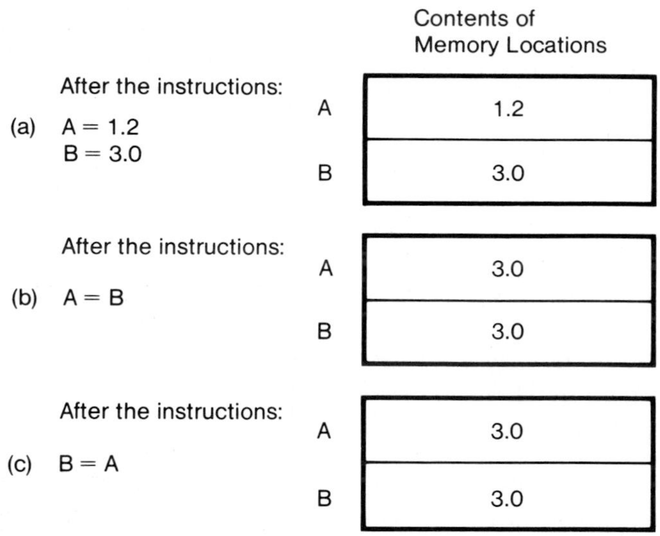

Contents of
Memory Locations

After the instructions:

(a)   A = 1.2
       B = 3.0

A	1.2
B	3.0

After the instructions:

(b)   A = B

A	3.0
B	3.0

After the instructions:

(c)   B = A

A	3.0
B	3.0

Assigning a value to a memory location destroys the previous value. Thus, the instructions:

A = B
B = A

do *not* interchange the values of A and B, because the instruction

A = B

destroys the previous value of A. To interchange the values of A and B, an additional variable is needed (see Figure 1.15).

The instruction "Let Y equal 1 divided by X + 1" is written

$$Y = 1/(X + 1)$$

You can use parentheses to group terms in FORTRAN expressions, just as in algebra.
    In the algorithm for averaging numbers, one of the instructions said "Add 1 to COUNT." The corresponding FORTRAN statement is

$$COUNT = COUNT + 1$$

FIGURE 1.15

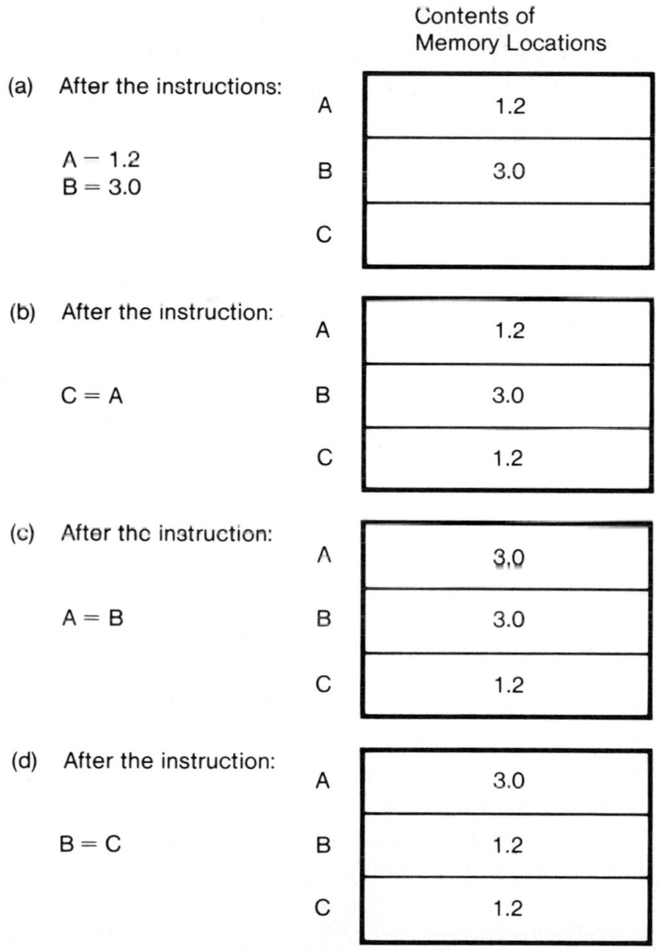

Contents of
Memory Locations

(a) After the instructions:

        A $-$ 1.2
        B = 3.0

A	1.2
B	3.0
C	

(b) After the instruction:

        C = A

A	1.2
B	3.0
C	1.2

(c) After the instruction:

        A = B

A	3.0
B	3.0
C	1.2

(d) After the instruction:

        B = C

A	3.0
B	1.2
C	1.2

Three assignment statements are needed to interchange the values of A and B. The extra variable, C is needed to temporarily store the old value of A.

This statement emphasizes the difference between FORTRAN and algebra. As an algebraic equation, this is nonsense. But an assignment statement is not an equation to be solved; it is an instruction that tells the computer to do something.

Table 1.1 gives some further examples.

TABLE 1.1
THE ASSIGNMENT STATEMENT

Form

variable = expression

where *variable* is a variable name (which can be a letter or a word of six or fewer characters), and *expression* is made up of numbers, variables, and mathematical operations

Meaning

Compute the value of the expression and store the result in the variable

Examples	
A = 0	Store the value zero in the variable A
A = 1.2 − R	Subtract the value of R from 1.2 and store the result in the variable A
SUM = A + B	Add the values of A and B and store the result in the variable SUM
TWICE = 2 * AMOUNT	Multiply AMOUNT by 2 and store the result in TWICE
CHANGE = 100 * A/(B − A)	Multiply 100 by the value of A, divide by the value of B − A, and store the result in the variable CHANGE
TOTAL = TOTAL + 1	Add 1 to TOTAL and store the result in the variable TOTAL

Input and Output

You can also instruct a computer to read in data. Data to be read by a program is called **input data**, or simply **input**. To tell the machine to read, you use an **input instruction** in your program.

On a hand calculator, you enter numbers by pressing the keys. On a computer system, you might use punch cards instead. You first type the data on a keypunch machine, which has a typewriter-like keyboard. The keypunch is not part of the computer itself, but the punch cards it produces are put in the computer's **card reader**. An input instruction in your program tells the card reader to read a punch card.

When you want your program to write out results, you use an **output instruction**. For instance, you can instruct the machine to print results on a **line printer**. Data written by a program is called **output**.

You will probably use only the card reader and line printer at first, but several other devices are used for input and output. Each has advantages that make it suitable for certain applications. A **computer terminal** has a keyboard that you can use to enter data directly without using punch cards. Some terminals have a cathode-ray tube (CRT) display similar to a television screen. Instead of printing results on paper, you can have your program write on the CRT screen. **Magnetic tape recorders** are used for both input and output. Large volumes of data can be recorded very compactly on magnetic tape. Although the tapes cannot be read directly by a person, they can be read by a computer program for further processing. For example, a commercial bank might run a program each day to record the day's transactions on a magnetic tape. At the end of the month, another program could read the tapes and print statements for the customers. Other common media are **magnetic disk**, **paper tape**, and **microfilm**. See Figures 1.16 and 1.17 for these devices.

FIGURE 1.16
SOME DEVICES USED FOR INPUT AND OUTPUT

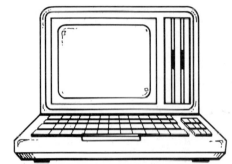

A computer terminal has a
keyboard for input and a
display screen for output.

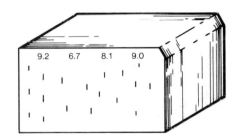

Punch card input is prepared
on a keypunch and read on a
card reader.

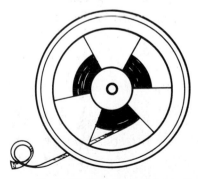

Printed output is produced
on a line printer.

Magnetic tape is used for both
input and output.

FIGURE 1.17
SCHEMATIC DIAGRAM OF A MAGNETIC DISK UNIT

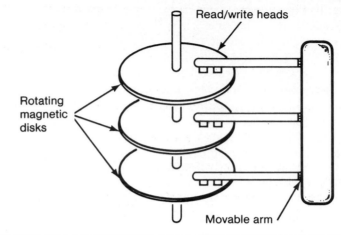

The movable read/write heads are electromagnetics that selectively magnitize areas of the rotating disks.

The FORTRAN instruction for input is the **READ statement**. An example is

READ ∗, VALUE

This instruction says to read a number and store it in the variable VALUE. Every time you read a number you must store it in some variable.

The FORTRAN instruction for output is the PRINT statement. An example is

PRINT ∗, TOTAL

which means to print the value of the variable TOTAL. The statement

PRINT ∗, 'THE SUM IS', SUM

means to print the words 'THE SUM IS', followed by the value of the variable SUM. If SUM is equal to 100, this statement will print the output line:

THE SUM IS 100.0

Tables 1.2 and 1.3 give some more examples.

TABLE 1.2
THE READ STATEMENT

Form
READ *, *list*

where *list* is a list of variable names. If there is more than one variable, separate them by commas.

Meaning

Read values from the input unit (cards or terminal), and store the values in the variables listed.

Examples

```
READ *, A
READ *, CONVER, FACTOR, NUMBER
READ *, X, NUMBER
```

TABLE 1.3
THE PRINT STATEMENT

Form
PRINT *, *list*

where *list* is a list of items to be printed. If there is more than one item in the list, separate them by commas. Each item can be a variable, a title enclosed in single quote marks, or a mathematical expression.

Meaning

Write the values in the list on the standard output unit (printer or terminal).

Examples

```
PRINT *, 'THE ANSWER IS ', B
PRINT *, PCT, 'PERCENT'
PRINT *, 'ALL NUMBERS ARE IN CENTIMETERS'
PRINT *, A, B, C, D
PRINT *, A, B, ' SUM = ', A + B
```

Control Instructions

The statements in a FORTRAN program are normally carried out in the order in which they are written. You can modify that order with control instructions.

To represent a decision, for example, you can use an **IF-THEN-ELSE** construct of the form

```
IF (condition) THEN
      statement 1
ELSE
      statement 2
END IF
```

In this example, *statement 1* and *statement 2* represent any FORTRAN statements, and *condition* represents some simple condition that a computer can test electronically to determine whether it is true or false.

For example, a computer can test a variable A and a variable B to see if their values are equal. You would write this condition as

```
A .EQ. B
```

The symbol ".EQ." is the FORTRAN symbol for "equal to." Similarly, ".NE." means "not equal to."

In the algorithm for averaging numbers, one of the steps said, "If COUNT is not zero, then let AVERAGE equal SUM divided by COUNT; otherwise, let AVERAGE equal zero." The corresponding FORTRAN statements are;

```
IF (COUNT .NE. 0) THEN
      AVERAG = SUM/COUNT
ELSE
      AVERAG = 0
END IF
```

(See Table 1.4.) Note that we dropped the E from AVERAGE since FORTRAN variables can be at most six characters long.

TABLE 1.4
THE IF-THEN-ELSE STATEMENTS

Form

```
IF (condition) THEN
      statement 1
ELSE
      statement 2
END IF
```

Meaning

If the *condition* is true, execute *statement 1*; otherwise, execute *statement 2*.

Example

```
IF (COUNT .NE. 0) THEN
      AVERAG = SUM/COUNT
ELSE
      AVERAG = 0
END IF
```

Another kind of control statement is the **GO TO statement**, which you can use for a loop. Here is an example

```
10    READ *, X
      PRINT *, X
      GO TO 10
```

The number "10" here is a **statement label**. The first two statements read and print a number, using a variable X to store it. The GO TO statement says to return to statement 10, the READ statement. (See Table 1.5.)

TABLE 1.5
THE GO TO STATEMENT

Form
GO TO *n*

where *n* is a statement label

Meaning
Branch to the statement with statement label *n*.

Examples
```
GO TO 1000
GO TO 7
GO TO 99
```

In the algorithm for averaging numbers there is a loop that is performed for every input value. You can write this procedure in FORTRAN by using a GO TO statement in conjunction with a special form of the READ statement, as follows.

```
10    READ (*, *, END = 20) VALUE
      SUM = SUM + VALUE
      COUNT = COUNT + 1
      GO TO 10
20    IF (COUNT .NE. 0) THEN
```

This form of the READ statement is a combination input and control instruction. If there is more input data, the READ statement reads the next number, stores it in the variable VALUE, and proceeds to the following assignment statement. However, if there is no more input data, the READ statement causes the program to branch to statement 20, the IF statement. That is the meaning of the symbol "END = 20" in the READ.

The last line in any FORTRAN program is an **END statement**, which you write simply as

```
END
```

This instruction indicates the end of your program and tells the computer to halt.

Putting It All Together

Using the statements just covered, you can write a complete program. The following program finds the average of a set of numbers. We have added a few small embellishments to the algorithm given earlier. First, we included a PRINT statement right after the READ statement to print each input value. This technique is called **echo checking**. This way, you get a listing of your data along with the output. Second, we included PRINT statements at the beginning to provide titles for the output. Finally, we included statements to print the sum and the count of the numbers as well as the average. Each of these three values will be labeled in the output. Here is the complete program.

```
        INTEGER COUNT
        REAL VALUE, SUM, AVERAG
        PRINT *, 'AVERAGE NUMBER PROGRAM'
        PRINT *, 'INPUT VALUES:'
        SUM = 0
        COUNT = 0
10          READ (*, *, END = 20) VALUE
        PRINT *, VALUE
        SUM = SUM + VALUE
        COUNT = COUNT + 1
        GO TO 10
20      IF (COUNT .NE. 0) THEN
            AVERAG = SUM/COUNT
        ELSE
            AVERAG = 0
        END IF
        PRINT *, 'THE SUM IS ', SUM
        PRINT *, 'THE COUNT IS ', COUNT
        PRINT *, 'THE AVERAGE IS ', AVERAG
        END
```

SUMMARY

An algorithm is a step-by-step procedure for solving a problem. Each step must be a meaningful instruction. The order in which the steps are performed must be precisely determined, and the algorithm must eventually terminate.

In the top-down method of designing an algorithm, you begin by describing the overall plan of your solution. You refine the top-level design by adding more detail. As you develop the algorithm, you continually validate it to make sure that it is correct.

A structured flowchart is a diagram of an algorithm. Instructions are written in boxes, and the boxes are arranged to indicate the order in which the instructions are carried out.

FORTRAN is a precise language that can be used to write an algorithm in a form that a computer can carry out. There are only a few different kinds of statements in FORTRAN, each of which has a certain prescribed form.

A typical computer system consists of a central processor, memory unit, and peripheral devices. The instructions that a computer can perform fall into four categories: storing and recalling from memory, computation, input and output, and program control.

The assignment statement in FORTRAN tells the machine to carry out computations and store the result in memory. Each variable in FORTRAN is a name for some memory location.

Several kinds of devices are used for input and output. The FORTRAN statements READ and PRINT tell the machine to perform input and output.

Control instructions specify the order in which instructions are carried out. The IF-THEN-ELSE statements indicate decisions in a FORTRAN program. The GO TO statement causes a branch to some statement and can be used to program a loop.

VOCABULARY

address
algorithm
assignment statement
boundary condition
card reader
computer
computer terminal
conditional instruction
counter
cathode-ray tube
echo checking
END statement
exit from a loop
flowchart
FORTRAN
GO TO statement
if-then-else
increment
initialize
input
instruction set

iterate
line printer
loop
magnetic disk
magnetic tape
memory
microfilm
output
peripheral device
program
program control instruction
pseudocode
statement
statement label
store and recall from memory
system
top-down design
validation
value of a variable
variable

||||||||||||||||||||||||||||||||||||||||||||||||||||||||||||||||||||||||||||||||||||||||||||||||||||||||||||||||||||||||||||||||||||||||||

EXERCISES

1. Which of the following are algorithms that a person could carry out with a pencil and paper? Why, or why not.
   - (a) (1) Write the number 2.
     - (2) Multiply it by 5 and add 1.
     - (3) If there is life on other planets, subtract 3.
     - (4) Write the result.
   - (b) (1) Let N equal 512.
     - (2) Let N equal N divided by 2.
     - (3) Go to either Step 2 or Step 4.
     - (4) If N is greater than 10, go to Step 2.
     - (5) Write down the final value of N.
   - (c) (1) Let N equal 99.
     - (2) Let N equal N minus 2.
     - (3) If N equals zero, stop; otherwise, go to Step 2.
   - (d) (1) Let N equal 99.
     - (2) Let N equal N minus 1.
     - (3) If N equals zero, stop; otherwise, go to Step 2.

2. Is the number 1234567 even or odd? How did you know? Write down the procedure you used in the form of an algorithm to determine if any given number is even or odd.

3. When you leave the house in the morning, do you take your school books with you? Do you take an umbrella? Do you wear a coat? Could you write the procedure you use for deciding these matters as an algorithm?

4. In the year 1960, New Year's Day was a Friday. The Fourth of July was a Monday. If you know the day of the week of New Year's Day for any given year, is there an algorithm you can use to determine the day of the Fourth of July for the year?

5. Suppose you are teaching a friend to drive a car. "Your first exercise," you say, "is to start the car, back it out of the driveway, drive around the block, and park in the driveway again. I'll sit next to you and explain each step." What instructions would you give? Do you think that giving these instructions to a novice adult driver would be difficult? Do you think you could write the steps as an algorithm? If so, do you think a five-year-old child could follow the algorithm? Suppose your car were equipped with a computer that could operate the controls of the car (start the ignition, shift gears, turn the steering wheel, and so on). Do you think the computer could follow your algorithm? Do you think it is possible in theory to program the computer to chauffeur you around town? Why or why not?

6. The accompanying figure shows a construction from elementary geometry for bisecting a line segment—that is, for dividing the line AB into two equal parts, AC and CB. This figure represents an algorithm that a person can carry out using a pencil and paper, a straightedge, and a compass. Write down the steps in the algorithm in a form that you could read over a telephone to a person to explain how to bisect a line segment.

ALGORITHM FOR BISECTING A LINE SEGMENT

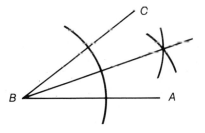

7. The accompanying figure shows a construction from elementary geometry to bisect a given angle—that is, to divide it into two equal angles. Write an algorithm, as in Exercise 6, that describes this construction. Are there any exceptional cases (boundary conditions) in this problem? Does your algorithm handle them correctly?

ALGORITHM FOR BISECTING AN ANGLE

Note: A famous result in mathematics is that it is impossible to trisect an angle, in general. This result asserts that no algorithm exists to divide any given angle into three equal angles using a straightedge and compass.

8. The computations below show how to express the numbers 1/2, 1/4, and 1/8 as decimal numbers, 0.5, 0.25, 0.125. The same procedure was used in each case. Could you write this procedure as an algorithm? Would your algorithm work for

finding the decimal expansion of 1/*n* for any positive integer *n*? In particular, would it work to find the decimal expansion of 1/3?

$$\begin{array}{r} 0.5 \\ 2\overline{)1.0} \\ 1\,0 \end{array} \qquad \begin{array}{r} 0.25 \\ 4\overline{)1.00} \\ 8 \\ 20 \\ 20 \end{array} \qquad \begin{array}{r} 0.125 \\ 8\overline{)1.000} \\ 8 \\ 20 \\ 16 \\ 40 \\ 40 \end{array}$$

9. Suppose you have a balance scale and a set of weights, as shown in the figure below. Write an algorithm you could use to determine the weight of any object, to within one gram. What is a boundary condition for this exercise? (*Hint:* Could you weigh a sack of flour?)

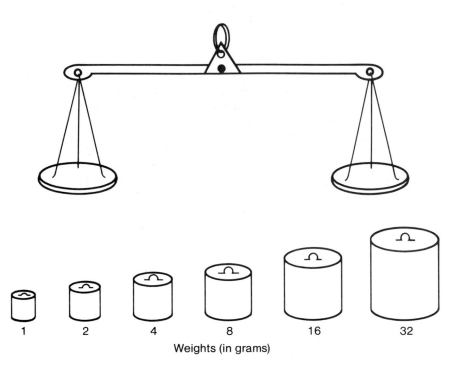

1   2   4   8   16   32

Weights (in grams)

10. Suppose you have a balance scale, like the one in Exercise 9, but no weights. You are given three pennies. Two of them are genuine and the other is counterfeit. Although the pennies look identical, the counterfeit penny is either a little heavier or a little lighter than a genuine penny. In two weighings on the balance, find the counterfeit penny. Write a structured flowchart for an algorithm to solve this problem.

11. Write the first and last names of 10 friends on a set of 10 index cards. Shuffle them, then put them in alphabetical order. Describe the algorithm you used to put the cards in order. Would you use the same algorithm to put 1000 cards in order?

12. Suppose you were handed a large set of index cards with one number written on each card and were asked to find the largest and the smallest numbers in the set. Write an algorithm you could use to solve this problem.

13. Write an algorithm that a computer could use to solve the problem in Exercise 12. That is, describe the algorithm in terms of variables and computer instructions of the kind covered in this chapter. Draw a structured flowchart to represent the algorithm.

14. Write an algorithm that a computer could follow to print the value

$$1 + 2 + 3 + 4 + 5 + \cdots + 98 + 99 + 100$$

Represent your algorithm with a structured flowchart.

15. Write an algorithm that a computer could follow to print the value

$$1 - \frac{1}{2} + \frac{1}{3} - \frac{1}{4} + \frac{1}{5} - \frac{1}{6} + \frac{1}{7} - \cdots + \frac{1}{99} - \frac{1}{100}$$

Represent your algorithm with a structured flowchart.

16. The *Fibonacci numbers* are the sequence of numbers

$$0 \quad 1 \quad 1 \quad 2 \quad 3 \quad 5 \quad 8 \quad 13 \ldots$$

Each number in this sequence is the sum of the previous two numbers (e.g., $8 = 5 + 3$). Write an algorithm that a computer could follow to print the first 20 numbers in this sequence. Represent your algorithm with a structured flowchart. Check your algorithm by carrying it out with paper and pencil (or a calculator).

17. The *factorial* of a positive integer n, written $n!$, is defined as the product of all the positive integers less than or equal to n. Thus, $5! = 1 \times 2 \times 3 \times 4 \times 5 = 120$. Write an algorithm that a computer could use to input a number n and print the number $n!$. Draw a structured flowchart. Carry out the steps in your algorithm using paper and pencil (or a calculator) to compute the value of $7!$.

18. Following is a sample dialogue between two people playing a game called "Guess the number."

"I am thinking of a number between 1 and 100."
"I guess 50."
"Too low."
"I guess 75."
"Too low."
"I guess 80."
"Too high."
"I guess 77."
"That's right. You got it in four guesses."

   Write an algorithm that a computer could use to play this game with you. The computer would "think of a number" by reading a number from an input source unknown to the human player. Thereafter, the computer reads the person's guess and responds appropriately.

19. *Nim* is a game that two people can play. In one of the more popular versions, you start with three rows of pennies, arranged as shown in the figure (on page 30). On each turn, a player takes one or more coins from any row (the player can take as

ARRANGEMENT OF PENNIES FOR THE GAME OF NIM

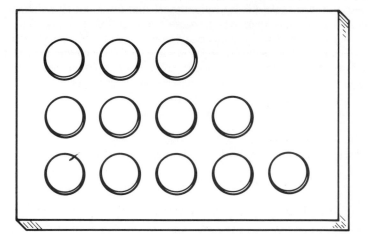

many coins as he chooses, but they must all come from the same row). Players alternate turns. Whoever takes the last penny wins.

Write an algorithm that a computer could use to play this game with you. Assume that you get to move first. You indicate your move by typing two numbers: the row number, and the number of pennies you remove. The computer should respond by typing two numbers for its move. If you enter an illegal move, the computer should tell you so and ask you to move again. If you win on your move, or if the computer wins on its move, the computer should tell you so. Have the computer decide on its move using some very simple strategy (such as taking one penny from the first row that has any pennies in it). A much more challenging version of this problem would be to have the computer play "intelligently," trying to win if possible.

20. A simple version of an old puzzle called the Tower of Hanoi is shown in the figure on page 31. There are three disks A, B, and C, stacked on peg number 1. The problem is to move all the disks to peg number 2. The rules are that you can move only one disk at a time from one peg to another, but you cannot set a disk on top of a smaller disk. Write an algorithm for solving this puzzle. Suppose you had a puzzle with four disks instead of three. Do not write a complete algorithm, but describe how you would solve the four-disk puzzle. How many steps would there be in a complete algorithm for the four-disk puzzle (i.e., how many moves would it take). Could you solve a five-disk puzzle the same way? How many moves would it take?

21. In the game of "Twenty-One", a player is dealt two cards and draws other cards from a deck. The object is to get a hand that totals as close as possible to 21, without going over 21. Face cards count 10. Aces count 1 or 11. Other cards count their face value. One simple way to play is to draw cards until your hand is 17 or better. Write an algorithm for a Twenty-One strategy.

22. A set of input cards has one number on each card, where each number represents a student's test score (0 to 100). The algorithm represented by the structured flowchart in the figure on page 31 reads these cards. What does the output represent?

TOWER OF HANOI PUZZLE

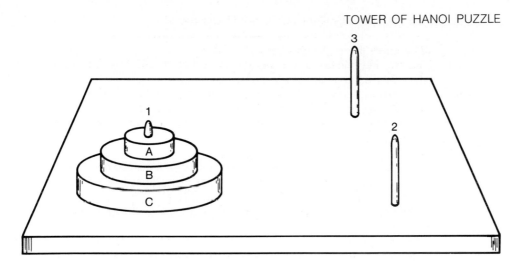

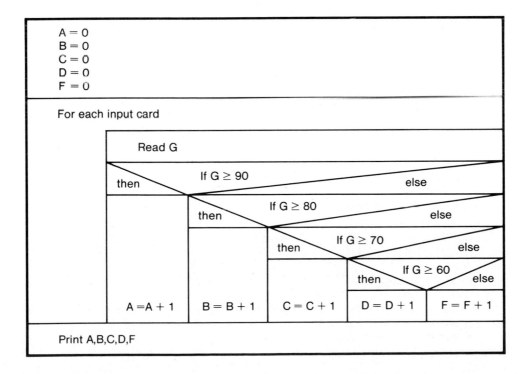

23. Carry out the following algorithm with a paper and pencil.

   Step 1   Write down the numbers from 2 to 100.
   Step 2   Find the first number in the list that is neither circled nor crossed out (to begin with none of them are) and circle it.
   Step 3   Cross out all multiples of the number you circled in Step 2. (If a number is already crossed out, just go on and cross out the next multiple).
   Step 4   If there are still some numbers that are neither circled nor crossed out, go to Step 2; otherwise stop.

   The numbers that are circled when the algorithm terminates are the *prime numbers* up to 100. This algorithm is called the Sieve of Erastosthenes, after the Greek mathematician who invented it in the third century B.C.

24. Write an algorithm to print a table of squares of numbers 1 through 100. Draw a structured flowchart for your algorithm.

25. If a FORTRAN program uses two variables, X and Y, that represent integer numbers, you can declare them by putting the following statement at the beginning:

   INTEGER X, Y

   To set Y equal to the square of X, you can use the FORTRAN statement

   Y = X * X

   To print X and Y, you can use the statement

   PRINT *, X, Y

   Using these statements, and the others you learned in this chapter, write a FORTRAN program to carry out your algorithm from Exercise 24.

26. If a program uses variables X, SMALL, and LARGE to represent real numbers, you can begin the program with the statement

   REAL X, SMALL, LARGE

   The following statement means, "Read a value into variable X but go to statement 20 if there are no more input values."

   READ (*, *, END = 20) X

   The following statement means, "If the value of X is less than the value of SMALL, set SMALL equal to X."

   IF (X .LT. SMALL) SMALL = X

   The symbol ".GT." means "greater than." What do you think the following statement means?

   IF (X .GT. LARGE) LARGE = X

      Put these statements together with others you learned in this chapter to write a
FORTRAN program to solve the problem described in Exercises 12 and 13.
27. Write a FORTRAN program to solve the problem described in Exercise 14.
28. Write a FORTRAN program to solve the problem described in Exercise 15.
29. Write a FORTRAN program to solve the problem described in Exercise 16.
30. Write a FORTRAN program to solve the problem described in Exercise 17.

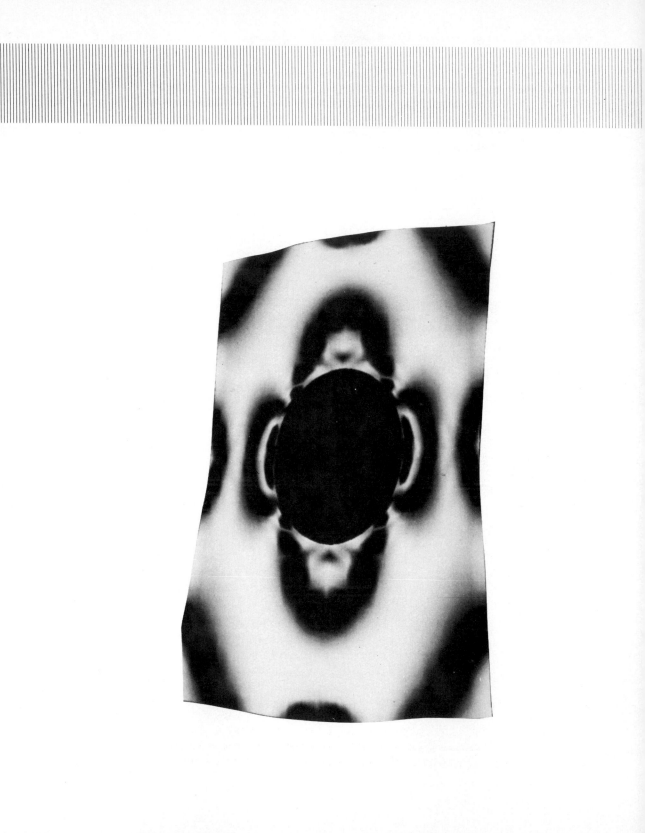

RUNNING
YOUR FIRST
PROGRAM

INTRODUCTION Now that you've seen what the FORTRAN language is like, let us see how to run a program on a computer.

The first step is to prepare your program in a form the computer can read. A common way is to punch the program on computer cards, using a keypunch machine. On a timesharing system, you might use a text editor to type FORTRAN statements at a terminal keyboard. In either case, the FORTRAN statements must be prepared in a certain form, which we will explain.

If your program reads input data, the data too must be prepared in a certain format.

When your program and data are properly set up, you run the program, or have a computer operator run it for you. Running the program consists of several distinct phases. If the job is not properly set up, or if something goes wrong in one of these phases, the computer will print a message to help you locate the problem.

Although the FORTRAN language is the same on all computers, the details of setting up a program and running it depend on the particular computer system you are using. You may wish to consult the reference manuals for your computer for further information.

PREPARING YOUR PROGRAM FOR THE COMPUTER

There are two common ways to prepare a program in machine-readable form. You can punch it on computer cards, or you can type the program on a computer terminal.

If you use cards, you keypunch each FORTRAN statement on a separate card. Table 2.1 shows the FORTRAN character set: the characters on your keypunch or terminal that you can use in a FORTRAN statement. Figure 2.1 shows how these characters look on a punch card. The printing on the card is for the convenience of the

TABLE 2.1
THE FORTRAN CHARACTER SET

Blank		(Also called a space or blank space)
Dollar sign	$	(Also called a currency symbol)
Single quote	'	(Also called an apostrophe or quote)
Left parenthesis	(	
Right parenthesis	)	
Asterisk	*	(Also called a star)
Plus sign	+	
Comma	,	
Minus sign	−	(Also called a hyphen)
Period	.	(Also called a decimal point)
Slash	/	
Digits	0 through 9	
Colon	:	
Equal sign	=	
Capital letters	A through Z	

FIGURE 2.1
A PUNCH CARD, SHOWING THE LEGAL FORTRAN CHARACTERS

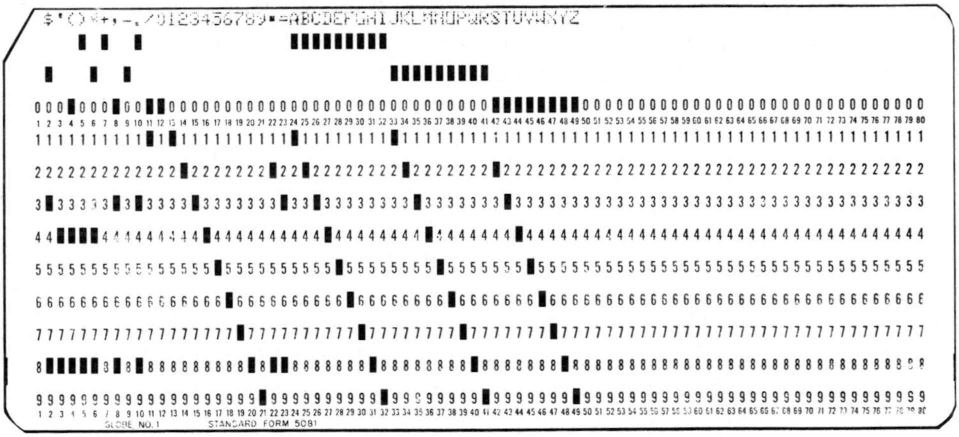

Each character is represented by a pattern of holes. (Note: The hole codes for special characters may be different on some computer systems.)

programmer; the computer senses only the holes. The punch card has 80 columns, so you can type up to 80 characters on a single card. The columns are numbered 1 through 80 from left to right.

If you use a computer terminal, there are no cards involved, but the principle is similar. Each line of input corresponds to one FORTRAN statement, and you can think of each line as having 80 columns (although the columns on a terminal are usually not numbered).

When typing FORTRAN statements at a computer terminal, you will probably use a **text-editing program** that lets you insert and delete lines, just as you could if you were preparing a deck of cards on a keypunch. Your program will be stored on the computer's disk unit, rather than on cards. Text-editing programs vary from one computer system to the next, so you will need to consult your system's reference manual for details. One point to note is that such programs often use a *line sequence number* to distinguish among the lines in your program. Do not confuse the line sequence number, which is used only by the text editor, with the FORTRAN statement number, which is part of your program.

Each FORTRAN statement must be typed in a certain format. You type the statement in columns 7 through 72 of the line. The other columns are used for different purposes, as we will explain.

You may find it helpful to use a **coding form** which has the columns marked on it, such as the one shown in Figure 2.2.

FIGURE 2.2
A FORTRAN STATEMENT WRITTEN ON A CODING FORM

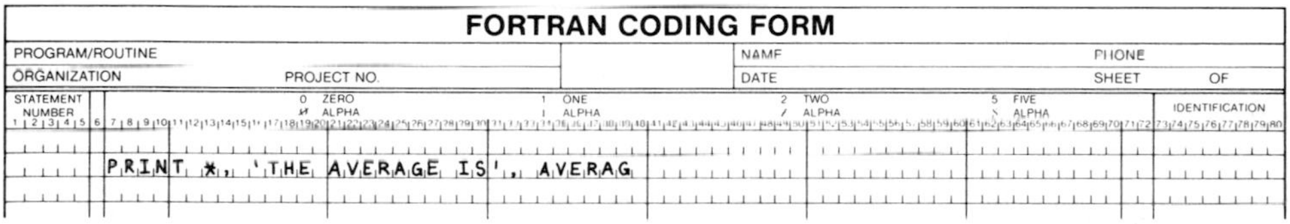

Sometimes a FORTRAN statement is too long to type on one line. You can use a **continuation line** to write a statement on two or more lines.

A continuation line (or **continuation card**, as it is often called) is a line with some character other than a blank space or a zero typed in column 6. Columns 7 through 72 of a continuation line are interpreted as though they were part of the previous line. Figure 2.3 shows a two-line statement. If necessary, a FORTRAN statement can be up to 20 lines long.

FIGURE 2.3

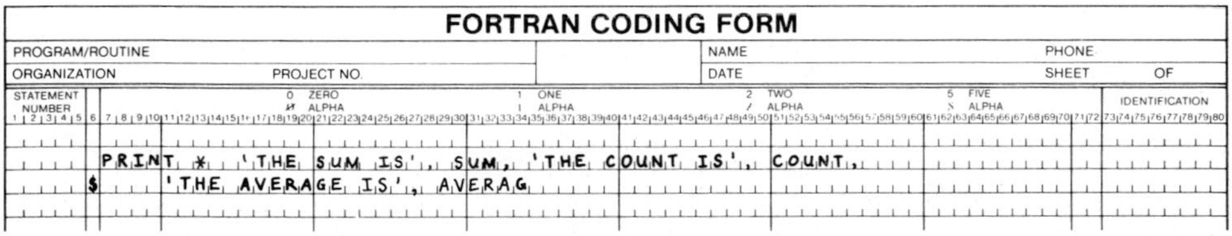

A statement can be continued on another line by using column 6.

FIGURE 2.4
COMMENT LINES

FORTRAN CODING FORM

PROGRAM/ROUTINE			NAME		PHONE	
ORGANIZATION		PROJECT NO.	DATE		SHEET	OF

STATEMENT NUMBER		0 - ZERO, ∅ - ALPHA	1 ONE, I ALPHA	2 TWO, Z ALPHA	5 FIVE, S ALPHA	IDENTIFICATION
*	ANY LINE WITH AN ASTERISK (*) OR THE					
C	LETTER 'C' IN COLUMN 1 IS A COMMENT LINE,					
*	AND IS IGNORED BY FORTRAN.					
*	A BLANK LINE IS ALSO A COMMENT.					

Indicating a continuation is the only thing column 6 is ever used for in FOR-
TRAN. Be careful not to type something accidentally in column 6 or the machine will
think you meant to continue the line, even though you may not have intended to.

Any line with an asterisk (*) or the letter C in column 1 is a **comment line**
(Figure 2.4). You can use comment lines to explain what your program does or how it
works. Comment lines are ignored in FORTRAN. You can put them anywhere in the
program without affecting the meaning of the FORTRAN statements. A blank line is
also a comment line and is ignored in FORTRAN. Although comments are always
optional, you will find them very helpful when you are reading a program or making
changes to it.

A FORTRAN statement does not have to have a statement label (statement
number), but if it does have one, you type the number in columns 1 through 5. You
can type the statement number starting in column 1, or you can precede the number
with one or more blank spaces. Spacing is not important as long as the number is
typed somewhere in columns 1 through 5. Figure 2.5 shows some examples.

Columns 73 through 80 of a line are ignored in FORTRAN. You can leave them
blank or use them for whatever you want. You might use them to type a sequence
number in each card. That way, if you drop your program cards, it will be easy to put
them back in order.

Figure 2.6 summarizes the form of a FORTRAN statement.

EXAMPLE 2.1 A Complete Program, Ready for Keypunching
Figure 2.7 shows the program to average numbers written on a coding form.

FIGURE 2.5
COLUMNS 1–5 ARE USED FOR THE STATEMENT NUMBER

FORTRAN CODING FORM

PROGRAM/ROUTINE			NAME		PHONE	
ORGANIZATION		PROJECT NO.	DATE		SHEET	OF

STATEMENT NUMBER		0 - ZERO, ∅ - ALPHA	1 ONE, I ALPHA	2 TWO, Z ALPHA	5 FIVE, S ALPHA	IDENTIFICATION
10	READ(*, *, END = 20) VALUE					
20	IF (COUNT .NE. 0) THEN					

FIGURE 2.6

THE PARTS OF A FORTRAN STATEMENT MUST BE KEYPUNCHED
IN CERTAIN COLUMNS

FIGURE 2.7
A FORTRAN PROGRAM, WRITTEN ON A CODING FORM

FORTRAN CODING FORM

PROGRAM/ROUTINE		NAME	PHONE
ORGANIZATION	PROJECT NO.	DATE	SHEET OF

STATEMENT NUMBER | 0 ZERO Ø ALPHA | 1 ONE I ALPHA | 2 TWO Z ALPHA | 5 FIVE S ALPHA | IDENTIFICATION

```
* PROGRAM TO AVERAGE NUMBERS .
      INTEGER COUNT
      REAL VALUE, SUM, AVERAG
      PRINT *, 'AVERAGE NUMBER PROGRAM'
      PRINT *, 'INPUT VALUES:'
      SUM = 0
      COUNT = 0
10          READ(*, *, END = 20) VALUE
            PRINT *, VALUE
            SUM = SUM + VALUE
            COUNT = COUNT + 1
            GO TO 10
20    IF (COUNT .NE. 0) THEN
            AVERAG = SUM / COUNT
      ELSE
            AVERAG = 0
      END IF
      PRINT *, 'THE SUM IS', SUM
      PRINT *, 'THE COUNT IS', COUNT
      PRINT *, 'THE AVERAGE IS', AVERAG
      END
```

STYLE MODULE—TYPING FORTRAN STATEMENTS

One of the unusual things about FORTRAN, as a language, is that spaces have no significance whatever, except within quote marks (as in the PRINT statements in Figure 2.8). Figure 2.8 shows four ways to write a FORTRAN statement. All four ways mean exactly the same thing.

Since FORTRAN ignores spaces, you can use them to improve the readability of your program. Type spaces on either side of an equal sign, and use spaces around plus and minus signs. When typing a long statement, do not try to crowd it all onto one line by omitting spaces. It is better to use spaces as necessary for readability and to continue the statement on another line. Remember that you can use up to 19 continuation lines.

Indentation means putting spaces at the beginning of a statement, like indenting the first line of a paragraph in English. You can use indentation to set off the statements in a program loop or in a conditional statement (as in Figure 2.8). The indentation is ignored in FORTRAN, but it will greatly improve the readability of your programs.

Another way to set off groups of statements is to put blank lines between them. You might use blank lines and other comment lines to break the program into sections of statements, where each section performs a specific task, such as initialization.

FIGURE 2.8

SPACING DOES NOT AFFECT THE MEANING OF A FORTRAN STATEMENT

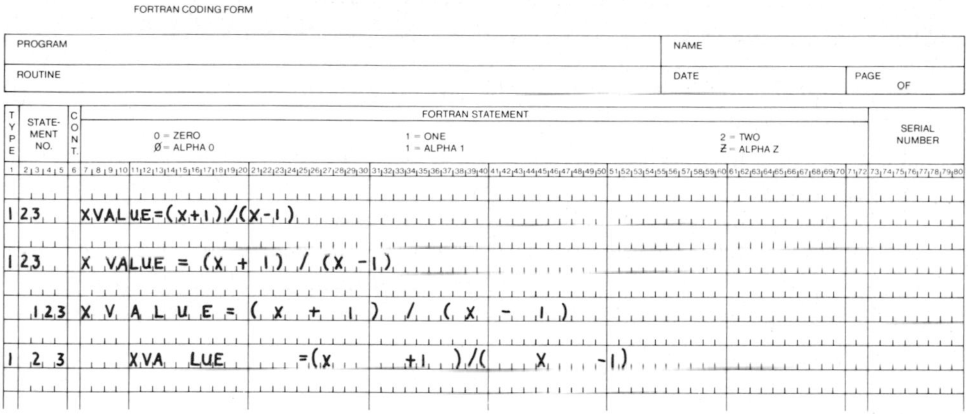

FORTRAN CODING FORM

PROGRAM		NAME	
ROUTINE		DATE	PAGE OF

The coding form shows the same statement written four different ways:

```
123    XVALUE=(X+1)/(X-1)
123    X VALUE = (X + 1) / (X -1)
   123 X V A L U E = ( X + 1 ) / ( X - 1 )
1 2 3    XVA  LUE      =(X    +1 )/(   X    -1)
```

You can indicate a continuation line by putting any character other than a blank or zero in column 6. All the continuation lines in this book have a dollar sign in column 6. The reason for using a dollar sign is that it is not used for anything else in FORTRAN. Thus there is no danger of misreading it as being part of the FORTRAN statement. If you used a plus sign in column 6, for instance, you might forget that the plus sign is not part of the FORTRAN statement.

You will find that continued lines are more legible if you indent them a few spaces. Put a dollar sign in column 6 and start the rest of the statement in column 10, for example.

You can break a continuation line anywhere—even in the middle of a word—but for readability it is best to break it at some natural place, such as after an operator

STYLE MODULE—USING COMMENTS

Since comment lines are ignored by FORTRAN, you might ask, "Why use them at all?" The fact is, comments are an important part of a program. They help you, the programmer, to read your program and figure out what it does. And they help you, or someone else who might use your program, to use the program correctly.

Professional programmers typically spend as much time *maintaining* programs as they spend writing programs. Maintaining a program can involve making minor changes to a program because of new requirements. It can also involve adding additional features to a program. It's a story familiar to every programmer: just when you think you've finished a job, the customer changes his or her mind about what was wanted, or dreams up some new requirement. And it's the same story when writing programs for your own use. You run the program a few times and you think of a new feature that would be nice to add.

The point is that even after a program is finished you will often have to read it, study it, and figure out how it works. This is where good comments become invaluable. If you ever have to modify or to run a program written by someone else (or even a program that you yourself wrote a long time ago), you will especially appreciate the importance of comments.

What you choose to comment on, and how you choose to do so, are matters of style. Here are some general guidelines.

Begin each program with a section of comments that lists the author's name, the date written, the purpose of the program, the required input, and a brief description of how it works. If the program uses methods described in published articles, give references.

This sort of information is often called **program documentation**. Many programmers will write a program, then write the documentation later (if they get around to it), and have it typed up and filed away somewhere. It is preferable to write the documentation first, before writing the program, and to type it as comment cards right in the program.

The reason for writing the documentation first is that it helps you to get a clear idea of what you are supposed to be doing before you do it. This, of course, is the whole purpose of top-down design.

Including the documentation as comments will help to keep it from getting lost or out-of-date. Inaccurate documentation is almost as bad as none at all. Keep the documentation right with your program. If you change the program, change the documentation too.

In Chapter 5 you will see an example of a program that can read a set of program cards and list only the documentation. This points out another good reason for keeping documentation as comment cards in a program: it is easy to revise the documentation and get a new listing of it.

When you write your own algorithm for a program, include your top-level design as comments at the start of your program.

Use comments (and blank lines, which are also comments) to subdivide your program into sections of related statements. For example, the comments

```
      *
      * THE FOLLOWING STATEMENTS COMPUTE
      * THE MINIMUM INPUT VALUE, XMIN.
      *
```

could introduce a sequence of FORTRAN statements that perform the indicated task. An excellent practice is to use one such section for each step in your top-level program design. It will then be easy to relate your FORTRAN statements to the overall program design.

Do not comment on the obvious. Consider some examples:

```
      * THE FOLLOWING STATEMENT ADDS 1 TO N
            N = N + 1
```

```
* READ A VALUE FOR X
     READ *, X
* IF N IS NEGATIVE, GO TO 100
  IF (N .LT. 0) GO TO 100
```

In each case, the comment adds nothing to your understanding of the program. Comments should not merely restate the FORTRAN instructions. They should supplement the instructions to describe more generally what the program does.

The programming examples in this book often will have fairly brief comments. In particular, we will often omit the program documentation part of the comments, since the examples are explained in the text. When writing programs of your own, however, you should include the appropriate documentation in the comments.

EXAMPLE 2.2 The Same Program with Comments Added

Figure 2.9 shows the final version of the program to average numbers, with comment lines added. Compare this with Figure 2.7. Which version is more legible?

PREPARING YOUR DATA

The cards on which you keypunch your program are called **program cards**. If your program does any input operations, you will also need a set of **data cards** containing the values to be read.

If you are using a computer terminal, rather than a keypunch, you may type a line of data directly on the terminal, instead of on a card. The principle is the same.

You put all your data cards together at the end of your program. Each time your program executes a READ statement, the program reads a new data card. The values on the card are stored in the variables specified in the READ.

An easy way to type your data is to put one number on each data card. For the READ statement we have been using, it doesn't matter what columns in the card you use. You can begin in column 1 of the card, or you can leave some blank spaces in front of the number.

If the data value is a negative number, you type a minus sign in front of it. Do not leave a blank space after the minus sign. That is, you can keypunch the number −12 as

```
−12
```

but *not* as

```
−  12
```

The statement

```
READ *, A, B, C
```

FIGURE 2.9

FORTRAN CODING FORM

| PROGRAM/ROUTINE **PROGRAM to AVERAGE NUMBERS** | | NAME | | PHONE | |
| ORGANIZATION | PROJECT NO. | DATE | | SHEET **1** OF **2** | |

STATEMENT NUMBER		0 – ZERO / Ø – ALPHA	1 – ONE / I – ALPHA	2 – TWO / Z – ALPHA	5 – FIVE / S – ALPHA	IDENTIFICATION

```
*
*  PROGRAM TO AVERAGE NUMBERS.
*
*  AUTHOR: M. MERCHANT
*
*  THIS PROGRAM READS A SET OF INPUT DATA,
*  WITH ONE NUMBER ON EACH INPUT LINE.
*  IT PRINTS THE VALUE OF EACH NUMBER READ.
*  AT THE END OF THE OUTPUT, IT PRINTS THE
*  SUM OF THE INPUT VALUES, THE NUMBER OF
*  INPUT VALUES, AND THEIR AVERAGE.
*
       INTEGER COUNT
       REAL VALUE, SUM, AVERAGE

*  PRINT THE TITLES.

       PRINT *, 'AVERAGE NUMBER PROGRAM'
       PRINT *, 'INPUT VALUES:'

*  INTIALIZE THE SUM AND COUNT.

       SUM = 0
       COUNT = 0
```

FORTRAN CODING FORM

| PROGRAM/ROUTINE **PROGRAM to AVERAGE NUMBERS** | | NAME **M. MERCHANT** | | PHONE | |
| ORGANIZATION | PROJECT NO. | DATE | | SHEET **2** OF **2** | |

STATEMENT NUMBER		0 – ZERO / Ø – ALPHA	1 – ONE / I – ALPHA	2 – TWO / Z – ALPHA	5 – FIVE / S – ALPHA	IDENTIFICATION

```
*  FOR EACH INPUT NUMBER, READ AND PRINT THE
*  VALUE, ADD IT TO THE SUM, AND INCREMENT THE COUNT.

10     READ(*, *, END = 20) VALUE
       PRINT *, VALUE
       SUM = SUM + VALUE
       COUNT = COUNT + 1
       GO TO 10

*  AT THE END OF INPUT, COMPUTE THE AVERAGE.

20     IF (COUNT .NE. 0) THEN
          AVERAG = SUM / COUNT
       ELSE
          AVERAG = 0
       END IF

*  OUTPUT THE RESULTS.

       PRINT *, 'THE SUM IS', SUM
       PRINT *, 'THE COUNT IS', COUNT
       PRINT *, 'THE AVERAGE IS', AVERAG

       END
```

says to read three numbers. You could provide three data cards, with one number on each card, or you could put all three numbers on one card, with a blank space or a comma (or both) separating the numbers. Thus if you want to read the numbers 11, 12, and 13 for A, B, and C, you can type three data cards:

    11
    12
    13

or just a single data card:

    11, 12, 13

or without the commas:

    11 12 13

You can type a whole number with or without a decimal point. Integer variables (declared in an INTEGER statement) are allowed to have *only* integer values. You must *not* type a decimal point in an integer input value. Thus the number "two" can be typed on a data card as

    2.0

or just as

    2

If the number is not a whole number, you must type it with a decimal point. The number "three and a half" is typed as

    3.5

The number "one-third" must be approximated by a decimal fraction such as

    0.333333

SETTING UP YOUR JOB DECK*

In addition to your FORTRAN program and your data cards, you will need some **control cards** to tell the computer system to run your program. Control cards are used, for example, to tell the computer that you are running a FORTRAN program, rather than a program written in some other language, such as COBOL. Each

*Optional section.

computer system has a control language of its own. You will need only a few control language statements to run a FORTRAN program. Your instructor or your computer center can tell you the exact statements to use. Write them down in the back of this book.

The control cards together with the program and data cards comprise the **job deck** which you submit to be run on the computer. Again, the exact format of the job deck depends on the particular computer you are using, but typically you will put a few control cards in front of your program cards, followed by your data cards, as shown in Figure 2.10.

FIGURE 2.10
TYPICAL JOB DECK SETUP

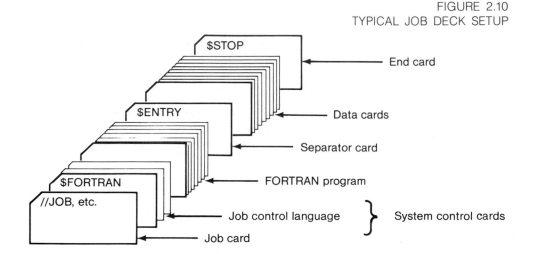

EXAMPLE 2.3 Data to Be Averaged
One week in July, the high temperatures in Cleveland were 78.2°F, 76.9°F, 76.0°F, 80.1°F, 79.1°F, 77.4°F, and 78.5°F. Set up this data so that the program of Example 2.1 can find the average high temperature for the week.

The data coding form in Figure 2.11 shows how to punch the data cards. Figure 2.12 shows how these data cards and the program would be set up in a job deck.

RUNNING YOUR PROGRAM*

When you have set up your job deck, you can run it on the computer (or have a computer operator run it for you). You need not be concerned with exactly what happens when your job is run, but in order to understand your output, you should be aware that there are three phases in running any FORTRAN program: compilation, linking, and execution.

Compilation (sometimes called **translation**) is the process of translating your FORTRAN program into machine-language instructions. We said in Chapter 1 that

*Optional section.

FIGURE 2.11
DATA CARDS FOR EXAMPLE 2.3

80 COLUMN ENTRY											
PROGRAMMER			PROBLEM						DATE	PAGE	OF

1	5	6	10	11	15	16	20	21	25	26	30	31	35	36	40	41	45	46	50	51	55	56	60	61	65	66	70	71	73	80
78.2																														
76.9																														
76.0																														
80.1																														
79.1																														
77.4																														
78.5																														

every computer has an instruction set, consisting of a few basic operations. A program called the FORTRAN **compiler** translates your FORTRAN program into an equivalent program in the machine instruction set for your computer.

During compilation, the computer will print a listing of your program. It may also print a **cross-reference map**, which is a table giving information about your program, such as the names of the variables you used in it. If the compiler detects any errors in

FIGURE 2.12
INPUT FOR EXAMPLE 2.3

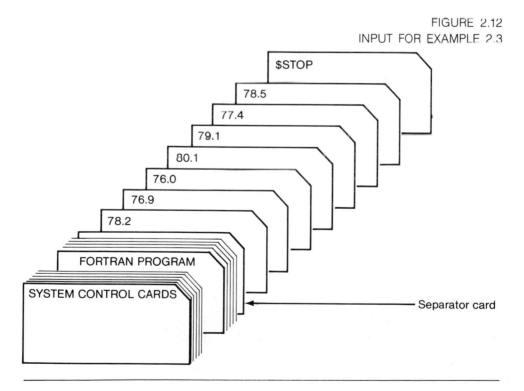

The exact form of the system control cards, separator card, and end card will depend on the particular computer system you are using.

the program, it will print an error message to help you find and correct the errors.

The compiler usually stores the machine-language program on a disk unit. In the **linking** phase, a program called the **linker** reads this machine-language program back into computer memory. The linker might also read in instructions from a program library. For example, if your FORTRAN program uses one of the FORTRAN-supplied functions that you will study in Chapter 6, the linker will retrieve the machine-language instructions for the function from a program library.

When the linker completes its work, your program begins the **execution** phase. This is the step where the instructions in your program are actually carried out.

If all goes well, your program runs for a few seconds, produces the desired results, then stops, at which time the computer may compile, link, and execute someone else's program. The operator will deliver your output, which typically will consist of a banner page identifying your output, a listing of your program, a list of any error diagnostics, and a cross-reference map from the compiler, as well as the output from your program (Figure 2.13).

EXAMPLE 2.4 Sample Output

The output produced by the program in Example 2.3 would consist of a listing of the program, as in Figure 2.11, followed by the program output shown below.

```
AVERAGE NUMBER PROGRAM
INPUT VALUES:
     78.2
     76.9
     76.0
     80.1
     79.1
     77.4
     78.5
THE SUM IS 546.2
THE COUNT IS 7
THE AVERAGE IS 78.028571
```

RUNNING ON AN INTERACTIVE SYSTEM*

When you use a computer system that lets you type commands directly to a terminal, you are *interacting* with the computer. Such a computer is called an **interactive** or **timesharing** system. Many computer systems will accept both batch input (that is, card decks), and interactive commands.

The steps in running a program on an interactive system are the same as on a batch system. Instead of preparing control cards in advance, however, you can control the process by typing commands at your terminal.

---

*Optional section

FIGURE 2.13
TYPICAL OUTPUT FORMAT

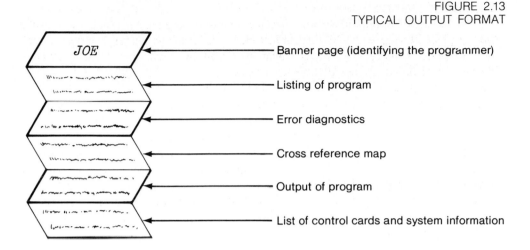

Banner page (identifying the programmer)

Listing of program

Error diagnostics

Cross reference map

Output of program

List of control cards and system information

Suppose you have used a text-editing program to create a copy of your program on the computer's disk storage unit under the name AVPROG. To compile the program, you might type the command

COMPILE AVPROG/FORTRAN

You might then link and execute the program with the command

EXECUTE AVPROG

When your program begins running, it will print out the titles

AVERAGE NUMBER PROGRAM
INPUT DATA:

You would then type your input data, pressing the RETURN key on your terminal after each number. After the last number you would press a special key on the terminal to signal the end of input. On some systems, end of input is indicated by a CONTROL-Z, which you type by pressing the CONTROL key and the letter Z key together. Your program would then print its final output and stop, and the terminal would be ready for you to type another command.

EXAMPLE 2.5 Output from an Interactive System
The following output is what you would see on your terminal when running the program to average numbers on an interactive system. The lines starting at the left margin show the commands and data you type on the terminal. The indented lines are output from the computer. Note that each input value is printed twice: once when you type it, and once again when the program prints it. On an interactive system, the echoing is thus superfluous.

```
COMPILE AVPROG/FORTRAN
      NO FORTRAN ERRORS
      0.20 SECONDS COMPILATION TIME
EXECUTE AVPROG
      (BEGINNING EXECUTION)
AVERAGE NUMBER PROGRAM
INPUT VALUES:
78.2
      78.200000
76.9
      76.900000
76
      76.000000
80.1
      80.100000
79.1
      79.100000
77.4
      77.400000
78.5
      78.500000
(CONTROL-Z)
      THE SUM IS 546.200000
      THE COUNT IS 7
      THE AVERAGE IS 78.028571
      (END OF EXECUTION)
      EXECUTION TIME 0.07 SECONDS
```

ERRORS AND DIAGNOSTICS*

It is a fact of life that programs frequently contain mistakes. There are several things that can go wrong. A **compilation error** is a mistake detected by the FORTRAN compiler. The program may have statements of incorrect form, for example. The statement

```
W = 2K + 3
```

is incorrect because 2K is an illegal variable name. Probably, the programmer intended to write 2∗K instead of 2K. Having no common sense, the compiler is merciless and simply marks the statement to be in error.

This particular kind of compilation error is a **syntax error**: the statement has an illegal **syntax** (form). Another kind of compilation error is a statement label that is referenced but not defined. For example,

```
GO TO 100
```

*Optional section.

is a legal FORTRAN statement, but if there is no statement 100 in the program, the compiler cannot translate the statement in a sensible way.

When the compiler detects an error, it prints an error message. Such messages are called **diagnostics**: they help you to diagnose the problem. When the program has compilation errors, it will not execute. All you get back in your output is the program listing and the error listing. Learning to understand the diagnostics is an important part of a programmer's education.

Another type of error is an **execution error**. This happens when a program compiles correctly and begins execution but then tries to do something impossible. Consider the statements:

```
N = 1
M = 5 + K/(N - 1)
```

These statements are valid FORTRAN statements and so could be part of a valid program. But when the computer tries to execute the second statement, it has to divide K by zero. Since division by zero is undefined, most computers would terminate execution and display some sort of error message. It is up to the programmer to read the error message and figure out what happened.

The worst kind of error is when a program compiles and executes all the way through but produces the wrong answers. We say it is the worst because it is usually the most difficult type to diagnose and correct, since no error messages at all are printed out. Frequently in such cases, the programmer has made a mistake in basic reasoning about the problem. Consider the following example from a student program to compute the circumference of a circle.

```
C = 3.2426 * D
```

This is a valid statement; but due to a keypunching error, the wrong value of π was used. So, of course, the circumference was incorrectly computed, although the computer gave no hint of this. The only way to detect this kind of mistake is to proofread the program carefully and run it with some sample data for which the correct answers are known.

Errors of one sort or another are usually called **bugs** in a program, and the process of finding them is called **debugging**. Even the best and most careful programmers spend a considerable amount of time debugging programs. Occasionally, the process can be an interesting challenge—like solving a puzzle (the puzzle being to figure out why the computer isn't doing what you thought it would). Mostly, though, debugging is not nearly as much fun as programming.

The best way to deal with bugs is to prevent them. Although there is a natural tendency to dash off a program and run it immediately in hope that it might work, you will find that it saves time in the long run to design programs carefully, using the top-down approach, and to validate programs carefully before running them.

If, for some reason, your output is still not what you expected, don't throw it away in disgust. Study it. Figure out what the program really did. Then figure out why. When you take the time to discover why a program failed, you can avoid the problem in the future. Each computer run, whether it works or not, can be a profitable learning experience.

If you have difficulty understanding a diagnostic message, consult the reference manuals for your computer system. If you still cannot understand the diagnostic message, ask someone to explain it to you. Most computing centers have consultants who can answer this kind of question.

It is usually fairly easy to find the cause of a syntax error or of an execution error that prints a diagnostic message. It may be more difficult to discover why a program produces erroneous output. A good approach is to form conjectures about what might be wrong, and test the conjectures by including FORTRAN statements to do so. For example, you might suspect that a program is failing because the value of a variable X is zero, although it is not supposed to be. You could test this conjecture by including a PRINT statement at an appropriate place in your program to print the value of X. Or, you might combine a PRINT statement with an IF statement to print the value of X only if it is less than 1. Thus you can have the computer itself assist in validating your program.

On many computer systems, there are **debugging packages** that can assist in locating certain kinds of errors. For example, your FORTRAN compiler might have a debugging option that will cause your program to print more complete diagnostics in case of an execution error, such as dividing a number by zero. Find out if such features are available and learn to use them.

EXAMPLE 2.6 Some Possible Problems
Suppose you keypunch the program in Example 1 and the data cards in Example 2, provide the necessary control cards, and run the program. Here are some things that might go wrong.

You get no output at all. Maybe you used the wrong control cards. One of the control cards tells the computer system to compile your FORTRAN program. If you make a mistake keypunching this card, the system does not even try to compile the program (much less execute it).

You get a listing of your program, but no answers. Most likely there was a compilation error. For example, in keypunching the statement

```
IF (COUNT .NE. 0) THEN
```

you might have left off a period and keypunched it as

```
IF (COUNT .NE 0) THEN
```

The FORTRAN compiler will recognize that this is an incorrect statement and it will print an error diagnostic on your listing.

Your program executes normally and prints out all the numbers it should, but the average is wrong. In this case, you have to read the listing of the program and analyze what the program is actually doing. For example, if you accidentally left out the statement

```
SUM = SUM + VALUE
```

then the program would always print out zero for the average.

OPERATING SYSTEMS*

In modern computer systems, except on very small machines, the computer is always under the control of a large, complicated program called the **operating system**. The operating system controls the programs that are running on the machine and manages all of the computer's resources, such as the computer itself, the disk storage units, the card reader, the printer, and the terminals.

In the early days of computing, if two students (we'll call them Alice and Fred) wanted to use the computer, they would have to decide between themselves how to schedule their work. Alice might run her program, look at her printout, decide it was correct, then tell Fred it was his turn. Meanwhile, Fred sat around drumming his fingers, waiting for Alice to finish up. Modern computers are so fast that this approach is not practical. It is quite possible that a large computer could run Alice's program from start to finish before she could say, "It's your turn, Fred."

On today's computers, Alice and Fred would probably type their programs on cards and put them in a card reader. Under control of the operating system, the computer will automatically read in both programs and store them somewhere (probably on a disk unit) along with many other programs waiting to be run. As soon as the computer finishes what it is doing, it will search the disk unit for the next program to run and begin working on it. Alice and Fred can take a coffee break while they wait for their output.

Unless it requires some special operator action (like mounting a magnetic tape) Alice's job can proceed from start to finish without human intervention. The operator just reads in the cards and delivers the output when it is printed. The system control cards in the job deck direct the operating system to compile, link, and execute Alice's program, then go on to the next job: Fred's perhaps. Her output will be waiting for her when she finishes her coffee—unless there are many other programs waiting to be run, in which case she will have to wait a bit longer.

The elapsed time from when a job is read in until the output is delivered is called the **turnaround time**. It depends, among other things, on how many jobs are waiting to be run: that is, on how many other people are trying to use the system.

If Alice and Fred are using a **timesharing system**, they can each sit down at a computer terminal, type in their programs, and run them at the same time.

How can a computer do two things at once? Actually, it does only one thing at a time. It may work on Alice's program for a fraction of a second, then work on Fred's program for a fraction of a second, then work on Alice's again, and so on. Thus the computer is sharing its time among all the users. This process is carried out automatically by the operating system. The computer might work on a dozen different programs in the time it takes Fred to type one line at his terminal, but because the machine is so fast, Fred will notice hardly any delay.

The operating system is complex, but it is really just a large program, made up of the same kinds of instructions that Fred and Alice use in their programs. Its main purpose is to let many people use the computer efficiently and easily.

Thus a modern computer system consists of **hardware**: the computer itself, and

*Optional section.

its peripheral devices, such as the card reader and printer; and **software**: the programs that run the system. The word *software* can mean any program or set of programs, but it is usually reserved for large programs, such as the operating system and the FORTRAN compiler. Such system software is usually purchased from the same company that makes the computer hardware.

As a FORTRAN programmer, you need to know very little about the operating system. As far as you are concerned, the computer, with its system software, is just a machine that will run your FORTRAN programs for you and manage the scheduling of system resources so that you need not be concerned with such details.

|||||||||||||||||||||||||||||||||||||||||||||||||||||||||||||||||||||||||||||||||||||||||||||||||||||||||||||||||||||

SUMMARY

FORTRAN statements are keypunched or typed into a computer terminal according to the rules given on page 37. The parts of each statement must be typed in certain columns: columns 7–72 for the statement, and columns 1–5 for the statement label, as shown in Figure 2.6, page 39. If a statement is too long to fit on one line, it can be continued as shown in Figure 2.3, page 37.

You can use comment cards to add documentation to your program. Any card with a C or an * in column 1 is a comment as shown in Figure 2.4, page 38.

For the READ statements we have been using thus far, you can prepare data cards in a simple way. Keypunch one card for each READ operation, with as many numbers per card as there are variables in the READ statement. The numbers in the data card can be keypunched in any columns, as long as numbers on the same data card are separated by a blank or a comma.

You will need to supply some control cards with your job deck, directing the computer's operating system to compile, link, and execute your program. Consult the reference manual for your particular computer system for details.

On a timesharing system, you enter FORTRAN statements under control of a text editor, creating a disk file. You type commands to the operating system to have it compile and execute your program. You type data directly to the program, rather than using punch cards.

A program called the FORTRAN compiler translates your FORTRAN program into machine language. The compiler will diagnose any errors it can detect. If it finds none, your program will begin execution: the phase in which your instructions to the computer are carried out.

Finding and correcting errors in a program is called debugging. Errors can occur during compilation or execution of a program. Learning to understand the diagnostics produced by the computer system will help you to master the art of debugging.

The operating system is a complex program that controls the compilation and execution of all other programs. It also schedules jobs and manages computer resources so that the system can be used in a convenient, efficient manner by many people.

VOCABULARY

bug	execution
character set	execution error
columns	hardware
comment line	job deck
compilation	linking
compilation error	operating system
compiler	program cards
continuation line	software
control card	syntax error
cross-reference map	text editor
data card	timesharing
debugging	translation
diagnostic	turnaround time

EXERCISES

1. From your instructor, or from the system reference manual, find out the job control language statements needed to run a job on your system. Write them down in the back of this book. Which statements cause compilation? Which statements cause execution? Is there a separate statement that causes linking, or is linking implied by the statement that causes execution?

2. If you will be using punch cards in your class, study the keyboard of a keypunch. Locate the FEED key. Depress it twice. A card is now ready for punching. Hold down the NUM (numeric) key and type the digits 0123456789. Press the space bar until the column indicator (the red arrow in the window) points to column 20. Punch all the letters A to Z in order. Press the space bar until column 50 is reached. Type the special characters

   + − * / . , ( ) = $ ' :

   Press the REL (release) key, the REG (register) key, and the REL key again. Remove the card and compare it to the one shown in Figure 2.1. Are the holes the same? In which column is the letter Z punched?

3. If you will be using a terminal for your class, find out from your instructor how to log in on the computer. Locate the RETURN key on your terminal and press it. What does the computer type (if anything) when it is expecting a command? Type the letters ABCDE and press the BACKSPACE or RUBOUT key. Can you erase

mistakes with this key? Is there a key you can type to erase the entire line? Locate the SHIFT key and the CONTROL key. What do these keys do? Type the digits, letters, and special characters listed in Exercise 2.

4. Using a keypunch or terminal, type the program in Figure 2.9, substituting your own name for the author's name. Type the control statements needed to run the program. Type the data cards shown in Example 2.3. Now run the program.

5. On your output from Exercise 4, locate the program listing. Make a check mark beside each line that the compiler printed in addition to your input lines. What is the purpose of each of these lines? Did your program compile successfully? Were there any diagnostic messages? Is there a load map? Is there a list of the control statements you used? Is there any program output? Is it the same as the answer in the text? If not, correct the errors and rerun the job. How much time did the computer use to compile your program? To execute it? How much memory was needed?

6. Suppose that Thomas Jefferson had opened a savings account 200 years ago with $2.00 earning 8% interest, compounded quarterly. How much would that account be worth today? The answer is given by the following FORTRAN program.

```
*  THOMAS JEFFERSON'S SAVINGS ACCOUNT
   *
      REAL AMOUNT
      AMOUNT = 2.00 * (1 + 0.08/4) ** (4 * 200)
      PRINT *, 'VALUE TODAY = $ ' , AMOUNT
      END
```

Run this program on the computer.

7. The purpose of this exercise is to familiarize you with diagnostics. Run the program in Exercise 6, *but*: make a deliberate mistake in each line. For example, you can keypunch the program as follows:

```
   THOMAS JEFFERSON'S SAVINGS ACCOUNT
        *
   REAL, AMOUNT
   AMOUNT = 2.00 * 1 + 0.08/4) ** 4 * 20
   PRINT, 'VALUE TODAY = $, ' AMOUNT
```

Study the diagnostic messages produced by the compiler. Next to each such message, write down the problem you think caused it. Consult the system reference manuals to see if there is a list of diagnostics. If you find any message you do not understand, have someone explain it to you. Were there any mistakes in the program that were not diagnosed? To find out, correct only the mistakes that were diagnosed and run the program again.

8. Suppose you are playing a gambling game for a penny a game. You lose the first game. You and your opponent agree to make it "double or nothing," meaning that if you lose again, you will owe 2 cents, but if you win, you will be even. Suppose you continue this and lose 30 times in a row. How much will you owe? The answer, in pennies, is 2 raised to the 30th power. The following program computes this number and prints it (as dollars). Run the program.

```
* DOUBLE OR NOTHING
      REAL X
      X = (2.0 ** 30)/100
      PRINT *, 'YOU OWE $', X
      END
```

9. This exercise will acquaint you with execution error diagnostics. The following program prints a table of square roots.

```
* PRINT A SHORT TABLE OF SQUARE ROOTS.
*
      REAL X
      X = 50
10    IF (X .GT. −5) THEN
          PRINT *, 'X = ', X, ' SQUARE ROOT = ', X ** 0.5
          X = X − 1
          GO TO 10
      END IF
      END
```

According to the program, what is the last value of X that should be printed? Since the square root of a negative number cannot be computed in the ordinary way, what do you think the last value of X actually printed will be? Run the program. Examine the output carefully. What was the value of X when the program halted? Is there a message that tells you that the program terminated abnormally? Is this message in the same place as a message that diagnoses a syntax error?

10. Find out the answers to the following questions.
    (a) What model computer are you using?
    (b) How much memory does it have?
    (c) How much disk storage space does it have?
    (d) What kinds of input/output devices does it have, and how many of each are there?
    (e) What is the name of the operating system you use?
    (f) Where is the reference manual for the operating system available?
    (g) Where is the reference manual for the FORTRAN compiler available?
    (h) What are some features of the FORTRAN compiler (such as, debugging options) that might be of use to you in this class?

CONSTANTS, VARIABLES, AND EXPRESSIONS

INTRODUCTION   When it comes to arithmetic, computers are so much faster than humans that it is almost incredible. You can blink your eyes in about one-fifth of a second. In that time, even a modestly priced small computer can do about 10,000 multiplications! Thus mathematical computation, which most people find a tedious chore, is done easily by a computer. And FORTRAN makes it easy for you to set up a problem for the machine.

The FORTRAN instruction for carrying out a computation is the **assignment statement**. An example is

    X = 2.54*(A + 1)

The form of an assignment statement is always the same. On the left of the equal sign is a variable name. On the right is an **expression**. The expression

    2.54*(A + 1)

contains **constants** 2.54, and 1; a **variable**, A; **operators**, *, and +; and parentheses. For doing numerical calculation FORTRAN provides four kinds of constants and variables. The two most common types are **integer** and **real**. The other types, **double precision** and **complex**, are useful for certain special kinds of computation, and are covered in Chapter 10. This chapter explains how to use integer and real variables, and you will learn the rules for combining them into expressions.

CONSTANTS

You can write a FORTRAN constant the same way you ordinarily write numbers—with a few exceptions. For example, 10,000 is not a legal FORTRAN constant because it contains a comma. The number 3 1/2 is not a legal constant because it is not written as a decimal number.

Rule for FORTRAN Constants
A FORTRAN constant consists of one or more numbers, 0 through 9. It may have an initial plus or minus sign to indicate whether it is positive or negative. If it has no sign, it is positive. The constant may be written with or without a decimal point. Commas are not allowed. You can write zeros before a number without affecting the value.

Table 3.1 shows some examples of FORTRAN constants.

TABLE 3.1
SOME FORTRAN CONSTANTS

Number	*FORTRAN Form*	*Comments*
1,000	1000	No comma
1,000,123	1 000 123	Blanks are allowed
8 1/2	8.5	Must be written in decimal form
1/3	0.333333	Must use an approximation to write in decimal form
π	3.14159	Must use an approximation to write in decimal form
0 ˜	0 or 0.0 or 0.	All are acceptable ways of writing it
−6.2	−6.2	

TABLE 3.2
SOME FORTRAN CONSTANTS

Constant	*Type*
31.1	Real
31.0	Real
31.	Real
31	Integer
0	Integer
0.0	Real
+1	Integer
−0.33333	Real
−1.2E−1	Real
333E−3	Real

FORTRAN distinguishes between two types of numeric data: **integer** and **real**. An integer is a whole number such as −2, −1, 0, 1, 2, 3. A real number is one which may not be a whole number, such as 4.6 or −3.01.

A FORTRAN constant may be an **integer constant** or a **real constant**. You can tell the difference by the following simple rule.

> Rule for Integer and Real Constants
> A FORTRAN integer constant does *not* have a decimal point. A FORTRAN real constant *does* have a decimal point.

Table 3.2 gives some examples of integer and real constants.

EXPONENTIAL FORM

Numbers that are very large or very small are often written in **scientific notation**. In this notation, a number is written with a multiplier that is a power of 10 (Table 3.3).

TABLE 3.3
EXAMPLES OF SCIENTIFIC NOTATION

Number	Scientific Notation	
365	3.65×10^2	(Days in a year)
86,400	8.64×10^4	(Seconds in a day)
31,536,000	3.1536×10^7	(Seconds in a year)
0.0022	2.20×10^{-3}	(Pounds in a gram)
0.000001	1.0×10^{-6}	(Meters in a micron)
0.0000000667	6.67×10^{-8}	(Gravity constant in centimeter-gram-second system)

The FORTRAN equivalent of scientific notation is called the **exponential form** or **E form** of a constant. Instead of using a superscript, FORTRAN exponential form uses the letter E followed by the power of 10 multiplier. For example, in FORTRAN

    5.975E27

can represent the number 5.975×10^{27}.

Numbers written in exponential form are always real constants in FORTRAN, although you can omit the decimal point before the E. Thus,

    12.0E2   and   12E2

are both FORTRAN real constants equal to 1200.0.

The **exponent** (the number following the letter E) may be positive or negative. For example,

    −1.23E2   or   −1.23E+2

both mean $-1.23 \times 10^2 = -123.0$. And,

    −1.23E−2

means $-1.23 \times 10^{-2} = -0.0123$.

Table 3.4 shows some more examples of FORTRAN E-form constants with the equivalent values in scientific notation.

TABLE 3.4
EXPONENTIAL FORM OF REAL NUMBERS IN FORTRAN

FORTRAN Number	Scientific Notation	Value
2.0E4	2.0×10^4	20,000
2.E4	2.0×10^4	20,000
2E4	2.0×10^4	20,000
2 E 4	2.0×10^4	20,000
+02.00E+4	2.0×10^4	20,000
2.0E04	2.0×10^4	20,000
1.63E1	1.63×10^1	16.3
1.63E−1	1.63×10^{-1}	0.163
.163E0	0.163×10^0	0.163
163.0E−3	163.0×10^{-3}	0.163
1.0E−6	1.0×10^{-6}	0.000001
7.E13	7.0×10^{13}	70,000,000,000,000

WHY INTEGERS AND REAL NUMBERS ARE DIFFERENT*

You may wonder why we bother with two kinds of numbers, or why integer variables and real numbers are different. After all, in mathematics, a number is a number, is it not?

Yes—but the mathematics of computers is slightly different from ordinary mathematics. Remember that a variable in FORTRAN is just a name for a memory location. Since each memory location can store only a certain number of digits, there are some numbers that can be represented only approximately.

For instance, 1 divided by 3 is an infinite series of digits: 0.33333 . . . . A computer memory can store only a finite number of digits, so the number 1/3 must be rounded to an approximation, such as 0.333333. A typical computer provides seven-place accuracy, so for practical purposes, you can usually forget about the slight inaccuracy of the computer. Still, there are some cases where you need an exact result—for example, in counting the number of times a program loop was executed.

This, then, is the dilemma of computer arithmetic: We want some numbers to be exact, yet some numbers must be approximate. The resolution, as you may have guessed, is to have two kinds of numbers.

Integer numbers are exact. The only restriction on integers is that their values be within certain limits: on a typical computer system, an integer number may have any value between $-2^{35} + 1$ and $2^{35} - 1$.

*Optional section.

Real numbers are not necessarily exact. In order that real arithmetic may be as accurate as possible, real numbers are stored in computer memory using a kind of scientific notation in which each number has a fraction part and an exponent part which are stored separately. (See Figure 3.1.) The real constant

12345678987654321.0

might be stored in the computer memory as

1.23457 × 10¹⁶

On a typical computer, a real number can have any value for which the exponent part is between −78 and +75. The machine may, however, store only seven significant digits of the number. You can force the machine to store more digits of a number by using double precision constants, covered in Chapter 10. Mathematicians have found that this method of storing numbers in two parts helps to minimize the inaccuracy that results from computation with approximate numbers.

FIGURE 3.1

Integer number: 1234
In computer memory:

Real number: 33.33333 = 0.3333333 × 10²
In computer memory:

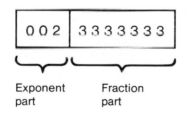

Exponent part   Fraction part

If you could look into computer memory you would see that integer numbers are stored differently than real numbers. An integer is stored in one part, but a real number is stored in two parts: an exponent and a fraction.

VARIABLES

In algebra you generally represent a variable with a single letter, such as x or y. A FORTRAN variable name can be a letter, such as X, or a word, such as WEIGHT. The rule is this:

Rule for FORTRAN Variable Names
A variable name must begin with a letter. It can consist of from one to six characters. Only letters (A – Z) and numbers (0 – 9) may be used in the name. Special symbols such as +, ., or / are not allowed.

Table 3.5 gives some examples of FORTRAN variable names.

TABLE 3.5
EXAMPLES OF VARIABLE NAMES

Some Correct Variable Names

A	LETTER
I	ALPHA
MASS	WW7777
TAX	NNN
X1234	HELLO

Some Incorrect Variable Names

IJKLMNOPQ	(Too many characters)
I+J	(Illegal symbol)
4H	(Does not start with a letter)
NAME.1	(Illegal symbol)
AMOUNTDUE	(Too many characters)

Like constants, each FORTRAN variable has a certain type. An integer variable stores integer values, and a real variable stores real values.

You can choose, for each variable in your program, whether to make it integer or real. If you make it an integer variable, it will be an integer variable throughout the program, and will contain only integer values. If you make it a real variable, it will be a real variable throughout the program, and will contain only real values. You can indicate your choice by using an **INTEGER** or a **REAL statement**.

Suppose that you want the variables COUNT, TICKS, and N to be integer variables. At the beginning of the program, you can write the FORTRAN statement

    INTEGER COUNT, TICKS, N

Similarly, if you want the variables X, L, and BETSY to be real variables in a program, use the following statement at the beginning:

    REAL X, L, BETSY

EXECUTABLE AND NONEXECUTABLE STATEMENTS

The INTEGER and REAL statements are classified as **type statements**: statements that tell the *type* (integer or real) of certain variables. Type statements are one kind of **specification statement** in FORTRAN. A specification statement gives information about the variables used in a program. You will learn about other specification statements later on.*

All specification statements are **nonexecutable**. Nonexecutable statements do not cause the machine to do anything when the program runs. They provide information about the program that is used when the program is compiled.

Assignment statements, READ statements, and PRINT statements, on the other hand, are examples of **executable statements**. Executable statements *do* cause something to happen when the program is run. Executable statements are your instructions to the computer. Nonexecutable statements are instructions to the FORTRAN compiler, giving supplemental information about how to carry out your instructions.†

We mentioned before that INTEGER and REAL statements go at the beginning of a program. To be more precise, the rule is this:

Rule for Location of Specification Statements
All the specification statements in a program must come before the first executable statement in the program.

IMPLICIT TYPE DECLARATION

The INTEGER and REAL statements let you *explicitly* declare the types of each variable in your program. There is another way to specify the type of a variable.

Suppose you decide to adopt the following convention in writing a certain program: All variables whose names begin with the letter "A" will be integer variables, and all variables whose names begin with the letter "B" will be real variables. Rather than listing each variable in an INTEGER or REAL statement, you can include the following **IMPLICIT statement** at the beginning of your program:

IMPLICIT INTEGER (A), REAL (B)

This specification statement defines variable types *implicitly*. The type of a variable is implied by its name. Variables named APPLE, or A, or ALVIN will be integer variables in the program, since their names begin with A. Variables named B12, or BILL, or BTU will be real variables, since their names begin with B.

An IMPLICIT statement consists of the word IMPLICIT followed by a type, which may be INTEGER, or REAL (or any of the other types you will study in this book), followed by a set of parentheses that tell which letters are associated with the type. You can use a single letter, as in

IMPLICIT INTEGER (X)

---

*The FORTRAN type statements are: INTEGER, REAL, DOUBLE PRECISION, COMPLEX, LOGICAL, and CHARACTER. The other specification statements are: DIMENSION, EQUIVALENCE, COMMON, IMPLICIT, PARAMETER, EXTERNAL, INTRINSIC, and SAVE.

†In addition to the specification statements already listed, the following FORTRAN statements are nonexecutable: PROGRAM, FUNCTION, SUBROUTINE, ENTRY, BLOCK DATA, DATA, FORMAT, and statement function definition.

meaning that all variables beginning with letter X are integer variables. You can give a sequence of letters, separated by commas, as in

    IMPLICIT INTEGER (A, B, C, D, E)

meaning that all variables beginning with letters A, B, C, D, or E are integer variables. Another way to write this is

    IMPLICIT INTEGER (A − E)

In an IMPLICIT statement, the notation "A − E" means "A through E."

If you use an IMPLICIT statement, it must be the very first statement in your program. To be more precise, the rule is:

Rule for Position of Implicit Statements
All IMPLICIT statements must precede all other specification statements and all executable statements.

You can override (or confirm) the effect of an IMPLICIT statement by including an explicit type declaration. For example, the two statements

    IMPLICIT REAL (A − Z)
    INTEGER I, N

mean that all variables in the program will be real variables, *except* for I and N, which are integer variables.

DEFAULT TYPE DECLARATION

FORTRAN does not require that every variable be declared in a type statement. When you do not declare the type of a variable, the variable has a **default type**, either integer or real, depending on the variable's name.

Rule for Default Types
Unless otherwise specified (by a type statement or an IMPLICIT statement), if a variable name begins with the letter I, J, K, L, M, or N, it is an integer variable. If the name begins with a letter A through H, or O through Z, it is a real variable.

In other words, unless you specify otherwise, variable types are determined as though you began the program with the statement

    IMPLICIT REAL (A — H), INTEGER (I — N), REAL (O — Z)

This convention comes from the standard practice in mathematics of using variables *i*, *j*, *k*, *l*, *m*, and *n* for subscripts or for variables that take only integer values.

STYLE MODULE—CHOOSING VARIABLE NAMES

It is usually a challenging mental exercise, when writing a program, to keep track of the variables you have used. Many bugs turn out to be due to a misunderstanding of the exact definition of a variable, or to using a variable in two slightly different ways in different parts of the program.

A good way to avert this problem is to choose variable names that mean something. If you need a variable to represent time, you could call it T, but a better choice is TIME. If a variable represents a street address, call it STREET, rather than A. Avoid variable names that are too similar. If your program uses variables for State and Federal Tax, you could call them TAX1 and TAX2; better names would be STATAX and FEDTAX. Do not use randomly chosen names like X9.

Another helpful practice is to write a definition of each variable and to include the dictionary as comments in your program. The program on page 74 gives an example. If you use top-down program design methods, making such a dictionary should be easy, since your top-level program outline will define the data being processed.

If your FORTRAN compiler can produce a cross-reference list of variable names, learn to use this feature. Glancing through such a list can help to quickly locate typographic errors. In a cross-reference list, some compilers will mark variables that have been used but not defined. For instance, if a variable X2 appears in only one statement such as

    Y = X2

it is almost certainly an error. Perhaps the programmer intended to write

    Y = X*2

As another example, if you see a variable named PRINT in your listing when you know that you have used no such variable (intentionally), you should suspect that some PRINT statement in the program was incorrectly typed.

STYLE MODULE—USING TYPE STATEMENTS

You have seen three ways to declare the type of a variable:

1. Use an explicit type statement (INTEGER or REAL).
2. Use the default type, which depends on the first letter of the name.
3. Use an IMPLICIT statement to create your own default types.

All three methods are commonly used. In fact, you can use them all in the same program. There are some stylistic considerations you should be aware of in making your choice.

Method 2 is the most common among most FORTRAN programmers. One drawback is that default type variables are either integer or real. Character variables, which are covered in Chapter 5, always require an explicit type declaration.

If you use default typing at all, use it consistently. If you make an exception to the usual naming conventions, you may forget that you have done so, leading to possible confusion. For example, do not make a variable X an integer variable in a program where all the other variables have the default type.

Method 3, using an IMPLICIT statement, is especially useful in programs where all the variables (or almost all of them) have the same type. In some applications, it is common for a program to use all integer variables. In that case you could use the specification

```
IMPLICIT INTEGER (A — Z)
```

This gives you the freedom to think up meaningful variable names that begin with something other than I, J, K, L, M, or N.

Remember that you can override the effect of an IMPLICIT statement with explicit type declarations. If all the variables in some program are integer type, except for a few that are real type, you might use the statements

```
IMPLICIT INTEGER (A — Z)
REAL AMOUNT, WEIGHT
```

Our recommendation is to declare all variables explicitly. The effort required will pay off in a more readable program. Note that this method fits well with our recommendation of using comments to make a dictionary of variable definition. For instance:

```
* NUMBER OF CASES
      INTEGER NCASES
* MAXIMUM X VALUE, Y VALUE
      REAL XMAX, YMAX
* NUMBER OF SAMPLES
      INTEGER N
```

All of the programs in this book use explicit type declarations for the variables. In short examples that are not complete programs, you can assume that variables have their default types unless otherwise specified.

THE ASSIGNMENT STATEMENT

The **assignment statement** is used to assign a value to a variable. An example is

APPLE = 1.0

which says to store the value of the constant 1.0 in the variable APPLE. The variable receiving the new value is always written to the *left* of the equal sign. To the right of the equal sign you write a constant (as above), a variable, or, in general, an *expression*. As you saw in Chapter 1, the value of the expression is stored in the variable, destroying any previous value it may have held.

EXPRESSIONS

An **expression** can be a constant or a variable or a combination of constants, variables, and expressions joined by **operators**, and possibly grouped by parentheses.

The expression

A + B

consists of two variables joined by the operator "+." The expression

2*(X + 1)

is made up of a constant, 2, and an expression (X + 1), joined by the operator *. Table 3.6 lists the FORTRAN operators for arithmetic computations.

TABLE 3.6
FORTRAN OPERATORS

+	Addition
	Subtraction (or changing sign)
*	Multiplication
/	Division
**	Exponentiation (raising to a power)

The minus sign can denote subtraction, as in the statement

Y = A − 1.0

or it can mean to change the sign of a quantity, as in the statement

X = −A

which means to take the negative of A and store it in X.

FORTRAN does not permit one mathematical operator to come right after another. For example,

A + / B

is an incorrect expression. If you ever need to use two operators in a row, use parentheses to separate them. For instance, to multiply X by the negative of WEIGHT, you *cannot* use the expression

    X * − WEIGHT

but you *can* use the expression

    X *(−WEIGHT)

Note that the symbol for exponentiation (∗∗) is considered to be a single operator. Table 3.7 gives some more examples.

TABLE 3.7
EXAMPLES OF FORTRAN EXPRESSIONS

Algebra Form	FORTRAN Expression
profit − 10% of sales	PROFIT − 0.10∗SALES
$\dfrac{1}{x-1}$	1.0/(X − 1.0)
$1/2\ at^2 + vt$	0.5∗A∗T∗∗2+V∗T
$\dfrac{a\ -\ 1}{b\ -\ 2}$	(A−1.0)/(B−2.0)

Evaluating an expression means carrying out the indicated mathematical operations to compute the value. For example, when the computer evaluates the expression

    N + 1

it recalls the value of the variable N and adds the value of the constant 1. The assignment statement:

    variable = expression

tells the computer to evaluate the expression on the right and store the resulting value in the variable on the left.

There are rules that specify the order in which operations are evaluated in a FORTRAN expression. These rules are similar to the usual conventions of algebra. For example, in algebra, the expression

$$2x + 1$$

means to multiply 2 by x, then add 1. That is, $2x + 1$ means the same as

$$(2x) + 1$$

vhich is different from

$$2(x + 1)$$

Similarly, in evaluating the FORTRAN expression

    2 * X + 1

the multiplication is carried out before the addition.

Specifically, the rules for evaluating expressions are as follows:

Rules for Order of Evaluation

Parentheses may be used to group the terms in an expression. Any expression inside parentheses is completely evaluated before evaluating any expression of which it is a part.

Unless otherwise grouped by parentheses, operations are carried out in the following order:

    exponentiations
    multiplications and divisions
    additions, subtractions, and negations

Consecutive exponentiations are carried out right to left. Thus,

    A ** B ** C

means the same as

    A ** (B ** C)

Subject to the above rules, operations are carried out left to right.*

To see how these rules work, consider the statement

    DELTA = A/B*C

This might seem ambiguous. Does it mean

$$\text{DELTA} = \frac{A}{B \cdot C}$$

or does it mean

$$\text{DELTA} = \frac{A}{B} \cdot C$$

*To be precise, the *effect* of a computation must be left-to-right evaluation. The computer may rearrange the order of operations in any mathematically equivalent manner.

The left-to-right rule means that the division (/) is evaluated before the multiplication (∗). Thus A is divided by B, then the result is multiplied by C, just as though we had written parentheses:

DELTA = (A/B)∗C

As another example, the statement

W = 2.0∗X + 3.0∗Y

means the same as

W = (2.0∗X) + (3.0∗Y)

because of the rule that says multiplication is done before addition.

EXAMPLE 3.1 Selling Price for a Given Profit Margin
A retail merchant paid $357 for 75 toys. What is the average cost of each item, and what should be the selling price if it is desired to make a 20% profit?

In writing FORTRAN statements to carry out this computation, it will be just as easy to use variable names for the quantities involved as to use their numerical values. We could let A be the average cost, P the price, etc. We prefer to use longer variable names that give more indication of what the variables stand for. We let

UNITS be the number of units
TCOST be the total cost
PMARG be the profit margin
UCOST be the unit cost
PRICE be the unit price

Now, the unit cost is the total cost divided by the number of units. The unit price, to attain a desired profit margin, is the unit cost divided by 1 minus the profit margin. If the profit margin is given as percent (for example, 20.0 represents 20%), it must be divided by 100 to give a decimal fraction (0.20 represents 20%). The following two assignment statements will perform this calculation.

UCOST = TCOST/UNITS
PRICE = UCOST/(1 − PMARG/100)

Here is a complete FORTRAN program that reads the number of units, the total cost, and the desired profit margin as input.

```
* PROGRAM TO COMPUTE THE UNIT COST AND
* THE UNIT PRICE FOR A GIVEN PROFIT MARGIN.
*
      REAL UNITS, TCOST, PMARG, UCOST, PRICE
*
* READ THE NUMBER OF UNITS, THE TOTAL COST,
* AND THE PROFIT MARGIN. THE PROFIT MARGIN
```

```
   * IS EXPRESSED IN PERCENT (FOR EXAMPLE, 20.0 MEANS 20 PERCENT)
   *
         READ *, UNITS, TCOST, PMARG
   *
   * COMPUTE AND PRINT THE UNIT COST
   * AND THE UNIT PRICE.
   *
         UCOST = TCOST/UNITS
         PRICE = UCOST/(1 - PMARG/100)
         PRINT *, 'UNITS: ', UNITS
         PRINT *, 'TOTAL COSTS: ' TCOST
         PRINT *, 'PROFIT MARGIN: ', PMARG, ' PERCENT'
         PRINT *, 'UNIT COST: ', UCOST
         PRINT *, 'UNIT PRICE: ', PRICE
         END
```

EXAMPLE 3.2 Another Way to Write the Same Program
You have seen examples of expressions in assignment statements. You can also use expressions
in other FORTRAN statements. For instance, you can use an expression in a PRINT statement
such as

```
   PRINT *, 'THE SUM IS', A + B
```

If you like, you can omit the variables UCOST and PRICE from the program in Example
3.1, writing the corresponding expressions as part of the PRINT statements. Here is the revised
program.

```
   * REVISED PROGRAM TO COMPUTE THE UNIT COST AND
   * THE UNIT PRICE FOR A GIVEN PROFIT MARGIN.
   * (IN THIS VERSION THE EXPRESSIONS ARE WRITTEN
   * AS PART OF THE PRINT STATEMENTS.)
   *
         REAL UNITS, TCOST, PMARG, UCOST, PRICE
   *
         READ *, UNITS, TCOST, PMARG
         PRINT *, 'UNITS: ', UNITS
         PRINT *, 'TOTAL COSTS: ', TCOST
         PRINT *, 'PROFIT MARGIN: ', PMARG, ' PERCENT'
         PRINT *, 'UNIT COST: ', TCOST/UNITS
         PRINT *, 'UNIT PRICE: ', (TCOST/UNITS)/(1 - PMARG/100)
         END
```

EXAMPLE 3.3 Compound Interest
A sum of money P (the principal) is invested at a rate of interest r given as a percent (for
example, 20.0 means 20%). The interest is compounded m times per year for n years. For
example, if the interest is compounded monthly for 4 years, then $m = 12$ and $n = 4$. The
accumulated amount, principal plus interest, is given by the formula

$$A_n = P \left(1 + \frac{r}{100m} \right)^{mn}$$

Write a program to read values of P, r, m, and n, and compute A_n.

First you must decide on legal names for the variables. A_n has a subscript, so it is not a legal FORTRAN variable name. There is really no need to use a subscript. You can call the amount A, or better yet, call it AMOUNT. Likewise, you can invent meaningful names for the other variables. The formula is easily translated into a FORTRAN expression. Here is a complete program.

```
* COMPOUND INTEREST PROGRAM.
* READ VALUES FOR THE FOLLOWING VARIABLES:
*     PRINCE = PRINCIPAL (AMOUNT INVESTED).
*     RATE = ANNUAL INTEREST RATE, IN PERCENT.
*     NTIMES = NUMBER OF TIMES PER YEAR THE MONEY IS
*         COMPOUNDED (12 FOR MONTHLY COMPOUNDING).
*     YEARS = NUMBER OF YEARS - MAY BE A DECIMAL FRACTION.
* THE PROGRAM COMPUTES THE ACCUMULATED PRINCIPAL PLUS
* INTEREST.

      REAL PRINCE, RATE, NTIMES, YEARS, AMOUNT
      READ *, PRINCE, RATE, NTIMES, YEARS
      PRINT *, 'PRINCIPAL $', PRINCE
      PRINT *, 'INTEREST RATE ', RATE, ' PERCENT'
      PRINT *, 'COMPOUNDED ', NTIMES, ' TIMES PER YEAR'
      PRINT *, 'FOR ', YEARS, ' YEARS'
      AMOUNT = PRINCE*(1 + RATE/(100*NTIMES))**(NTIMES*YEARS)
      PRINT *, 'YIELDS A TOTAL AMOUNT OF $', AMOUNT
      END
```

REAL AND INTEGER ARITHMETIC

If an arithmetic expression involves only integer numbers and integer variables, we call it an **integer expression**. For example, if LIMIT is an integer variable,

    2*LIMIT + 11

is an integer expression. When the computer evaluates this expression, the result will be an integer number.

If an arithmetic expression involves only real numbers and real variables, we call it a **real expression**. For example, if FISH and SCALE are real, then

    9.0*FISH/SCALE

is a real expression.

One difference between real and integer expressions is in the way division is performed. In integer arithmetic, a quotient is always an integer number, while in real arithmetic, decimal fractions are allowed. For example, the real expression

    3.0/2.0

would be evaluated as 1.5. However, in integer division, the decimal part is truncated, and

   3/2

is evaluated as 1. As another example, $10/(-3)$ is the integer -3 (the fractional part is truncated and the minus sign is retained).

   This property of integer arithmetic has some useful applications. It is a bit different from ordinary arithmetic. Consider the expression

   (5*3)/5

This is evaluated as $15/5 = 3$. However, if the parentheses are placed differently, as

   5*(3/5)

then the result is $5*0 = 0$ since $3.0/5.0 = 0.6$, which is truncated to zero in integer arithmetic.

   When an expression involves both real and integer variables, we call it a **mixed-mode expression**. An example of a mixed-mode expression is

   2.1 + (17/5)

Here 17 and 5 are integer numbers and 2.1 is a real number. In this expression, first 17/5 is evaluated in integer mode. The result is the integer value 3 (*not* 3.4). The computer cannot add the real number 2.1 directly to the integer number 3, so it converts the integer number to the equivalent real value 3.0, and then adds these two real numbers to get the real result 5.1. This example illustrates the following rule.

Rule for Mixed-Mode Arithmetic
If an addition, subtraction, multiplication, or division operation involves both an integer and a real number, the integer number is converted to real form, the operation is performed in real arithmetic, and the result is a real number.

   This means that the statements

   X = X + 1

and

   X = X + 1.0

will have exactly the same effect.

   Expressions involving raising to a power deserve some special attention. A real expression raised to an integer power is considered a real expression, not a mixed-mode expression. For example,

    X**3

is a real expression, since it means the same as

    X*X*X

Integer exponents should be used when raising a quantity to an integer power. To square the value of X, you should write

    X**2

not

    X**2.0

These may seem like the same thing, but these two expressions are evaluated differently. The second form is computed using logarithms, which is a comparatively slow method. The second form has one other drawback: it is illegal in FORTRAN to raise a negative number to a real power. So the expression X**2 (with an integer exponent) is legal whether X is positive, negative, or zero; but the expression X**2.0 (with a real exponent) will cause an execution error in the program if the value of X is not a positive number.

TYPE CONVERSION WITH AN ASSIGNMENT STATEMENT

An integer variable must always contain an integer number, and a real variable must always contain a real number. As you saw earlier, these types of numbers are stored differently in the computer memory. You can use an assignment statement to convert an integer value to real or vice versa.

For example, the statement

    X = 34

says to assign an integer value to the variable X. If X is a real variable, the computer will convert the integer value 34 to the real value 34.0 before storing it in X. Thus the statements

    X = 34

and

X = 34.0

have exactly the same effect.

You can also assign a real value to an integer variable, as in the statement

N = 7.3

Suppose N is an integer variable. Since 7.3 is not an integer, the computer discards the fraction part and stores the integer value 7 in N. Thus, the statements

N = 7.3

and

N = 7

have exactly the same effect.

In general, the rules for conversion are these:

Rules for Type Conversion
When setting a real variable equal to an integer expression, the value is simply converted to real form.

When setting an integer variable equal to a real expression, the value of the real expression is converted to integer form by truncating the decimal fraction part.

Table 3.8 gives some more examples of type conversions.

TABLE 3.8
EXAMPLES OF TYPE CONVERSION*

Assignment Statement	Value Stored
N = 7.9	7
KICK = −6.2	−6
K = −6.0	−6
LIMIT = 100.0	100
LIMIT = 100.001	100
X = 2 + 2	4.0
CROP = 2*(3 + 1)	8.0
C = 7/3	2.0

*Assume that variables have their default types.

SYMBOLIC CONSTANTS

You have seen how to write FORTRAN constants like

77 (an integer constant)
3.5 (a real constant)

In each case, the constant is represented by a specific value. In science and mathematics it is common to represent a constant by a *symbol*. Some examples are:

π The ratio of the circumference to the diameter of a circle
e The base of natural logarithms
c The speed of light

You can write the formula for the area of a circle as

$$A = 3.14159265r^2$$

or as

$$A = \pi r^2$$

In the first case, we used the *value* of the constant (rounded to an approximation). In the second case, we used the *symbol* π instead.

In FORTRAN, as in mathematics, it is often convenient to represent a constant by a symbol, rather than by a value. The **PARAMETER statement** gives you a way to do this. The following program illustrates its use.

```
      REAL RADIUS, PI
      PARAMETER (PI = 3.14159265)
10    READ (*, *, END = 20) RADIUS
      PRINT *, 'RADIUS = ', RADIUS
      PRINT *, 'DIAMETER = ', 2*RADIUS
      PRINT *, 'CIRCUMFERENCE = ', 2*PI*RADIUS
      PRINT *, 'AREA = ', PI*RADIUS**2
      GO TO 10
20    END
```

The PARAMETER statement here declares that PI is a **symbolic constant** with a value of 3.14159265. The last two PRINT statements use this value of PI in expressions for the circumference and area of a circle. The effect is exactly as though we had written the statements with the numerical value of PI.

The PARAMETER statement is a specification statement. It is nonexecutable, and must come before the first executable statement in a program.

You can write a PARAMETER statement in the form

PARAMETER (*constant* = *expression*)

where *constant* is a symbolic constant name, and *expression* is a constant expression.

A **symbolic constant name** has the same form as a FORTRAN variable name. It consists of one to six letters and digits, and must begin with a letter.

Like a variable, a symbolic constant has a certain type (such as integer or real). You specify the type of a symbolic constant the same way you specify the type of a variable: with a type statement, an IMPLICIT statement, or with a default implicit type. If you use a type statement to give the type of the symbolic constant, the type statement must come before the PARAMETER statement that defines the value of the symbolic constant. Thus, if you want SIZE to be a symbolic constant representing the integer value 100, you could use the statements

```
INTEGER SIZE
PARAMETER (SIZE = 100)
```

To the right of the equal sign in a PARAMETER statement, you write a **constant expression**, which is an expression that involves only constants.

You can define several symbolic constants with a single PARAMETER statement by separating the definitions with commas, as in

```
INTEGER ROWS, COLS, ZERO
PARAMETER (ROWS = 20, COLS = 100, ZERO = 0)
```

A constant expression in a PARAMETER declaration may involve symbolic constants that have been previously defined. For example:

```
INTEGER NCOL, LINSIZ, PAGSIZ
PARAMETER (NCOL - 80)
PARAMETER (LINSIZ = NCOL + 1, PAGSIZ = 50*LINSIZ)
```

Here is a complete program that uses PARAMETER statements.

```
* CONVERT YEARS TO SECONDS
      REAL SECMIN, SECHR, SECDAY, SECYR
      PARAMETER (SECMIN = 60)
      PARAMETER (SECHR = 60*SECMIN)
      PARAMETER (SECDAY = 24.*SECHR)
      PARAMETER (SECYR = 365.*SECDAY)
      READ *, YEARS
      PRINT *, YEARS, 'YEARS EQUALS ',
     $    SECYR*YEARS, ' SECONDS.'
      END
```

As this program illustrates, a constant expression need not be the same type as the symbolic constant being defined. The rules here are the same as for an assignment statement. Thus in the first PARAMETER statement in this example, the integer value 60 is converted to a real value to become the value of the symbolic constant SECMIN.

There are two restrictions on constant expressions: you cannot use exponentiation unless the exponent is an integer, and you cannot use function references (which we discuss in Chapter 7).

You may wonder, at this point, what the difference is between a symbolic constant, defined by a PARAMETER statement, and a variable defined by an assignment statement. In many respects, there is little difference. You can define a constant LIMIT with the specification statement

```
PARAMETER (LIMIT = 25 * 25)
```

or you can define a variable LIMIT with the executable statement

```
LIMIT = 25 * 25
```

One difference is that once the value of a symbolic constant is defined, you *cannot* redefine it, deliberately or accidentally. An even more important difference is that symbolic constants are permissible in certain cases where variables are not. For instance, you can use a constant expression to define the length of character variables, as you will see in Chapter 5.

STYLE MODULE—SYMBOLIC PROGRAMMING

It is good programming practice to use symbols, rather than numbers, for quantities that might change.

Suppose you are writing a program to update account balances for a Savings and Loan Company. Just as you finish, the president walks by your desk and says, "By the way, our interest rate on passbook savings is going up 1/4 percent next week. Will that cause you any problems in your program?" Ideally, you should be able to reply, "Not at all. I'll just change one line." You might have followed a convention in your program of calling the passbook interest rate by the name PBRATE wherever it is used. To change the rate, you would need only change the definition of the symbol at the beginning of the program.

On the other hand, if you had written the interest rate as an explicit constant in several places throughout the program, it might be difficult to make all the necessary changes.

Experienced programmers have learned that such modifications are the rule more often than the exception. Try to anticipate values that might change and represent them as symbols rather than as explicit constants.

Using symbols also improves program readability. Compare these two statements.

```
AREA = 3.1415965*RADIUS**2
AREA = PI*RADIUS**2
```

Using the symbol PI is preferable to using the constant 3.14159265. You can see at a glance that the second formula has the correct form. Did you notice that the first formula has an incorrect value for the constant π? Of course, the symbol PI must be assigned a value somewhere, as in the statement

    PARAMETER (PI = 3.14159265)

But this is the only place in the program you have to look to verify that you used the correct value.

One other reason to use symbols for constants is that you can easily change the precision of the constant. Although the value of π will never change, you might decide to use an approximation of more or fewer decimal digits, depending, possibly, on the computer you are using. Incidentally, it is always acceptable to specify a constant with more precision than the computer can handle. If your computer provides seven-place precision for a real constant, you can still write a constant with more than seven significant digits. Many compilers will print a warning diagnostic to notify you of possible roundoff error.

STYLE MODULE—WRITING EXPRESSIONS

Careful typography in writing expressions will improve the readability of your programs.

Recall that blank spaces can be used almost anywhere in a FORTRAN statement. In fact, as long as the statement is typed in columns 7–72 of the line, FORTRAN completely ignores spaces except within a character constant. Thus, it makes no difference whether you write

    X*(Y/2+3)

or

    X * (Y/2 + 3)

Spaces are ignored even within variable names. If you like, you can write some variables as two words. For instance

    X VALUE = 0.5 * Y VALUE
    PRINT *, FED TAX, SUM 1

Do not be deceived by the spaces; the variables are XVALUE, YVALUE, FEDTAX and SUM1.

Write all expressions in the form that is easiest for you to read. Never sacrifice clarity in an attempt to make a minor gain in efficiency.

Consider these two ways of computing the volume of a sphere.

    * METHOD 1
         VOLUME = 4.18879021*R**3
    * METHOD 2
            PARAMETER (PI = 3.14159265)
            VOLUME = 4.0/3.0*PI*R**3

The second formula is easy to read because it looks like the following algebraic formula

$$V = \frac{4}{3}\,\pi r^3$$

The constant in the first formula is equal to $\frac{4\pi}{3}$, so the formulas should be equivalent—but you need a calculator to check that.

You might feel that Method 2 is inefficient, since it requires the machine to do more arithmetic. A good FORTRAN compiler, however, will recognize 4.0/3.0*PI as a constant expression and evaluate it during compilation, so there is no difference in execution speed between the two methods.

For the same reason, use mixed-mode arithmetic when you find it convenient. If you want to divide a real variable X by 2, you can write the expression

        X/2

Some programmers would advocate writing

        X/2.0

or

        X*0.5

instead, since the mixed-mode expression requires an extra operation to convert the integer 2 to the real value 2.0. But a good FORTRAN compiler will perform the necessary conversion when the program is compiled, so there is no difference in the speed of computing the expressions.

Another false economy in programming is the use of **temporary variables** when they are not needed. For example, suppose you want to compute values of X and Y with the statements

        X = (B2*C1 − B1*C2)/(A1*B2 − A2*B1)
        Y = (A1*C2 − A2*C1)/(A1*B2 − A2*B1)

Observe that the denominator is the same in both expressions. To save the machine the trouble of computing the expression twice, you might store the value in a temporary variable T as follows:

        T = A1*B2 − A2*B1
        X = (B2*C1 − B1*C2)/T
        Y = (A1*C2 − A2*C1)/T

Is this use of a temporary variable really more efficient? Surprisingly, on many computers it would be *less* efficient.* If you want to break a long expression into several parts, that's fine. Using a temporary variable can help to eliminate key-punch errors when typing a long expression. But don't worry about doing so just for a small gain in efficiency.

A modern FORTRAN compiler can **optimize** your program. That is, it can generate highly efficient machine-language instructions to carry out your FORTRAN statements. It is not necessary for you to be overly concerned with program efficiency.

The important thing is make your program easy to read and easy to debug. If you can find a way to get the machine to do your work for you, use it—that is what computers are for.

SUMMARY

A FORTRAN integer or real constant has a certain form:

1. It consists of digits 0 through 9.
2. It may have a plus or minus sign in front of it.
3. Commas are not allowed.
4. It may or may not have a decimal point.

If the constant has a decimal point, it is a real constant; otherwise, it is an integer constant (except that E-form constants need not have a decimal point). An E-form constant is similar to scientific notation.

Variable names consist of one to six letters or digits, and must begin with a letter. Each variable has a certain type, which may be declared in one of three ways:

1. By using an INTEGER or REAL type declaration
2. By using an IMPLICIT type declaration
3. By using default typing

Type declarations are nonexecutable statements.

The assignment statement assigns to some variable the value of an expression. An expression can be a constant or a variable, or a combination of these, joined by operators and grouped by parentheses. There are FORTRAN operators corresponding to the mathematical functions of addition ($+$), subtraction ($-$), multiplication ($*$), division ($/$), and raising to a power ($**$). Certain rules in FORTRAN specify the order in which these operations are carried out. Expressions may be real, integer, or mixed-mode. The assignment statement can be used to convert one type of value to another.

Symbolic constants are defined by a PARAMETER statement. A symbolic constant

---

*Because, an optimizing compiler would recognize the common subexpression anyway, and could store it in a register, rather than in a memory location.

has the same form as a variable and may be either integer or real, but its value does not change in the program.

Good programming style in writing expressions and choosing variable names will improve the readability of a program.

||||||||||||||||||||||||||||||||||||||||||||||||||||||||||||||||||||||||||||||||||||||||||||||||||||||||||||||||||||||||||||||||||||||||

VOCABULARY

assignment statement	INTEGER statement
constant	mixed-mode expression
constant expression	nonexecutable statement
default type	operator
E form	PARAMETER statement
executable statement	real
exponential form	REAL statement
exponentiation	specification statement
expression	symbolic constant
IMPLICIT statement	type conversion
integer	variable

||||||||||||||||||||||||||||||||||||||||||||||||||||||||||||||||||||||||||||||||||||||||||||||||||||||||||||||||||||||||||||||||||||||||

EXERCISES

1. Write each of the following numbers as a FORTRAN constant and tell whether it is an integer or real constant.
   - (a) one-half
   - (b) 1,000
   - (c) π
   - (d) −1 1/2
   - (e) 1/3
   - (f) zero
   - (g) one million
   - (h) 98.6

2. Write each of the following numbers as a FORTRAN E-form constant.
   - (a) 0.123
   - (b) 1
   - (c) -4.5×10^{-6}
   - (d) one million
   - (e) 365
   - (f) 1/100
   - (g) 10^{-5}
   - (h) 186,000
   - (i) 300,000,000
   - (j) 0.0001

3. Which of the following are legal variable names?
   - (a) RENOIR
   - (b) PICASSO
   - (c) A.1
   - (d) A1
   - (e) 1A
   - (f) AAAAA
   - (g) A+B
   - (h) A−B
   - (i) HOURS
   - (j) TEACHER
   - (k) SCHOOL
   - (l) UP BEAT

4. Tell whether each of the following statements is executable or nonexecutable.
   (a) GO TO 7
   (b) INTEGER X, Y, Z
   (c) PRINT *, 'TITLE'
   (d) REAL GOOD
   (e) A = A
   (f) IF (A .EQ. 1) THEN
   (g) IMPLICIT INTEGER (A—Z)

5. Evaluate each of the following constant expressions.
   (a) 2*(2 + 1)   (i)   10/2
   (b) 2 * 2 + 1   (j)   10/3
   (c) 3 * 2 + 6 * 4   (k)   2/10
   (d) 10/2 + 1   (l)   2.0/10.0
   (e) 12/(3 + 1)   (m) 1/2 * 3
   (f) 2**3   (n)   3 * 1/2
   (g) 2**2 + 2   (o)   30/5/2
   (h) 1 + 8/2 + 1   (p)   30/(5/2)

6. Write an equivalent algebraic expression of each of the following FORTRAN expressions.
   (a) 2.1*X**2 + 3.6*X − 1.05
   (b) (A + B)/2*(A − B)
   (c) (1 + 1/R)**(M*N)
   (d) A + B/C + D
   (e) A**N*B**M/C**L
   (f) N*R*T/P

7. Write an equivalent FORTRAN expression for each of the following algebraic expressions.
   (a) r^2

   (b) $(a − b)x^3$

   (c) $\dfrac{1}{\dfrac{1}{R_1} + \dfrac{1}{R_2} + \dfrac{1}{R_3}}$

   (d) 1/3 bh

   (e) $\dfrac{10}{\text{max} − \text{min}}$

   (f) $\dfrac{a}{b + \dfrac{c}{d}}$

   (g) $\dfrac{a}{b + \dfrac{c}{d + \dfrac{e}{f}}}$

   (h) $\left(1 + \dfrac{1}{n}\right)^n$

8. Write a FORTRAN assignment statement to express each of the following formulas.
   (a) $d = (x^2 + y^2 + z^2)^{1/2}$
   (b) $f = x_1y_1 + x_2y_2 + x_3y_3$
   (c) area $= [s(s − a)(s − b)(s − c)]^{1/2}$
   (d) $F = −G\dfrac{m_1m_2}{r^2}$
   (e) $V = (eu)^{-1/2}$
   (f) $k = \dfrac{1}{\sqrt{1 − \dfrac{v^2}{c^2}}}$
   (g) $z = (x_2 − x_1)(1 − B^2)^{1/2}$

   (h) $E = J(J + 1)\dfrac{h^2}{8\pi^2}$

   (i) $Y_0 = \dfrac{2EM}{B^2qd^2}(x_2 − x_1)^2$

   (j) $T = Z − \dfrac{Z^3}{3} + \dfrac{Z^5}{5} − \dfrac{Z^7}{7} + \dfrac{Z^9}{9}$

   (k) $L = \dfrac{s}{(s − a)(s − b)}$

   (l) $f = \dfrac{a}{a^2 + b^2}$

9. For each of the following FORTRAN assignment statements, write an equivalent algebraic formula.
    (a) RESULT = (12*A**2 − 2*A + 31)/(4*A + 6)
    (b) Y = (2*X + 3.5*(1 − X))/9
    (c) Z = A − 2*B + 3*C − 6
    (d) DET = A*D − B*C
    (e) W = X**2 − 5*A*X + 6*A**2
    (f) Y = X**2 + (1 − 2*A**2)*X − 2*A**2

10. Find the values of all the symbolic constants defined by the following statements and indicate whether the constant is integer or real.

    REAL A, B, C, H, HBAR, PI
    INTEGER IP
    PARAMETER (A = 1.0, B = 2.0, C = A + B)
    PARAMETER (H = 6.6251E-27, PI = 3.14159265)
    PARAMETER (HBAR = H/(2*PI), IP = PI)
    INTEGER NC, M
    PARAMETER (NC = C + 1.5, M = NC + 0.5)

For each of the following problems, write a complete FORTRAN program and run it on the computer.

11. In a five-card poker hand, the number of ways of getting various possible hands is given in the table below.

Type of Hand	Number of Possible Hands
One pair	$\dfrac{52 \cdot 3 \cdot 48 \cdot 44 \cdot 40}{2 \cdot 6}$
Two pairs	$\dfrac{52 \cdot 3 \cdot 48 \cdot 3 \cdot 44}{2 \cdot 2 \cdot 2}$
Three of a kind	$\dfrac{52 \cdot 3 \cdot 2 \cdot 48 \cdot 44}{2 \cdot 2 \cdot 3}$
Straight (but not a straight flush)	$10 \cdot 4^5 - 10 \cdot 4$
Flush (but not a straight flush)	$\dfrac{52 \cdot 12 \cdot 11 \cdot 10 \cdot 9}{2 \cdot 3 \cdot 4 \cdot 5} - 4 \cdot 10$
Full house	$\dfrac{52 \cdot 3 \cdot 2 \cdot 48 \cdot 3}{2 \cdot 6}$
Four of a kind	$\dfrac{52 \cdot 3 \cdot 2 \cdot 48}{2 \cdot 3 \cdot 4}$
Straight flush	$4 \cdot 10$
Total possible poker hands	$\dfrac{52 \cdot 51 \cdot 50 \cdot 49 \cdot 48}{2 \cdot 3 \cdot 4 \cdot 5}$
Nothing (no pairs, etc.)	Total number of hands minus sum of the other numbers

Write a program that computes each of these numbers. Also, compute the probability of each of these types of hands. (That is, the probability of a straight is the number of ways of making a straight divided by the total number of poker hands.) Use *no variables* in your program; use symbolic constants instead.

12. Input cards for this program contain two "times:" a start time and a stop time. Each time is represented by three numbers: hours (an integer between 0 and 23, inclusive), minutes (an integer between 0 and 59, inclusive), seconds (a real number between 0 and 59.999...). Thus, the input card

    11 22 10.0,   13 40 5.0

    represents a start time of 11:22:10.0 and a stop time of 13:40:05.0. The program should calculate the difference in times in minutes. Thus, the output corresponding to the above input line should be:

    START 11 22 10.0   STOP 13 40 5.0
                         INTERVAL = 137.91667 MINUTES

    Have the program repeat the procedure for each input card, and print the average interval, in minutes, at the end of the output.

13. Write a program to print the value of X and N, where X is a real variable that takes on values 0.0, 0.1, 0.2, 0.3, ..., 4.8, 4.9, 5.0, and N is an integer variable given by the formula

    N = X + 0.5

    What do these numbers represent?

14. Write a program that reads a positive integer N and prints the value

    1 + 2 + 3 + 4 + ... + N

    (See Exercise 14, Chapter 1.)

15. Write a program that reads a positive integer N and prints the value

    $$1 - 1/2 + 1/3 - 1/4 + \cdots \pm 1/N$$

    (See Exercise 15, Chapter 1.)

16. Write a program that prints the first 30 Fibonacci numbers:

    $$0\ 1\ 1\ 2\ 3\ 5\ 8\ 13 \ldots$$

    where each number in the sequence is the sum of the previous two numbers. (See Exercise 16, Chapter 1.)

17. Write a program that prints a table of factorials for numbers 1 to 100:

    1! = 1
    2! = 2
    3! = 6
    4! = 24
    5! = 120
    $\vdots$ $\vdots$

    (See Exercise 17, Chapter 1.) The number 100! is very large, so this program will probably terminate with an execution error. What is the largest factorial that could be computed? Try this problem first using integer arithmetic, then using real arithmetic. Does it make a difference?

18. Write a program to determine the smallest power of 2 that can be represented on your computer. Do this by setting a real variable POWER equal to 1 and letting N equal 0. Divide POWER by 2 and add 1 to N until one of the following conditions occurs: (a) POWER equals 0, (b) N = 1000, or (c) the program terminates with an execution error. What was the value of N when the program halted?

19. An architect is making a scale model of a building. She has a blueprint giving all the dimensions, in feet, and she wants to know how many inches to make each dimension in the model. Write a program to do the conversions. The first input card is the scale, consisting of two numbers: inches and feet. It means that x inches in the model equal y feet in the building. The following input cards give dimensions, in feet. Print the input dimension followed by the model dimension in inches and in centimeters (2.54 centimeters = 1 inch).

    Example:
    Scale: 1 inch = 3 feet

    BLDG. DIMENSION = 24 FT
    MODEL DIMENSION = 8.0 IN. = 20.32 CM.

20. Write a program that prints a table of height conversions from feet and inches to centimeters. Give the equivalent of every inch from 2 feet to 7 feet. (2.54 centimeters = 1 inch).

    Example:
    2 FEET 0 INCHES = 60.96 CENTIMETERS
    2 FEET 1 INCHES = 63.5 CENTIMETERS
           . . .
    6 FEET 11 INCHES = 210.82 CENTIMETERS
    7 FEET 0 INCHES = 213.36 CENTIMETERS

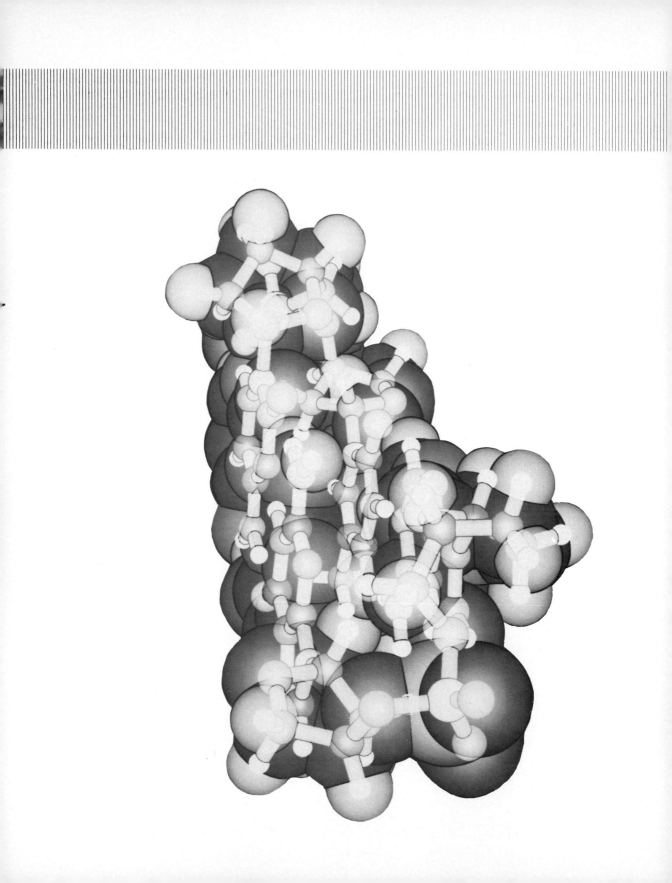

CONTROL STATEMENTS AND STRUCTURED PROGRAMMING

INTRODUCTION   One of the remarkable things about a computer is its ability to make decisions. Some computer programs make decisions so complex that the programs seem to exhibit almost human intelligence. Yet all programs, even the most complex, are made up of computations and elementary decisions like the ones you studied in Chapter 1. These elementary decisions enable a program to choose between alternative instruction sequences depending on the outcome of a single comparison of two quantities.

In FORTRAN, you program a decision using an IF statement. You were introduced to one form of the IF in Chapter 1. In this chapter you will learn about other forms of the IF, and about the related ELSE IF and ELSE statements.

An important use of decisions is in controlling program loops. One way of writing a loop is to use an IF statement in conjunction with a GO TO. Another method is provided by the DO statement.

This chapter also covers the other FORTRAN statements used to control the execution of a program: the STOP, PAUSE, and GO TO statements.

A main theme of this chapter is the need for structured programming. This chapter explains the basic control structures for writing program loops and decisions. Structured programming is a method of combining these control structures in an organized way that clearly reflects the program's meaning. The method is very important for writing programs that are easy to understand, and therefore reliable.

CONTROL STRUCTURES

The structured flowcharts we have been using are made up of rectangular boxes containing basic instructions. These boxes are assembled to show the order in which instructions are carried out. The various ways of assembling the boxes represent the different control structures used in expressing the logic of an algorithm.

We define a **basic block** in a structured flowchart to be either:

1. An empty box, or
2. A box containing an instruction that does not transfer control (for example, an assignment, or an output instruction)

Consider now how basic blocks can be combined in a structured flowchart. We can define a **block** in a structured flowchart through an indirect definition. A *block* in a structured flowchart is either:

1. A basic block, or
2. Any combination of basic blocks that can be constructed from the four rules shown in Figure 4.1

These four rules for constructing a block are the four basic control structures:

1. Sequential structure
2. If-then-else structure
3. While-loop structure
4. Repeat-loop structure

It may help you to understand the definition of a block if you think of it as a sort of puzzle. Suppose you have an assortment of boxes of various shapes and sizes cut out of paper. You can put them together, according to any of the four rules, to make a block. You can put one or more such blocks together, again according to any of the four rules, to make other blocks, and so on. The object of the puzzle is to make structured flowcharts. Figure 4.2 shows a specific example. The structured flowchart at the right of the figure is made in six steps by applying the rules.

You can try this puzzle for yourself. Draw any structured flowchart you can think of, then try to construct it from basic blocks by applying the rules, as in Figure 4.1. With a little experimentation, you can convince yourself of a basic fact: Any structured flowchart can be constructed in this manner. To be more precise, we can state this fact as follows:

Principle of Structured Programming
Any algorithm can be represented by a structured flowchart constructed from basic blocks according to the four rules listed in Figure 4.1.

One way of looking at this principle is that it provides a definition of a structured flowchart: A *structured flowchart* is the same thing as a *block*, as previously defined. But the real significance of the principle is that four control structures are all we need. Any program, no matter how long or how complex, can be written by using these four

FIGURE 4.1
FOUR BASIC CONTROL STRUCTURES

Rule 1: Sequential Structure
A block can be made by joining
two blocks to indicate sequential execution:

Block 1
Block 2

Rule 2: If-Then-Else Structure
A block can be made by joining two
blocks under a condition:

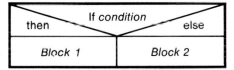

Block 1	*Block 2*

Rule 3: While-Loop Structure
A block can be made by putting
a block inside a while-loop bracket:

While *condition*

Block

Rule 4: Repeat-Loop Structure
A block can be made by putting
a block inside a repeat-loop bracket:

Block

Repeat while *condition*

control structures in an organized way. Later in this chapter we will reexamine this principle to see how it applies to writing structured programs in FORTRAN.

THE GO TO STATEMENT

The **GO TO statement** transfers control to another statement in the program. To specify which statement is to be performed next, you use a **statement label**. A statement label (sometimes called a **statement number**) is just a one- to five-digit number written in columns 1 through 5 of the line. Figure 2.5 on page 38 gives

FIGURE 4.2

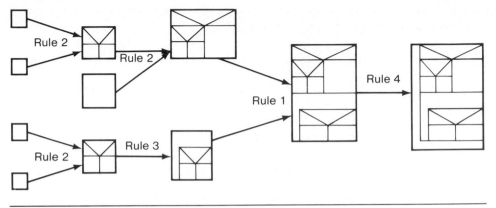

Any structured flowchart can be constructed by applying four rules which correspond to the basic control structures.

examples of statement labels. The form of the GO TO statement is

GO TO *n*

where *n* is a statement label. This causes program control to transfer to the statement with label *n*.

Any statement can have a label. However, no two statements in a program can have the same label. Also, although a nonexecutable statement (such as INTEGER) may have a label, a control statement must not transfer to a nonexecutable statement.

STYLE MODULE—USING STATEMENT LABELS

It will improve the readability of your programs if you use statement labels in increasing order. Statement 20 should come after statement 10. Statement 30 should come after statement 20. This is not required in FORTRAN, but it will help you to find your way through your program. When you read a statement that says GO TO 100, you will know whether to look down the page or up the page for statement 100.

It is a good idea also to skip some numbers between statement labels. Label your statements 10, 20, 30, rather than 1, 2, 3. That way, if you modify your program, you can insert new statement labels and still keep them in increasing order.

STOP, PAUSE, AND END STATEMENTS

The FORTRAN statement

STOP

simply tells the machine to stop executing your program. This **STOP statement** is an executable statement which can appear at any point in your program.

The **END statement** also has a simple form:

```
END
```

Every program must contain one and only one END statement, which must be the last line of the program.

The END statement serves a dual purpose. It is an executable statement that tells the machine to stop running; in this respect it is identical to the STOP statement. But the END statement is also a declarative statement that marks the end of your FORTRAN program, so that the FORTRAN compiler knows when it has read all your program cards.

The following program contains both a STOP and an END statement:

```
REAL X
READ *, X
IF (X .EQ. 0) THEN
      PRINT *, 'THE VALUE IS ZERO'
      STOP
END IF
PRINT *, 'THE VALUE IS NOT ZERO'
END
```

If the number read is zero, the STOP statement terminates execution. Otherwise, the END statement terminates execution.

A STOP statement can include a character string in quotes, such as

```
STOP 'PROGRAM FINISHED'
```

The character string may or may not be used for anything, depending on your particular computer system. On some systems, the character string is printed at the end of your output when the STOP statement is executed. This feature is useful for debugging—especially if you have several different STOP statements in the program.

The **PAUSE statement** serves almost exactly the same purpose as the STOP statement. The form is

```
PAUSE
```

or

```
PAUSE 'character string'
```

The effect of this statement is like a STOP, except that after a PAUSE statement, the computer operator can manually restart the program, which then continues at the statement following the PAUSE.

The exact effect of the PAUSE statement depends on the particular computer system you use. On a timesharing system, it may suspend execution of your program and wait for you to type a command to continue the program execution or end it. This statement can be useful for debugging on a timesharing system.

THE END-OF-FILE SPECIFIER
IN THE READ STATEMENT

Figure 4.3 shows a procedure to read a number from a card then print the number and repeat the process.

FIGURE 4.3
A NEVER-ENDING LOOP

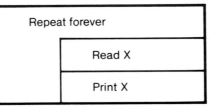

You can write this procedure with three FORTRAN statements:

```
10    READ *, X
      PRINT *, X
      GO TO 10
```

After reading each number and printing it, the GO TO statement branches back to the beginning of the loop. This will work fine—as long as there are more data cards to read. However, after the last card is read, the READ statement has nothing to read. This will cause an error condition, and the program will stop after printing some error message.

It would be better to have the program determine automatically that there are no more data cards to read, as in Figure 4.4.

FIGURE 4.4
A LOOP THAT EXITS WHEN ALL THE DATA HAS BEEN READ

While there is more data

Read X

Print X

To do this in FORTRAN, you can include an **end-of-file specifier** in the READ statement. An example is:

    READ (*, *, END = 20) X

The symbol

    END = 20

is the end-of-file specifier. This READ statement is like a combination READ and GO TO statement. It means to read a value for X, *but* if there is no more input data, to go to statement number 20. Using this form of the READ, you can write the procedure in Figure 4.4 like this:

    10   READ (*, *, END = 20) X
          PRINT *, X
          GO TO 10
    20   END

If there are 10 data cards to be read, the end-of-file specifier has no effect the first 10 times through the loop. The program just reads a value for X, and then goes on to the PRINT statement. The eleventh time the READ is executed, there is no more data, so the program branches to statement 20, the END statement, which stops execution.

The general form of the READ statement with an end-of-file specifier is

    READ (*, *, END = n) list

where n is a statement label, and *list* is the list of variables to read. It means: "Read values for the variables, but branch to statement n if there is no more data to read."

In a structured flowchart, you can represent the end-of-file specifier in the looping condition as in Figure 4.4, or by a decision as in Figure 4.5.

FIGURE 4.5
ANOTHER WAY TO DIAGRAM THE END-OF-FILE SPECIFIER

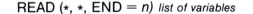

READ (*, *, END = n) list of variables

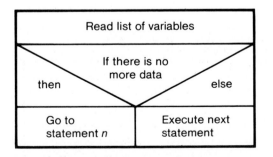

THE IF-THEN-ELSE STATEMENTS

To decide between two paths in a program you can use an **IF-THEN statement** (also called a **block IF statement**) along with an **ELSE statement** and an **END IF statement**. Figure 4.6 shows an example. In the figure, *condition* represents some condition that is either true or false, while *Block 1* and *Block 2* represent any FORTRAN statement or group of FORTRAN statements. If the condition is true, the program executes *Block 1*; if the condition is false, the program executes *Block 2*. Figure 4.7 shows a specific example which corresponds to the following FORTRAN statements.

```
IF (N .EQ. 0) THEN
      PRINT *, 'ERROR: N WAS ZERO'
ELSE
      PRINT *, 'NUMBER OF VALUES = ', N
      PRINT *, 'SUM = ', SUM
      PRINT *, 'AVERAGE = ', SUM/N
END IF
```

The ELSE and END IF statements, by themselves, do nothing. Technically, they are executable statements, but they cause no machine action when executed. They serve only to delimit the **IF block** and the **ELSE block**, which are the two groups of statements between which the IF statement chooses.

To be precise, the IF block consists of all the executable statements following a block IF statement up to, but not including, the ELSE or END IF statement that goes with the block IF. The ELSE block consists of all the executable statements following the ELSE statement up to, but not including, the END IF statement that goes with the ELSE.

The only legal way to enter an IF block or an ELSE block is by executing the block IF or ELSE statement:

Rule for Transfer into a Block
A program may not transfer into an IF block or an ELSE block (or an ELSE IF block, covered later) from outside the block.

This rule implies that the following statements are not allowed.

```
* ILLEGAL TRANSFER INTO AN IF BLOCK
      IF (N .EQ. 0) THEN
          PRINT *, X
100       Y = X**2
          PRINT *, Y
      END IF
      GO TO 100
```

FIGURE 4.6
THE IF, ELSE, AND END IF STATEMENTS REPRESENT A DECISION

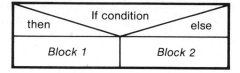

	If condition	
then		else
Block 1		Block 2

```
IF  (condition) THEN
        Block 1
    ELSE
        Block 2
    END IF
```

The GO TO statement is illegal because it transfers control from outside an IF block to inside the block. Note that the rule does not forbid branching *out of* an IF block, nor does it forbid branching from one point to another *within* an IF block.

RELATIONAL EXPRESSIONS

Within the parentheses of an IF statement you write a condition, such as

A .GT. 10

This kind of condition is called a **relational expression**. The symbol

.GT.

is called a **relational operator**. There are six such operators in FORTRAN. Table 4.1 lists them. You can use these operators to compare any two arithmetic expressions.

FIGURE 4.7

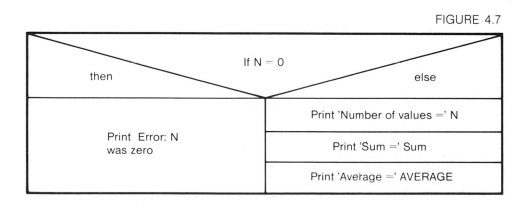

	If N = 0	
then		else
Print Error: N was zero	Print 'Number of values =' N	
	Print 'Sum =' Sum	
	Print 'Average =' AVERAGE	

For example,

    N + 1 .LT. 2*A + 3*B

means "Is N + 1 less than 2A + 3B?" In algebra, you would write this as:

$$(N + 1) < (2A + 3B)$$

TABLE 4.1
RELATIONAL OPERATORS

FORTRAN Symbol	Mathematical Symbol	Meaning
.LT.	$<$	Less than
.LE.	$\leq$	Less than or equal to
.GT.	$>$	Greater than
.GE.	$\geq$	Greater than or equal to
.EQ.	$=$	Equal to
.NE.	$\neq$	Not equal to

If you compare two expressions of different types, a type conversion takes place, just as in mixed-mode arithmetic. For example, suppose that N is an integer variable and X is a real variable. Then to evaluate the relational expression

    N .GE. X

FORTRAN converts N to a real value, subtracts the real value of X, and compares the result to zero.

All of the examples of IF statements that you have seen thus far have used simple relational expressions. The condition in an IF can be any relational expression, or, in fact, any *logical expression*.

LOGICAL EXPRESSIONS

Relational expressions are one kind of **logical expression**. A logical expression in FORTRAN is an expression that is either *true* or *false*. Such expressions are called *logical* because they are like the expressions used in the mathematical study of symbolic logic.*

The two simplest logical expressions in FORTRAN are the two **logical constants**, which represent the values *true* and *false*. In FORTRAN, you write these constants as:

---

*Symbolic logic, in its modern form, was invented by George Boole in his *Laws of Thought* (1854). Symbolic logic is sometimes called Boolean logic, and logical expressions are sometimes called *Boolean expressions*.

.TRUE.

and

.FALSE.

The periods around each of these words are part of the symbol for the logical constants.

Another kind of logical expression is a **logical variable**. Just as an integer variable takes on integer values, a logical variable takes on logical values. Thus there are only two possible values for a logical variable: .TRUE. and .FALSE..

You can declare certain variables to be logical by using a **LOGICAL statement**, like the following:

LOGICAL P, Q

This statement means that P and Q are logical variables in the program.

The LOGICAL statement (like the INTEGER and REAL statements) is a declarative statement that must come before the first executable statement in the program.

You can assign a value to a logical variable using a **logical assignment statement** of the form:

variable = expression

where *variable* is a logical variable and *expression* is a logical expression. For example,

LOGICAL YES
YES = .TRUE.

Logical operators in FORTRAN join logical expressions together to form new logical expressions. Suppose you want to know if the value of the real variable X is between 1 and 10. In algebra you would write this condition as

$$1 \leq X \leq 10$$

In FORTRAN, you use the logical operator

.AND.

to join two relational expressions, as follows:

1 .LE. X .AND. X .LE. 10

The machine computes the value of this logical expression to be either .TRUE. or .FALSE.. It is true if and only if both of the relations are true.

The logical operator

.OR.

tests whether at least one of two logical expressions is true. The logical expression

N .LT. 1 .OR. N .GT. MAX

has the value .TRUE. if N is less than 1 or if N is greater than MAX. In everyday speech, the word "or" sometimes means "one or the other, but not both." If a menu says, "soup or salad," it usually means you cannot have both. But in FORTRAN, the .OR. operator means "one or the other, or possibly both."

The operator

.NOT.

gives a logical expression its opposite value. You write this operator in front of an expression to change its value from true to false, or vice versa. For example,

.NOT. I .LT. J

is true if I is *not* less than J.

The logical operator

.EQV.

tests whether two logical expressions are equivalent; that is, whether they have the same value.

P .EQV. Q

is true if P and Q are both true or both false.

The logical operator

.NEQV.

is the opposite of the .EQV. operator. It tests whether two logical expressions are *not* equivalent. The expression

P .NEQV. Q

is true if P is true and Q is false, or if P is false and Q is true. The .NEQV. operator is sometimes called an **exclusive or** operator because another interpretation of it is that

P .NEQV. Q

is true if P is true or Q is true but *not* both. Thus, it is like .OR., but it *excludes* the case where both are true.

Table 4.2 is called a **truth table**. It shows all possible outcomes of applying any of the logical operators to two logical expressions P and Q.

TABLE 4.2
TRUTH TABLE FOR FORTRAN LOGICAL OPERATORS

P	Q	.NOT. P	P .OR. Q	P .AND. Q	P .EQV. Q	P .NEQV. Q
.TRUE.	.TRUE.	.FALSE.	.TRUE.	.TRUE.	.TRUE.	.FALSE.
.TRUE.	.FALSE.	.FALSE.	.TRUE.	.FALSE.	.FALSE.	.TRUE.
.FALSE.	.TRUE.	.TRUE.	.TRUE.	.FALSE.	.FALSE.	.TRUE.
.FALSE.	.FALSE.	.TRUE.	.FALSE.	.FALSE.	.TRUE.	.FALSE.

In Chapter 3, you saw the rules for evaluating arithmetic expressions. One of these rules said that multiplication is done before addition, unless otherwise specified by parentheses. There are similar rules for evaluating logical expressions.

Rules for Evaluating Logical Expressions
Parentheses can be used to group parts of a logical expression.

All arithmetic operators (+, −, *, /, **) are evaluated first, according to the rules in Chapter 3.

Relational operators (.LT., .GT., .LE., .GE., .EQ., .NE.) are evaluated before logical operators.

Unless otherwise grouped by parentheses, logical operators are evaluated in the following order:

1. .NOT.   3. .OR.
2. .AND.   4. .EQV. OR .NEQV.

Subject to the preceding rules, expressions are evaluated left to right.

The first rule means that you can always use parentheses if you are not sure how to write a logical expression. The other rules tell you what happens if you leave off the parentheses. For example, the rules imply that

    .NOT. I + 1 .EQ. 5 .OR. N .EQ. 1

means the same as

    (.NOT. ((I + 1) .EQ. 5)) .OR. (N .EQ. 1)

The most common use of logical expressions is in IF statements. When the IF is executed, the logical expression in parentheses is evaluated to yield a value of ".TRUE." or ".FALSE.". This value determines whether the IF statement then transfers control to the IF block or the ELSE block.

OTHER FORMS OF THE IF STATEMENT

Figure 4.8 illustrates a procedure that says, "If N is less than 0, print the word 'ERROR' and set N equal to 0; otherwise, do nothing." You can write this in FORTRAN as follows:

```
IF (N .LT. 0) THEN
     PRINT *, 'ERROR'
     N = 0
ELSE
END IF
```

The ELSE block in this example is empty. In this case, you can omit the ELSE statement entirely, and write the procedure as

```
IF (N .LT. 0) THEN
     PRINT *, 'ERROR'
     N = 0
END IF
```

Note that the END IF statement is still needed to terminate the IF block.

It is also allowable to have an empty IF block. For example, Figure 4.9 shows a procedure that says, "If $XMIN \leq X \leq XMAX$, do nothing; otherwise print an error message and stop." You can write this in FORTRAN as follows.

```
IF (XMIN .LE. X .AND. X .LE. XMAX) THEN
ELSE
     PRINT *, 'ERROR: X OUT OF RANGE'
     STOP
END IF
```

Another way to write this is to reverse the condition and put the statements in the IF block.

```
IF (.NOT. (XMIN .LE. X .AND. X .LE. XMAX)) THEN
     PRINT *, 'ERROR: X OUT OF RANGE'
     STOP
END IF
```

There is a short form of the IF statement which you can use to conditionally execute a single statement. An example is

```
IF (N LT. 100) N = N + 1
```

In place of the word "THEN" is the FORTRAN statement "N = N + 1." This assignment statement is executed if the condition "N .LT. 100" is true. Otherwise, the assignment statement is simply bypassed.

FIGURE 4.8
A CONDITIONAL STATEMENT WITH AN EMPTY ELSE BLOCK

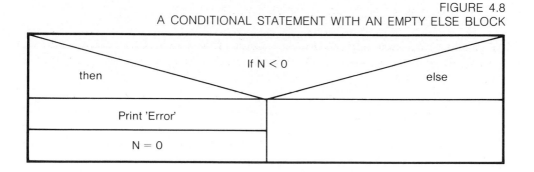

This one-line IF statement is called a **logical IF statement**.* Figure 4.10 shows the general form. The condition in this statement can be any logical expression. The statement can be any executable statement except the following: DO, block IF, ELSE IF, END IF, END, or another logical IF. (Some of these are discussed later in this chapter.)

EXAMPLE 4.1 Percent Increase or Decrease
Dingles Drug Store has compiled sales figures for each item in their inventory. For each item, they prepared a data card giving:

1. The item number (an integer),
2. The dollar amount of sales for last month, and
3. The dollar amount of sales for this month.

Last month's sales might be zero if it is a new item. This month's sales might be zero if it is a discontinued item. Write a program that will compute the percent increase (or decrease) in sales for each item. On each line of output, print the item name, the sales figures, and the percent increase followed by the words PERCENT INCREASE (or print the percent decrease, followed by the words PERCENT DECREASE).

FIGURE 4.9
A CONDITIONAL STATEMENT WITH AN EMPTY IF BLOCK

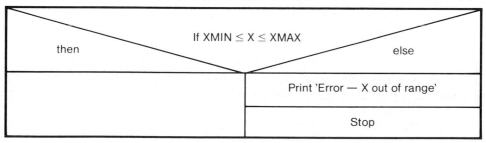

*"One-line IF statement" would be a better name; for historical reasons, it is called the logical IF to distinguish it from the older arithmetic IF.

FIGURE 4.10

IF *(condition) statement*
Next statement

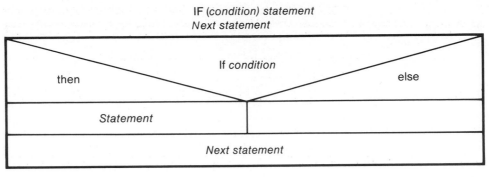

The logical (one-line) IF statement can select one statement to be executed if a condition is true.

Figure 4.11 shows a top-level design. To carry out this procedure, you can use three variables: ITEM, an integer variable for the item name, OLD AMT and NEW AMT, real variables for the sales amounts. To compute the percent increase in sales, you subtract the old amount from the new amount, then divide by the old amount. Multiply the result by 100 to give percent increase. The FORTRAN statement is:

PCT INC = 100*(NEW AMT − OLD AMT)/OLD AMT

There is one special case to watch out for. When OLD AMT is zero, the formula is invalid, because it calls for division by zero. You can use an ELSE statement to define the percent increase to be zero when OLD AMT is zero.

You can also use an ELSE statement to choose whether to print the words PERCENT INCREASE or PERCENT DECREASE.

Figure 4.12 shows the complete procedure. Here is the corresponding FORTRAN program.

```
* DINGLES DRUG STORE PROGRAM
* COMPUTE PERCENT INCREASE OR PERCENT DECREASE IN SALES
* FOR EACH ITEM.
      INTEGER ITEM
      REAL OLD AMT, NEW AMT, PCT INC
```

FIGURE 4.11
TOP-LEVEL DESIGN FOR THE PROGRAM IN EXAMPLE 4.1

While there is more input data
Read the data
Compute the percent increase (or decrease)
Print the data followed by the words 'percent increase' (or 'decrease')

FIGURE 4.12
SECOND-LEVEL DESIGN FOR THE PROGRAM IN EXAMPLE 4.1

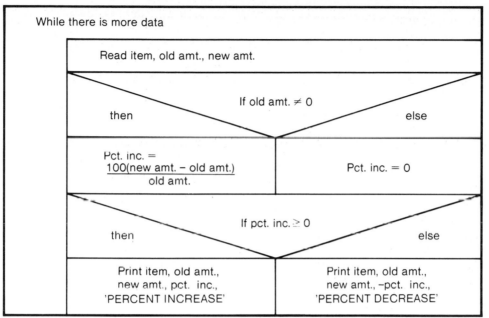

```
10      READ (*, *, END = 900) ITEM, OLD AMT, NEW AMT
        IF (OLD AMT .NE. 0) THEN
            PCT INC = 100 * (NEW AMT − OLD AMT)/OLD AMT
        ELSE
            PCT INC = 0
        END IF
        IF (PCT INC .GE. 0) THEN
            PRINT *, ITEM, ' LAST MONTH: $', OLD AMT,
    $           ' THIS MONTH: $', NEW AMT, ' ',
    $           PCT INC, ' PERCENT INCREASE'
        ELSE
            PRINT *, ' LAST MONTH: $', OLD AMT,
    $           ' THIS MONTH: $', NEW AMT, ' ',
    $           PCT INC, ' PERCENT DECREASE'
        END IF
        GO TO 10
900     END
```

STYLE MODULE—STRUCTURED PROGRAMMING

One of the greatest difficulties facing the beginning programmer is how to express program logic clearly. Without care, even a simple program can become a confused tangle of statements. Consider the following example:

```
      REAL X, LIMIT, DX, Y
      READ *, X, LIMIT, DX
 5    IF (X .LE. LIMIT) GO TO 15
      STOP
 10   X = X + DX
      GO TO 5
 15   Y = X**2 + X
      PRINT *, X, Y
      GO TO 10
      END
```

Each statement in this program is easy to understand. But what does the program do? It is difficult to tell. The procedure, though basically simple, is confusing because of the way it is written. See how much clearer the same procedure is when we rewrite it as follows:

```
      REAL X, Y, START, LIMIT, DX
      READ *, START, LIMIT, DX
      X = START
 10   IF (X .LE. LIMIT) THEN
         Y = X**2 + X
         PRINT *, X, Y
         X = X + DX
         GO TO 10
      END IF
      END
```

Structured programming is a technique of building a program in an organized way by combining statements according to the basic control structures listed at the beginning of this chapter. We defined a *block* in a structured flowchart by using an indirect definition that gave rules for building blocks from other blocks. We can define a *program block* in a similar manner:

Definition of a Program Block
A **program block** is either:

1. A single executable statement that does not transfer control, or
2. Any combination of such statements that can be formed by the following rules.

Rule 1: Sequential structure. A program block can be made by joining two program blocks in sequence:

```
  Block 1
  Block 2
```

Rule 2: If-then-else structure. A program block can be made using the block IF, ELSE, and END IF statements in any of the following forms:

```
(a) IF (condition) THEN
        Block
    END IF

(b) IF (condition) THEN
    ELSE
        Block
    END IF

(c) IF (condition) THEN
        Block 1
    ELSE
        Block 2
    END IF
```

Rule 3: WHILE-loop structure. A program block can be made by putting a program block inside a while loop in the form:

```
label   IF (condition) THEN
            Block
            GO TO label
        END IF
```

Rule 4: Repeat-loop structure. A program block can be made by putting a program block inside a repeat loop in the form:

```
label   Block
        IF (condition) GO TO label
```

These rules are simply the FORTRAN version of the rules for making structured flowcharts. The principle of structured programming given earlier has the following counterpart for FORTRAN programs:

Principle of Structured Programming
Any algorithm can be written in FORTRAN by combining executable statements into a block according to the four rules given above.

We define a **structured program** to be a program that follows the rules of FORTRAN and in which all the executable statements form a block.

In Chapter 2 we said that *indentation* of statement groups can improve program readability. What we have actually been doing in our examples is indenting each structured program block. This practice lets you see at a glance just where each block in your program begins and ends. Thus, indentation of blocks is a typographical way of highlighting your program's control structure.

You may ask why structured programming is important. After all, if a computer carries out a set of instructions and comes up with the right answer, does it matter whether the instructions are written in structured form? The answer is that it certainly does not matter to the computer, and possibly does not matter to the end user of the output data, but it may matter a great deal to the programmer. Structured programs are by far easier to read and easier to understand than unstructured ones.

In a structured program, control flows from *top to bottom*. You can read a structured program like you read a book, starting at the beginning, ending at the end. Reading a highly unstructured program is like reading a book with a dozen footnotes per page. Your train of thought is constantly interrupted as your eyes dart about the page in seemingly random fashion. The logic behind the statements is obscure. A structured program is easier to read, and therefore much easier to validate. Validating a program—constructing an informal mental proof, or perhaps a formal written proof, of correctness—is ultimately the only way you have of knowing that the program works as you intended. Structured programming is your greatest asset in program validation.

EXAMPLE 4.2 Constructing a Structured Program
In the structured flowchart of Figure 4.13, *condition 1*, *condition 2*, and so on, can be any logical expressions, and *statement 1*, *statement 2*, and so on, can be any executable statements that do not transfer control. According to our definition, each of the statements are program blocks. Then by Rule 2, the following is a program block.

FIGURE 4.13

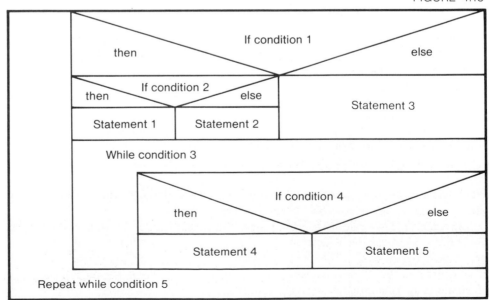

```
IF (condition 2) THEN
     statement 1
ELSE
     statement 2
END IF
```

By Rule 2 again, the following is a program block.

```
IF (condition 1) THEN
     IF (condition 2) THEN
          statement 1
     ELSE
          statement 2
     END IF
ELSE
     statement 3
END IF
```

In fact, you can continue to apply the rules for constructing a program block in the same way that the structured flowchart was built up in Figure 4.2 to show that the algorithm can be written as a structured program in the following form.

```
100   IF (condition 1) THEN
          IF (condition 2) THEN
               statement 1
          ELSE
               statement 2
          END IF
      ELSE
          statement 3
      END IF
200   IF (condition 3) THEN
          IF (condition 4) THEN
               statement 4
          ELSE
               statement 5
          END IF
          GO TO 200
      END IF
      IF (condition 5) GO TO 100
      END
```

Note that the form of this program—its structure—is the same regardless of the particular statements and conditions used.

Of course, to write a structured program you do not have to actually apply the rules in this mechanical fashion. With a little practice, you will learn to recognize the structured forms and use them automatically in your work. Your final result, though, is a program that could be built up step by step in the manner indicated by this example.

STYLE MODULE—LOOPS WITH AN EXIT
IN THE MIDDLE

Consider the procedure in Figure 4.14. This is an example of a loop with an exit in the middle. The loop contains an instruction that exits if *condition 2* is true.

At first glance, this algorithm does not appear to fit into any of the patterns we covered; it is neither a while-loop structure nor a repeat-loop structure. We can, however, transform the algorithm into a while-loop structure by the technique of **introducing a control variable**.

Suppose that P is a logical variable which is not used anywhere else in the algorithm. To begin with, let P be true. Then modify the loop control condition to execute the loop while

  condition 1 .AND. P

is true. Within the loop, if *condition 2* is true, let P be false. This makes the loop control condition false, so that the loop terminates on the next iteration (Figure 4.15).

You should trace the logic of the algorithms in Figures 4.14 and 4.15 to convince yourself that they are equivalent.

A similar technique can be used to transform a repeat loop with an exit in the middle into a repeat loop with no such exit (Exercise 17). In fact, a similar technique

FIGURE 4.14
A LOOP WITH AN EXIT IN THE MIDDLE

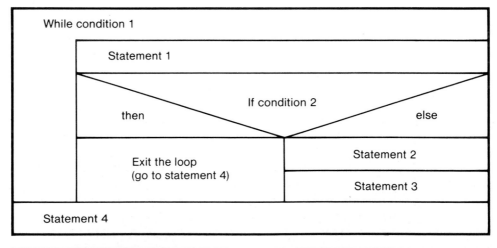

```
10      IF (condition 1) THEN
            Statement 1
            IF (condition 2) GO TO 20
            Statement 2
            Statement 3
            GO TO 10
        END IF
20      Statement 4
```

FIGURE 4.15

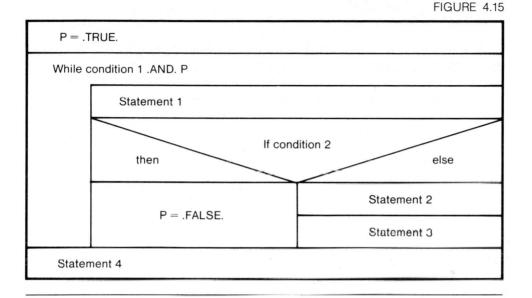

Using a logical variable P, the procedure in Figure 4.14 can be written so that the exit condition is incorporated into the looping condition.

```
        P = .TRUE.
10      IF (condition 1 .AND. P) THEN
            Statement 1
            IF (condition 2) THEN
                P = .FALSE.
            ELSE
                Statement 2
                Statement 3
            END IF
            GO TO 10
        END IF
        Statement 4
```

can be used to transform a while loop into a repeat loop, or vice versa (Exercise 18).

Another kind of loop with an exit in the middle is a loop that terminates when end of data is reached on a READ operation. This case can also be handled by introducing a control variable, using the IOSTAT specifier, which is discussed in Chapter 9. It is often more convenient in FORTRAN to use an end-of-file specifier that branches to the end of the block. A good way to organize such procedures is to make the READ the first statement of a block and have the end-of-file specifier branch to the first statement of the following block. You can use the form:

```
label 1   READ (*, *, END = label 2) list
          Block
          GO TO label 1
label 2   Next Block
```

For all practical purposes, this can be considered a while loop, since the block is executed while there is more input data.

EXAMPLE 4.3 Quadratic Equations
A *quadratic equation* is an equation of the form

$$ax^2 + bx + c = 0$$

where a, b, and c are constants, and x is a variable. In algebra, you learn that this equation has two solutions, x_1 and x_2, given by the formulas

$$x_1 = \frac{-b + \sqrt{b^2 - 4ac}}{2a}$$

$$x_2 = \frac{-b - \sqrt{b^2 - 4ac}}{2a}$$

For example, you can solve the equation

$$x^2 - 3x + 2 = 0$$

by applying the above formula to find $x_1 = 2$, $x_2 = 1$. Let us write a program to read three numbers, a, b, c, and print out solutions to the corresponding quadratic equation.

To make the program convenient to use, we can have it read a set of data cards, where each data card contains three values: a, b, and c. For each data card, the program determines the corresponding solutions and prints them. Thus, the top-level design is that shown in Figure 4.16.

To make the program work correctly for all possible values of a, b, and c, there are several special cases to consider.

If a is zero, the equation is not really a quadratic equation; it is a linear equation:

$$bx + c = 0$$

which we must solve by a different formula. Thus, the top-level design can be expanded as shown in Figure 4.17.

The solution of the linear equation is

$$x = -\frac{c}{b}$$

This formula, however, does not work if $b = 0$, in which case the equation to be solved has the form:

$$0x = c$$

This equation is true for all x if $c = 0$ (the trivial case), and true for no x if $c \neq 0$ (the impossible case). Thus, the procedure for solving the linear equation is as shown in Figure 4.18.

The solution of the quadratic case ($a \neq 0$) is given by the formulas, but again there are three separate cases. The quantity under the square root sign

$$b^2 - 4ac$$

is called the *discriminant* of the equation. If $b^2 - 4ac > 0$, then the equation has two distinct

FIGURE 4.16
TOP-LEVEL DESIGN FOR SOLVING QUADRATIC EQUATIONS

While there is more input

Read values of a, b, c

Print the equation to be solved

Print the solutions (if any) to the equation

solutions given by the formulas. If $b^2 - 4ac = 0$, then the equation has one solution given by

$$x = -\frac{b}{2a}$$

If $b^2 - 4ac < 0$, the equation has two solutions, but they are *complex numbers*, of the form

$$x + yi \qquad x - yi$$

where i is the base of the imaginary numbers $(i = \sqrt{-1})$ and x and y are given by the formulas

$$x = -\frac{b}{2a}$$

$$y = \frac{\sqrt{-(b^2 - 4ac)}}{2a}$$

FIGURE 4.17
SECOND-LEVEL DESIGN FOR SOLVING QUADRATIC EQUATIONS

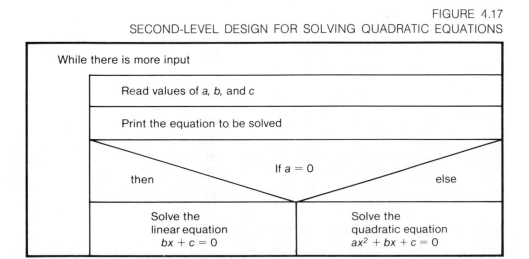

While there is more input

Read values of a, b, and c

Print the equation to be solved

If a = 0

then

else

Solve the
linear equation
bx + c = 0

Solve the
quadratic equation
ax² + bx + c = 0

FIGURE 4.18
SOLUTION OF THE LINEAR CASE ($a = 0$)

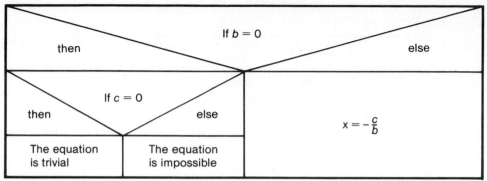

Thus, the procedure for solving the quadratic case is as shown in Figure 4.19. Putting these parts together, we have the complete structured flowchart shown in Figure 4.20.

You can translate this procedure into FORTRAN using the structured forms previously described. There is only one point which we have not yet covered: finding square roots. The square root of a nonnegative value X is the same as X raised to the power 1/2. Thus, the square root of DISC is given by the FORTRAN expression

DISC**0.5

The complete program is as follows.

```
* SOLVE THE QUADRATIC EQUATION
*
*     A*X**2 + B*X + C = 0
*
* FOR ANY VALUES OF A, B, AND C.
*
* THIS PROGRAM READS ANY NUMBER OF DATA CARDS. EACH DATA CARD
* CONTAINS THREE NUMBERS AS VALUES OF A, B, AND C. THE PROGRAM
* PRINTS EACH SET OF INPUT VALUES ALONG WITH THE SOLUTION TO THE
* CORRESPONDING EQUATION.
*
      REAL A, B, C, DISC
10    READ (*, *, END = 90) A, B, C
      PRINT *, 'THE EQUATION'
      PRINT *, A, 'X**2 + ', B, 'X + ', C, ' = 0'
      IF (A .EQ. 0) THEN
          IF (B .EQ. 0) THEN
              IF (C .EQ. 0) THEN
                  PRINT *, 'IS TRIVIAL'
              ELSE
                  PRINT *, 'IS IMPOSSIBLE'
              END IF
```

FIGURE 4.19
SOLUTION OF THE QUADRATIC CASE ($a \neq 0$)

DISC $= b^2 - 4ac$

If DISC ≥ 0

then   else

If DISC > 0

then   else

Two complex solutions:

Two solutions:

$$\frac{-b + \sqrt{\text{DISC}}}{2a}$$

and

$$\frac{-b - \sqrt{\text{DISC}}}{2a}$$

One solution:

$$\frac{-b}{2a}$$

$$\frac{-b}{2a} \pm \left(\frac{\sqrt{-\text{DISC}}}{2a} \right) i$$

FIGURE 4.20
COMPLETE ALGORITHM FOR THE PROGRAM TO SOLVE QUADRATIC EQUATIONS

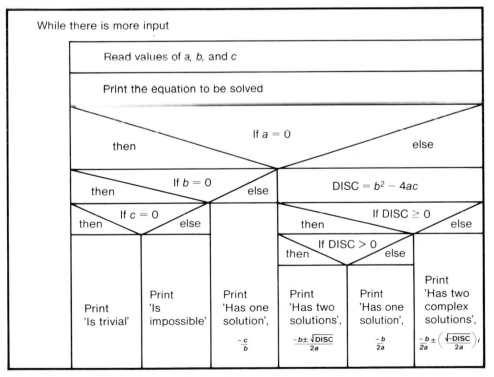

While there is more input

Read values of a, b, and c

Print the equation to be solved

If $a = 0$

then   else

If $b = 0$ DISC $= b^2 - 4ac$

then   else

If $c = 0$ If DISC ≥ 0

then   else   then   else

If DISC > 0

then   else

Print   Print   Print   Print   Print   Print
'Is trivial'   'Is   'Has one   'Has two   'Has one   'Has two
                  impossible'   solution',   solutions',   solution',   complex
                                                                                    solutions',

$$\frac{-c}{b}$$ $$\frac{-b \pm \sqrt{\text{DISC}}}{2a}$$ $$\frac{-b}{2a}$$ $$\frac{-b}{2a} \pm \left(\frac{\sqrt{-\text{DISC}}}{2a} \right) i$$

```
              ELSE
                  PRINT *, 'HAS ONE SOLUTION'
                  PRINT *, 'X = ', -C/B
              END IF
          ELSE
              DISC = B**2 - 4*A*C
              IF (DISC .GE. 0) THEN
                  IF (DISC .GT. 0) THEN
                      PRINT *, 'HAS TWO SOLUTIONS'
                      PRINT *, 'X1 =',
     $                    (-B + DISC**0.5)/(2*A)
                      PRINT *, 'X2 =',
     $                    (-B - DISC**0.5)/(2*A)
                  ELSE
                      PRINT *, 'HAS ONE SOLUTION'
                      PRINT *, 'X =', -B/(2*A)
                  END IF
              ELSE
                  PRINT *, 'HAS TWO COMPLEX SOLUTIONS'
                  PRINT *, -B/(2*A), ' + OR - ',
     $                    (-DISC)**0.5/(2*A), ' *I'
              END IF
          END IF
          GO TO 10
   90     END
```

THE ELSE IF STATEMENT

Often you may need to use a whole series of conditions in a procedure. Figure 4.21 shows a procedure that executes one of four statements based on tests of three conditions. You can write this procedure in FORTRAN as follows:

```
IF (condition 1) THEN
    statement 1
ELSE
    IF (condition 2) THEN
        statement 2
    ELSE
        IF (condition 3) THEN
            statement 3
        ELSE
            statement 4
        END IF
    END IF
END IF
```

These statements are perfectly correct. There is, however, a more compact way of writing the procedure using the **ELSE IF statement**, as follows:

```
IF (condition 1) THEN
     statement 1
ELSE IF (condition 2) THEN
     statement 2
ELSE IF (condition 3) THEN
     statement 3
ELSE
     statement 4
END IF
```

This procedure means exactly the same thing as the one previously given. The first ELSE IF statement terminates the IF block and begins a new block, called an **ELSE IF block**. Thus, the ELSE IF combines the functions of an ELSE and an IF statement. Written this way, the procedure requires only one END IF statement, rather than three.

Using a structured flowchart, there is a more compact way of writing this kind of procedure. Figure 4.22 is a short way of writing the procedure in Figure 4.21. The instruction in the upper box means to test the conditions from left to right. If any condition is true, control passes to the instructions written under that condition.

Figure 4.23 shows a specific example of a procedure to select among one of three cases. As often happens in practice, the cases here are *mutually exclusive*—that is, exactly one of the conditions must be true. Thus, the order in which the conditions are tested does not matter, and you can diagram the selection of the case in the even simpler form shown in Figure 4.24. The corresponding FORTRAN statements are as follows:

FIGURE 4.21

CHAIN OF DECISIONS TO SELECT AMONG FOUR ALTERNATIVES

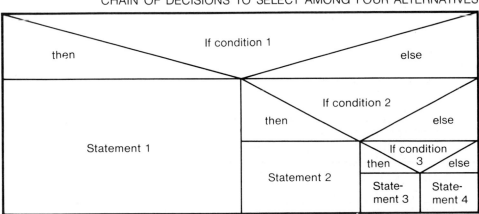

```
READ *, N
IF (N .LT. 0) THEN
    PRINT *, 'THE NUMBER IS NEGATIVE'
ELSE IF (N .EQ. 0) THEN
    PRINT *, 'THE NUMBER IS ZERO'
ELSE
    PRINT *, 'THE NUMBER IS POSITIVE'
END IF
PRINT *, 'THE END'
END
```

EXAMPLE 4.4 Tax Computation
The following table shows a hypothetical table for figuring income tax.

If income is OVER	But NOT OVER	Tax is
$0	$4000	15% of income
$4000	$6000	$600 + 19% of excess over $4000
$6000	$10,000	$980 + 23% of excess over $6000
$10,000	$12,000	$1900 + 25% of excess over $10,000
$12,000	$18,000	$2400 + 32% of excess over $12,000
$18,000	$20,000	$4320 + 35% of excess over $18,000
$20,000	$30,000	$5020 + 38% of excess over $20,000
$30,000	—	$8820 + 45% of excess over $30,000

FIGURE 4.22
ANOTHER WAY OF WRITING A CHAIN OF DECISIONS

If Condition 1	Else If Condition 2	Else If Condition 3	Else
Statement 1	Statement 2	Statement 3	Statement 4

FIGURE 4.23
AN IF . . . ELSE IF . . . ELSE STRUCTURE TO SELECT ONE OF THREE CASES

Read N		
If N < 0	Else If N = 0	Else
Print 'The number is negative'	Print 'The number is zero'	Print 'The number is positive'

FIGURE 4.24
A SIMPLER WAY OF DIAGRAMMING THE PROCEDURE OF FIGURE 4.23

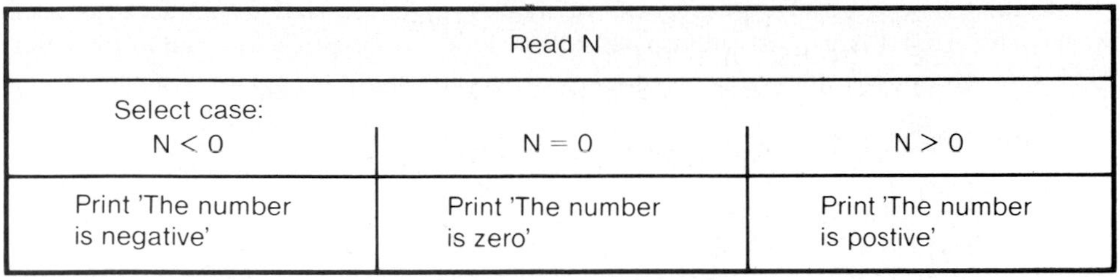

Read N		
Select case: N < 0	N = 0	N > 0
Print 'The number is negative'	Print 'The number is zero'	Print 'The number is postive'

The taxpayer is allowed a $500 deduction from his or her net income for each dependent. A set of data cards contains data on taxpayers. The data on the card is:

Social security number (written as three numbers with a space between them, that is, 111 22 3333)
Number of dependents (an integer)
Net income, in dollars (a real number)
Amount withheld, in dollars (a real number)

Write a program to compute each person's tax and the refund due (or amount owed). Some sample output is

```
SOCIAL SECURITY NUMBER 111 - 22 - 3333
INCOME              $ 10000.0
DEDUCTIONS           2
TAXABLE INCOME $ 9000.0
TAX                 $ 1670.0
AMT  WITHHELD   $ 1700.0
REFUND  DUE      $ 30.0
```

Figure 4.25 shows a top-level design for the program.

FIGURE 4.25
TOP-LEVEL DESIGN FOR EXAMPLE 4.4

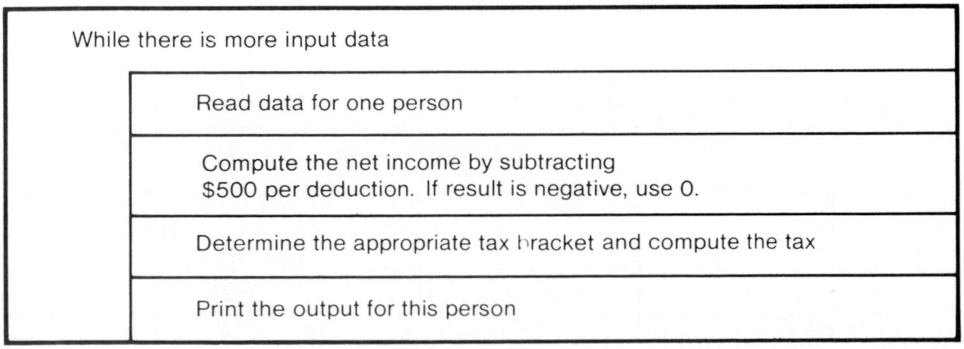

While there is more input data	
	Read data for one person
	Compute the net income by subtracting $500 per deduction. If result is negative, use 0.
	Determine the appropriate tax bracket and compute the tax
	Print the output for this person

   To determine which range the adjusted income falls in, you can use a series of ELSE IF
statements. You can expand step 4 of the top-level outline as shown in Figure 4.26.
   In the following FORTRAN program, we used symbolic constants for all the numbers in
the tax table. CUT 1 is the first cutoff point, $4000. PCT 1 is the percentage rate in formula 1.
AMT 2 is the constant amount in formula 2, and so on. Here is the complete program.

```
* INCOME TAX COMPUTATION
*
      REAL INCOME, NET INC, WTHOLD
      INTEGER DEDUC, SOC 1, SOC 2, SOC 3
      REAL CUT 1, CUT 2, CUT 3, CUT 4, CUT 5, CUT 6, CUT 7
      REAL PCT 1, PCT 2, PCT 3, PCT 4, PCT 5, PCT 6, PCT 7, PCT 8
      REAL AMT 2, AMT 3, AMT 4, AMT 5, AMT 6, AMT 7, AMT 8
      PARAMETER (CUT 1 = 4000, CUT 2 = 6000, CUT 3 = 10000,
   $     CUT 4 = 12000, CUT 5 = 18000, CUT 6 = 20000
   $     CUT 7 = 30000)
```

FIGURE 4.26
PROGRAM DESIGN FOR EXAMPLE 4.4

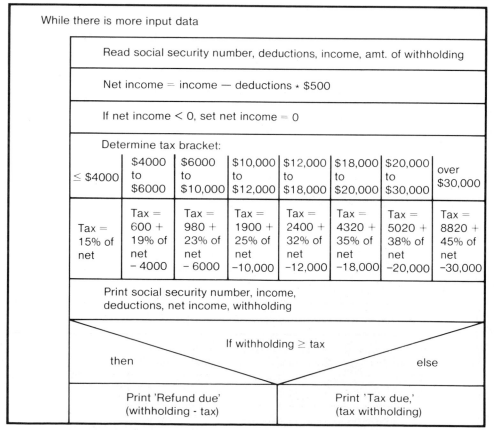

```
      PARAMETER (PCT 1 = 0.15, PCT 2 = 0.19, PCT 3 = 0.23,
  $       PCT 4 = 0.25, PCT 5 = 0.32, PCT 6 = 0.35,
  $       PCT 7 = 0.38, PCT 8 = 0.45)
      PARAMETER (AMT 2 = 600, AMT 3 = 980, AMT 4 = 1900,
  $       AMT 5 = 2400, AMT 6 = 4320, AMT 7 = 5020,
  $       AMT 8 = 8820)
*
* REPEAT THE FOLLOWING FOR EACH INPUT CARD.
*
100   READ (*, *, END = 900) SOC 1, SOC 2, SOC 3
  $       DEDUC, INCOME, WTHOLD
*
* COMPUTE THE NET INCOME BY SUBTRACTING $500 PER DEDUCTION.
* IF THE RESULT IS NEGATIVE, MAKE IT ZERO.
*
      NET INC = INCOME − 500*DEDUC
      IF (NET INC .LT. 0) NET INC = 0
*
* COMPUTE THE TAX
*
      IF (NET INC .LE. CUT 1) THEN
          TAX = PCT 1 * NET INC
      ELSE IF (NET INC .LE. CUT 2) THEN
          TAX = AMT 2 + PCT 2 * NET INC
      ELSE IF (NET INC .LE. CUT 3) THEN
          TAX = AMT 3 + PCT 3 * NET INC
      ELSE IF (NET INC .LE. CUT 4) THEN
          TAX = AMT 4 + PCT 4 * NET INC
      ELSE IF (NET INC .LE. CUT 5) THEN
          TAX = AMT 5 + PCT 5 * NET INC
      ELSE IF (NET INC .LE. CUT 6) THEN
          TAX = AMT 6 + PCT 6 * NET INC
      ELSE IF (NET INC .LE. CUT 7) THEN
          TAX = AMT 7 + PCT 7 * NET INC
      ELSE
          TAX = AMT 8 + PCT 8 * NET INC
      END IF
*
* PRINT THE RESULTS.
*
      PRINT *, 'SOCIAL SECURITY NUMBER ',
  $       SOC 1, ' − ', SOC 2, ' − ', SOC 3
      PRINT *, 'INCOME          $', INCOME
      PRINT *, 'DEDUCTIONS       ', DEDUC
      PRINT *, 'TAXABLE INCOME $', NET INC
      PRINT *, 'AMT WITHHELD    $', WTHOLD
      IF (WTHOLD .GE. TAX) THEN
          PRINT *, 'REFUND DUE               $', WTHOLD − TAX
```

```
        ELSE
            PRINT *, 'TAX DUE                  $', TAX – WTHOLD
        END IF
        GO TO 100
  900   END
```

THE DO STATEMENT

One of the most common types of program loops is one in which a variable counts the number of times the loop has been executed. The **DO statement** provides an easy way to write this kind of loop. A **DO loop** is actually just a while-loop structure in which a counter variable, called the **DO variable**, is incremented or decremented automatically on each iteration. Thus, you can use a DO loop to form structured programs in the same way as you would use the equivalent while loop.

The following program uses a DO statement to print a table of squares.

```
        INTEGER X
        DO 10, X = 1, 20
  10        PRINT *, X, ' SQUARE = ', X**2
        END
```

This DO statement means to execute statement number 10, the PRINT statement, first with X = 1, then with X = 2, then with X = 3, and so on, until X = 20. Thus the PRINT statement executes 20 times, and the output includes the squares of the numbers 1 through 20. You can represent this procedure with the structured flowchart shown in Figure 4.27.

Figure 4.28 shows the parts of the DO statement. After the word DO comes a statement label. The comma following this label is optional. Next comes the name of the **DO variable**, then an equal sign, then two or three arithmetic expressions, separated by commas. These expressions are called the **initial parameter**, the **terminal parameter**, and the **incrementation parameter**.

The statement label after the word DO is the label of the terminal statement of the loop. All the statements following the DO, up to and including the terminal statement, form the **range** of the DO loop. A DO loop can consist of a single statement, as in our first example, or it can include many statements.

The DO variable may be any real or integer variable name. The value of this variable changes as the DO loop executes. To begin with, the value of the DO variable is set to the value of the initial parameter. When the loop has executed once, the value of the incrementation parameter is added to the DO variable, and the loop repeats, starting with the first statement after the DO statement. This process continues. On each iteration of the DO loop, the value of the incrementation parameter is added to the DO variable. When the value of the DO variable is greater than the value of the terminal parameter, the program **exits** the DO loop, branching to the first statement after the terminal statement of the DO loop.

FIGURE 4.27

Do for X = 1, 20	
	Print X, X^2

Each of the initial, terminal, and incrementation parameters may be a constant, or variable, or expression. For example,

DO 70, X = 1, 2∗N + 1, INC/2

You can omit the incrementation parameter entirely (along with the comma before it). Omitting the incrementation parameter is the same as specifying a value of 1. Thus,

DO 100, I = 1, 20

means the same as

DO 100, I = 1, 20, 1

The incrementation parameter can be positive, or negative, but not zero. If it is negative, the DO variable counts "backward." For example,

DO 100, X = 50, 0, −1

means to execute the DO loop with X equal to 50, then 49, then 48, 47, and so on.

FIGURE 4.28
PARTS OF THE DO STATEMENT

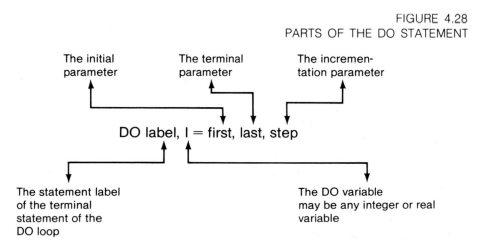

The three parameters and the DO variable itself each may be of either integer or real type. For instance,

```
REAL X
DO 100, X = 0, 1.2, 0.1
```

means to execute the loop with X = 0.0, 0.1, 0.2, 0.3, . . . , 1.1, 1.2.

Let's see in more detail how the DO statement works. Consider the statement in its general form:

DO *label*, *var* = e_1, e_2, e_3

Executing the DO loop consists of nine steps.

Step 1: *Evaluate the parameters.* The values of the expressions e_1, e_2, and e_3 are computed. If the DO variable is an integer variable, the values of the parameters are converted to integer numbers. Similarly, if the DO variable is real, the values of the parameters are converted to real numbers. Remember that if you leave off the incrementation parameter, e_3, it is assumed to have the value 1.

Step 2: *Initialize the DO variable.* This has the effect of the assignment statement

$$var = e_1$$

Step 3: *Compute the iteration count.* The **iteration count** is the number of times the DO loop is to be executed. For example, the statement

```
DO 100, I = 1, 20
```

says to execute the DO loop 20 times, so the iteration count is 20. For the statement

```
DO 100, I = −10, 10
```

the iteration count is 21. For the statement

```
DO 100, I = 100, 0, −1
```

the iteration count is 101. In general, FORTRAN figures the iteration count using the formula

$$iteration\ count = (e_2 - e_1 + e_3)/e_3$$

If the result is not an integer, it is converted to an integer, truncating any fractional part. If the iteration count is less than zero, FORTRAN uses an iteration count of zero.

Step 4: *Test the iteration count.* If the count is zero, the program exits the DO loop, beginning with the statement following the terminal statement of the loop. If the count is positive, the program goes on to Step 5. Note that the iteration count might be zero the very first time it is tested, in which case the DO loop is not executed at all.

Step 5: *Execute the DO loop.* If there are no control statements in the loop, the program executes all the statements up to the terminal statement. If the loop contains control statements, it is possible that the program will exit the loop by branching to a statement outside the loop, in which case the DO loop is said to be **inactive**, and the loop processing is no longer controlled by these steps. For iteration to continue, the program must eventually go on to Step 6.

Step 6: *Execute the terminal statement.* Of course, if the DO loop consists of a single statement, then this is the same as Step 5. A more complicated DO loop may contain many statements, including control statements that branch within the loop. Whatever happens within the loop, the terminal statement must be executed before loop processing can continue.

Step 7: *Increment the DO variable.* The value of the incrementation parameter is added to *var*.

Step 8: *Decrement the iteration count.* The new value of the iteration count is the old value minus 1.

Step 9: Go back to Step 4.

The effect of these nine steps is shown in Figure 4.29.

FIGURE 4.29
EFFECT OF THE STATEMENT DO *label, var* $= e_1, e_2, e_3$

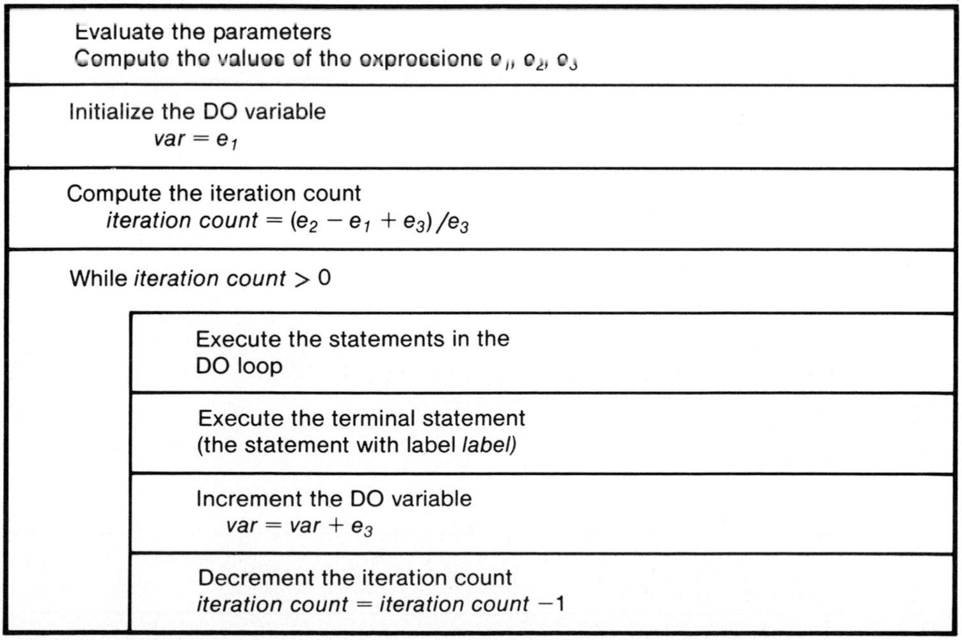

Evaluate the parameters Compute the values of the expressions e_1, e_2, e_3
Initialize the DO variable $var = e_1$
Compute the iteration count $iteration\ count = (e_2 - e_1 + e_3)/e_3$
While *iteration count* > 0

Execute the statements in the DO loop
Execute the terminal statement (the statement with label *label*)
Increment the DO variable $var = var + e_3$
Decrement the iteration count $iteration\ count = iteration\ count - 1$

THE CONTINUE STATEMENT

The **CONTINUE statement** has a simple form:

CONTINUE

This statement has a simple purpose, too. It does nothing. It is an executable statement that has no effect when it is executed.

As a matter of style, we generally use a CONTINUE statement as the terminal statement for a DO loop. For instance, the DO loop

```
      DO 20, I = 1, N
20        PRINT *, I
```

can also be written like this:

```
      DO 20, I = 1, N
          PRINT *, I
20        CONTINUE
```

These two DO loops have exactly the same effect.

As you will see in the following section, there are a few cases where a CONTINUE statement must be used to avoid certain restrictions of DO loops. In most cases, we just use it to make the program easier to read.

RULES FOR DO LOOPS

There are a few restrictions on the use of the DO statement, and a few points that need special attention.

> The value of the DO variable must not be redefined within the loop.

The value of the DO variable changes according to the incrementation procedure discussed earlier. You cannot circumvent that procedure by assigning a new value to the DO variable within the loop. Thus, the following loop is illegal.

```
* ILLEGAL DO LOOP
      DO 10, J = 1, L
          IF (J .EQ. K) J = J + 1
10        PRINT *, J
```

> A program must not branch into a DO loop from outside the loop.

This rule implies that the following program is illegal.

```
        DO 100, COUNT = 1, N + 1
50      PRINT *, COUNT
100  CONTINUE
*  ILLEGAL GO TO STATEMENT.
        GO TO 50
```

The GO TO statement is *outside* the DO loop, but it branches to a statement *inside* the loop.

It is easy to see why this rule is necessary. If branching into a DO loop were allowed, then the values of the DO variable and the iteration count would be undefined at the end of the loop.

Certain statements are not allowed as the terminal statement of a DO loop. They are:

GO TO
assigned GO TO
arithmetic IF
block IF
DO
ELSE IF
ELSE
END IF
RETURN
STOP
END

A logical IF statement is allowed to be the terminal statement but only if it does not contain any of the above statements.

For completeness, this list of illegal terminal statements includes some statements we have not yet discussed.

This rule implies that the following DO loop is illegal.

```
*  ILLEGAL DO LOOP
        DO 10, I = 1, L
10         IF (I**2 .EQ. J) GO TO 20
```

You can make this loop legal by using a CONTINUE statement, as follows.

```
*  LEGAL DO LOOP
        DO 10, I = 1, L
            IF (I**2 .EQ. J) GO TO 20
10         CONTINUE
```

Although the CONTINUE statement itself does nothing, it is a legal terminal statement for a DO loop, whereas the IF statement is not.

DO loops and IF blocks, ELSE IF blocks, or ELSE blocks must not overlap. If a DO loop contains a block IF statement, then the corresponding END IF statement must be within the DO loop. If a block IF statement contains a DO loop, then the entire DO loop must be inside the IF block.

The following statements violate this rule.

```
* ILLEGAL DO LOOP AND IF BLOCK
      IF (A .GT. B) THEN
         DO 10, I = 1, N
            READ *, X
            A = A − X
         END IF
10       CONTINUE
```

MORE RULES FOR DO LOOPS*

In this section we cover three rules that apply when you write one DO loop inside another DO loop, as illustrated in Figure 4.30. This arrangement is sometimes called **nested DO loops**. The **inner** DO loops are nested inside the **outer** one.

If two DO loops overlap, then one of them must be entirely inside the other.

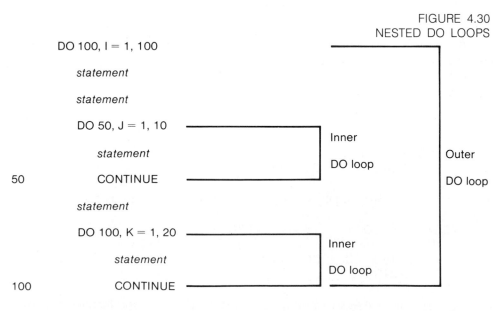

FIGURE 4.30
NESTED DO LOOPS

*Optional section.

According to this rule, the loops shown in Figure 4.31 are illegal. The rule does *not*, however, forbid two DO loops from having the same terminal statement. The third DO statement in this figure has the same terminal statement label (100) as the first DO statement in the figure.

Two or more DO loops may have the same terminal statement. Each time the terminal statement is executed, incrementation of the DO variable and testing of the iteration count are carried out for each loop, in turn, just as though each loop ended with a separate terminal statement.

In other words, the statements

```
        DO 20, I = 1, 10
        DO 20, J = 1, 10
20          PRINT *, I, J
```

have the same effect as they would if written like this:

```
        DO 20, I = 1, 10
        DO 10, J = 1, 10
        PRINT *, I, J
10      CONTINUE
20      CONTINUE
```

The rules we gave earlier for DO loops apply to *each* loop in a set of nested DO loops. In particular, they forbid an inner DO loop from changing the value of the DO variable in an outer DO loop. To be specific:

Two nested DO loops may not use the same DO variable.

FIGURE 4.31
ILLEGAL NESTING OF DO LOOPS

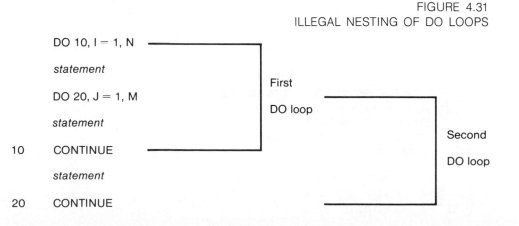

```
        DO 10, I = 1, N

        statement

        DO 20, J = 1, M

        statement

10      CONTINUE

        statement

20      CONTINUE
```

First
DO loop

Second
DO loop

Thus the following DO loops are *not* permitted.

```
        DO 20, I = 1, 10
        DO 10, I = 1, 10
        statement
10      CONTINUE
20      CONTINUE
```

STYLE MODULE—MISUSE OF THE DO STATEMENT

Not all loops are DO loops. The DO statement is useful for some kinds of loops, but sometimes you should use GO TO and IF statements instead.

Consider the following short program. This program is supposed to read a deck of cards, with one number on each card, and print the sum of all the numbers.

```
* POOR PROGRAM TO ADD NUMBERS
        REAL SUM, X
        INTEGER I, N
        SUM = 0
* READ THE NUMBER OF DATA CARDS
        READ, N
*
        DO 10, I = 1, N
            READ *, X
            SUM = SUM + X
10          CONTINUE
        PRINT *, N, ' CARDS WERE READ'
        PRINT *, 'THE SUM IS ', SUM
        END
```

This use of a DO loop makes things easy for the programmer, but it makes things hard for the user of the program. Suppose you wanted to add up the numbers on about 200 cards. You would have to count all the cards before you could run this program. And if you made a mistake in counting, the program would not work.

It is much better to let the computer do the counting. That is what computers are good at. Here is one way to do it.

```
* BETTER PROGRAM TO ADD NUMBERS
        REAL SUM, X
        INTEGER N, INFIN
        PARAMETER (INFIN = 50000)
        SUM = 0
        DO 10, N = 1, INFIN
            READ (*, *, END = 20) X
            SUM = SUM + X
10          CONTINUE
```

```
20      PRINT *, N − 1, ' CARDS WERE READ'
        PRINT *, ' THE SUM IS ', SUM
        END
```

This program uses a DO loop with a large upper limit. The upper limit was chosen to be so large that it would never be reached. The program should always exit the loop via the END = branch on the READ statement.

It is just as easy to write this program without using a DO loop at all. This is what we've done in the third version.

```
*  IMPROVED PROGRAM TO ADD NUMBERS
        REAL SUM, X
        INTEGER N
        SUM = 0
        N = 0
10          READ (*, *, END − 20) X
            N = N + 1
            SUM = SUM + X
            GO TO 10
20      PRINT *, N, ' CARDS WERE READ'
        PRINT *, 'THE SUM IS ', SUM
        END
```

There are two lessons to be learned from this example, the first lesson is this:

Use DO loops where appropriate. Use other kinds of loops where they are better suited to the program.

A DO loop is fine if you know in advance how many times the loop needs to be executed. But if you want a loop to repeat until some condition is true—for instance until the program runs out of data cards—then you should consider using a different control structure.

The second lesson is of a more general nature.

Make your program easy to use.

Of course you want to make your program easy to write. That is fine. But do not do so at the expense of making it hard to use. For example, do not make the user count the data cards by hand. Computers have gotten a bad reputation over the years. Some people see them as inflexible, obstinate machines. In most cases, the programmer, not the computer, is to blame. The first program in this section is only a small example of the problem. But many large programs written by professional programmers are just as bad. As your skill in programming increases, you may very likely begin writing programs for others to use. As a programmer, whether student or professional, it is your responsibility to look out for the interests of the user.

STYLE MODULE—COMPARISON OF REAL EXPRESSIONS FOR EQUALITY

You can run into difficulty when you use a relational expression of the form

    A .EQ. B

where A and B are real expressions. The following program illustrates the problem.

```
* TEMPERATURE CONVERSION TABLE
* (INCORRECT METHOD)
      REAL C, F
      F = 95
100      C = 5.0/9.0 * (F − 32)
      PRINT *, 'FAHRENHEIT:', F, ' CELSIUS:', C
      F = F + 0.1
      IF (F .EQ. 105.1) STOP
      GO TO 100
      END
```

This is a legal program, but on many computers it would get stuck in the loop. The reason is that F may never be equal to 105.1. Mathematically, F should be 105.1 on the 102nd iteration of the loop. But F is a real variable, and there is some inherent error in real variables because of the way they are stored in the computer. On the 102nd trip through the loop, F might be equal to 105.099999, which is very close to 105.1, but not exactly equal, so the loop repeats again, with F approximately equal to 105.2. The program might run forever unless stopped by the computer operator. (Usually, the computer operating system will automatically stop student jobs that run for more than a few seconds.)

To avoid this problem, observe the following practice:

Do not use relational expressions of the form

    A .EQ. B

or

    A .NE. B

where A or B is a real expression that might be approximate. Rewrite the program to use one of the forms

    A .LT. B   A .LE. B
    A .GT. B   A .GE. B

or use a DO loop instead.

STYLE MODULE—REAL DO VARIABLES

When you use a DO loop with a real DO variable, the value of the variable will be approximate. Consider the temperature conversion program in the previous example. We can rewrite this using a DO loop, as follows:

```
* TEMPERATURE CONVERSION PROGRAM
      REAL C, F
      DO 100, F = 95, 105, 0.1
          C = 5.0/9.0 * (F − 32)
          PRINT *, ' FAHRENHEIT:', F, ' CELSIUS:', C
100       CONTINUE
      END
```

This program is legal and it does not get stuck in a loop (because the DO loop tests the iteration count, not the value of F). But the output may look a bit strange. On a certain computer, the program might produce the following output.

```
FAHRENHEIT 95.00000      CELSIUS 32.00000
FAHRENHEIT 95.09999      CELSIUS 35.05555
FAHRENHEIT 95.19998      CELSIUS 35.11110
FAHRENHEIT 95.29997      CELSIUS 35.16665
   . . .                     . . .
```

The programmer may have wanted the Fahrenheit temperatures to be exactly 95.0, 95.1, 95.2, 95.3, and so on. But there is a cumulative roundoff error that results from adding 0.1 to F on each iteration. So the values of F are slightly inaccurate and the output is hard to read.

The way around this problem is to use integer arithmetic. It is less convenient to use, but it is more precise, and in some applications, that is important.

Instead of a real DO variable, you can use an integer DO variable N that varies from 0 to 100. You can compute F from N with the statement

$$F = 95.0 + N/10.0$$

This method eliminates the cumulative round-off error. Here is the complete program.

```
* TEMPERATURE CONVERSION TABLE
      REAL F, C
      INTEGER N

      DO 100, N = 0, 100
          F = 95 + N/10.0
          C = 5.0/9.0 * (F − 32)
          PRINT *, 'FAHRENHEIT: ', F, ' CELSIUS:', C
100       CONTINUE
      END
```

‖‖

SUMMARY

Control statements determine the order in which your FORTRAN statements are executed.

The GO TO statement is used to branch from one point to another within your program.

The STOP and PAUSE statements terminate execution of a program. The last line of any program must be an END statement, which is a directive to the FORTRAN compiler, as well as an executable statement similar in purpose to STOP.

The logical IF, block IF, ELSE IF, and ELSE statements are used to choose among different paths in a program. They can select a particular sequence of statements to execute, depending on the value of some logical expression.

A logical expression is composed of logical constants, logical variables, or relational expressions. There are only two possible values for a logical expression: .TRUE., and .FALSE.. A relational expression is a certain kind of logical expression that compares two quantities.

The DO statement provides a way to write loops that are controlled by a counter variable.

Programming style is especially important in organizing the logic of a program to clearly reflect the programmer's thinking. Good program organization is aided by choosing the appropriate control statement for a particular purpose.

Structured programming means using a certain limited set of control structures in writing a program. For decisions, use the *if-then-else* or *if-else-if-else* structures. For loops, use *while loop* or *repeat loop* structures. For loops controlled by a counter, use a DO loop. Use GO TO statements only for programming the basic control structures.

‖‖

VOCABULARY

block IF statement
Boolean variable
CONTINUE statement
DO statement
DO variable
ELSE block
ELSE IF block
ELSE IF statement
ELSE statement
empty block
END statement
exit a DO loop

GO TO statement
IF block
IF-THEN-ELSE structure
inactive DO loop
incrementation parameter
initial parameter
inner DO loop
iteration count
logical assignment statement
logical constant
logical expression
logical IF statement

logical operator	repeat loop
logical operator	repeat loop
LOGICAL statement	statement label
logical variable	STOP statement
nested DO loops	structured programming
outer DO loop	terminal parameter
PAUSE statement	terminal statement of a DO loop
relational expression	top-to-bottom control flow
relational operator	while loop

EXERCISES

1. Write FORTRAN statements for the following instructions.
   (a) Halt execution of the program.
   (b) Branch to statement number 20.
   (c) Suspend execution temporarily to wait for operator action.
   (d) Stop the program if N is equal to NTOP.
   (e) Branch to statement 1 if X is less than or equal to X2.
2. Write FORTRAN statements for the following instructions.
   (a) If C is equal to A, set X equal to Y; otherwise, set X equal to zero.
   (b) If A equals B, read a new value for A; otherwise write the value of A.
   (c) If INPUT is negative, read a new value of INPUT and repeat this step.
   (d) If I is less than J, do nothing; otherwise, set I equal to J.
   (e) Set X equal to the maximum of A and B.
3. Write FORTRAN statements for the following instructions.
   (a) Read values for the variable D until either D is positive or there is no more input data.
   (b) While N is less than M, multiply N by 2.
   (c) If X is between 0 and 10, set N equal to 1; otherwise, set N equal to 0.
   (d) If X is between 0 and 10, set N equal to 1; if X is between 10 and 100, set N equal to 2; otherwise, set N equal to 3.
   (e) Based on the value of X, set N equal to some number according to the following table.

If X Is At Least	But Less Than	Let N Equal
0.0001	0.001	−4
0.001	0.01	−3
0.01	0.1	−2
0.1	1	−1
1	10	0
10	100	1

If X is outside all these ranges, set N = 1.

4. Write FORTRAN logical expressions for each of the following conditions.
   (a) $0 \leq x < 10$
   (b) $n > 100$ or $N < 0$
   (c) x is not less than y.
   (d) x is not less than either y or z.
   (e) $x = y = z$
   (f) Both i and j are greater than k or else both i and j are less than or equal to 10.
   (g) x and y are not equal.
   (h) Neither x nor y is greater than 100.
   (i) x is between a and b (where a is not necessarily less than b).
   (j) x is not between a and b.
5. Complete the following truth tables by filling in the value of the FORTRAN logical expression given the value of the logical variables.

(a)

P	Q	P .NEQV. A
.TRUE.	.TRUE.	
.TRUE.	.FALSE.	
.FALSE.	.TRUE.	
.FALSE.	.FALSE.	

(b)

P	Q	.NOT. P .NEQV. Q
.TRUE.	.TRUE.	
.TRUE.	.FALSE.	
.FALSE.	.TRUE.	
.FALSE.	.FALSE.	

(c)

P	Q	.NOT. P .OR. Q
.TRUE.	.TRUE.	
.TRUE.	.FALSE.	
.FALSE.	.TRUE.	
.FALSE.	.FALSE.	

(d)

P	Q	.NOT. P .AND. .NOT. Q
.TRUE.	.TRUE.	
.TRUE.	.FALSE.	
.FALSE.	.TRUE.	
.FALSE.	.FALSE.	

(e)	P	Q	R	P .OR. Q .AND. R
	.TRUE.	.TRUE.	.TRUE.	
	.TRUE.	.TRUE.	.FALSE.	
	.TRUE.	.FALSE.	.TRUE.	
	.TRUE.	.FALSE.	.FALSE.	
	.FALSE.	.TRUE.	.TRUE.	
	.FALSE.	.TRUE.	.FALSE.	
	.FALSE.	.FALSE.	.TRUE.	
	.FALSE.	.FALSE.	.FALSE.	

6. Write a FORTRAN program for the following procedure.

While there is more input data

Read a temperature F (in Fahrenheit)

Convert to Celsius using the formula
$$C = \frac{5}{9}(F - 32)$$

Print F and C

Select case:

$C \leq 0$	$0 < C \leq 10$	$10 < C \leq 20$	$20 < C \leq 30$	$30 < C \leq 40$	$40 < C$
Print 'freezing'	Print 'cold'	Print 'cool'	Print 'room temperature'	Print 'warm'	Print 'hot'

7. Write a FORTRAN program that reads a set of numbers and prints them. If the numbers are in ascending order print the message 'NUMBERS ARE IN ORDER.' at the end of the output. However, if any number is less than the previous number, print the message 'OUT OF ORDER' next to the number and print the message 'SOME NUMBERS ARE OUT OF ORDER' at the end of the output.

8. Data has been prepared for a class with one card for each student who took a test. Each card contains the student identification number (an integer), followed by the test score (an integer). The students are to receive number grades of 4, 3, 2, 1, or 0. The first data card contains the four cutoff grades: the lowest test score qualifying for a grade of 4, the lowest score for a 3, and so on. Thus, if the cutoff grades were 91, 81, 71, and 61, the first few input cards might look like this:

```
    91, 81, 71, 61
113322    75
121212    87
413277    80
```

Write a program that lists each student's identification number, test score, and grade. Some sample output is:

STUDENT: 115322   SCORE: 75   GRADE: 2
STUDENT: 121212   SCORE: 87   GRADE: 3
STUDENT: 413277   SCORE: 80   GRADE: 3

9. Modify the program in Exercise 8 so that at the end of the output it also prints the grade ranges, the number of grades in each range, and the average grade, as in the following sample:

GRADE: 4   RANGE: 91 AND ABOVE   NUMBER: 14 (12.4 PERCENT)
GRADE: 3   RANGE: 81 to 90   NUMBER: 35 (31.0 PERCENT)
GRADE: 2   RANGE: 71 to 80   NUMBER: 47 (41.6 PERCENT)
GRADE: 1   RANGE: 61 to 70   NUMBER: 10 (8.8 PERCENT)
GRADE: 0   RANGE: 60 AND BELOW   NUMBER: 7 (6.2 PERCENT)
                              TOTAL: 113 (100 PERCENT)
AVERAGE GRADE: 76.735

10. Write FORTRAN DO statements to execute program loops for each of the following sets of values:
   (a) N = 1, 3, 5, 7, . . . , 19
   (b) X = 0.0, 5.0, 10.0, 15.0, . . . , 100.0
   (c) ALPHA = −10, −9, −8, . . . , 0, 1, 2, . . . , 10
   (d) EPSILN = 0.01, 0.02, 0.03, 0.04, . . . , 2.0
   (e) J = 10, 9, 8, 7, . . . , 0
   (f) UNIT = 100.0, 99.5, 99.0, 98.5, . . . , 75.0
   (g) K = all odd integers between −100 and +100, starting with the largest
   (h) ITEST = all positive even numbers less than or equal to 500

11. For each of the following DO statements, assuming that the DO loop contains no control statements, how many times will the loop be executed? What is the value of the DO variable when the loop is complete?
   (a) DO 1000, K = 1, 50, 20
   (b) DO 99, X = 10.0, 0.0, −0.5
   (c) DO 5, L = 10, 5
   (d) DO 200, ZED = −10, 10
   (e) DO 80, N = N − 3, N + 3
   (f) DO 75, VAR = −3∗N, 3∗N, N

12. In the sequence of fractions:

$$\frac{2}{1}, \frac{3}{2}, \frac{5}{3}, \frac{8}{5}, \frac{13}{8}, \frac{21}{13}, \cdots$$

the numerator of each fraction is the sum of the numerator and denominator of the previous fraction. Using real arithmetic, compute the value of the first 40 terms of this sequence.

13. The number of combinations of n things taken k at a time is given by the formula

$$C = \frac{n!}{k! \, (n-k)!} = \frac{(n-k+1) \, (n-k+2) \, \ldots \, (n-1) \, n}{1 \cdot 2 \cdot 3 \cdots (k-1)k}$$

That is, $C = \dfrac{\text{TOP}}{\text{BOTTOM}}$ where TOP is computed by multiplying together all the integers from $n-k+1$ to n, and BOTTOM is computed by multiplying together all the numbers from 1 to k. Write a program to read pairs of values, for n and k, and print n, k, and C. Use your program to compute the number of possible five-card poker hands ($n = 52$, $k = 5$).

14. Rewrite the following procedure so that it uses no GO TO statements.

```
        IF (X .GE. 1) GO TO 20
            Y = 1.71828 * X + 1.0
            GO TO 100
 20     IF (X .GE. 2) GO TO 30
            Y - 4.67077 * X - 1.95249
            GO TO 100
 30     IF (X .GE. 3) GO TO 40
            Y = 12.69648 * X - 18.00391
            GO TO 100
 40     IF (X .GE. 4) GO TO 50
            Y = 34.51261 * X - 83.45230
            GO TO 100
 50     Y = 93.81501 * X - 320.66189
100     CONTINUE
```

15. Rewrite the following procedure to use only one GO TO statement.

```
* FIND SUMPOS - SUM OF POSITIVE NUMBERS
* AND SUMNEG = SUM OF NEGATIVE NUMBERS.
        N = 0
        SUMPOS = 0
        SUMNEG = 0
 10     READ (*, *, END = 90) A
        IF (A .EQ. 0) GO TO 90
        IF (A .LE. 0) GO TO 20
        SUMPOS = SUMPOS + A
        GO TO 30
 20     SUMNEG = SUMNEG + A
 30     N = N + 1
        GO TO 10
 90     PRINT *, N, SUMPOS, SUMNEG
```

16. The following program was deliberately written to violate every rule of structured programming. Rewrite it as a structured program.

```
        REAL C, N, S, X, Z
        GO TO 100
  5     STOP
 10     C = C*(N - 2)/(N - 1)
        GO TO 50
 20     IF (-1E-3 .LT. Z/N) GO TO 60
        GO TO 40
```

```
30    IF (Z/N .LT. 1E−3) GO TO 20
40    N = N + 2
      GO TO 10
50    Z = Z*X**2
      GO TO 70
60    PRINT *, X, S
      GO TO 5
70    S = S + C*Z/N
      GO TO 30
80    IF (X .LE. −1) GO TO 5
      GO TO 95
90    IF (X .GE. 1) GO TO 5
      GO TO 80
95    N = 1
      C = 1
      Z = X
      S = X
      GO TO 30
100   READ *, X
      GO TO 90
      END
```

17. The accompanying figure shows a repeat-loop structure with an exit in the middle. Use the technique of introducing a control variable to transform this algorithm into a repeat-loop structure with no such exit.

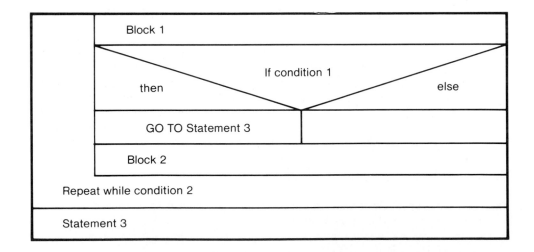

18. Using the technique of introducing a control variable, show how a repeat-loop structure can be transformed into an equivalent while-loop structure. Then show how a while-loop structure can be transformed into an equivalent repeat-loop structure.

19. Write a program for the algorithm shown in the accompanying figure. Run the program and analyze the output. What does this program do?

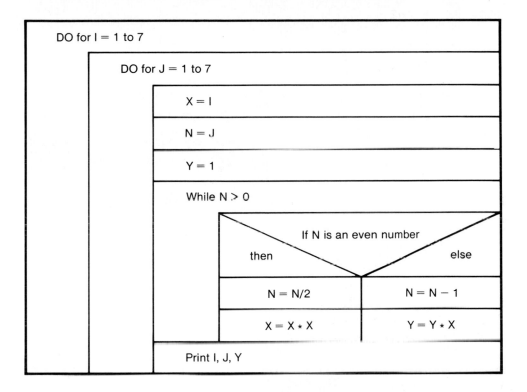

20. A popular example of elementary probability theory is to compute the probability that two people out of a randomly chosen group of *n* people have the same birthday. Ignoring leap years, the probability of any two people *not* having the same birthday is 364/365; the probability that a third person's birthday will differ from the first two is (364/365)(363/365); and so forth. For 10 people, there are 10 such fractions to be multiplied together to give the probability that all have different birthdays. This result subtracted from 1 is the probability that at least two have the same birthday. Write a program to find the probability that at least two out of *n* people have the same birthday, where *n* ranges from 2 to 50.

CHARACTER DATA

INTRODUCTION   A computer is more than just a "number cruncher" that carries out mathematical computations. It is a general-purpose machine that can process symbols of all types. Many important computer applications are nonnumerical, involving very little arithmetic. For instance, consider the problem of compiling a telephone directory for a city with 200,000 phones. Sorting the customer's names in alphabetical order is an enormous job but one that involves processing not of numbers, but of character data.

In this chapter you will learn how to use character data in FORTRAN. There are **character constants, character variables**, and **character expressions** similar to the arithmetic expressions covered in Chapter 3. One programming consideration in dealing with such data is that each character expression has a certain length: that is, it consists of a certain number of characters.

In forming character expressions from constants and variables, you can use the **concatenation operator** to join two character strings. The reverse operation, in a sense, is extracting characters from a string by using **substring expressions**.

Using these simple tools, you can write a variety of interesting nonnumerical applications.

CHARACTER CONSTANTS

A **character** is a single letter, digit, or symbol. The collection of all the characters that a computer can represent is called the computer's **character set**. For instance, the FORTRAN character set includes the capital letters A, B, C, . . . , Z, the digits 0, 1, 2, . . . , 9, a blank space, and the symbols $+ - * / . , ( ) = : '$ and \$. Many computers also include small letters a, b, c, . . . , z, and other special symbols in their character sets.

A **character string** is a sequence of one or more characters. A **character constant** in FORTRAN is a character string enclosed in quotes ('). For example:

'ABC'

is a character constant representing the character string ABC. The number of characters in a character string is called its **length**. Thus 'ABC' has length 3.

145

A **space** character (sometimes called a **blank space** or a **blank**) is a character. Thus the character constant

'A B'

consists of three characters: A, space, B. Although spaces are usually ignored in FORTRAN, they are significant within a character constant.

Any character in the machine's character set may be part of a character constant. You can even include a quote mark as a part of a character constant by representing it as two consecutive quotes:

'DON''T'

This character constant consists of five characters: D, O, N, quote T.

CHARACTER VARIABLES

Integer variables store integer values, and real variables store real values. To store a character string value, you use a **character variable**.

You can picture a character variable as a sequence of empty boxes in computer memory (Figure 5.1).

FIGURE 5.1

A

NAME

STREET

You can picture a character variable as a sequence of empty boxes in computer memory, where each box can hold one character. The type statement

CHARACTER A*1, NAME*20, STREET*15

sets up the three variables depicted here, having lengths 1, 20, and 15 characters.

Each "box," or **character storage unit**,* as it is more properly called, can hold one character. The number of such boxes in a character variable is called the **length** of the variable.

You can use a **CHARACTER statement** in FORTRAN to declare variables to be character variables. An example is:

CHARACTER NAME*20

This statement says two things: that NAME is a character variable, and that the length of NAME is 20 characters.

The CHARACTER statement is a type statement, like INTEGER and REAL. That means that a CHARACTER statement is nonexecutable, and must come at the beginning of your program.

You can use a CHARACTER statement to declare a single variable, as in the previous example, or to declare several character variables, as in the following statement:

CHARACTER A*1, NAME*20, STREET*15

This statement says that A, NAME, and STREET are character variables having lengths 1, 20, and 15.

The **length specification** that follows the asterisk after each variable name can be an integer constant, as in the previous examples, or it can be an integer expression, enclosed in parentheses, as in this statement

CHARACTER LINE* (2 * 40 + 1)

You can give a character variable any length you choose.

You can give a **default length specification**, after the word CHARACTER, which applies to all the variables in the CHARACTER statement. For example:

CHARACTER *10 X, Y, Z

means that X, Y, and Z are each character variables having length 10.

The default length is the length of each character variable for which you do not give an explicit length. In the statement

CHARACTER *10 X, Y*2, Z

the variables X and Z have the default length 10, but Y has length 2, since its length is declared explicitly.

---

*Another name for a character storage unit is a **byte**, meaning a group of **bits** (binary digits). Although *character storage unit* is the correct FORTRAN terminology, the word *byte* is in common use in computing literature.

If you provide no length specification at all, each variable has the default length of 1. Thus, the statement

```
CHARACTER A, B, C
```

means the same as

```
CHARACTER A*1, B*1, C*1
```

As with integer and real variables, you can declare character variables implicitly. For example, the statement

```
IMPLICIT CHARACTER (C, X)
```

says that unless otherwise specified, variables beginning with the letters C or X will be character variables, having the default length of 1.

You can declare character variable lengths, as well as names, implicitly. The statement

```
IMPLICIT CHARACTER *2 (A − C), CHARACTER *10 (X)
```

says that variables beginning with the letters A, B, or C are character variables of length 2, and variables beginning with the letter X are character variables of length 10.

SYMBOLIC CHARACTER CONSTANTS

In Chapter 3 you saw how to use the PARAMETER statement to define symbolic integer and real constants, as in the following example.

```
INTEGER MAXSIZ
REAL PI
PARAMETER (MAXSIZ = 100, PI = 3.1416)
```

Similarly, you can define symbolic character constants, as in the following statements.

```
CHARACTER TITLE*32
PARAMETER (TITLE = 'ACME COMPANY SALES REPORT')
```

The length of 32 was used because there are 32 characters in the constant TITLE. Another, more convenient way to set up the symbolic constant is this:

```
CHARACTER TITLE *(*)
PARAMETER (TITLE = 'ACME COMPANY SALES REPORT')
```

The difference is that the length of TITLE is given as an asterisk enclosed in parentheses. This has the same effect as the previous definition, but it is more convenient because you need not count the characters in the constant. In general, the declaration

CHARACTER *name* *(*)

can be given to specify that *name* is a symbolic character constant. The actual length of *name* is then determined from the PARAMETER statement that defines its value.

EXAMPLE 5.1 Simple Grading Program
In a chemistry class, there were five laboratory assignments with 100 points possible on each. A data card has been prepared for each student, giving the student's name followed by the five laboratory grades, as in the following sample:

'PAULING, L.' 95, 95, 90, 87, 92

Notice that the name is enclosed in quotes on the data card. A student needs a total of 380 points or more to pass. A total of 450 or more is considered excellent. Write a program that prints each student's name, grades, total grade, and the word FAIL, PASS, or EXCELLENT. Some sample output is:

```
PAULING, L.    95   95   90   87   92   TOTAL   459   EXCELLENT
BOHR, N.       80   82   75   86   81   TOTAL   404   PASS
SMITH, X.      60   62    0   50   60   TOTAL   232   FAIL
```

To store the name, you can use a character variable NAME of length sufficient to store the longest name. The declaration

CHARACTER NAME * 25

allows for a name of up to 25 characters. If any name is longer than 25 characters, the excess characters will just be truncated. You can read a data card with the statement

READ (*, *, END = 100) NAME, G1, G2, G3, G4, G5

There are three kinds of output line, depending on the rating of the student: FAIL, PASS, or EXCELLENT. One way to make the selection is to choose among three PRINT statments:

```
   IF (TOTAL .GE. 450) THEN
       PRINT *, NAME, G1, G2, G3, G4, G5,
$          ' TOTAL:', TOTAL, ' EXCELLENT'
   ELSE IF (TOTAL .GE. 380) THEN
       PRINT *, NAME, G1, G2, G3, G4, G5,
$          'TOTAL:', TOTAL, ' PASS'
   ELSE
       PRINT *, NAME, G1, G2, G3, G4, G5,
$          ' TOTAL', TOTAL, ' FAIL'
   END IF
```

A more concise method, however, is to use a single PRINT statement with a character variable RATING to which one of three values has been assigned. This method is illustrated in the following complete program.

```
* PROGRAM TO TOTAL LAB GRADES.
*
      CHARACTER NAME *25, RATING*10
      INTEGER G1, G2, G3, G4, G5, TOTAL
10    READ (*, *, END = 100) NAME, G1, G2, G3, G4, G5
         TOTAL = G1 + G2 + G3 + G4 + G5
         IF (TOTAL .GE. 450) THEN
            RATING = 'EXCELLENT'
         ELSE IF (TOTAL .GE. 380) THEN
            RATING = 'PASS'
         ELSE
            RATING = 'FAIL'
         END IF
         PRINT *, NAME, G1, G2, G3, G4, G5
      $       ' TOTAL', TOTAL, ' ' , RATING
      GO TO 10
100   END
```

CHARACTER EXPRESSIONS

Since character data is stored in memory differently than numeric data, you cannot add or subtract character data as you would numeric data. The character constant

'123'

is *not* the same as the integer constant

123

The two constants look similar on paper, but in computer memory they are entirely different. You cannot mix character with numeric data as in the *incorrect* FORTRAN statement:

X = '123' + 1

Both character constants and character variables are types of **character expressions**. Although the usual mathematical operations are not valid in character expressions, there is one operator you can use to combine character expressions. It is called the **concatenation operator**, and it is represented in FORTRAN by a double slash (//).

The word **concatenation** (sometimes called **catenation**) comes from the Greek word *catenula*, meaning *chain*. To concatenate two strings means to chain them together. If C1 and C2 are two character expressions, then

C1 // C2

is the character string obtained by joining C2 to the end of C1.

Here is an example:

```
CHARACTER F*3, C*7
F = 'FOR'
C = F // 'TRAN'
PRINT *, C
```

The second assignment statements concatenates 'FOR' and 'TRAN', assigning the value 'FORTRAN' to C.

SUBSTRINGS

As you have seen, you can think of a character variable as a sequence of boxes in computer memory. Sometimes you may want to deal with the individual boxes, or groups of boxes, that make up a character variable. That is what **substrings** are used for. You can think of a substring as an individual box or a group of adjacent boxes within the variable (Figure 5.2). More formally, we can define a substring of a character variable as a sequence of one or more consecutive character storage units of the variable.

Character storage units within a variable are numbered 1, 2, 3, . . . , starting with the leftmost character. To specify a substring, you need to specify the name of the

FIGURE 5.2
A SUBSTRING NAME REFERS TO PART OF A CHARACTER VARIABLE

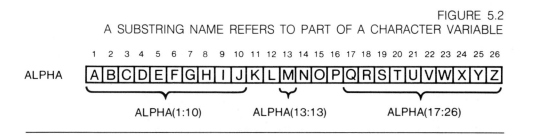

In this figure, ALPHA is a character variable consisting of 26 character storage units. The substring name ALPHA(1:10) refers to the first 10 character storage units of ALPHA. The substring name ALPHA(13:13) refers to the 13th character storage unit. ALPHA(17:26) refers to the last 10 character storage units.

variable and the number of the first and the last character storage units. The FOR-
TRAN notation for this is:

    NAME(I:J)

This notation represents a **substring name**. NAME is the name of a character
variable. I and J are integer expressions which are called **substring expressions**. The
value of I is the number of the first character, and the value of J is the number of the
last character in the substring. Notice that the substring expressions are separated by a
colon.

The following example illustrates substrings.

```
* EXAMPLE OF SUBSTRINGS
    CHARACTER ALPHA*26, S*10, C*1
    ALPHA = 'ABCDEFGHIJKLMNOPQRSTUVWXYZ'
    S = ALPHA(1:10)
    PRINT *, S
    S = ALPHA(17:26)
    PRINT *, ALPHA(1:5) // S
    PRINT *, ALPHA(1:5) // ALPHA(22:26)
    C = ALPHA(2:2)
    PRINT *, C
    END
```

The output from this program is:

```
ABCDEFGHIJ
QRSTUVWXYZ
ABCDEQRSTUVWXYZ
ABCDEVWXYZ
B
```

In this example the substring expressions are integer constants, but they could be
integer expressions instead, as in the following statements.

```
N = 10
PRINT *, ALPHA(N − 5: N + 5)
```

The **length** of a substring name is the number of characters it contains. You can
refer to the individual character storage units using substring names of length 1, like
the following:

```
C(1:1)
ALPHA(N:N)
NAME(I + 1:I + 1)
```

A substring can have any length. There is only one restriction.

Rule for Substring Expressions
Whenever you use a substring name

   NAME(I:J)

the values of the substring expressions I and J must obey the relations

   $1 \leq I \leq J \leq$ length of NAME

Thus if you use a variable C defined by

   CHARACTER C*10

it would be illegal to use substring names

   C(9:11)

or

   C(0:5)

because they refer to nonexistent character storage units.

   A substring name always contains a colon, but you can omit either of the integer substring expressions. The notation

   NAME(I:)

means the substring of NAME consisting of character number I through the end of NAME. Likewise, the notation

   NAME(:I)

means the substring of NAME consisting of all the characters up to character I. For example, the statements

```
CHARACTER VOWEL*5
VOWEL = 'AEIOU'
PRINT *, VOWEL(3:)
PRINT *, VOWEL(:4)
```

will print the characters

   IOU
   AEIO

EXAMPLE 5.2 Shifted Output Lines
Write a program that prints the following output.

```
FORTRAN 77
 FORTRAN 77
  FORTRAN 77
   FORTRAN 77
    FORTRAN 77
         .
         .
         .
```

There are a total of 50 output lines, each line being shifted one character to the right from the previous line.

An easy way to produce the desired output is this: For each N from 1 to 50, print N blank spaces followed by the string FORTRAN 77. If BLANK is a character variable consisting of 50 blank spaces, you an use the substring expression

    BLANK(:N)

to print the first N spaces.

```
    * PRINT SHIFTED OUTPUT LINES.
    *
          INTEGER N
          CHARACTER BLANK*50
          DO 10, N = 1, 50
             BLANK(N:N) = ' '
             PRINT *, BLANK(:N)//'FORTRAN 77'
    10       CONTINUE
          END
```

CHARACTER ASSIGNMENT

A **character assignment statement** stores character strings, much like an arithmetic assignment statement stores numeric values. For example,

    MONTH = 'JANUARY'

stores the character string JANUARY in the character variable MONTH. You have already seen several examples of the character assignment statement. This section explains its effect in more detail.

The first rule for character assignment says that you cannot mix character and numeric data in an assignment.

Rule for Character Assignment
If the left side of an assignment statement is a character variable, then the right side must be a character expression.

Thus, the following statements are illegal because 123 is an integer.

```
* ILLEGAL CHARACTER ASSIGNMENT
      CHARACTER C*3
      C = 123
```

You can use a character assignment statement to store a value in a substring. Here is an example.

```
* EXAMPLE OF STORING A VALUE
* IN A SUBSTRING.
      CHARACTER S*10
      S(1:3) = 'ABC'
      S(4:6) = 'DEF'
      S(7:) = 'GHIJ'
      PRINT *, S
      END
```

This program prints the string

```
ABCDEFGHIJ
```

In general, the rule is this:

Rule for Character Assignment
A character assignment statement has the form

name = expression

where *name* is a character variable or substring name, and *expression* is a character expression.

The variable or substring name on the left of the equal sign has a certain length, as does the expression on the right of the equal sign. If these lengths are the same, the entire value of the expression is stored. If the lengths are different, the effect is determined by the following rules.

Rules for Character Assignment
If the length of the variable is greater than the length of the expression, the value of the expression is stored in the left part of the variable and spaces are stored in the remaining characters.

If the length of the variable is less than the length of the expression, then only the leftmost characters are stored.

The following example illustrates these two rules.

```
CHARACTER LONG *10, SHORT *3
LONG = 'ABCDE'
SHORT = 'ABCDE'
PRINT *, LONG//SHORT
END
```

The characters printed are

ABCDE   ABC

Figures 5.3 and 5.4 show the effect of the assignment statements.

FIGURE 5.3

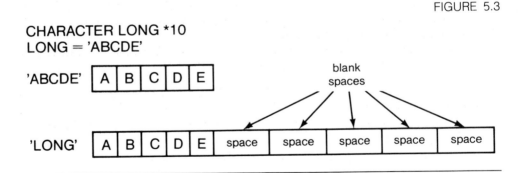

When the variable is longer than the value being stored, the value is stored in the left part of the variable and the right part is filled with blank spaces.

ANOTHER LOOK AT INPUT AND OUTPUT

Chapter 2 explained how to prepare data cards for your program. Now that you know how to write FORTRAN constants, we can give a more precise description of data card format.*

---

*In this section we discuss reading from a *card*, but the principle is the same if your program reads data from a computer terminal. Each line of terminal input corresponds to one card.

FIGURE 5.4

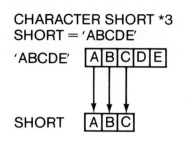

CHARACTER SHORT *3
SHORT = 'ABCDE'

When the variable is shorter than the value being stored, only the leftmost characters of the value are stored.

Remember that the input list of a READ statement consists of variable names. As you now know, each variable has a certain type (integer, real, or character). The first rule for preparing input data is this:

Rule for List-Directed Input Data
Each value on the data card must be a constant of the same type as the corresponding variable in the input list.

Thus when reading an integer variable, you would supply an integer constant on the data card. When reading a real variable, you supply a real constant, which you can type in the usual form or in exponential form.

There is a convenient exception to this rule. When reading a real value, you can leave off the decimal point. To be precise:

Rule for List-Directed Input Data
When reading a value for a real variable, the corresponding data value may have the form of an integer constant.

You can read a value for a character variable or a substring name. The corresponding value on the data card must be a character constant, enclosed in quotes. The following statements read two substring names and a character variable name.

```
CHARACTER NAME *20, CLASS *10
READ *, NAME(11:20), NAME(1:10), CLASS
```

You could prepare a data card like this:

```
'JOHN' 'JONES' 'SOPHOMORE'
```

When reading character values, the length of the value is adjusted to fit the length of the variable or substring, according to the following rule.

> *Rule for List-Directed Input Data*
> If the length of a character variable or substring name in an input list is greater than the length of the corresponding data value, then the value is stored in the leftmost character positions and the remaining characters are filled with blank spaces. If the length of the variable or substring name is less than the length of the data value, only the leftmost characters are stored.

In other words, reading a value for a character variable has the same effect as storing the value in the variable with an assignment statement.

You can type one value or several values on each data card. Specifically, the rules are:

> *Rules for List-Directed Input Data*
> Each READ statement begins reading a new card. The computer will read as many cards as necessary to supply values for each new variable in the input list.
>
> If you type more than one value on a data card, you should separate the values by a comma, or by one or more blank spaces, or by a comma and one or more blank spaces.

For example, suppose you are preparing data to be read by the following statements.

```
CHARACTER CITY *10, STATE*2
INTEGER N
REAL X
READ (*, *, END = 100) CITY, STATE, N, X
```

You could prepare data on one card like this:

```
'MIAMI', 'FL', 47, 3.5
```

Or, you could type the data without the commas, like this:

```
'MIAMI' 'FL' 47 3.5
```

Or, you could read the data from two or more cards, like this:

```
'MIAMI' 'FL'
47
3.5
```

Sometimes you may want to read several identical values from a card. Suppose you want to read five values, all zero. You could type the card like this:

```
0  0  0  0  0
```

There is a shorter way to type this input, using a **repetition factor**. You just type:

    5*0

In input data, the asterisk does not indicate multiplication. It means to repeat the following value. So 5*0 means five values of zero. The number 5 is the repetition factor. In general, we have:

Rule for List-Directed Input Data
In input data you can write an integer number, followed by an asterisk, followed by a constant (of any type) to indicate a sequence of identical input values.

Output data format is similar to input data format. Certain details of the output format will depend on the particular computer you use. For example, the statement:

    PRINT *, 'ABC', 1, 2.2

might print the three values separated by spaces, or separated by commas, or by both spaces and commas. Thus on one system the output might look like this:

    ABC   1   2.2

while on another system, the output might look like this:

    ABC,1,2.2

Details such as how many decimal places to print for a real number are also dependent on the particular computer system you use.

One difference between input and output data formats is that on output (to a terminal or to a line printer), there are no quotes around character values, while on input, quotes are required. The statements:

    CHARACTER C*10
    C = 'COMPUTER'
    PRINT *, C

will print the word

    COMPUTER

(with no quotes). But to read a value with the statements

    CHARACTER C*10
    READ *, C

you need to type quotes around the input data, like this:

'COMPUTER'

Typing quotes around character input may sometimes be inconvenient. There is a way to read character data without quotes. You can use a *format* in a READ statement. Here is an example.

READ (*, '(A)', END = 100) C

You have seen similar READ statements before. But this one, instead of having two asterisks, has the symbol

'(A)'

in place of the second asterisk. This symbol represents a format specifier consisting of an A type edit descriptor. This is often called an A format, for short.

In Chapter 8, you will learn all about formats. There are many different kinds. You can use them to specify exactly how you want your input or output data to look. For now, we will need only one kind of format: the A format illustrated above. The following rule explains how to use it.

Rule for List-Directed Input Data
Suppose that *var* is a character variable (or substring name) having a length of *n* characters. The statement

READ (*, '(A)', END = 900) *var*

reads the first *n* characters from a card and stores them in *var*. Any remaining characters on the card are ignored. If there are no more input cards, the program branches to statement 900 (or to whatever statement label you supply after the END =).

The following example illustrates this form of the READ statement.

EXAMPLE 5.3 Listing a Card Deck
Write a program that will read a deck of cards and list them on the printer. You could use this program to get a listing of your FORTRAN programs or data sets.

Here is a simple program that does the job. The READ statement reads all 80 characters of the card into the substring LINE(11:90). The first 10 characters of LINE are blank spaces that provide a left margin when LINE is printed.

```
* PROGRAM TO LIST A CARD DECK
      CHARACTER LINE *90
      LINE (1:10) = ' '
```

```
10      READ (*, '(A)', END = 90) LINE(11:90)
        PRINT *, LINE
        GO TO 10
90      END
```

EXAMPLE 5.4 Program Documentation Lister

Whenever you write a program to be used more than once, you will need to write some documentation telling how to use the program or how to change it. Often it is useful to include such documentation as comments within the program itself.

Not all of the comments in a program will be part of the general program documentation. Suppose you adopt the following convention:

1. Begin each block of general documentation with a comment card having a plus sign in column 2.
2. End each block of general documentation with a comment card having a minus sign in column 2.

Here is an example.

```
*+ PROGRAM TO LIST DOCUMENTATION.
*  AUTHOR: M. MERCHANT.
*  THIS PROGRAM READS A DECK OF INPUT CARDS AND PRINTS
*  ALL THE DOCUMENTATION BLOCKS. A DOCUMENTATION BLOCK IS
*  DEFINED TO BE ALL OF THE LINES BETWEEN A 'START' LINE AND
*  A 'STOP' LINE (INCLUDING BOTH THE START LINE AND THE STOP
*  LINE).
*  A START LINE IS A COMMENT LINE WITH A PLUS SIGN (+) IN
*  COLUMN 2.
*  A STOP LINE IS A COMMENT LINE WITH A MINUS SIGN (-) IN
*- COLUMN 2.
*+
*  A PROGRAM MAY HAVE MORE THAN ONE DOCUMENTATION
*  BLOCK. NOTE THAT ALL LINES IN THE DOCUMENTATION BLOCK,
*- NOT JUST COMMENTS, ARE LISTED.
```

The principle of the program is to read all the input lines, list all lines that are inside a documentation block, and skip all lines that are not. Thus, as the program reads the input, there are two possible "states:" it is either inside or outside of a documentation block. Figure 5.5 shows the top-level program design.

An important point to note is that the end of a documentation block is signalled by a "stop" line, but the stop line is itself part of the block. That is why the transition from being in a block to being out of a block must take place *after* the line is printed.

The program needs some way to "remember" whether it is inside a documentation block. You can use a logical variable INSIDE which is true when inside a block and false otherwise.

According to the definition, a block begins with a comment line having a plus sign in column 2. The equivalent FORTRAN condition can be written:

```
LINE(1:2) .EQ. '*+' .OR. LINE(1:2) .EQ. 'C+'
```

FIGURE 5.5
PROGRAM DOCUMENTATION LISTER—TOP-LEVEL DESIGN

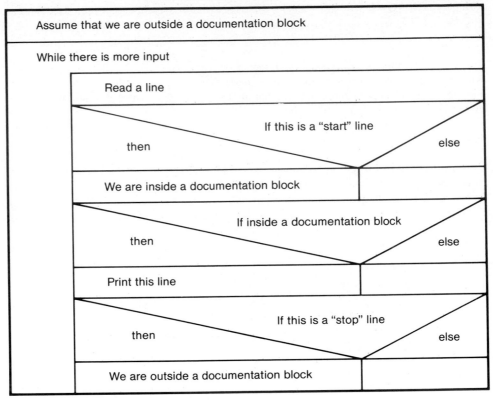

Here is the complete FORTRAN program.

```
      LOGICAL INSIDE
      CHARACTER LINE * 80

      INSIDE = .FALSE.

      READ (*, '(A)', END = 900) LINE
100      IF (LINE(1:2) .EQ. '*+' .OR. LINE(1:2) .EQ. 'C+')
     $         INSIDE = .TRUE.

         IF (INSIDE) PRINT *, LINE

         IF (LINE(1:2) .EQ. '*−' .OR. LINE(1:2) .EQ. 'C−')
     $         INSIDE = .FALSE.

      GO TO 100
900   END
```

COMPARING CHARACTER EXPRESSIONS

The relational operators, .LT., .EQ., and so on, can be used to compare two character expressions. With character expressions,

A .LT. B

means, especially, that A comes before B in alphabetical order. For example, the relation:

'APPLE' .LT. 'BANANA'

is true, because APPLE comes before BANANA in *alphabetical order*. To see how alphabetical order works in FORTRAN, let us start with the simplest case: comparing two characters.

Alphabetic characters compare according to the usual alphabetical order. Thus the following relations are all true.

'A' .LT. 'B'
'B' .LT. 'C'
'A' .LT. 'Z'

What happens when you compare nonalphabetic characters? For example, how can you tell whether the relation

'*' .LT. '='

is true or false? The answer depends on the particular computer system you are using.

Suppose you took all the characters in your computer's characer set and put them in their generalized alphabetical order, so that the first character is less than the second, the second character is less than the third, and so on. This arrangement is called the **collating sequence** of the computer's character set.

Here is one possible collating sequence for the FORTRAN character set:

space $ ' ( ) *+, − ./0123456789: = ABCD ... Z

This is the collating sequence specified by the American Standard Code for Information Interchange (ASCII), which is used on many computers.

The ASCII collating sequence, however, is only one possible choice. Most IBM computers use the Extended Binary Coded Decimal Interchange Code (EBCDIC). This is a different character set, with a different collating sequence.

Although the exact collating sequence may vary among computers, certain relations will always be true in standard FORTRAN. As we said earlier, uppercase alphabetical characters compare according to the usual alphabetical order. The characters corresponding to the digits 0 through 9 compare in the usual numerical order.

Thus, the following relations are all true:

```
'0' .LT. '1'
'1' .LT. '2'
'2' .LT. '3'
'9' .GT. '8'
```

A blank space is less than both the letter 'A' and the character '0'. Thus, the following relations are true.

```
' ' .LT. 'A'
' ' .LT. '0'
```

There are no standard rules for determining the order of other special characters. That is, the relation

```
'+' .LT. '*'
```

might be true on one computer system and false on another. Similarly, all of the following relations might be either true or false, depending on the particular collating sequence your computer uses.

```
' ' .LT. '*'
'.' .LT. 'A'
'A' .LT. '3'
'9' .LT. '−'
```

If your computer has lowercase alphabetic characters, they will probably compare in alphabetical order, but they have no standard relation to uppercase characters. Thus,

```
'a' .LT. '
```

might be either true or false, depending on your computer.

The preceding discussion deals with comparing two single characters, but you can compare two longer character expressions as well. Suppose that C1 and C2 are character expressions having the same length. Then the relation

```
C1 .EQ. C2
```

is true if and only if each character of C1 is equal to the corresponding character of C2.

To determine whether the relation

```
C1 .LT. C2
```

is true, you can use the same algorithm you use for putting two words in alphabetical order: Compare each character of C1 with the corresponding character of C2. Keep comparing until you come to a character that is different (or until you come to the end of the string). If the strings are different, then their alphabetical order is the same as the alphabetical order of the first different character. Thus the relation

'AAA1' .LT. 'AAA2'

is true because the fourth character of the first expression is less than the fourth character of the second.

You can also compare character expressions having different lengths. The effect of such a comparison is as though the shorter string were padded on the right with blank spaces to make it the same length as the longer string. Thus the relation

'A' // 'X' .GT. 'ABC'

is true.

It is illegal to compare a character expression with a numeric expression. Thus, the relation

'123' .EQ. 123

is illegal.

One final note about comparing character strings: Besides using relational operators, there are two other useful ways to do it. One way is to use the intrinsic functions LLT, LGT, LLE, and LGE, which compare strings according to the ASCII collating sequence. Another way is to use the intrinsic functions CHAR and ICHAR, which make it possible to define your own collating sequence. We will discuss intrinsic functions in Chapter 7.

EXAMPLE 5.5 Classifying Characters
The object of this example is to read lines of text and, for each line, to produce output like the following:

DELAWARE RATIFIED THE U.S. CONSTITUTION ON DEC. 7, 1787.
16 VOWELS.
22 CONSONANTS.
5 DIGITS.
5 PUNCTUATION MARKS.

The first line of output is the input line. The following four lines of output show how many characters of each type were present in the input: vowels (A, E, I, O, U), consonants (other letters of the alphabet), digits (0 through 9), and punctuation marks (which, for this example, will mean any character other than a letter, a digit, or a blank space). We assume that alphabetic letters are all uppercase.

FIGURE 5.6
PROGRAM TO CLASSIFY CHARACTERS

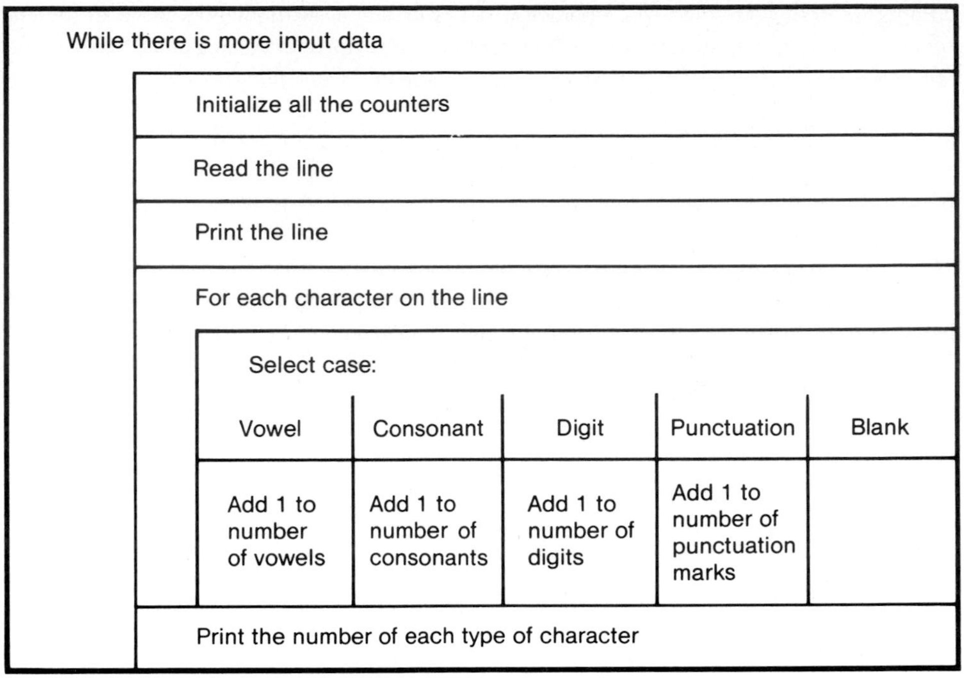

While there is more input data				
Initialize all the counters				
Read the line				
Print the line				
For each character on the line				
Select case:				
Vowel	Consonant	Digit	Punctuation	Blank
Add 1 to number of vowels	Add 1 to number of consonants	Add 1 to number of digits	Add 1 to number of punctuation marks	
Print the number of each type of character				

A top-level design for this program is shown in Figure 5.6. For each input line, you inspect each character, figure out what type it is, then add 1 to the appropriate counter.

To determine the type of a particular character C, suppose that CSET is a character variable in which the character set has been stored as follows:

CSET = ' AEIOUBCDFGHJKLMNPQRSTVWXYZ0123456789 '

You can use a while-loop structure to compare C with each character of CSET as follows:

```
       J = 1
20     IF (J .LE. 37 .AND. C .NE. CSET(J:J)) THEN
           J = J + 1
           GO TO 20
       END IF
```

The final value of J determines the type of the character C. If $J = 1$, C is a blank space. If $2 \le J \le 6$, C is a vowel. If $7 \le J \le 27$, C is a consonant. If $28 \le J \le 37$, C is a digit. If $J > 37$, C is not equal to any of the characters in CSET, therefore, C is a punctuation mark. Here is the complete program.

```
      *
        PROGRAM TO READ A SET OF CARDS AND PRINT THE NUMBER
      * OF VOWELS, CONSONANTS, DIGITS, AND PUNCTUATION MARKS.
      *
      * VARIABLES:
      ** LOOP COUNTERS:
          INTEGER I, J
      ** COUNTERS FOR EACH TYPE OF CHARACTER:
          INTEGER NVOWEL, NCONS, NDIGIT, NPUNC
      ** STORAGE FOR THE INPUT LINE, FOR ONE CHARACTER, AND FOR THE
      ** CHARACTER SET:
          CHARACTER LINE*80, C*1, CSET*38
      *
          CSET = ' AEIOUBCDFGHJKLMNPQRSTVWXYZ0123456789
   10     READ (*, '(A)', END = 900) LINE
          PRINT *, LINE
      *
      * INITIALIZE THE COUNTERS.
      *
          NVOWEL = 0.
          NCONS = 0
          NDIGIT = 0
          NPUNC = 0
      *
      * INSPECT EACH CHARACTER OF THE LINE AND DETERMINE THE TYPE.
      *
          DO 100, I = 1, 80
              C = LINE(I:I)
              J = 1
   20         IF (J .LE. 37 .AND. C .NE. CSET(J:J)) THEN
                  J = J + 1
                  GO TO 20
              END IF
              IF (J .EQ. 1) THEN
      *           (IT IS A SPACE)
              ELSE IF (2 .LE. J .AND. J .LE. 6) THEN
      *           (IT IS A VOWEL)
                  NVOWEL = NVOWEL + 1
              ELSE IF (7 .LE. J .AND. J .LE. 27) THEN
      *           (IT IS A CONSONANT)
                  NCONS = NCONS + 1
              ELSE IF (28 .LE. J .AND. J .LE. 37) THEN
      *           (IT IS A DIGIT)
                  NDIGIT = NDIGIT + 1
              ELSE
      *           (IT IS SOMETHING ELSE, THEREFORE PUNCTUATION)
                  NPUNC = NPUNC + 1
              END IF
   100    CONTINUE
```

```
*
* OUTPUT THE RESULTS FOR THIS LINE.
*       PRINT *, NVOWEL, ' VOWELS,'
        PRINT *, NCONS, ' CONSONANTS,'
        PRINT *, NDIGIT, ' DIGITS,'
        PRINT *, NPUNC, ' PUNCTUATION MARKS.'
        GO TO 10
900  END
```

EXAMPLE 5.6 Counting Words

The input data to this program consists of a paragraph of English prose, typed on cards. The problem is to count the number of words in the paragraph. Also count the number of nonblank characters in the paragraph and compute the average word length, in characters per word. Print the paragraph, as well as the three numbers. Here is some sample output.

```
WHAT A PIECE OF WORK IS MAN
HOW NOBLE IN REASON
HOW INFINITE IN FACULTY
IN FORM AND MOVING HOW
EXPRESS AND ADMIRABLE


23 WORDS, 94 CHARACTERS,
AN AVERAGE OF 4.08696 CHARACTERS PER WORD.
```

(The quotation is Shakespeare: *Hamlet*, Act II.)

For simplicity, assume that the text contains no numbers or special characters such as punctuation marks. In particular, assume that words are not hyphenated at the end of a line. Figure 5.7 shows the top-level design.

The only difficult part of this procedure is to determine when you have reached the end of a word. The problem can be simple if you adopt a simple definition of "word." We will assume that a word is a sequence of nonblank characters followed by either a blank character or by the end of the line. With this definition, you can write a more detailed and slightly modified version of the inner loop as shown in Figure 5.8.

This method *almost* works, but it has one flaw. In the bottom decision, what happens when you look at the last character of the line? There is no "following character," so you cannot carry out the instruction. You could deal with this problem by making the condition more complicated, to take into account whether this is the last character on the line. An easier resolution is to make sure that every line has an extra blank character at the end. Suppose the input line is 80 characters long. You can read the line into a variable LINE that is defined to have not 80, but 81 characters, and you initialize the last character with the statement

```
LINE(81:81) = ' '
```

You can then write the condition that controls the inner loop as follows.

Starting with the first character in the line, look at each character except the last (the extra blank).

The bottom decision now makes sense, because there is a "following character" for every character being looked at. This technique is frequently used in processing character data. Figure 5.9 shows the revised algorithm.

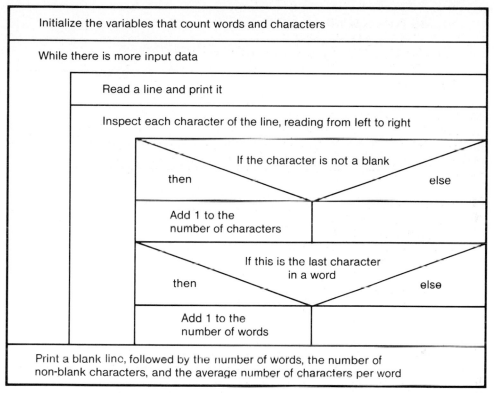

FIGURE 5.7
PROGRAM TO COUNT WORDS—TOP-LEVEL DESIGN

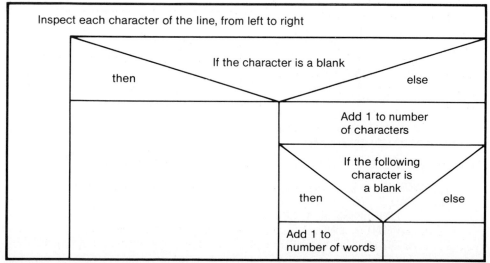

FIGURE 5.8
DETAIL OF PROCEDURE FOR COUNTING WORDS

FIGURE 5.9
PROGRAM TO COUNT WORDS

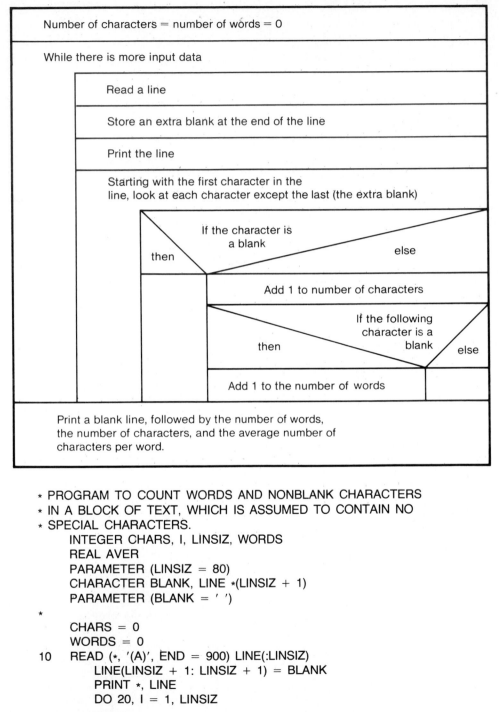

```
* PROGRAM TO COUNT WORDS AND NONBLANK CHARACTERS
* IN A BLOCK OF TEXT, WHICH IS ASSUMED TO CONTAIN NO
* SPECIAL CHARACTERS.
      INTEGER CHARS, I, LINSIZ, WORDS
      REAL AVER
      PARAMETER (LINSIZ = 80)
      CHARACTER BLANK, LINE *(LINSIZ + 1)
      PARAMETER (BLANK = ' ')
*
      CHARS = 0
      WORDS = 0
10    READ (*, '(A)', END = 900) LINE(:LINSIZ)
          LINE(LINSIZ + 1: LINSIZ + 1) = BLANK
          PRINT *, LINE
          DO 20, I = 1, LINSIZ
```

```
            IF (LINE(I:I) .EQ. BLANK) THEN
                CONTINUE
            ELSE
                CHARS = CHARS + 1
                IF (LINE(I + 1: I + 1) .EQ. BLANK) THEN
                    WORDS = WORDS + 1
                END IF
            END IF
20          CONTINUE
        GO TO 10
900     PRINT *, BLANK
        AVER = CHARS
        AVER = AVER/WORDS
        PRINT *, WORDS, ' WORDS, ',
     $          CHARS, ' CHARACTERS, '
        PRINT *, ' AN AVERAGE OF ', AVER, 'CHARACTERS PER WORD.'
        END
```

SUMMARY

A character constant is a string of characters enclosed in quotes. You can also define symbolic character constants with a PARAMETER statement.

A character variable consists of a sequence of character storage units, and is declared by a CHARACTER statement. Every character variable, and, in fact, every character expression, has a certain length which is the number of character storage units it contains. You define the length of a character variable in the CHARACTER statement. The variable has the same length throughout the program.

A substring is a sequence of adjacent character storage units of a character variable. You can use a substring to extract part of a character string. The substring expressions that define the substring must be within the proper range or an execution error will result.

A character expression can be a character constant, variable, or substring name. Character expressions can be combined using the concatenation operator, which joins two strings to form a longer string.

When a value is read into a character variable or assigned to it, the length is adjusted to fit the variable. If the value is too long for the variable, the rightmost characters are truncated. If the value is shorter than the variable, blank spaces are added to the right.

When using list-directed input, each value read must be a constant of the same type as the corresponding variable. You can use an A format to read an entire input line as a single character value.

You can use relational operators to compare character expressions. For the operators .EQ. and .NE., the result of a comparison is always determined, but for the other relational operators, the result is only partially determined by the rules of standard FORTRAN. Basically, character expressions compare according to alphabetical order.

VOCABULARY

A format
byte
character assignment statement
character constant
character expression
character set
CHARACTER statement
character storage unit
character variable

collating sequence
concatenation
default length specification
length
length expression
repetition factor
space
substring
substring expression

EXERCISES

1. In each case below, what value is assigned to the character variable X?
   (a) CHARACTER X*5
        X = 'A' // 'B' // 'C'
   (b) CHARACTER X*5, A, B
        A = '123'
        B = '456'
        X = A // B
   (c) CHARACTER X
        X = 'ABC'
   (d) CHARACTER*3 X, A
        A = 'ABC'
        X = A
        X = X // X
   (e) CHARACTER*3 A, X*5
        A = 'ABCDE'
        X = A

2. In each case below, what value is assigned to the character variable X?
   (a) CHARACTER X*5, A*5
        A = 'ABCDE'
        X = A(4:5) // A(:3)
   (b) CHARACTER X*5
        X = 'ABCDE'
        X = X(5:5)//X(4:4)//X(3:3)//X(2:2)//X(1:1)
   (c) CHARACTER *5 X, A
        A = 'ABCDE'
        X = A(4:) // A(:4)
   (d) CHARACTER X*5
        X = 'ABCDE'
        X = X(4:)
   (e) CHARACTER X*5
        X = 'ABCDE'
        X(4:) = X
        X(:4) = X(2:)
   (f) CHARACTER *5 X
        X(5:5) = 'A'
        X(4:4) = 'B'
        X(3:3) = 'C'
        X(2:2) = 'D'
        X(1:1) = 'E'

3. What is the value of each of the following logical expressions? If the value is not determined specifically by the rules of standard FORTRAN, indicate that fact.
   (a) 'A' .NE. 'A '
   (b) 'A' .NE. ' A '
   (c) 'AX' .LT. 'AXE'
   (d) '2' .EQ. 'A'

(e) '2' .LT. 'A'
(f) ' ' .GT. 'ABC'
(g) '+' .LT. 'ABC'
(h) 'ABC' .EQ. 'ABCD'
(i) 'ABC' .LT. 'ABCD'
(j) 'XYZ' // 'ABC' .LT. 'ABC' // 'XYZ'

4. What values are stored in the variables by the following statements, given the input data shown?

```
INTEGER I, J, K
REAL A, B, C
CHARACTER*5 X, Y, Z
READ *, A, B, C, I, I
READ *, X
READ *, Y, Z, J, K
```

Input data:

```
1 2 3 4
5 6 7 8
'ALABAMA', 'ALASKA'
'ARIZONA', 'ARKANSAS'
5*2, 2*5
```

5. A set of data cards has been prepared in the following format.

Card Column	Item
1 – 10	First Name
12	Middle Initial
14 – 25	Last Name
31 – 39	Social Security Number (for example, 111223333)

Write a program that lists these cards in the following format.

Print Column	Item
1 – 11	Social Security Number, with hyphens inserted (for example, 111-22-3333)
14 – 25	Last Name
27 – 36	First Name
38	Middle Initial

6. Columns 73 – 80 of a FORTRAN program are not used by FORTRAN. They may be used for some identification. For example, the first three cards in a program might contain the identifiers

```
PDLA0001
PDLA0002
PDLA0003
```

where PDLA is an identifier of the program (perhaps Program Documentation Lister, Version A), and 0001, 0002, 0003 are sequence numbers. Write a program that reads a set of cards and checks that columns 73 – 80 are in alphabetical order. Also check that columns 73 – 76 are the same in every card. If all cards are in order, print 'CARDS IN SEQUENCE'. If not, print 'CARDS OUT OF SEQUENCE' and stop.

7. Write a program that prints the following pattern of characters.

```
            *
            **
            ***
            ****
        . . . (total of 50 lines)
```

8. Write a program that prints the following pattern of characters.

```
            +
          +++
         +++++
        +++++++
        . . . (total of 50 lines)
```

9. The figure below shows a 4 × 4 checkerboard pattern made up of X's. Write a program that prints an 8 × 8 checkerboard pattern large enough for playing checkers. Assume that the printer prints 10 characters per inch horizontally and 6 lines per inch vertically. Make each small square one inch on a side.

```
        XXXXXXXXXX          XXXXXXXXXX
        XXXXXXXXXX          XXXXXXXXXX
        XXXXXXXXXX          XXXXXXXXXX
        XXXXXXXXXX          XXXXXXXXXX
        XXXXXXXXXX          XXXXXXXXXX
        XXXXXXXXXX          XXXXXXXXXX
                  XXXXXXXXXX          XXXXXXXXXX
                  XXXXXXXXXX          XXXXXXXXXX
                  XXXXXXXXXX          XXXXXXXXXX
                  XXXXXXXXXX          XXXXXXXXXX
                  XXXXXXXXXX          XXXXXXXXXX
                  XXXXXXXXXX          XXXXXXXXXX
        XXXXXXXXXX          XXXXXXXXXX
        XXXXXXXXXX          XXXXXXXXXX
        XXXXXXXXXX          XXXXXXXXXX
        XXXXXXXXXX          XXXXXXXXXX
        XXXXXXXXXX          XXXXXXXXXX
        XXXXXXXXXX          XXXXXXXXXX
                  XXXXXXXXXX          XXXXXXXXXX
                  XXXXXXXXXX          XXXXXXXXXX
                  XXXXXXXXXX          XXXXXXXXXX
                  XXXXXXXXXX          XXXXXXXXXX
                  XXXXXXXXXX          XXXXXXXXXX
                  XXXXXXXXXX          XXXXXXXXXX
```

10. Write a program that prints a pattern of X's in a circle, 10 inches in diameter.

11. In the program to count words (Example 5.6), some simplifying assumptions were made: that there were no punctuation marks, and that there were no hyphenated words. Modify the program to work even if there are punctuation marks. Count a hyphenated word as one word. Take into account the possibility that a word might be hyphenated at the end of a line.

12. A simple way of enciphering a message is to use a letter substitution code. For example, if you use the letter substitution:

```
A B C D E F G H I  J K L M N O P Q R S T U V W X Y Z
Z Y X W V U T S R Q P O N M L K J I  H G F E D C B A
```

then the message

THE QUICK BROWN FOX JUMPS OVER THE LAZY DOG

becomes:

GSV JFRXP YILDM ULC QFNKH LEVI GSV OZAB WLT

Write a program that reads two lines, representing a letter substitution code. The third and following lines are the message which the program should encipher and print. Write the program so that it can decipher a coded message if you interchange the first two cards.

13. Write a program that reads input lines containing text and prints each word on a separate line. For example, if the input is the line:

APPLY YOURSELF TO WHAT YOU ARE ABOUT

then the output should be

APPLY
YOURSELF
TO
WHAT
YOU
ARE
ABOUT

14. Write a program that reads a list of words, such as the list produced by the program in Exercise 13, and writes them on one or more lines such that as many words as possible fit on the line without making the line more than 65 characters long. Put a blank space between words.

15. This program performs conversion from English to metric units. Some sample input is

```
180     'INCHES'
16      'FEET'
2       'YARDS'
1.5     'MILES'
```

For each input line, print the input followed by the equivalent metric value as shown in the following table.

If Input Is	Multiply By	To Obtain
Inches	2.54	Centimeters
Feet	30.48	Centimeters
Yards	0.9144	Meters
Miles	1.609344	Kilometers

16. Write a program that reads lines of text and prints the length of the longest line. Length in this case means the length of the line not counting any trailing blank spaces. Assume that no input line is longer than 200 characters.

17. Write a program that reads character input and prints it with all blank spaces removed. Thus, if an input line is:

DEL TAX = (A + B)/2

the output line would be

DELTAX=(A+B)/2

18. A histogram is a bar graph that shows the relative frequency of occurrence of a set of measurements. For example, the following table shows the results of a hypothetical survey of users of laundry soap.

Brand of Laundry Soap	Percentage of People Surveyed Who Use Brand
Brand A	10
Brand B	15
Brand C	5
Brand D	31
Brand E	2
Brand X (all others)	37

The histogram in the figure on page 177 displays these results graphically. The length of each bar is proportional to the percentage of people who use the brand. Write a program that prints a histogram. The first input line is a title for the histogram. Each following input line consists of a character label (up to 20 characters) followed by a percentage (0 to 100). Thus, input prepared from the table above would be

'SURVEY RESULTS OF LAUNDRY SOAP USERS'
'BRAND A' 15
'BRAND C'   5
'BRAND D' 31
'BRAND E'   2
'BRAND X (OTHER)' 37

The program should print the input, giving the total percentage, followed by a labeled histogram. Use on asterisk for each percentage point. Make the bars three lines wide and skip a line between bars. Sample output is shown in the figure on page 178.

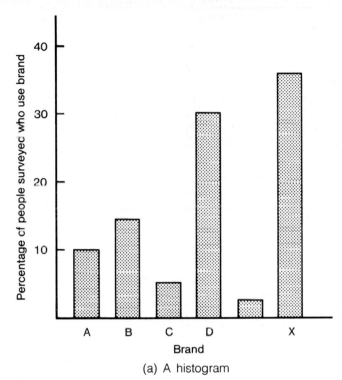

(a) A histogram

19. The figure on page 179 shows an example of a printer plot: a graph of a mathematical equation done on a line printer or terminal. For this exercise you will write a simple example of a printer plot. The problem is to plot the mathematical equation:

$$y = x^2$$

for values of x from -10 to 10, adding 1/3 to x on each iteration. Define a character variable PLOT of size 101, and store blank spaces in it. For each value of x, starting at -10, compute the corresponding y. Set the integer variable I equal to Y + 1.5. Now store an asterisk in PLOT(I:I) and print the value of PLOT. Store a blank space in PLOT(I:I), then repeat the procedure for the next X.

20. To generate the printer plot shown in the figure for Exercise 19, plot the equation:

$$y = x(x-3)\ (x-5)$$

for values of x from -1 to 6. The basic technique is the same as for Exercise 19, but you must determine how to *scale* the data so that when you compute the index I from the corresponding Y value, I will be within the proper limits to be used as an index for the character variable you print.

SURVEY RESULTS OF LAUNDRY SOAP USERS

```
                 **********
BRAND A          **********        10 PERCENT
                 **********


                 ***************
BRAND B          ***************        15 PERCENT
                 ***************


                 *****
BRAND C          *****          5 PERCENT
                 *****


                 ******************************
BRAND D          ******************************        31 PERCENT
                 ******************************


                 **
BRAND E          **          2 PERCENT
                 **


                 *************************************
BRAND X (OTHER)  *************************************        37 PERCENT
                 *************************************
```

(b) Sample output from histogram program (Exercise 18)

A COMPUTER-GENERATED GRAPH

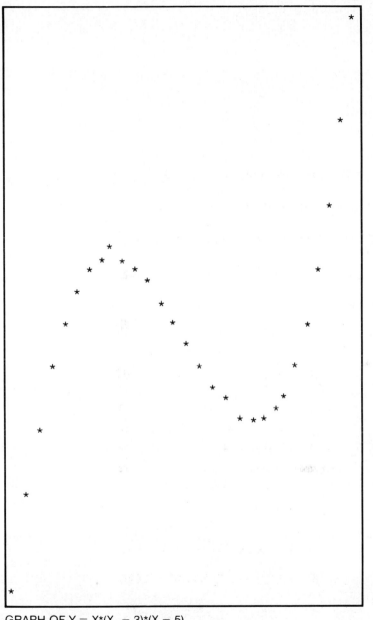

GRAPH OF Y = X*(X − 3)*(X − 5)
OVER THE RANGE −1 TO 6

ARRAYS

INTRODUCTION In mathematics, a variable is often written with a **subscript**. For instance,

$$X_2$$

(read "X sub 2") is a subscripted variable with the subscript 2. Subscripted variables are extremely useful in programming, too, because they allow you to deal systematically with a large number of variables.

Consider an example. Suppose you want a program that will read 100 numbers and print them in the reverse order. Since the program cannot begin printing until it finishes reading, it will have to store the input in 100 different variables. The easy way to do this is to set up an **array** X consisting of the 100 variables.

$$X_1, X_2, X_3, \ldots, X_{99}, X_{100}$$

Then you can use a variable I for the subscript and write the procedure as shown in Figure 6.1

The examples in this chapter illustrate important programming techniques, such as sorting and searching, which would be practically impossible without arrays.

In addition to arrays with one subscript, FORTRAN allows arrays with two subscripts, like:

$$A_{1,1} \quad A_{1,2} \quad A_{1,3}$$
$$A_{2,1} \quad A_{2,2} \quad A_{2,3}$$

Such an array is sometimes called a **matrix**. As a matter of fact, FORTRAN allows arrays with up to seven subscripts.

Arrays are a simple yet powerful feature of the FORTRAN language. They allow the programmer to organize and manipulate data in complex ways. In fact, as you will see, the careful choice of **data structures**, of which an array is one example, goes hand in hand with the choice of control structures in designing an algorithm. Both are vital to achieving a well-structured program.

FIGURE 6.1
PROCEDURE TO PRINT 100 NUMBERS IN REVERSE ORDER

Do for I = 1,2,3,..., 100
Read X_I
Do for I = 100,99,98,..., 1
Print X_I

ARRAYS AND SUBSCRIPTS IN FORTRAN

An **array** in FORTRAN is a set of variables. You give a name, such as X, to the entire array. Then you use a **subscript** to distinguish among the variables in the array.

On a keypunch, and on most computer terminals, there is no way to type a subscript. Instead, you represent a subscript expression by enclosing it in parentheses. Thus, instead of writing

$$X_I$$

as in algebra, you write "X sub I" in FORTRAN as

The X in this expression is the **array name**, which has the same form as any FORTRAN variable name: it begins with a letter and can be up to six characters long. The **subscript expression**, which is the part within the parentheses, can be any integer expression (Table 6.1).

TABLE 6.1
A SUBSCRIPT EXPRESSION WHICH IS ENCLOSED
IN PARENTHESES CAN BE AN INTEGER EXPRESSION

Algebraic Notation	Equivalent FORTRAN Expression
a_i	A(I)
a_{i+1}	A(I + I)
x_{2k}	X(2*K)
ΔX_{i+j}	DELTAX (I + J)
$y_{n/2}$	Y(N/2)

The expression X(I) represents an **element** of the array X. That is, the array X is a set of variables, and each element X(I) is a variable (Figure 6.2).

FIGURE 6.2

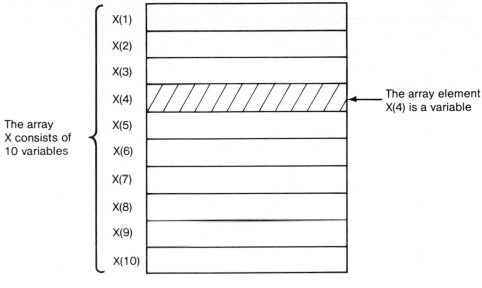

The array element X(4) is a variable

The array X consists of 10 variables

An array is a set of variables that is stored in a sequence of memory locations. Each array element is one variable.

All the elements in an array have the same type. A real array consists of real elements. Thus, if ABC is a real array, then ABC(1), ABC(2), and so on, are real variables. Likewise, an integer array or a character array consists of all integer variables or all character variables. You can declare the type of an array with a type statement just as with other variables. Alternatively, you can use an IMPLICIT statement or default typing to determine the type of an array.

An array element can be used in an expression, just like any other FORTRAN variable. For instance, if A and B are arrays, then you could use the following expression in a program:

$$A(I + 1) = 2 *A(I) + B(I - 1)$$

DIMENSION DECLARATIONS

Suppose that you want to use an array consisting of the real variables

X(1), X(2), X(3), . . . , X(99), X(100)

You need to include in your program a declarative statement that tells the FORTRAN compiler two things:

1. X is an array.
2. The subscripts for X range from 1 to 100.

You can specify this information with a **DIMENSION statement** like the following:

    DIMENSION X(100)

The expression

    X(100)

in this statement is called an **array declarator**. The number 100 is the **upper dimension bound** of the array X. That is, 100 is the maximum allowable subscript value for X. A DIMENSION statement consists of the word DIMENSION, followed by an array declarator or a series of array declarators, separated by commas.

The purpose of the DIMENSION statement is simply to declare arrays and their dimension bounds. It is a declarative statement that goes at the beginning of the program (before the first executable statement). When the FORTRAN compiler sees a DIMENSION statement, it reserves storage locations for the array. Thus, the statement

    DIMENSION A(11)

causes FORTRAN to set aside eleven memory locations for the array A (Figure 6.3).

You can use a DIMENSION statement in conjunction with a type statement to declare the dimension bounds and type of an array. For example, the statements

    REAL X
    INTEGER VECT
    DIMENSION X(100), VECT(10)

set up two arrays: X and VECT. X is a real array, consisting of 100 real variables:

    X(1), X(2), X(3), . . . , X(99), X(100)

while VECT is an integer array, consisting of 10 integer variables:

    VECT(1), VECT(2), VECT(3), . . . , VECT(9), VECT(10)

If you prefer, you can omit the DIMENSION statement and write the array declarator as part of the type statement itself. Instead of the three statements given above, you could write

    REAL X(100)
    INTEGER VECT(10)

These statements have exactly the same effect. They declare X to be a real array of 100 elements and VECT to be an integer array of 10 elements.

In addition to the upper dimension bound, you can specify a **lower dimension bound** in an array declarator. In the statement

    DIMENSION B(−5:5)

FIGURE 6.3

THE DIMENSION STATEMENT IS A DECLARATIVE STATEMENT THAT RESERVES STORAGE FOR ARRAYS

DIMENSION A(11)

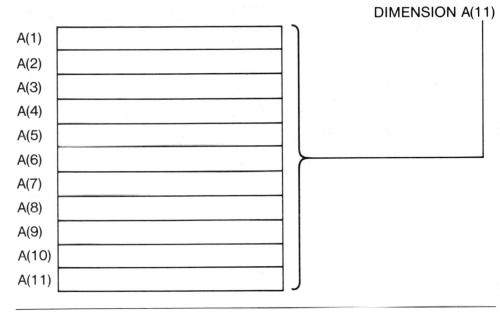

The DIMENSION statement shown here reserves 11 memory locations for the array A.

the array declarator contains two numbers, separated by a colon. The first of these numbers is the lower dimension bound: the minimum value of a subscript for the array B. The second number is the upper dimension bound. Thus, this statement declares B to be an array of 11 elements: B(−5) through B(5) (Figure 6.4).

If you do not specify a lower dimension bound in the array declarator, then the lower dimension bound is assumed to be 1. Thus, the statements

    DIMENSION X(25)

and

    DIMENSION X(1:25)

mean the same thing.

Both the lower and upper dimension bounds can be any integer constant expressions. For example, the following statements are legal.

    INTEGER MAX
    PARAMETER (MAX = 25)
    REAL A(MAX), B(2*MAX), C(2*MAX + 1)
    INTEGER X(−MAX:MAX), P(−2:MAX + 1)

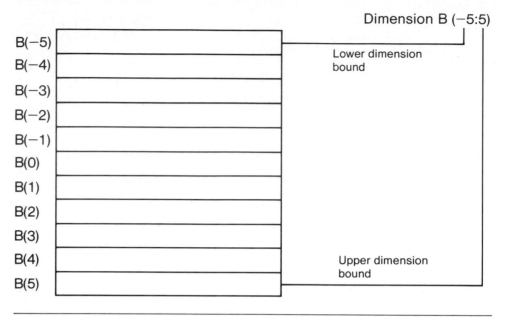

FIGURE 6.4

A dimension declarator can give both a lower dimension bound and an upper dimension bound to specify the minimum and maximum allowable subscript values for an array.

In an array of character variables, each element has the same length. That is, each element consists of the same number of characters. For example, the statements

    CHARACTER C*6
    DIMENSION C(5)

declare that C is a character array consisting of 5 elements, and that each element of the array is a character variable consisting of 6 characters (Figure 6.5).

Another way to declare this array is with the single statement

    CHARACTER C(5)*6

In any CHARACTER statement you can write an array declarator followed by a length specification to set up a character array.

Each element of a character array can be used just like any other character variable. In the array shown in Figure 6.6, C(1) is a character variable of length 6, so the statement

    C(1) = 'APPLE'

stores the character constant in the first element of the array C.

FIGURE 6.5
IN A CHARACTER ARRAY, EACH ARRAY ELEMENT HAS THE SAME LENGTH

CHARACTER C(5)*6

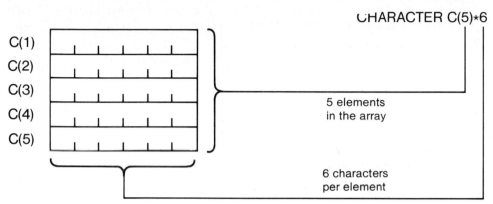

5 elements
in the array

6 characters
per element

You can use substring expressions with character array elements, just as you do for other character variables. For example, the substring expression

C(3)(3:5)

refers to characters 3 through 5 of the third element of the array C. The expression

C(5)(4:4)

refers to the fourth character of the fifth element of C (Figure 6.6).

EXAMPLE 6.1 Reversing an Array
In the introduction to this chapter, we gave an example of a simple problem that uses arrays. The problem is to read a list of values and to print them in reverse order. Let us see how this can be done in FORTRAN.

The program shown below will read a deck of input cards and list them in reverse order. A

FIGURE 6.6
SUBSTRING EXPRESSIONS CAN BE USED WITH CHARACTER ARRAYS

C(1) A P P L E   ◄——————————————— C(1)
C(2) O R A N G E
C(3) P E A R   ◄——————————————— C(3) (3:5)
C(4) G U A V A
C(5) M A N G O   ——————————————— C(5) (4:4)

The substring expressions, enclosed in parentheses, are written after the array element name.

DO loop varies the subscript I from 1 up to the maximum value MAX (MAX is a symbolic constant that represents the size of the array.) When the program detects end of input, it exits the first DO loop and begins the second DO loop, which varies the subscript from its highest value down to 1 to print the array elements in reverse order.

```
* PROGRAM TO LIST A DECK OF CARDS IN REVERSE ORDER.
*
      INTEGER I, MAX
* MAX IS THE MAXIMUM NUMBER OF CARDS THIS PROGRAM WILL READ.
      PARAMETER (MAX = 100)
      CHARACTER LINE(MAX)*80
* READ THE INPUT INTO THE ARRAY LINE.
      DO 10, I = 1, MAX
          READ(*, '(A)', END = 20) LINE(I)
10        CONTINUE
20    CONTINUE
* THE VALUE OF I IS NOW ONE PLUS THE ACTUAL NUMBER OF INPUT
* CARDS.
* NOW PRINT THE ARRAY IN REVERSE ORDER.
      DO 30, I = I − 1, 1, − 1
          PRINT *, LINE(I)
30        CONTINUE
      END
```

EXAMPLE 6.2 Counting Letters

Some letters are more frequent than others in English words. The letter E, for instance, occurs in many words, while words containing X or Z are comparatively rare. Write a program that reads a set of data cards containing character input and counts the number of times each letter of the alphabet occurs in the input.

This program can be written easily using an integer array, which we shall call COUNT. Each array element COUNT(J) represents the number of times the Jth letter of the alphabet was read. That is, COUNT(1) is the number of A's in the input, COUNT(2) is the number of B's, and so on. For simplicity, we will assume that the input consists of uppercase letters. We will let COUNT(0) be the number of "other" characters: spaces, punctuation marks, or anything other than an uppercase alphabetic character.

The algorithm is to look at each character on the input line, convert it to a number that can be used as a subscript, then to add 1 to the corresponding element of COUNT (Figure 6.7).

To convert a character to a number you can use a DO loop that compares the character of the input line with each character of the alphabet. If the characters of the alphabet are stored in a character variable ALPHA, this procedure can be carried out with the statements

```
      DO 30, J = 26, 1, − 1
          IF (LINE(I:I) .EQ. ALPHA(J:J)) GO TO 35
30        CONTINUE
35    CONTINUE
```

If LINE(I:I) is equal to ALPHA(J:J) for some J, then J will be the desired subscript when the program branches to CONTINUE statement 35. If LINE(I:I) is not equal to any of the characters ALPHA(J:J), then the value of J will be zero when the program reaches CONTINUE statement 35. In either case, you can count the character with the statement

FIGURE 6.7

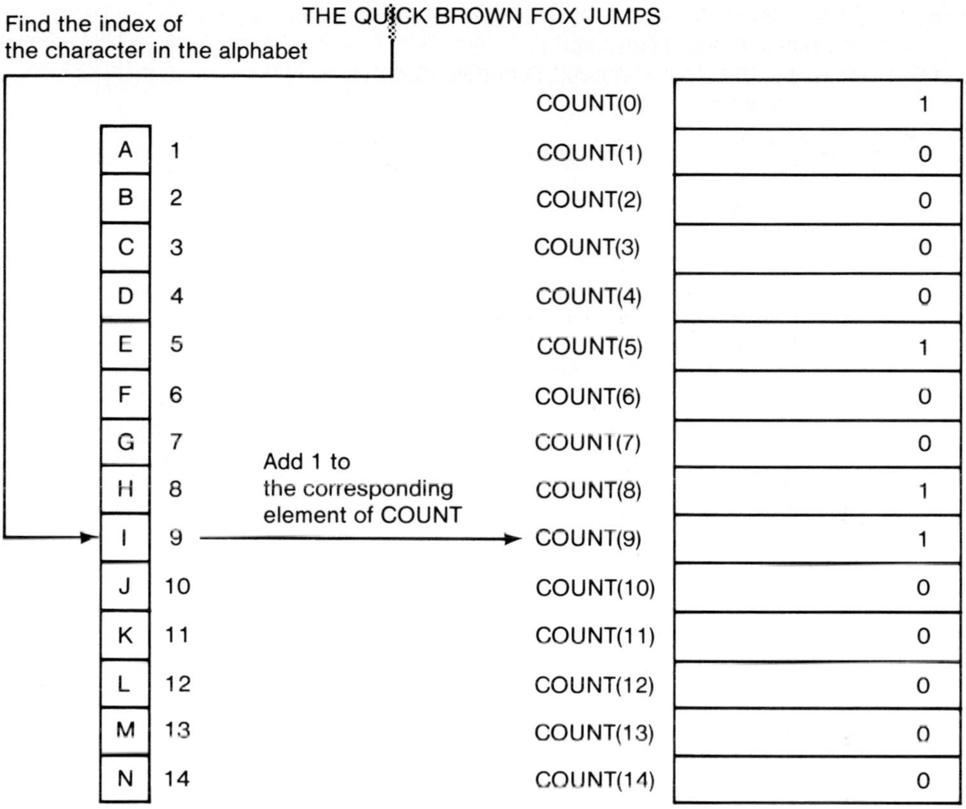

In the letter frequency count program, each letter in the input line is associated with an integer which is then used as a subscript to the array COUNT.

$$COUNT(J) = COUNT(J) + 1$$

The complete FORTRAN program is as follows.

```
* PROGRAM TO COUNT THE NUMBER OF TIMES EACH LETTER OCCURS
* IN THE INPUT TEXT.
* VARIABLES:
* I, J      SUBSCRIPTS
* COUNT   AN ARRAY TO STORE THE COUNTS. AT THE END OF THE
* COUNT   PROGRAM, COUNT(J) EQUALS THE NUMBER OF TIMES THE
* COUNT   JTH CHARACTER OF THE ALPHABET WAS READ. COUNT(0)
* COUNT   IS THE NUMBER OF CHARACTERS THAT WERE NOT IN THE
* COUNT   ALPHABET.
* ALPHA   A CHARACTER VARIABLE CONTAINING THE ALPHABET.
* LINE    THE INPUT LINE.
* CONSTANTS:
* LIMIT   THE NUMBER OF CHARACTERS IN ALPHA.
* LINSIZ  THE NUMBER OF CHARACTERS IN LINE.
```

```
        INTEGER I, J, LIMIT, LINSIZ
        PARAMETER (LIMIT = 26, LINSIZ = 80)
        INTEGER COUNT(0: LIMIT)
        CHARACTER LINE*(LINSIZ), ALPHA*(LIMIT)
*  INITIALIZATION.
*
        ALPHA = 'ABCDEFGHIJKLMNOPQRSTUVWXYZ'
        DO 10, I = 0, LIMIT
            COUNT(I) = 0
10          CONTINUE
*
*  WHILE THERE IS MORE INPUT, READ A LINE,
*
20      READ (*, '(A)', END = 50) LINE
*
*  FOR EACH CHARACTER ON THE INPUT LINE, FIND THE INDEX OF THE
*  CHARACTER IN ALPHA AND ADD 1 TO THE CORRESPONDING ELEMENT
*  OF COUNT.
*
        DO 40, I = 1, LINSIZ
            DO 30, J = LIMIT, 1, -1
                IF (LINE(I:I) .EQ. ALPHA(J:J)) GO TO 35
30              CONTINUE
35          CONTINUE
            COUNT(J) = COUNT(J) + 1
40          CONTINUE
        GO TO 20
*
*  PRINT THE RESULTS.
*
50      DO 60, I = 1, LIMIT
            PRINT *, 'LETTER', ALPHA(I:I), ', COUNT ', COUNT(I)
60          CONTINUE
        PRINT *, 'OTHER CHARACTERS ', COUNT(0)
        END
```

EXAMPLE 6.3 Sorting an Array

The problem of sorting an array is one that arises in many applications. Suppose you have an array of character items. The problem is to rearrange the entries of the array so that they appear in alphabetical order (Figure 6.8).

There are several ways you can approach this problem. The method described in this example is called **linear selection with exchange**. This is the way most people sort a hand of cards. Although not the fastest possible method, it is easy to understand. To see how it works, let us go through an example.

Step 1. Go through the array to find the element that comes first in alphabetical order. In Figure 6.8, you look at the first element, 'SACRAMENTO' and compare it with the second, 'AUSTIN.' 'AUSTIN' comes before 'SACRAMENTO,' so you make a mental note of 'AUSTIN.' Looking at the third element, 'ATLANTA,' you note that it

FIGURE 6.8

Initital Contents of the Array			After Sorting	
1	SACRAMENTO		1	ATLANTA
2	AUSTIN		2	AUSTIN
3	ATLANTA		3	BOSTON
4	PORTLAND		4	COLUMBUS
5	TALLAHASSEE		5	LANSING
6	BOSTON		6	PORTLAND
7	TOPEKA		7	SACRAMENTO
8	COLUMBUS		8	SPRINGFIELD
9	SPRINGFIELD		9	TALLAHASSEE
10	LANSING		10	TOPEKA

Sorting an array consists of rearranging the values so that they appear in alphabetical order.

comes before 'AUSTIN' in alphabetical order, so you make a mental note of 'ATLANTA.' Then you look at the other elements: 'PORTLAND,' 'TALLAHASSEE,' . . . , 'LANSING,' and you find that none comes before 'ATLANTA' in alphabetical order.

Step 2. You now know that 'ATLANTA' should come first in the list, so you put 'ATLANTA' in the first element of the array, and you put 'SACRAMENTO' in the third element, where 'ATLANTA' was. In other words, you *interchange* the values of the first element and the smallest element. (Figure 6.9).

Step 3. Now you look at array elements 2 through 10 to find the smallest of these ('smallest' in the sense of alphabetical order). This turns out to be 'AUSTIN,' which is already in the right place, so you go on to the next step.

Step 4. Now you look at array elements 3 through 10 to find that the smallest element there is 'BOSTON,' which is array element 6. You interchange elements 3 and 6 so that 'BOSTON' comes third in the list (Figure 6.10).

At this point, the first three elements of the array contain the three alphabetically smallest values, in their correct alphabetical order. You can continue in the same manner, examining elements 4 through 10, then 5 through 10, then 6 through 10, and so on. After you have examined elements 9 through 10 and put them in their correct order, the entire array will be sorted.

In general, you can sort an array A of N elements by executing a loop a total of N − 1 times, as shown in Figure 6.11.

There are two basic steps in the loop: finding the *smallest* element (in alphabetical order) and exchanging its value with another element.

To carry out the first of these steps, you can use a variable JMIN which represents the subscript of the smallest element found so far. You can use a loop within the outer loop to set

FIGURE 6.9
THE FIRST STEP IN SORTING

1	SACRAMENTO
2	AUSTIN
3	ATLANTA
4	PORTLAND
5	TALLAHASSEE
6	BOSTON
7	TOPEKA
8	COLUMBUS
9	SPRINGFIELD
10	LANSING

The first step in sorting is to find the value that comes first in alphabetical order (in this case, ATLANTA) and to interchange its value with the value of the first array element.

FIGURE 6.10
THE THIRD STEP IN SORTING

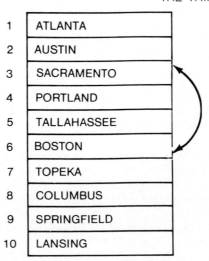

1	ATLANTA
2	AUSTIN
3	SACRAMENTO
4	PORTLAND
5	TALLAHASSEE
6	BOSTON
7	TOPEKA
8	COLUMBUS
9	SPRINGFIELD
10	LANSING

The third step in sorting is to find the value among elements 3–10 that comes first in alphabetical order (in this case BOSTON) and to interchange its value with the value of the third array element.

JMIN equal to the subscript of the smallest of all the elements A(I), A(I + 1), . . . , A(N), as
shown in the more detailed algorithm of Figure 6.12.

The FORTRAN statements to carry out this procedure are as follows.

```
* THE FOLLOWING STATEMENTS SORT THE ARRAY ELEMENTS
* A(1) THROUGH A(N) IN ASCENDING ORDER, USING THE
* METHOD OF LINEAR SELECTION WITH EXCHANGE.
*
      DO 20, I = 1, N - 1
*
* FIND THE SUBSCRIPT JMIN SUCH THAT A(JMIN)
* IS THE MINIMUM OF A(I) THROUGH A(N)
*
      JMIN = I
      DO 10, J = I + 1, N
          IF (A(J) .LT. A(JMIN)) JMIN = J
10        CONTINUE
*
* EXCHANGE THE VALUES OF A(I) AND A(JMIN)
*
      TEMP = A(I)
      A(I) = A(JMIN)
      A(JMIN) = TEMP
20    CONTINUE
```

Although Figures 6.8 through 6.10 illustrated the sort procedure for a character
array, these same FORTRAN statements could be used to sort an integer or real array
A. The only requirement is that the variable TEMP must be the same type as the array
A. If A is a character array, then the size of TEMP must be at least the size of an
element of A.

The following example shows how the sort procedure can be used in a complete
program.

EXAMPLE 6.4 An Application of Sorting
We can use the sorting procedure just described to read a set of input cards and print them in
alphabetical order. Suppose a set of data cards contains names and telephone numbers, for
instance. Some sample data cards might be as follows.

```
TYLER, JOHN            853-1808
POLK, JAMES K.         242-1795
ADAMS, J. Q.           611-1761
PIERCE, FRANK          423-1804
```

We would like to list the input cards just as they are, but in alphabetical order by name. Note
that for the sorting to work correctly, the names should be written with the last name first.
Otherwise, the output would be sorted by first names. The program can treat the entire data card
as one item. Since the name is the first thing on the card, the presence of the telephone numbers
will not affect the order of the sorted output. In fact, this same program could be used to sort
any kind of input in a similar fashion.

FIGURE 6.11
PROCEDURE TO SORT ARRAY ELEMENTS A(I) THROUGH A(N)—TOP-LEVEL DESIGN

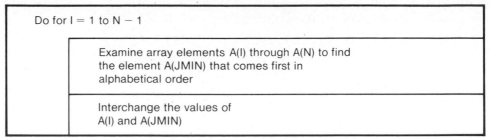

Do for I = 1 to N − 1

> Examine array elements A(I) through A(N) to find
> the element A(JMIN) that comes first in
> alphabetical order
>
> Interchange the values of
> A(I) and A(JMIN)

FIGURE 6.12
PROCEDURE TO SORT ARRAY ELEMENTS A(1) THROUGH A(N)

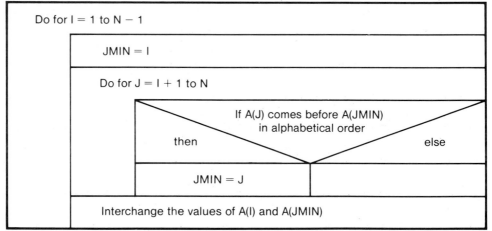

Do for I = 1 to N − 1

> JMIN = I
>
> Do for J = I + 1 to N
>
> > If A(J) comes before A(JMIN)
> > in alphabetical order
> > then   else
> >
> > JMIN = J
>
> Interchange the values of A(I) and A(JMIN)

FIGURE 6.13
PROGRAM TO PRINT A SET OF INPUT DATA IN ALPHABETICAL ORDER—TOP-LEVEL
DESIGN

Read cards into elements of an array A(1), A(2),..., A(N)

Sort the array A(1), A(2),..., A(N)

Print the elements of the array A

A top-level design for the program is shown in Figure 6.13. You can use the sort procedure of Example 6.3. The only programming detail of any complexity is how to read input into the array. You must take care not to exceed the maximum size of the array. The details are shown in the revised design in Figure 6.14.

The complete FORTRAN program follows.

```
* SORT PROGRAM
* THIS PROGRAM READS INPUT LINES, SORTS THEM IN ALPHABETICAL
* ORDER, AND PRINTS THE SORTED LINES.
*
* LINSIZ = THE SIZE OF EACH INPUT LINE
* MAXLIN = THE MAXIMUM NUMBER OF LINES THAT THIS
*          PROGRAM CAN HANDLE
*
      INTEGER LINSIZ, MAXLIN
      PARAMETER (LINSIZ = 80, MAXLIN = 200)
      CHARACTER A(MAXLIN) *(LINSIZ), TEMP * (LINSIZ)
      INTEGER I, J, JMIN, N
*
* READ THE INPUT LINES, BUT DO NOT READ MORE THAN
* MAXLIN LINES. LET N BE THE ACTUAL NUMBER OF LINES.
*
```

FIGURE 6.14
PROGRAM TO PRINT A SET OF INPUT DATA IN ALPHABETICAL ORDER

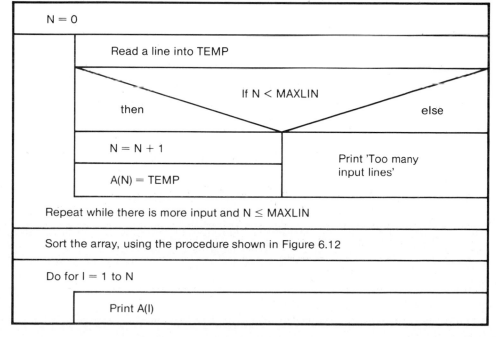

```
        N = 0
10      READ (*, '(A)', END = 20) TEMP
        IF (N .LT. MAXLIN) THEN
            N = N + 1
            A(N) = TEMP
            GO TO 10
        ELSE
            PRINT *, 'TOO MANY INPUT LINES.'
            PRINT *, 'ONLY ', MAXLIN, ' WERE READ.'
        END IF
20      CONTINUE
*
* SORT THE ARRAY IN ASCENDING ORDER.
*
        DO 40, I = 1, N - 1
            JMIN = I
            DO 30, J = I + 1, N
                IF (A(J) .LT. A(JMIN)) JMIN = J
30          CONTINUE
            TEMP = A(I)
            A(I) = A(JMIN)
            A(JMIN) = TEMP
40      CONTINUE
*
* PRINT THE SORTED ARRAY.
*
        DO 50, I = 1, N
            PRINT *, A(I)
50      CONTINUE
        END
```

STYLE MODULE—SUBSCRIPT ERRORS AND HOW TO PREVENT THEM

As you have seen, when you declare an array, you give dimension bound expressions that specify the range of permissible subscript values. Suppose a program contains the statement

REAL X(1:3)

This says that throughout the program the subscripts of the array X will have values between 1 and 3. The question arises: What happens if your program has a **subscript error**—that is, uses a subscript that is out of range? For instance, what would the statement

X(4) = 0

do?

To answer this question, let us consider what computer memory looks like when a program is running (Figure 6.15). A certain part of memory is allocated as storage for the array X. Any other arrays and variables used by the program will also have memory locations allocated to them for storage. The machine language instructions for the program itself are also stored in memory. As a FORTRAN programmer, you have no control over how your machine instructions, variables, and arrays are actually arranged in memory. That job is taken care of automatically by the system software,* and you need not be concerned with how it works. The important fact is that each area of computer memory is allocated for a specific purpose. If you use some memory location for the wrong purpose, the result can be disastrous.

Suppose that your program carries out the instruction

$$X(4) = 0$$

where X is an array whose upper dimension bound is 3. The computer executes this instruction by storing a zero in the memory location 4, counting from the beginning of the array X. The trouble is, of course, that this location is not part of the array X. It may have been allocated to some other variable, in which case you will change the value of the other variable. Worse yet, it may be in the area of memory reserved for your machine language instructions, in which case you will alter the program itself. Without a detailed knowledge of the memory layout,† there is no way of predicting the exact effect, but one thing is certain: it isn't going to work right.

Finding the cause of a subscript error can be one of the most difficult debugging

FIGURE 6.15

TYPICAL ARRANGEMENT OF INSTRUCTIONS AND DATA IN COMPUTER MEMORY

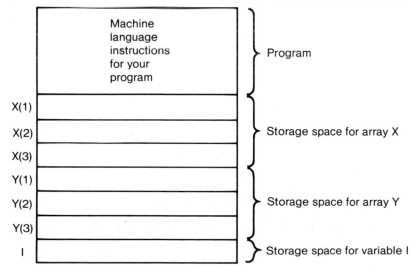

---

*Generally by the *loader* program—see Chapter 2.

†Which you can get from a **load map**, produced by the loader—consult your system reference manual for details.

problems, since the effect of such an error may seem totally unrelated to the actual cause. Your best recourse is to prevent such errors from happening in the first place. Write your FORTRAN statements in such a way that subscript errors are impossible. The following suggestion will help.

Use symbolic constants for dimension bounds.

For example, instead of declaring an array as

```
REAL X(100)
```

and having a DO loop such as

```
        DO 70, I = 1, 100
70          X(I) = 0
```

use a symbolic constant, such as MAXX, in both the array declarator and the DO statement:

```
        PARAMETER (MAX X = 100)
        REAL X(MAX X)
        . . .
        DO 70, I = 1, MAX X
70          X(I) = 0
```

This practice improves program readability. It also helps you avoid subscript errors that might arise if you change the size of an array in a revision of your program. You would only need to redefine the parameter MAX X in this example to make X a larger array.

Whenever a subscript value is read in or computed, check that it is within range before using it.

For example, the following statement is legal, but dangerous.

```
READ *, I, A(I)
```

If a data card contains the values 2 and 3000 this statement will read the value 3000 into the array element A(2). But suppose that through a keypunching error, the input values are reversed. Then the statement says to read the number 2 into the array element A(3000), which might be a huge subscript error. It is much safer to set up the data and the program so that you can check the value of the subscript before using it, as in the following example.

```
READ *, I
IF (1 .LE. I .AND. I .LE. ASIZE) THEN
    READ *, A(I)
ELSE
    PRINT *, 'SUBSCRIPT OUT OF RANGE', I
    STOP
END IF
```

Use any available debugging tools to check for subscript errors.

Many FORTRAN compilers have the capability to provide run-time subscript checking, which means they can automatically include machine-language statements that will check subscripts when your program runs to see that the subscripts are within range. If your system provides such a feature, learn to use it. The only disadvantage of run-time subscript checking is that it might slow down program execution. But this drawback is greatly outweighed by the advantage of automatically protecting against subscript errors.

A note of caution: run-time subscript checking systems are not foolproof. It is possible, especially when using arrays in subprograms (Chapter 7), to cause a subscript error that will go undetected. Therefore, use such automatic debugging tools to *supplement* your own good programming practices, but do not rely on them to catch all possible mistakes.

EXAMPLE 6.5 A Table Lookup Procedure
A set of data cards contains billing data for customers of a small business. Each card contains three values:

1. An account number, which is a character value such as 'MS1234'
2. A customer name, which is a character value such as 'SMITH, M.'
3. An amount of purchase, which is a real number such as 10.42

If a customer made several purchases during the month, there will be several input cards with his or her account number and name. The input cards are in no particular order, however. The problem is to read all the input cards and print the total amount of purchases for each customer. Some sample output is shown below.

```
CUSTOMER ACCOUNT TOTALS
ACCOUNT: MS1234    NAME: SMITH, M.    TOTAL PURCHASES: $17.63
ACCOUNT: AB3761    NAME: BROWN, A.    TOTAL PURCHASES: $23.31
ACCOUNT: JJ9532    NAME: JONES, J.    TOTAL PURCHASES: $43.74
ACCOUNT: WW2702    NAME: WHITE, W.    TOTAL PURCHASES: $65.13
```

Our solution to this problem uses three arrays:

```
ACCTNO      array of customer account numbers
NAME        array of customer names
AMOUNT      array of purchase amounts
```

Each time the program reads a data card, it compares the account number read from the card (which we call CD ACCT) with each of the account numbers stored in the array ACCTNO. If the account number is different from all of the account numbers in the array, the program puts the new account number into the array and initializes the corresponding elements of the arrays NAME and AMOUNT. If the account number on the card is equal to some account number already in the array, the program adds the amount of purchase from the card to the corresponding element of the array AMOUNT. This top-level design is illustrated in Figure 6.16.

To refine this top-level design, we need to define what is meant by finding an account number in the array ACCTNO. We will use the symbolic constant MAXLEN to represent the actual size of the three arrays. The integer variable LENGTH will represent the number of elements that are actually used in each array. Initially, LENGTH is equal to zero. Each time we add a new item to the arrays, we add 1 to LENGTH and use the new value of LENGTH as a subscript for the arrays. To avoid possible subscript errors, we always check that the value of LENGTH is less than or equal to MAXLEN.

FIGURE 6.16
CUSTOMER ACCOUNT TOTALS; TOP-LEVEL DESIGN

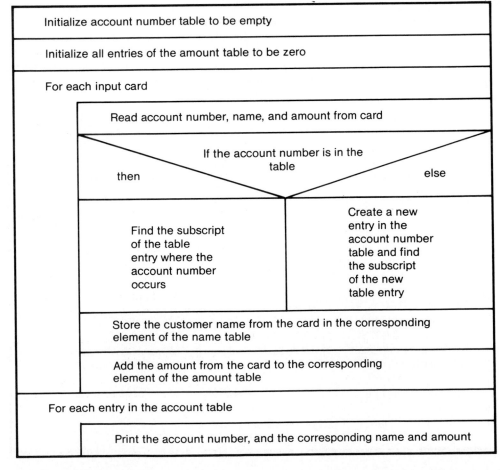

Searching the ACCTNO array for a particular account number is an example of a **table lookup procedure**. The easiest way to program such a procedure is with a **linear search**, in which the program simply examines each item in the table until it either finds the item being sought or reaches the end of the table. If the item is not found in the table, a new entry is created at the end of the table—provided there is room for one. Figure 6.17 shows the outline of the table lookup.

The complete FORTRAN program is as follows.

```
* CUSTOMER ACCOUNT TOTALS.
      INTEGER LENTAB
      PARAMETER (LENTAB = 200)
      CHARACTER*7 CD ACCT, ACCTNO(LENTAB)
      CHARACTER*15 CD NAME, NAME(LENTAB)
      REAL CD AMT, AMOUNT(LENTAB)
      INTEGER I, LENGTH
*
* INITIALIZE ACCTNO ARRAY TO BE EMPTY (LENGTH
* IS THE NUMBER OF ITEMS USED IN THE ARRAY).
*
      LENGTH = 0
```

FIGURE 6.17
TABLE LOOKUP BY THE LINEAR SEARCH METHOD

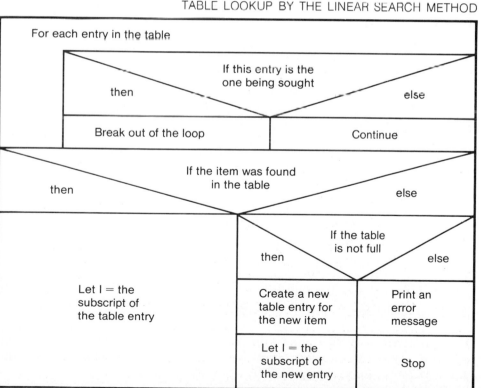

```
*
* INITIALIZE AMOUNT TABLE.
*
      DO 10, I = 1, LENTAB
          AMOUNT(I) = 0
10        CONTINUE
*
* FOR EACH INPUT CARD, FIND OR CREATE AN ACCOUNT
* TABLE ENTRY, THEN UPDATE THE CUSTOMER NAME AND
* AMOUNT TABLES.
*
20    READ (*, *, END = 50) CD ACCT, CD NAME, CD AMT
*
* SEARCH THE ACCTNO ARRAY FOR THIS ACCOUNT
*
      DO 30, I = 1, LENGTH
          IF (CD ACCT .EQ. ACCTNO(I)) GO TO 40
30        CONTINUE
*
* ACCOUNT NUMBER NOT FOUND — PUT IT IN THE ARRAY.
*
      LENGTH = LENGTH + 1
      IF (LENGTH .GT. LENTAB) THEN
          PRINT *, 'MAXIMUM ARRAY SIZE EXCEEDED'
          STOP
      END IF
      ACCTNO(LENGTH) = CD ACCT
      I = LENGTH
*
40    NAME(I) = CD NAME
      AMOUNT(I) = AMOUNT(I) + CD AMT
      GO TO 20
*
* AT END OF INPUT, PRINT THE ARRAYS
*
50    PRINT *, 'CUSTOMER ACCOUNT TOTALS'
      DO 60, I = 1, LENGTH
          PRINT *, 'ACCOUNT: ', ACCTNO(I), ' NAME: ', NAME(I),
      $          ' TOTAL PURCHASES: $', AMOUNT(I)
60        CONTINUE
      END
```

STYLE MODULE—A SUBTLE SUBSCRIPT ERROR

There are several possible ways of writing the table lookup procedure used in Example 6.5. One way that might occur to you is to use a "while" loop construction, rather than a DO loop, for searching the table, as in Figure 6.18.

FIGURE 6.18

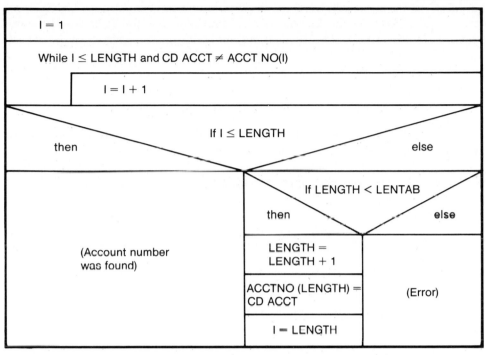

In this algorithm for the table lookup procedure, a subscript error will occur when LENGTH is equal to the size of the array.

In FORTRAN, you can write this procedure according to the following outline.

```
      I = 1
10    IF (I .LE. LENGTH .AND. CD ACCT .NE. ACCTNO(I)) THEN
          I = I + 1
          GO TO 10
      END IF
      IF (I .LE. LENGTH) THEN
*         *** ACCOUNT NUMBER WAS FOUND ***
      ELSE
          IF (LENGTH .LT. LENTAB) THEN
              LENGTH = LENGTH + 1
              ACCTNO(LENGTH) = CD ACCT
              I = LENGTH
          ELSE
              PRINT *, 'ERROR'
              STOP
          END IF
      END IF
```

The trouble with this method is that it can result in a subscript error. Suppose that CD ACCT is not in the table and that the table is already full—that is, LENGTH is equal to LENTAB. On the last iteration of the loop, the condition will be false because I is greater than LENGTH. The program will still check the second part of the condition:

```
CD ACCT .NE. ACCTNO(I)
```

In this case, however, I is equal to LENTAB + 1, which is an illegal subscript value.

This example illustrates a general class of bugs known as **boundary condition errors**. The program works correctly when the table is not full—that is, when LENGTH is less than LENTAB. Also, LENGTH will never be greater than LENTAB, because the program stops if an attempt is made to insert an entry into a full table. It is only at the boundary condition, when LENGTH = LENTAB, that the subscript error can occur.

Errors of this type are easy to overlook. When designing any algorithm, try to identify boundary conditions and check that they work correctly. For programs that use arrays, ask yourself: What are the largest and smallest possible values for each subscript? What does the program do when these values are used?

In the example above, there are several easy ways to avert the potential error. One way is to set up an extra element in the ACCNO array by declaring it with the statement

```
CHARACTER*7 CD ACCT, ACCTNO(LENTAB + 1)
```

Another method is to use two IF statements in the loop, rather than one:

```
      I = 1
10    IF (I .LE. LENGTH) THEN
          IF (CD ACCT .NE. ACCTNO(I)) THEN
              I = I + 1
              GO TO 10
          END IF
      END IF
```

The difference here is that the second IF statement is not executed if the first condition is false.

TWO-DIMENSIONAL ARRAYS

An array with two subscripts is called a **two-dimensional array**. Another name for such an array is a **matrix**. You can think of a matrix as having rows and columns. Figure 6.19 shows a matrix with three rows and four columns. Each element of the

FIGURE 6.19

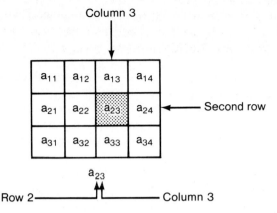

A two-dimensional array can be thought of as a rectangular grid with the subscripts giving the row and column

array has two subscripts. The first subscript specifies the row, and the second subscript specifies the column.

In FORTRAN, you can set up a two-dimensional array by giving an array declarator with two dimension bound expressions, separated by a comma. For example, a real array A with three rows and four columns can be declared with the statement (see Figure 6.20).

    REAL A(3, 4)

FIGURE 6.20
A 3 BY 4 ARRAY HAS THREE ROWS AND FOUR COLUMNS

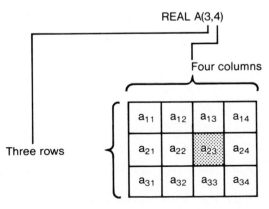

As with one-dimensional arrays, each of the two size declarations can be a single number or a pair of numbers, separated by a colon. Thus,

    INTEGER MAT (−2:2, 0:1)

sets up an array of five rows and two columns for which the first subscript may vary between −2 and 2, and the second subscript may be 0 or 1.

You specify an element of a two-dimensional array by writing the array name followed by a pair of subscript expressions, separated by a comma and enclosed in parentheses. For example,

    A(2, 3)

means the element of the array A in the 2nd row, 3rd column. Each subscript expression can be any integer expression. For example,

    A(I + 1, MIN(I* J, K))

The value of each subscript expression must be within the range given by the array declarator that defines the array. Thus, for an array PAGE defined by the statement

    CHARACTER PAGE(50, 100)

the value of the first subscript *must* be between 1 and 50, and the value of the second subscript *must* be between 1 and 100. If either subscript expression is out of range, a subscript error is possible. As mentioned before, you should take care to avoid such errors.

HIGHER-DIMENSIONAL ARRAYS

FORTRAN allows the use of three-dimensional arrays in a manner analogous to the two-dimensional case. For example, the statement

    REAL B(4, 4, 4)

declares B as a three-dimensional real array having 64 elements ($64 = 4 \times 4 \times 4$). You specify an element of this array with an expression of the form

    B(I, J, K)

where each of the three subscripts is an integer expression having a value between 1 and 4.

Similarly, you can use arrays with up to seven subscripts. For example, the statement

LOGICAL Z(2, 2, 2, 2, 2, 2, 2)

declares Z to be a logical array with seven subscripts, each of which may have a value of 1 or 2. Use of such higher-dimensional arrays is less common, in practice, than use of one- or two-dimensional arrays.

IMPLIED DO LOOPS

An **implied DO loop** is used to represent a list of variables or values in an input or output list. It can be particularly useful when reading or printing a sequence of array elements. For example, suppose that X is a real array having 10 elements, and you want to print all 10 elements on a single line of output. You could simply list each of the elements in the output list, as follows:

```
PRINT *, X(1), X(2), X(3), X(4), X(5), X(6),
$ X(7), X(8), X(9), X(10)
```

A shorter way is to use an implied DO loop, like this:

```
PRINT *, (X(I), I = 1, 10)
```

The expression

```
(X(I), I = 1, 10)
```

is the implied DO loop. It means "X sub I, for I equals 1 to 10." The integer variable I in this example is the **implied DO variable**. As in a DO statement,

```
I = 1, 10
```

means that I ranges from 1 to 10, counting by 1.

The implied DO loop just given contained a single output variable, X(I). Here is an example of an implied DO loop with two input variables, A(J) and B(J).

```
READ *, (A(J), B(J), J = 1, 5)
```

This means to read A(J) and B(J), for J from 1 to 5. Thus, it means the same as the statement

```
READ *, A(1), B(1), A(2), B(2), A(3), B(3),
$          A(4), B(4), A(5), B(5)
```

In general, an implied DO loop can be used as an element of an input or output list, representing a sequence of variables or values. Table 6.1 shows the general form.

TABLE 6.1
IMPLIED DO LOOPS

Form

(*list*, *var* = *first*, *last*, *step*)

or

(*list*, *var* = *first*, *last*)

where   *list* is a list of variables, expressions, or implied DO loops. If there is more than one
item in the list, the items are separated by commas.
var is a real or integer variable called the implied DO variable.
first, *last*, and *step* are expressions giving the range of the implied DO variable.

Meaning

first, *last*, and *step* are used to define iteration processing of the implied DO in exactly the same
way as for a DO statement. Each iteration of the implied DO loop defines a list of variables or
expressions that are substituted in the input or output list where the implied DO loop appears.

Examples
```
READ *, X, Y, (A(I), I = 1, 5), Z
READ *, N, (ARRAY(I), I = 1, N)
PRINT *, (I A(I), I+10, A(I+10), I = 1, 9)
PRINT *, (I, ' VALUE = ', X(I), I = N, 1, −1)
PRINT *, (X, 1.0/X, X = 1.0, 10.0, 0.5)
READ *, (A(I), I = 2*N, 3*N, INC/2)
```

The implied DO loop functions in a manner similar to a DO statement. The *first*,
last, and *step* expressions are evaluated, an iteration count is computed, and values are
assigned to the implied DO variable, just as in processing a DO statement. Each
iteration of an implied DO loop defines a list of variables or expressions that are used
in the READ or PRINT statement just as though they had been written out the long
way. Wherever the implied DO variable appears in the list of the implied DO loop, its
value is defined by the iteration processing of the loop. Zero-trip implied DO loops are
legal. If the iteration count in an implied DO loop is zero, the effect is as though the
implied DO loop had been omitted altogether.

Implied DO loops are very useful for input and output of arrays. For example, the
following statement reads one row of an array named MATRIX.

```
READ *, (MATRIX(I, J), J = 1, N)
```

The value of J is incremented on each iteration of the implied DO loop to read the
variables MATRIX(I, 1), MATRIX(I, 2), . . . , MATRIX(I, N).

An implied DO loop may itself be used as an element in a list of an implied DO loop. For example, the following statement reads an entire two-dimensional array named A.

    READ *, ((A(I, J), J = 1, 4), I = 1, 3)

The inner implied DO loop

    (A(I, J), J = 1, 4)

specifies the variables

    A(I, 1), A(I, 2), A(I, 3), A(I, 4)

This inner DO loop is nested within an outer DO loop which iterates with values of I ranging from 1 to 3. The effect is to read the 12 variables:

    A(1, 1), A(1, 2), A(1, 3), A(1, 4)
    A(2, 1), A(2, 2), A(2, 3), A(2, 4)
    A(3, 1), A(3, 2), A(3, 3), A(3, 4)

Implied DO loops have other uses, besides reading and printing arrays. For instance, the following statement prints a line of 50 asterisks.

    PRINT *, ('*', I = 1, 50)

As this statement demonstrates, the implied DO variable does not have to be used in the input or output list element. In this case, it simply counts the number of times that the output list element '*' is to be repeated.

The implied DO variable can also be used as part of an expression. In the following example, the variable L appears in the expressions L and L**2.

    PRINT *, (L, L**2, L = 1, 5)

The output produced is:

    1 1 2 4 3 9 4 16 5 25

EXAMPLE 6.6 Average Test Grades

A class of students took four tests during the semester. For each student, a data card was prepared giving the student's name followed by the four test grades. Some sample input is as follows.

    'JONES',   87, 52, 75, 90
    'SMITH',   74, 60, 65, 80
    'ADAMS',   95, 85, 89, 92
    'BAKER',   88, 70, 80, 85

Write a program to compute each student's average grade and also the average grade for all students on each test. Sample output is shown in Table 6.2.

TABLE 6.2
SAMPLE OUTPUT FROM EXAMPLE 6.6

JONES	87	52	75	90	AVERAGE = 76.00
SMITH	74	60	65	80	AVERAGE = 69.75
ADAMS	95	85	89	92	AVERAGE = 90.25
BAKER	88	70	80	85	AVERAGE = 80.75

AVERAGE = 86.00 66.75 77.25 86.75

This program can be written using a two-dimensional array to store the grades. If you let G(I, J) represent the grade that student number I received on test number J, then you can compute the averages by summing each row and column of the array G (Figure 6.21).

FIGURE 6.21

```
G(1, 1)   G(1, 2)   ...   G(1, J)   ...   G(1, N)

G(2, 1)   G(2, 2)   ...   G(2, J)   ...   G(2, N)

...

G(I, 1)   G(I, 2)   ...   G(I, J)   ...   G(I, N)   ROWSUM(I) = sum of row I
...

G(M, 1)  G(M, 2)   ...   G(M, J)   ...   G(M, N)
                          ↑
                       COLSUM(J) =
                       sum of column J
```

Summing the rows and columns of a two-dimensional array:

$$ROWSUM (I) = G(I,1) + G(I,2) + \cdots + G(I,N)$$
$$COLSUM(J) = G(1,J) + G(2,J) + \cdots + G(M,J)$$

The following complete program uses implied DO loops for both input and output.

```
* AVERAGE GRADES FOR EACH STUDENT AND EACH TEST.
*
* M = NUMBER OF STUDENTS, COMPUTED FROM THE INPUT DATA
* N = NUMBER OF TESTS TAKEN, A CONSTANT.
* MMAX = MAXIMUM NUMBER OF STUDENTS THIS PROGRAM CAN HANDLE.
* G(I, J) = GRADE THAT STUDENT NUMBER I RECEIVED ON TEST J
* NAME(I) = NAME OF STUDENT NUMBER I.
* ROWSUM(I) = SUM OF ROW I OF THE ARRAY G.
* COLSUM(J) = SUM OF COLUMN J OF THE ARRAY G.
* I, J USED AS SUBSCRIPTS.
*
```

```
          INTEGER I, J, M, MMAX, N
          PARAMETER (MMAX = 100, N = 4)
          REAL G(MMAX, N), ROWSUM(MMAX), COLSUM(N)
          CHARACTER*10 NAME(MMAX)
     *
     * READ THE INPUT DATA.
     *
          DO 10, I = 1, MMAX + 1
              READ (*, *, END = 15) NAME(I), (G(I, J), J = 1, N)
     10       CONTINUE
          STOP 'TOO MANY STUDENTS — INCREASE VALUE OF MMAX'
     15   M = I - 1
     *
     * COMPUTE THE ROW AND COLUMN SUMS
     *
          DO 20, I = 1, M
              ROWSUM(I) = 0
     20       CONTINUE
          DO 30, J = 1, N
              COLSUM(J) = 0
     30       CONTINUE
          DO 50, I = 1, M
              DO 40, J = 1, N
                  ROWSUM(I) = ROWSUM(I) + G(I, J)
                  COLSUM(J) = COLSUM(J) + G(I, J)
     40           CONTINUE
     50       CONTINUE
     *
     * PRINT THE RESULTS
     *
          DO 60, I = 1, M
              PRINT *, NAME(I), (G(I, J), J = 1, N), ' AVERAGE = ',
         $          ROWSUM(I)/N
     60       CONTINUE
          PRINT *, 'AVERAGE = ', (COLSUM(J)/M, J = 1, N)
          END
```

STYLE MODULE—DATA STRUCTURES
AND TOP-DOWN DESIGN

Structured programming, as we defined it in Chapter 4, means using *control structures* that simplify the program control flow, making it easy to understand. But there is another aspect of structured programming that is equally important: the *data structures* used by the program.

In general, a **data structure** is a systematic method of representing information in a program. When writing programs in which the information is complex, it is important to consider carefully how the information is organized. In many cases, designing a suitable data structure is as difficult as designing an algorithm to manipulate the data.

In previous chapters, data structures used have been simple. Arrays, however, provide a means of dealing with much more complicated types of information.

As an example, suppose you are writing a program to play a game of chess against a human opponent. When two people play chess, they move pieces on a chessboard. The location of the pieces is the information that the people use in deciding on their moves. To write a chess program, you would need to invent some way of representing this information in a program. Perhaps you could represent the chessboard as an 8 by 8 matrix. You could use different numbers to represent the different chess pieces for each player. The program could represent the process of making a move by assigning different values to elements of the 8 by 8 matrix. You would also need to represent the moves of the game in some way that the human could understand. If the human wants to make the chess move "pawn to king 4," he or she might type the character string "P-K4" on a terminal. Thus, another data structure used by the program would be the set of text strings representing allowable moves, and the program would have to convert information represented in this form to an equivalent representation as a value of some matrix element.

Writing a chess program, of course, would be an immensely difficult job, because the algorithm for determining the computer's move would be very complicated (assuming that you want the machine to play well). But the point is that apart from designing the algorithm, it is a difficult job just to design the data structure used to represent the information that the algorithm deals with. Even for a relatively simple program, the choice of a data structure is an important resposibility of the programmer.

You can usually develop a precise definition of a data structure as you proceed through the steps of the top-down program design. In your top-level design of an algorithm you may not specify the data structure in computer terms. For example, in a top-level design for a chess program, part of the procedure might be:

> If the human player has a piece that can be captured, capture the piece and remove it from the board.

At some point in the process of stepwise refinement, you would need to define the data structure precisely so that you could translate the procedure into operations that a program can carry out. You would need to define what a "piece" means in the computer memory, what "capturing" means, and so on. And you would need to choose among various possible data structures by considering how the information is to be processed by your proposed algorithm.

Thus, the design of data structures and the design of algorithms go hand in hand, and the top-down method of stepwise refinement applies to both processes. A structured program uses both control structures and data structures in a clearly organized way.

Each program you write will have its own particular data structure. But certain general types of data structures are so common in programming that they have names. Example 6.7 illustrates the concept of a *pointer*. Other data structures, such as *stacks* and *buffers*, can be implemented in FORTRAN using arrays, as indicated in Exercises

16 through 22 at the end of Chapter 7. In Chapter 7 you will learn to manipulate these data structures using subprograms.

EXAMPLE 6.7 Sorting with an Array of Pointers

In programming, a **pointer** is a variable that *points to*, or indicates, another variable. For example, a variable that is used as a subscript points to an array element. The data structure in this example consists of an array of such pointers.

Suppose you have an array of character values, as in Figure 6.8. In Example 6.3, you saw how to sort this array by rearranging the elements of the array. It is possible, however, to sort the array *without* rearranging the elements, by using an array of pointers. Initially, the first element in the array POINTR points to the first element in the array CITY, and so on, as indicated by the arrows in Figure 6.22.

If you rearrange the pointers as shown in Figure 6.23, then you have, in effect, sorted the array of cities. The first element of the array POINTR points to the city that comes first in alphabetical order. The second element of the array POINTR points to the city that comes second in alphabetical order, and so on. Of course, the arrows in Figure 6.23 are not part of the data structure used by the computer. They only help to visualize the meaning of the POINTR array.

With the POINTR array sorted as in Figure 6.23, the following FORTRAN statements will print the names of the cities in alphabetical order

```
      DO 10, I = 1, 10
         PRINT *, CITY (POINTR (I))
10       CONTINUE
```

FIGURE 6.22

	POINTR			CITY
1	1		→	SACRAMENTO
2	2		→	AUSTIN
3	3		→	ATLANTA
4	4		→	PORTLAND
5	5		→	TALLAHASSEE
6	6		→	BOSTON
7	7		→	TOPEKA
8	8		→	COLUMBUS
9	9		→	SPRINGFIELD
10	10		→	LANSING

Initially, the elements of the array POINTR point to successive elements of the array CITY.

FIGURE 6.23

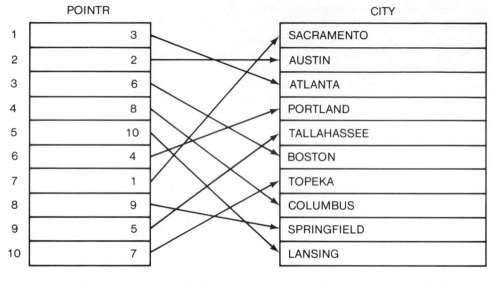

When the elements of the array POINTR are rearranged as shown they point to elements of the array CITY in alphabetical order. For instance, CITY(POINTR(1)) = CITY(3) = ATLANTA. Thus, sorting the pointers as shown is equivalent to sorting the array CITY.

Suppose that A is the character array to be sorted and that it has N elements. We want to write FORTRAN statements to store the integers 1 to N in an integer array POINTR in an order such that

A(POINTR(1)), A(POINTR(2)), A(POINTR(3)), . . . , A(POINTR(N))

are in alphabetical order.

With a few modifications, you can use the same algorithm as in Example 6.3. You start by initializing the POINTR array so that POINTR(I) = I, for I between 1 and N. Next you examine the array of pointers to find the one that points to the element of the array A that comes first in alphabetical order. In the POINTR array, you exchange this pointer with POINTR(1). The algorithm continues in a manner similar to the one shown in Figure 6.12, except that you manipulate the array of pointers, rather than the elements of the character array itself. Figure 6.24 shows the top-level design. You can expand on the top-level design in a manner similar to Example 6.3. To find the value JMIN required in Figure 6.24 (on page 216), you let JMIN = I, then you examine all successive values in POINTR, storing a new value in JMIN whenever you find a pointer that points to an element of A that is less than the A(POINTR(JMIN)). The expanded procedure is shown in Figure 6.25.

The FORTRAN statements to carry out this procedure are as follows.

* THE FOLLOWING FORTRAN STATEMENTS CREATE AN ARRAY OF
* POINTERS TO SORT THE ARRAY ELEMENTS A(1) THROUGH A(N). THE

```
    * NUMBERS 1 THROUGH N ARE STORED IN THE INTEGER ARRAY
    * POINTER IN AN ORDER SUCH THAT
    *    A(POINTR(1)), A(POINTR(2)), . . . , A(POINTR(N))
    * ARE SORTED IN ASCENDING ORDER.
    * THE ELEMENTS OF THE ARRAY A ARE UNCHANGED.
    * I, J, JMIN, N, AND TEMP ARE INTEGER VARIABLES.
    * POINTR IS AN INTEGER ARRAY.
    * THE ARRAY A CAN BE ANY TYPE.
    *
    * INITIALIZE THE ARRAY OF POINTERS.
    *
        DO 10, I = 1, N
            POINTR(I) = I
10        CONTINUE
    *
    * FOR EACH I, LET JMIN BE THE SUBSCRIPT SUCH THAT
    * A(POINTR(JMIN)) IS THE MINIMUM (OR FIRST IN ALPHABETICAL
    * ORDER) AMONG A(POINTR(I)), A(POINTR(I+1)), . . . , A(POINTR(N)).
        DO 30, I = 1, N − 1
            JMIN = I
            DO 20, J = I + 1, N
                IF (A(POINTR(J)) .LT. A(POINTR(JMIN))) JMIN = J
20            CONTINUE
    *
    *        INTERCHANGE THE VALUES OF
    *        POINTR(JMIN) AND POINTR(I)
    *
            TEMP = POINTR(I)
            POINTR(I) = POINTR(JMIN)
            POINTR(JMIN) = TEMP
30        CONTINUE
    *
    * END OF SORT PROCEDURE
```

EXAMPLE 6.8 An Application of Sorting with Pointers

Example 6.5 showed a program to print customer account totals. The last step in that program was to print the three tables used. Suppose you wanted to enhance the program to print the output with the customer names in alphabetical order. Sorting the NAME array directly would not be sufficient, since that would destroy the correspondence between the three arrays ACCTNO, NAME, and AMOUNT. The problem is solved easily using pointers. To the program in Example 6.5, you add a new array defined by

```
    INTEGER POINTR(LENTAB)
```

At the end of input, you create the array of sorted pointers using the technique of Example 6.7. The pointer array can then be used to print the output in alphabetical order. The complete program is given on pages 217 to 218.

FIGURE 6.24
ALGORITHM TO CREATE AN ARRAY OF POINTERS THAT SORTS THE ARRAY A IN
ALPHABETICAL ORDER—TOP-LEVEL DESIGN

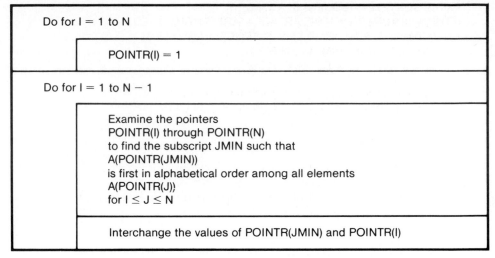

FIGURE 6.25
ALGORITHM TO CREATE AN ARRAY OF POINTERS THAT SORTS THE ARRAY A IN
ALPHABETICAL ORDER

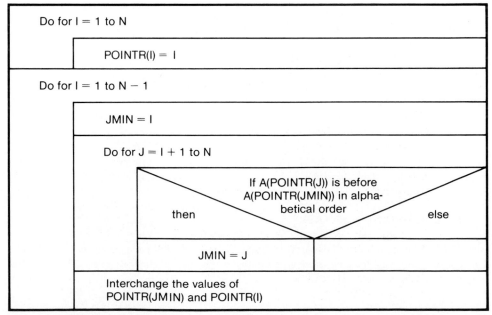

```
*  CUSTOMER ACCOUNT TOTALS, WITH THE OUTPUT IN ALPHABETICAL
*  ORDER BY NAME.
      INTEGER LENTAB
      PARAMETER (LENTAB = 200)
      CHARACTER*7 CD ACCT, ACCTNO(LENTAB)
      CHARACTER*15 CD NAME, NAME(LENTAB)
      REAL CD AMT, AMOUNT(LENTAB)
      INTEGER I, J, JMIN, LENGTH, POINTR(LENTAB)
*
*  INITIALIZE ACCTNO ARRAY TO BE EMPTY (LENGTH
*  IS THE NUMBER OF ITEMS USED IN THE ARRAY).
*
      LENGTH = 0
*
*  INITIALIZE AMOUNT TABLE.
*
      DO 10, I = 1, LENTAB
         AMOUNT(I) = 0
10       CONTINUE
*
*  FOR EACH INPUT CARD, FIND OR CREATE AN ACCOUNT
*  TABLE ENTRY, THEN UPDATE THE CUSTOMER NAME AND
*  AMOUNT TABLES.
*
20    READ (*, *, END = 50) CD ACCT, CD NAME, CD AMT
*
      DO 30, I = 1, LENGTH
         IF (CD ACCT .EQ. ACCTNO(I)) GO TO 40
30       CONTINUE
*
*  ACCOUNT NUMBER NOT FOUND – PUT IT IN THE ARRAY.
*
      LENGTH = LENGTH + 1
      IF (LENGTH .GT. LENTAB) THEN
         PRINT *, 'MAXIMUM ARRAY SIZE EXCEEDED'
         STOP
      END IF
      ACCTNO(LENGTH) = CD ACCT
      I = LENGTH
*
40    NAME(I) = CD NAME
      AMOUNT(I) = AMOUNT(I) + CD AMT
      GO TO 20
*
*  AT THE END OF INPUT, CREATE AN ARRAY OF POINTERS TO
*  SORT THE NAME ARRAY IN ALPHABETICAL ORDER.
*
50    DO 60, I = 1, LENGTH
         POINTR(I) = I
60       CONTINUE
```

```
        DO 80, I = 1, LENGTH - 1
            JMIN = I
            DO 70, J = I + 1, LENGTH
                IF (NAME(POINTR(J)) .LT. NAME(POINTR(JMIN))) JMIN = J
70              CONTINUE
            TEMP = POINTR(I)
            POINTR(I) = POINTR(JMIN)
            POINTR(JMIN) = TEMP
80          CONTINUE
*
* PRINT THE ARRAYS.
*
        PRINT *, 'CUSTOMER ACCOUNT TOTALS'
        DO 90, I = 1, LENGTH
            PRINT *, 'ACCOUNT: ', ACCTNO(POINTR(I)),
     $            ' NAME: ', NAME(POINTR(I)),
     $            ' TOTAL PURCHASES: $ ', AMOUNT(POINTR(I))
90          CONTINUE
        END
```

SUMMARY

An array is a collection of variables, all of the same type, which are stored in consecutive memory locations. To specify a particular array element, you write the array name, which has the form of a FORTRAN variable name, followed by a subscript expression enclosed in parentheses. The subscript expression can be any integer expression. Each array element is a variable and can be used in any statement where an ordinary variable name would be used.

To set up an array in a program or subprogram, you declare the array either in a DIMENSION statement or in a type statement having a dimension declarator. The dimension declarator gives an upper dimension bound, and optionally, a lower dimension bound. These bounds specify the range of subscripts for the array.

In a subprogram, an array name may be used as a dummy argument. In this case, the size of the array can be specified with an adjustable-array declaration or an assumed-size array declaration. The actual size of the array is then determined by the calling program.

If the value of a subscript expression is not within the dimension bounds given by the array declarator, a subscript error is the result. Subscript errors are often difficult to locate. It is advisable to include statements in your program to detect potential subscript errors and prevent them.

A two-dimensional array, or matrix, is established by a dimension declarator having two dimension bound expressions. An element of a two-dimensional array is specified by a pair of subscript expressions, separated by a comma. Three-dimensional and higher-dimensional arrays can be used analogously. The rules for using such arrays are similar to the rules for one-dimensional arrays. In particular, each subscript must be within the limits established by the dimension bound expression.

A data structure is a systematic method of representing information in a program.

An array is one example of a data structure. Other types can be defined for particular applications. In FORTRAN, complex data structures are usually implemented using arrays.

VOCABULARY

array	matrix
array declarator	pointer
array name	sort an array
assumed-size array declarator	subscript
data structure	subscript error
dimension bound expressions	subscript expression
DIMENSION statement	table lookup
element of an array	two-dimensional array
implied DO loop	type of an array
lower dimension bound	upper dimension bound

EXERCISES

1. Write a declaration statement to set up each of the following arrays.
   (a) A real array VECTOR whose subscripts range from 1 to 100.
   (b) An integer array NUMBER whose subscripts range from −10 to 10.
   (c) A character array LETTER of 26 elements, where each element is one character storage unit.
   (d) A character array PAGE of MAXLIN elements where each element has LINLEN characters.
   (e) A two-dimensional integer array BOARD with eight rows and eight columns.
   (f) A three-dimensional real array CUBE in which each subscript ranges from 0 to 3.
2. For each of the arrays in Exercise 1, write statements that initialize the entire array to zeros (or blank spaces, as appropriate).
3. Run the following program on your computer system. What happens? Why? What messages, if any, does the machine produce to help you diagnose the problem? Are the messages produced when the program compiles, loads, or executes?

```
      REAL X(10)
      INTEGER I
      DO 10, I = 1, 10000
         X(I) = 0
10       CONTINUE
      STOP 'NORMAL COMPLETION'
      END
```

4. Run the following program on your computer system. What happens? Why? Is this a legal program? What messages, if any, does the machine produce to help you diagnose the problem? Are the messages produced when the program compiles, loads, or executes?

```
        REAL XX(10), Y
        INTEGER I
        DO 10, I = 1, 10
            XX(I) = 0
10          CONTINUE
        Y = 0
        DO 20, I = 1, 10
            Y = Y + X(I)
20          CONTINUE
        STOP 'NORMAL COMPLETION'
        END
```

5. Run the following program on your computer system. The output indicates whether arrays are initialized to zero by your operating system. Do you think that initializing arrays in your own program is necessary?

```
        INTEGER N, ARRAY(500), COUNT
        COUNT = 0
        DO 10, N = 1, 500
            IF (ARRAY(N) .NE. 0.0) THEN
                PRINT *, N, ARRAY(N)
                COUNT = COUNT + 1
            END IF
10          CONTINUE
        PRINT *, COUNT, ' ELEMENTS WERE NON-ZERO'
        END
```

6. Suppose that $x_1, x_2, \ldots, x_n$ represents a set of measurements. The *mean value*, $\bar{x}$, (read "x bar") is given by

$$\bar{x} = \frac{x_1 + x_2 + \cdots + x_n}{n}$$

The *sample standard deviation*, s, is given by

$$s = \sqrt{\frac{SSQ - \frac{1}{n}(SX)^2}{n - 1}}$$

where $SX = x_1 + x_2 + \cdots + x_n$
$SSQ = x_1^2 + x_2^2 + \cdots + x_n^2$

Write a program that reads a set of up to 200 measurements, one per input line, and computes the mean and standard deviation.

7. Modify the program in Exercise 6 to list all of the measurements that differ from the mean value by more than one standard deviation in either direction.

8. A **polynominal** is an expression of the form

$$a_n x^n + a_{n-1} x^{n-1} + a_{n-2} x^{n-2} + \cdots + a_2 x^2 + a_1 x + a_0$$

where $a_n, a_{n-1}, \ldots, a_0$ are constants called the **coefficients** of the polynomial, and x is a variable. The integer n is called the **degree** of the polynomial. For example,

$$x^3 - 2.3x^2 + 1.9x + 0.5$$

is a polynomial of degree 3 with coefficients 1.0, −2.3, 1.9, and 0.5. To **evaluate** a polynomial means to find the value of the expression for a particular value of x. For example, to evaluate the above polynomial for $x = 1.5$, you substitute 1.5 for x to obtain

$$(1.5)^3 - 2.3(1.5)^2 + 1.9(1.5) + 0.5 = 1.55$$

The most efficient computational method for evaluating a polynomial is to group the terms as in the following example.

$$[(1.0 x - 2.3) x + 1.9] x + 0.5$$

This is equivalent to the polynomial above, but it can be evaluated with fewer multiplications. The general algorithm, called *Horner's method*, is shown in the accompanying figure.

HORNER'S METHOD FOR EVALUATING THE POLYNOMIAL

$$Y = A(N)*X**N + A(N - 1)*X**(N - 1) + \cdots + A(1)*X + A(0)$$

Y = 0
I = N
While I ≥ 0
Y = Y*X + A(I)
I = I − 1

Write a program that reads an array of coefficients and prints values of the polynomial for values of X in a given range. Input consists of three data cards.

CARD 1 the degree of the polynomial
CARD 2 the array of real coefficients, starting with a_n
CARD 3 the first value, the last value, and the incremental value of the variable X

For the input

2
1.0, 2.0, 3.0
0.0, 1.0, 0.2

the program output sould look like this:

VALUES OF THE POLYNOMIAL
    $Y = 1.0X^{**}2 + 2.0X^{**}1 + 3.0$
    X = 0.0   Y = 3.0
    X = 0.2   Y = 3.44
    X = 0.4   Y = 3.96
    X = 0.8   Y = 5.24
    X = 1.0   Y = 6.0

9. Write a program that reads two numbers. The first represents an amount of purchase and the second represents the amount you give the clerk. Print the exact change you should receive. For example:

PURCHASE $11.23
AMOUNT GIVEN $20.00
CHANGE $ 8.77 =
    1   FIVE DOLLAR BILLS
    3   ONE DOLLAR BILLS
    1   FIFTY CENT PIECE
    1   QUARTER
    2   PENNIES

10. The program in Example 6.3 sorts an array of alphabetical data. Using a similar algorithm, write a program that reads an array of real numbers, sorts them in ascending order, and prints them.

11. In Roman numerals,

M stands for 1000   X stands for 10
D stands for 500   V stands for 5
C stands for 100   I stands for 1
L stands for 50

The numeral XXVII stands for 27. However, XXIV is 24; since the I comes before the V, the value of the V is reduced by the value of I. Write a program that reads a Roman numeral and prints the equivalent number.

12. A set of data cards was prepared for a class of students. The first item on each card is a six-character student identification number. Print a list of all students for which there is more than one data card.

13. Peter the Postman works in a small post office in which there are 200 mailboxes, numbered 1 to 200. One night, out of sheer boredom, he opened every mailbox. Then he shut every second mailbox (2, 4, 6, . . .). Then he went to every third mailbox (3, 6, 9, . . .). If it was open, he shut it; if it was shut, he opened it. Then he went back to every fourth mailbox (4, 8, 12, . . .) and did the same thing. He continued this odd routine all night, going to every fifth mailbox, then to every sixth mailbox, and so on. On each round, if he found a box open, he shut it; if he found it

shut, he opened it. In the morning, which boxes were open and which were shut?

14. There is a story that the famous mathematician Hardy once went to visit the great Indian mathematician Ramanujan, who was in the hospital. Hardy mentioned the number of the cab he had arrived in, and remarked that it was an uninteresting number. Ramanujan immediately replied, "Not at all. It is the smallest number that can be written as the sum of two cubes in two different ways." What was the number? You can solve this problem by writing a table lookup procedure similar to the one in Example 6.5, for numeric items. Then create a table of numbers that can be written as the sum of two cubes, that is, numbers of the form $a^3 + b^3$ for integers a and b, where $b \geq a$. When you find a number that is already in the table, you will have the answer.

15. A **prime number** is a number greater than 1 that is not divisible by any number except 1 and itself. For example, 17 is a prime, but 25 is not, since $25 = 5 \times 5$. It can be shown that a number is prime if and only if it is not divisible by any prime number less than its square root. That observation is the basis for the algorithm shown in the following figure, which stores prime numbers in the integer array P(1), P(2), . . . , P(MAXLEN). All variables are integer variables. Write this algorithm as a FORTRAN program to print the first 200 prime numbers. *Note*: An integer N is divisible by an integer P(I) if N equals (N/P(I))*P(I) in integer arithmetic.

ALGORITHM TO STORE PRIME NUMBERS IN P(1), P(2), . . . , P(MAXLEN)

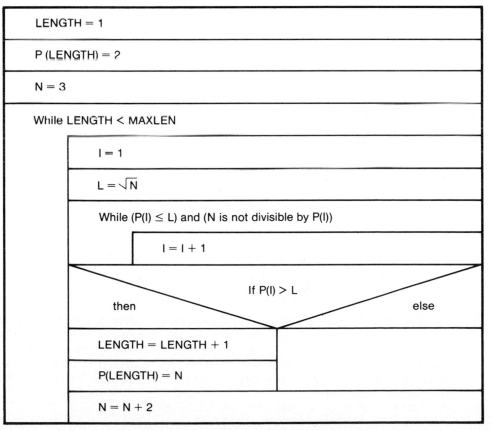

16. A central problem in calculus is finding the area under a curve. In the figure below, C is a curve given by some equation $y = f(x)$. The points $x_0, x_1, x_2, \ldots, x_n$ are equally spaced points on the x axis. That is,

$$x_i = x_0 + ih$$

for some positive number h.

Let $y_0, y_1, \ldots, y_n$ be the corresponding y values. To find the area under the curve C between the lines $x = y_0$ and $x = x_n$, you can use *Simpson's rule for numerical integration*:

$$\text{Area} = \frac{h}{3}\left[(y_0 + y_n) + 4(y_1 + y_3 + y_5 + \cdots + y_{n-1}) + 2(y_2 + y_4 + y_6 + \cdots + y_{n-2})\right]$$

In this formula, the number n must be an even number. Write a program that computes the area under the curve $y = 1/x$ from $x = 1$ to $x = 2$ using 1000 intervals.

WHAT IS THE AREA OF THE SHADED REGION UNDER THE CURVE?

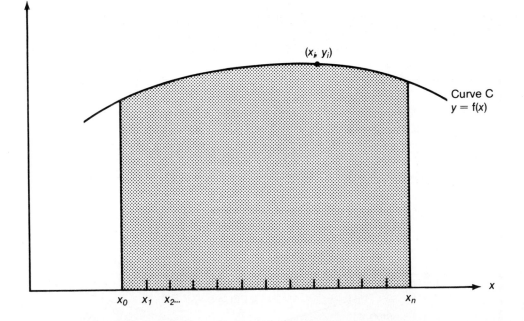

17. The International Morse Code represents each letter or number with a sequence of dots and dashes, as shown in the table on page 225. Write a program that reads a card and prints out the message in Morse code, using an asterisk for a dot and an equal sign for a dash. Print one or more blank spaces between letters and an extra blank space between words. (*Hint*: Use a character array to store the code, which you can read from cards.)

THE MORSE CODE

A	. —	M	— —	Y	— . — —	
B	— . . .	N	— .	Z	— — . .	
C	— . — .	O	— — —	1	. — — — —	
D	— . .	P	. — — .	2	. . — — —	
E	.	Q	— — . —	3	. . . — —	
F	. . — .	R	. — .	4	. . . . —	
G	— — .	S	. . .	5	. . . . .	
H	. . . .	T	—	6	—	
I	. .	U	. . —	7	— — . . .	
J	. — — —	V	. . . —	8	— — — . .	
K	— . —	W	. — —	9	— — — — .	
L	. — . .	X	— . . —	0	— — — — —	

18. In the following 3 by 3 matrix, the question marks stand for unknown numbers.

$$? \quad 1 \quad ?$$
$$3 \quad 5 \quad 7$$
$$? \quad 9 \quad ?$$

There is one way of replacing the question maks by the numbers 2, 4, 6, and 8 such that the matrix becomes a **magic square** in whlch the sum of the numbers in each row, column, and diagonal is the same. Write a program to solve this problem and print the solution.

19. Suppose you wish to find X and Y that satisfy both of the equations

$$a_{11} X + a_{12} Y = b_1$$
$$a_{21} X + a_{22} Y = b_2$$

where the a's and b's are known constants. This is the simplest case of the mathcmatical problem called solving a system of simultaneous linear equations. The solution is given by **Cramer's rule:**

$$X = \frac{a_{22} b_1 - a_{12} b_2}{a_{11} a_{22} - a_{12} a_{21}}$$

$$Y = \frac{a_{11} b_2 - a_{21} b_1}{a_{11} a_{22} - a_{12} a_{21}}$$

Write a program that reads values for the arrays a and b and prints the solutions for X and Y. Test your program by finding X and Y such that

$$3X + 5Y = -11$$
$$-2X + Y = 16$$

20. A physics student conducts an experiment to measure the relationship of two variables, which we shall call X and Y. He made 10 measurements, for various values of X, and recorded the corresponding Y values. The 10 pairs of measure-

ments (X_1, Y_1) are listed in the table and plotted on the graph in the accompanying figure. As you can see, the points lie approximately on a straight line. Thus, the student conjectures that X and Y are approximately related by the formula

$$Y = a + bX$$

What are the values of a and b that give the best approximation of this relationship? The solution is given by the statistical technique called the **method of least squares**. The formulas are

$$a = (SY*SX2 - SX*SXY)/(N*SX2 - SX2*SX2)$$
$$b = (N*SXY - SX*SY)/(N*SX2 - SX2*SX2)$$

where

N = number of (X, Y) pairs
SX = $X_1 + X_2 + X_3 + \cdots + X_N$
$SX2$ = $X_1{}^2 + X_2{}^2 + X_3{}^2 + \cdots + X_N{}^2$
SY = $Y_1 + Y_2 + Y_3 + \ldots + Y_N$
SXY = $X_1Y_1 + X_2Y_2 + X_3Y_3 + \cdots X_NY_N$

Write a program that reads a set of up to 200 (X, Y) measurements and computes the numbers a and b that give the best line according to the above formulas. Test your program with the data shown.

FITTING A LINE TO A SET OF POINTS

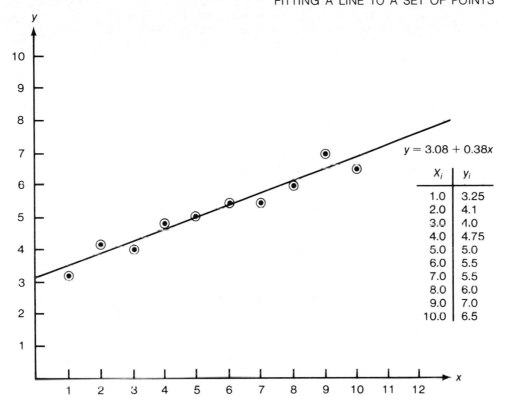

$y = 3.08 + 0.38x$

X_i	y_i
1.0	3.25
2.0	4.1
3.0	4.0
4.0	4.75
5.0	5.0
6.0	5.5
7.0	5.5
8.0	6.0
9.0	7.0
10.0	6.5

SUBPROGRAMS

INTRODUCTION   A **subprogram**, as the name implies, is a set of instructions that forms part of a program. As an example, suppose that in a certain program you need to find the square root of a number. One possible approach would be to devise an algorithm and write FORTRAN statements to carry out the square root computation. If you needed to carry out a similar computation in a different program, you could copy the same statements—that is, the same subprogram—to calculate a square root. Fortunately, this work has already been done for you. A subprogram to compute square roots is a built-in feature of the FORTRAN language. To use it, you simply write a statement such as

    Y = SQRT(X)

which sets Y equal to the square root of X.

The square root computation may be fairly complicated, consisting of many instructions, but you can use it easily, simply by referencing the SQRT subprogram. This kind of subprogram is called an **intrinsic function**. There is a whole library of such intrinsic functions to perform common mathematical operations.

Using intrinsic functions is so convenient that you may often wish there were more of them. You might say to yourself, "It's too bad they didn't include a function to do such and such, because then I could have written this program easily." No matter how many intrinsic functions there were, you could always wish for one more. The real answer is to learn to write functions of your own. That is exactly what you will do in this chapter.

A **function** is one kind of FORTRAN subprogram. The other kind of subprogram is a **subroutine**, which is very similar. The main difference between functions and subroutines is that subroutines do not return a value like functions do.

When you learn to use FORTRAN subprograms, you will be able to write a function (or subroutine) to carry out any sequence of FORTRAN instructions. Then you can use the function (or subroutine) in your program, or in another subprogram, just as though it were a FORTRAN intrinsic function.

Subprograms are a valuable tool in writing well-structured programs according to the principles of top-down design. Just as you can solve a problem by breaking it down into smaller pieces, you can often write a program by breaking it into several subprograms. You can write and debug the subprograms independently of each other, then put them together to solve your problem.

INTRINSIC FUNCTIONS

In mathematics, the notation

$$y = f(x)$$

is read "y equals f of x." It means that the variable y is a **function** of the variable x. A function is a rule that defines one variable in terms of another variable. For each value of x, the function f computes a value of $f(x)$. The variable x is called the **argument** of the function, and the number $f(x)$ that the function computes is called the **value** of the function.

An example is the square root function. Suppose we define a function $f(x)$ by the formula

$$f(x) = \sqrt{x}$$

That is, $f(x)$ is the square root of the number x. To evaluate the function for $x = 4$, you simply substitute 4 for x:

$$f(4) = \sqrt{4} = 2$$

If you substitute different values of the argument x, you get different values of the function $f(x)$. Thus

$$
\begin{aligned}
f(0) &= 0 \\
f(1) &= 1 \\
f(2) &= 1.4142 \quad \text{(approximately)} \\
f(3) &= 1.7321 \quad \text{(approximately)} \\
f(4) &= 2 \\
f(5) &= 2.2361 \quad \text{(approximately)}
\end{aligned}
$$

You can use functions in FORTRAN, too. FORTRAN provides a set of **intrinsic functions**—functions that are built-in feaures of the language—which you can use to compute common mathematical functions such as square root, absolute value, sine, and cosine.

The form of a FORTRAN function is similar to the mathematical notation. You write a function name followed by a set of parentheses that enclose the argument (or arguments).

Each intrinsic function has a certain name. The name of the intrinsic function for computing square roots is SQRT. To set Y equal to the square root of 2.0 you can use the assignment statement:

    Y = SQRT(2.0)

The number 2.0 is the argument and SQRT(2.0) is the value of the function, which is stored in Y.

To **reference** a function means to invoke execution of the subprogram that computes the function value. In the statement above, the expression SQRT(2.0) is called a **function reference** to the SQRT function. You can use an intrinsic function reference just like a variable name within an arithmetic expression. For example, the statement:

    Y = (1 + SQRT(X))/2

adds 1 to the square root of X and divides the result by 2.

The argument of an intrinsic function may be a constant, variable, or expression. The mathematical formula:

$$z = \sqrt{x^2 + y^2}$$

says that z is equal to the square root of the expression $x^2 + y^2$. You can write this in FORTRAN as

    Z = SQRT(X**2 + Y**2)

To evaluate the function reference, the machine first evaluates the argument expression, then it executes the SQRT subprogram.

When you use an intrinsic function, you must supply an argument of the correct type. The SQRT function requires a *real* argument, so the constant, variable, or expression inside the parentheses must be real. Thus,

    SQRT(2.0)

is a correct function reference because 2.0 is a real constant, but

    SQRT(2)

is incorrect, since 2 is an integer constant. The value of the SQRT function is a real number, like the argument.

There are some intrinsic functions for which you can choose the type of argument to supply. An example is the function ABS, which computes the *absolute value* of its argument (that is, the value of the function is the value of the argument converted to a nonnegative number). The argument of the ABS function can be either integer or real type. If you give it an integer argument, the value of ABS is an integer number. The value of

    ABS(−2)

is the integer number 2. If you give it a real argument, the value of ABS is a real number. The value of

    ABS(−2.0)

is the real number 2.0.

Actually, ABS is a **generic function name** that refers to several **specific intrinsic functions**. There is a specific function IABS that computes the integer absolute value of an integer argument. There is another specific function ABS that computes the real absolute value of a real argument. You never need to use the specific function names, though. You just use the generic name ABS and the FORTRAN compiler will figure out which specific function to use based on the type of argument you supply.

You do not need to declare intrinsic function names in a type statement. That is, you do *not* need a statement such as

    REAL ABS

to declare ABS to be a real function. In fact, since ABS is a generic function name, it could be used as both an integer and a real function in the same program. An IMPLICIT statement does not affect the type of intrinsic functions. Thus, in a program that begins with the statements

    IMPLICIT INTEGER (A − Z)
    REAL X

the function reference

    ABS(X)

would still be a real expression.

Appendix A lists all the FORTRAN intrinsic functions. Here is an introducton to some of the most useful ones. The function name given in each case is the generic name.

Absolute Value Function

    ABS(X)

is the **absolute value** of X, denoted in mathematics by the symbol

$$|x|$$

The definition is

$$|x| = \begin{cases} x & \text{if } x \geq 0 \\ -x & \text{if } x < 0 \end{cases}$$

The argument of ABS may be integer or real. The value of the function is the same type as the argument. Examples:

Function Reference	Value
ABS(2.0)	2.0
ABS(−2.0)	2.0
ABS(2)	2
ABS(−2)	−2
ABS(0)	0

Square Root Function

SQRT(X)

is the **square root** of X, denoted in mathematics by the symbol

$$\sqrt{x}$$

The argument of SQRT must be real. Since negative numbers do not have a real square root, the argument must also be nonnegative. Thus,

SQRT(−2.0)

is an illegal function reference. When a program tries to execute an illegal function reference like this, it will terminate with an execution error. On most systems, the machine would print a diagnostic message such as:

NEGATIVE ARGUMENT TO SQRT IN LINE 20
PROGRAM TERMINATED

Examples:

Function Reference	Value
SQRT(4.0)	2.0
SQRT(100.0)	10.0
SQRT(0.0)	0.0
SQRT(−1.0)	(illegal)
SQRT(2)	(illegal)

Exponential and Logarithmic Functions

EXP(X)

is the **exponential** function defined by the mathematical formula e^x, where e is the number 2.718281828 . . . , the base of natural logarithms. This function takes a real argument, which may be positive, negative, or zero.

The **natural logarithm** and **common logarithm** functions are

LOG(X)   and   LOG10(X)

corresponding to the mathematical notation $\log_e x$ and $\log_{10} x$. Each of these functions takes a real argument, which must be positive. Examples:

Function Reference	Value
EXP(1.0)	2.718282
EXP($-$1.0)	0.367879
LOG(2.718282)	1.0
LOG(1.0)	0
LOG10(1000.0)	3.0
LOG(2)	(illegal)
LOG($-$2.0)	(illegal)

Trigonometric and Inverse Trigonometric Functions

To find the **trigonometric sine** of x, use the function

SIN(X)

The argument must be real.

FORTRAN trigonometric functions use **radian measure** for angles. The angle 180° corresponds to π radians. If ANGLE represents some angle measured in degrees, you can convert it to radians by multiplying by π and dividing by 180. Thus, the sine of an angle in degrees is given by

SIN(PI/180.0 *ANGLE)

where PI = 3.14159265 . . . .

The **inverse trigonometric sine** or **arcsine** of X is given by

ASIN(X)

The argument is real and must have a value between -1 and 1.

There are similar intrinsic functions for other trigonometric relations:

COS(X)	Cosine of x
ACOS(X)	Arccosine of x
TAN(X)	Tangent of x
ATAN(X)	Arctangent of x
ATAN2(Y, X)	Arctangent of y/x

Note that there are two functions for computing inverse tangents. The function ATAN2 takes two real arguments and computes the arctangent of their quotient. It correctly handles the case where X = 0, and it is useful for converting an X, Y coordinate to polar coordinate form (Exercise 4). Examples:

Function Reference	Value
SIN(3.14159)	0.0
SIN(1.570796)	1.0
COS(0.0)	1.0
ATAN(1.0)	0.785398
ATAN2(1.0, 0.0)	1.570796

Type Conversion Functions

Occasionally you may need to convert a real value to an integer value, or vice versa. One way is to use an assignment statement such as

    N = X

As explained in Chapter 3, this would convert the real value X to integer form before storing the value in the integer variable N. The **integer value** function INT serves the same purpose. If X is a real expression, then

    INT(X)

is the integer value obtained by truncating any fractional part of X.

A similar function is the **nearest integer** function

    NINT(X)

Like the INT function, it converts the real argument to an integer value. Instead of truncating, however, NINT *rounds* the value to the nearest integer.

The **real value** function converts the value of an integer expression to a real number. If N is an integer expression,

    REAL(N)

is the equivalent real value. Examples:

Function Reference	Value
INT(3.2)	3
INT(3.6)	3
NINT(3.6)	4
INT(−2.5)	−2
NINT(−2.5)	−3
REAL(2)	2.0

Maximum and Minimum Functions

The function

    MAX(X, Y)

computes the **maximum value** of X and Y. For example

    MAX(5, 6)

is equal to 6. The arguments can be either integer or real, but all arguments must be of the same type. If you supply real arguments, the value is a real number; for integer arguments, the value is an integer.

The MAX function can have two or more arguments. If you want to find the maximum of three values A, B, and C, you can use the expression

    MAX(A, B, C)

The MIN function

    MIN(X, Y)

is similar, but it computes the **minimum value** of its arguments. Examples:

Function Reference	Value
MAX(1, 2, 3)	3
MIN(1, 2, 3)	1
MAX(−1, −2, −3)	−1
MIN(−1, −2, −3)	−3
MAX(1.1, 2.2)	2.2
MIN(1.1, 2.2)	1.1
MAX(1, 2.2)	(illegal)

Modulo Function

The **modulo function** computes the remainder when one number is divided by another. The function reference

MOD(M, N)

is equal to M modulo N; that is, it is the remainder when M is divided by N. The value of this function is the same as the value of the expression

M − INT(M/N) ∗N

The arguments can be integer or real, but both must be of the same type. The value of the function is the same type as the arguments. The value of the second argument must not be zero. Examples:

Function Reference	Value
MOD(5, 2)	1
MOD(6, 2)	0
MOD(7, 2)	1
MOD(100, 3)	1
MOD(−5, 2)	−1
MOD(3.2, 1.0)	0.2
MOD(3.2, 2.2)	1.0
MOD(2, 3)	2
MOD(1, 0)	(illegal)

Length Function

It is often necessary to know the length of a character variable or expression. The function reference

LEN(C)

computes an integer value which is the length of the character expression C. Examples:

Function Reference	Value
LEN('A')	1
LEN('AB')	2
LEN('I''M')	3
LEN('AB'//'CD')	4
LEN(C(1:5))	5

EXAMPLE 7.1 Using Intrinsic Functions

A function reference is an expression, so it can be used anywhere an expression can be used: in the output list of a PRINT statement, for instance, or as the terminal parameter in a DO statement, or as a subscript expression.

Suppose you want to print the value of x, e^x, and $\log_e x$. Using function references in a PRINT statement, you could write

    PRINT *, X, EXP(X), LOG(X)

Suppose you want to execute a loop for values of X between 0 and the square root of W. Using a function reference in a DO loop, you could write

    DO 100, X = 0.0, SQRT(W), DELTA X

You can even use a function reference as the argument of a function. Suppose that N is an integer variable. You want to execute a loop for I from 1 up to the integer nearest the square root of N. The expression

    SQRT(N)

is illegal, since SQRT requires a real argument, but you can use the REAL function to convert N to a real value. Thus the square root of N is

    SQRT(REAL(N))

The nearest integer value is found by applying the NINT function to the above expression:

    NINT(SQRT(REAL(N)))

Thus you could write the required DO statement as

    DO 100, I = 1, NINT(SQRT(REAL(N)))

The LEN function is often useful in substring expressions. For instance, to set the character variable TAIL equal to the last six characters of the character variable LINE, you could use the statement

    TAIL = LINE(LEN(LINE) − 5:)

As another example, suppose you want to store blank spaces in characters I through J of a character variable C. You could use the statement

    C(I:J) = ' '

To avoid possible substring errors, you might use the following procedure instead:

If J is less than I, do nothing.
If J is greater than the length of C, use the length of C in place of J.
If I is less than 1, use 1 in place of I.

Using intrinsic functions, you can write this procedure in one statement:

IF (I .LE. J) C(MAX(1, I):MIN(J, LEN(C))) = ' '

FUNCTION SUBPROGRAMS

A **function subprogram** is used the same way that an intrinsic function is used. The difference is that you write the function subprogram yourself. The concept can best be introduced through an example.

EXAMPLE 7.2 Factorial Function
For any positive integer n, the number $n!$ (read "n factorial") is defined as:

$$n! = 1 \times 2 \times 3 \times \ldots \times n$$

That is, $n!$ is the product of all the positive integers less than or equal to n. For example, $5! = 1 \times 2 \times 3 \times 4 \times 5 = 120$.

Suppose you want to write a program that prints the factorials of the numbers 1 to 10. Now suppose that there were an intrinsic function FACT(N) that computed the factorial of an integer N. (Since factorials are large numbers, we will suppose that the value of FACT is a real number—that way, we avoid the problem of computing integers that are too large for the machine to store.)

You could write the program as follows.

```
*
* PROGRAM TO PRINT A TABLE OF FACTORIALS.
*
      INTEGER N
      REAL FACT, F
      DO 10, N = 1, 10
         F = FACT(N)
         PRINT *, N, 'FACTORIAL = ', F
10       CONTINUE
      END
```

The trouble is, of course, that FORTRAN supplies no such intrinsic function. So in addition to the main program you have to write a function subprogram that computes FACT(N). The FORTRAN statements for this subprogram go after the END statement in the main program. Here is the complete program.

```
*
* PROGRAM TO PRINT A TABLE OF FACTORIALS
*
      INTEGER N
      REAL FACT, F
      DO 10, N = 1, 10
          F = FACT(N)
          PRINT *, N, 'FACTORIAL = ', F
10        CONTINUE
      END
*
* FACTORIAL FUNCTION.
* FACT(N) IS A REAL NUMBER EQUAL TO N FACTORIAL.
*
      REAL FUNCTION FACT(N)
      INTEGER I, N
      FACT = 1
      DO 10, I = 2, N
          FACT = FACT*I
10        CONTINUE
      END
```

When the program executes, the first statement to be carried out is the first executable statement in the main program, that is, the DO statement. On the first trip through the DO loop, the assignment statement

F = FACT(N)

tells the machine to compute the value of the FACT function with N equal to 1. At this point, control passes to the subprogram, as shown in Figure 7.1(a). The entire subprogram is executed, then control returns to the main program at the point where it left off in the process of carrying out the assignment statement. The value of the function is equal to the value of the variable FACT from the subprogram. A similar process occurs on the other iterations of the DO loop in the main program. Each time the value of the FACT function is called for, the entire subprogram is executed.

Figure 7.1(a) shows the main program and the factorial subprogram written separately. The function reference FACT(N) in the main program causes the subprogram to be executed. At the end of the subprogram, contol returns to the main program. The effect is as though the entire subprogram were included in the main program, as shown in Figure 7.1(b).

Executing a subprogram is a fundamental control structure, like the loop and decision structures discussed in Chapter 4. In a structured flowchart, the operation is represented by a single box that says to carry out the procedure shown in a different structured flowchart. In FORTRAN, this corresponds to a function reference or a subroutine call. As a tool in structured programming, subprograms are particularly useful for isolating separate procedures and breaking up a large program into small manageable parts. As you will see later in this chapter, subprograms can be used to structure a program according to your top-level design.

FIGURE 7.1

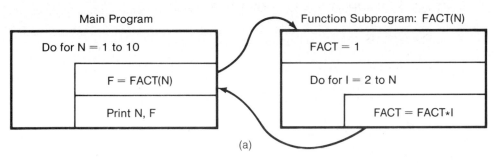

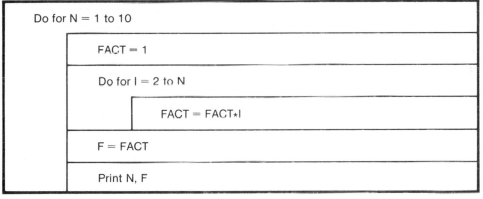

(b)

THE FUNCTION STATEMENT

The first line (after the comments) in the subprogram of Example 7.2 is the **FUNC-TION statement:**

    REAL FUNCTION FACT(N)

This declarative statement tells several things:

1. It says that the following lines (up to the next END statement) form a function subprogram.
2. The name of the function is FACT.
3. The function is a real function, so FACT is used as a real variable in the subprogram.
4. The function has one argument, N.

A function subprogram begins with a FUNCTION statement of the form

    type FUNCTION *name* (*arg*₁, *arg*₂, . . .)

where *type* is the function type (INTEGER, REAL or CHARACTER); *name* is the function name; and variables called arg_1, arg_2, . . . are the dummy arguments of the function.

Examples of FUNCTION statements are:

```
INTEGER FUNCTON NDAY(TIME)
REAL FUNCTION FREQ(L, R, C)
REAL FUNCTION F(A, NUMBER)
CHARACTER FUNCTION NCH(I)
LOGICAL FUNCTION OK(STRING)
INTEGER FUNCTION NRAND ( )
```

The function name has the same form as a variable name. In fact, within the function subprogram, you use the function name just like any other variable. If the function type is integer, then the function name is an integer variable within the subprogram (and similarly for other types: real, logical, and character).

At some point within the subprogram, the function name must be defined with some value. For instance, in the factorial function, the value of the function is defined by the statement

```
FACT = 1
```

or by the statement

```
FACT = FACT *I
```

The final value of the variable FACT is the **value of the function**. That is, it is the value of the expression

```
FACT(N)
```

in the main program.

Since FACT was declared in the subprogram to be a real function, it should also be declared as real in the program that references it. Thus, the main program in Example 7.2 contained the statement

```
REAL FACT
```

which makes the function reference

```
FACT(N)
```

a real expression.

PROGRAM UNITS

The program in Example 7.2 consists of two parts: a **main program** and a **subprogram**.

In general, a **program unit** is a sequence of FORTRAN statements terminated by an END statement. A **function subprogram** is a program unit that begins with a FUNCTION statement. Likewise, as you will see later, a **subroutine subprogram** is a program unit that begins with a SUBROUTINE statement. A **main program** is a program unit that is not a subprogram.

Each program unit is compiled independently of the others. That is, the FORTRAN compiler can translate each program unit into machine language without knowing anything about the other program units. Because of this fact, variables and statement numbers in different program units are not related. Thus, in Example 7.2, there is no conflict in having a statement number 10 in both the main program and the function subprogram. Similarly, if you use a variable X in two different program units, the two X's are two different variables.

ARGUMENTS

The variables that appear in the FUNCTION statement are called the **dummy arguments** of the function.

In a main program (or in another program unit), you **reference** the function with an expression of the form

name (arg$_1$, arg$_2$, . . .)

where *name* is the function name, and *arg$_1$*, *arg$_2$*, . . . are expressions, called the **actual arguments** of the function reference.

When the function subprogram is executed, the value of each actual argument replaces the value of the corresponding dummy argument (Figure 7.2).

Since the actual arguments may be expressions, the following statements form a legal program.

```
PRINT *, FACT(1)
N = 2
PRINT *, FACT(N)
PRINT *, FACT (N + 1)
PRINT *, FACT (2*N)
PRINT *, FACT(INT(FACT(3))+1)
END
```

There are two important rules about using function arguments.

FIGURE 7.2
DUMMY ARGUMENTS ARE THE VARIABLES USED IN THE SUBPROGRAM

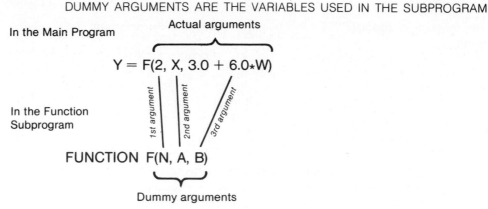

Actual agreements are the expressions whose values replace the dummy arguments when the subprogram is referenced.

Rule for Function Arguments
There must be the same number of actual arguments in the function reference as there are dummy arguments in the subprogram.

Thus, if a FUNCTION statement specifies four dummy arguments, you have to supply four actual arguments when you reference the function.

Rule for Function Arguments
Each actual argument in a function reference must have the same type as the corresponding dummy argument in the function subprogram.

The type of dummy arguments is determined by the type statements in the subprogram. For example, if a subprogram begins with the statements

```
REAL FUNCTION F(N, X)
INTEGER N
REAL X
```

then N is a integer variable in the subprogram, and X is a real variable. The rule means that it is incorrect to reference this function with a statement such as

```
Y = F(2, 5)
```

since 5 is an integer constant, and the function requires the second argument to be real. Be especially careful about following these rules. It is easy to violate them accidentally. Unfortunately, on most computer systems you get no diagnostic messages to warn you that you have done so.

If the function requires a real argument, but you give it an integer argument by mistake, the usual symptom is that the program behaves as though you had supplied a value of zero as an argument. If the function requires an integer argument, but you give it a real argument by mistake, the program might behave as though you had supplied a very large number. If you supply the wrong number of arguments, almost anything can happen—often the program just blows up; that is, terminates with some seemingly unrelated system error message.

There is one more important rule about referencing functions.

Rule for Referencing Functions
A function may not reference itself, either directly or indirectly.

In mathematics, a function that references itself in its definition is called **recursive.** For example, the function f defined by:

$$f(n) = \begin{cases} 1 & \text{if } n = 0 \\ n \times f(n-1) & \text{if } n > 0 \end{cases}$$

is a *recursive function*, because the function is defined in terms of itself. Recursive functions are *not allowed* in FORTRAN.

THE RETURN STATEMENT

The FORTRAN statement

    RETURN

in a function subprogram means to return to the place where the function was referenced. For example,

    IF (N .LT. 0) RETURN

means to return from the subprogram if N is less than zero.

Recall that in a main program, the END statement serves as a STOP instruction. Similarly, in a subprogram, the END statement serves as a RETURN instruction. Consider the following example.

```
REAL FUNCTION PIX(X)
REAL X
PIX = 3.14159 *X
RETURN
END
```

The RETURN statement tells the function to go back to the main program (or wherever the PIX function was referenced). If you left off the RETURN statement, the function would work exactly the same way, since the END statement implies a RETURN in a subprogram.

EXAMPLE 7.3 Factorial Function with Error Checking
The factorial of a negative number has no mathematical meaning.*

What should the FACT function in Example 7.2 do when the argument is negative? As it stands in Example 7.2, it just returns a value of 1. Let us rewrite it so that it prints an error message and then returns a value of -1.

While we are at it, we should make sure that the argument of FACT is not too large. If you try to compute the factorial of a large number, the value FACT will become so large that it cannot be stored in a computer word. This condition is called **arithmetic overflow**, and it will usually cause your program to terminate with an error message.

The maximum allowable value of N will depend on the machine you are using, so we will use a symbolic constant MAXN to represent this value. In the version of FACT below, we set MAXN equal to 69, which is the largest number n for which $n! < 10^{99}$.

If the argument of FACT is greater than 69, the program will print an error message and return the value of 69!.

One final note. By mathematical convention,

$$0! = 1$$

You should check that the following subprogram computes this value correctly.

```
* FACTORIAL FUNCTION.
* FACT(N) IS A REAL NUMBER EQUAL TO THE FACTORIAL OF N.
* THE VALUE OF N MUST BE BETWEEN 0 AND MAXN (INCLUSIVE).
* IF N IS LESS THAN ZERO, THE FUNCTION PRINTS AN ERROR
* MESSAGE AND SETS FACT EQUAL TO -1.
* IF N IS GREATER THAN MAXN, THE FUNCTION PRINTS AN ERROR
* MESSAGE AND SETS FACT EQUAL TO MAXN FACTORIAL.
*
      REAL FUNCTION FACT(N)
      INTEGER I, N, MAXN
      PARAMETER (MAXN = 69)

      IF (N .LT. 0) THEN
          PRINT *, 'ERROR - NEGATIVE ARGUMENT IN FACT.'
          FACT = -1
          RETURN
      ELSE IF (N .GT. MAXN) THEN
          PRINT *, 'ERROR - ARGUMENT IN FACT EXCEEDS', MAXN
      END IF
```

*Although in advanced calculus, there is a generalized factorial called the Gamma function, which is beyond the scope of this book.

```
        FACT = 1
        DO 10, I = 2, MIN(N, MAXN)
            FACT = FACT *I
10          CONTINUE
        END
```

CHARACTER DATA AS A FUNCTION ARGUMENT

Functions can use character variables, and they can return character values. The only thing unusual about using a character variable in a function is the way in which you determine its length.

Remember that the length of a character variable is defined by the CHARACTER statement. If the variable happens to be a dummy argument in a subprogram, you can specify its length with a statement like the following:

```
CHARACTER C *(*)
```

This means that the dummy argument C is a character variable whose length in the subprogram is equal to the length of the actual argument supplied when the function is referenced. The following example will illustrate this point.

EXAMPLE 7.4 Trimmed Length of a String
Remember that the intrinsic function LEN tells how long a character expression is. In this example, we will write a similar function, called LTRIM, that computes the length of a character expression trimmed of trailing blank spaces. That is,

```
LTRIM(C)
```

is an integer equal to the length of the character expression C minus the number of blank spaces at the right of C.

The algorithm for LTRIM is simple. Begin by setting LTRIM equal to the length of C. Then look at the last character of C. If it is not a blank space, return. Otherwise, subtract 1 from the value of LTRIM and go on to look at the next-to-last character of C, and so on.

This procedure can be written easily in FORTRAN using LTRIM as a DO variable in a loop that counts backwards from LEN(C) to 1. Here is the complete function subprogram.

```
* LTRIM — COMPUTE THE TRIMMED LENGTH OF A STRING.
        INTEGER FUNCTION LTRIM(C)
        CHARACTER *(*) C, SPACE
        PARAMETER (SPACE = ' ')
        DO 10, LTRIM = LEN(C), 1, −1
            IF (C(LTRIM:LTRIM) .NE. SPACE) RETURN
10          CONTINUE
        END
```

Notice the statement

CHARACTER *(*) C, SPACE

As you saw in Chapter 5, this statement means that the symbolic constant SPACE is a character constant whose length is determined by the PARAMETER statement that defines its value. The variable C is a dummy argument, so its length is determined when the function is referenced. If you reference the function with the statement

N = LTRIM('XYZ')

then the length of the actual argument is 3, so that will be the length of C in the function. Here is a short test program for this function.

```
* TEST OF THE LTRIM FUNCTION.

        CHARACTER TEST*10
        INTEGER I, LTRIM
        TEST = ' '

        PRINT *, TEST, LTRIM(TEST)
        DO 10, I = 1, 10
            TEST(I:I) = 'X'
            PRINT *, TEST, LTRIM(TEST)
10          CONTINUE
        END
```

This program produces the following output:

```
                    0
X                   1
XX                  2
XXX                 3
XXXX                4
XXXXX               5
XXXXXX              6
XXXXXXX             7
XXXXXXXX            8
XXXXXXXXX           9
XXXXXXXXXX          10
```

CHARACTER DATA AS A FUNCTION VALUE

To write a function that returns a character value, you begin the subprogram with a statement such as

CHARACTER FUNCTION F(X)

This declaration says that the value of F is a character value of length 1, so F is used as a character variable in the subprogram. The statement

    CHARACTER*5 FUNCTION F(X)

means that the value of the function F is a character value of length 5.

As with dummy arguments, you can give an unspecified length to a character function by using a FUNCTION statement such as

    CHARACTER *(*) FUNCTION F(X)

which means that the length of the character value F is defined in the program that references the function.

EXAMPLE 7.5 Case Conversion
Many computer systems let you type lowercase letters: a, b, c, . . . as well as uppercase: A, B, C, ... It is often useful to convert a character from one case to the other. We will write a function UC(X) that performs this conversion for a single character. The argument X and the function UC itself are both character values of length 1. The value of the function is simply the value of the argument, converted to uppercase if necessary. Thus,

    UC('a') is 'A'
    UC('b') is 'B'
    UC('A') is 'A'
    UC('$') is '$'

The function works by looking for the specified character within a lowercase alphabet, and, if found, replacing it by the corresponding character from an uppercase alphabet. The FORTRAN statements are as follow.

```
* UC — UPPERCASE VALUE OF THE ARGUMENT (A SINGLE CHARACTER).
      CHARACTER FUNCTION UC(X)
      CHARACTER X*1, UCALPH*26, LCALPH*26
      INTEGER I
*
      UCALPH = 'ABCDEFGHIJKLMNOPQRSTUVWXYZ'
      LCALPH = 'abcdefghijklmnopqrstuvwxyz'
      DO 10, I = 1, 26
         IF (X .EQ. LCALPH(I:I)) THEN
            UC = UCALPH(I:I)
            RETURN
         END IF
10       CONTINUE
      UC = X
      END
```

EXAMPLE 7.6 Case Conversion for a Variable

The function UC in the previous example converts a single character to uppercase. We can use UC to define a function UCASE that converts a whole string to uppercase.

The function begins with the declaration

```
CHARACTER *(*) FUNCTION UCASE(STRING)
```

which means that the length of UCASE is determined in the program that references the function. Likewise, the dummy argument STRING is defined by the statement

```
CHARACTER *(*) STRING
```

which means that the length STRING in the subprogram is equal to the length of the actual argument. For instance, a test program for UCASE could be as follows.

```
      CHARACTER *80 LINE, UCASE
10    READ (*, *, END = 20) LINE
      PRINT *, LINE
      PRINT *, UCASE(LINE)
      GO TO 10
20    END
```

When the subprogram UCASE is entered, the length of both UCASE and LINE will be 80 characters.

The procedure for UCASE is basically simple. Each character UCASE(I:I) is set equal to the uppercase value of the STRING(I:I).

There is one important point to consider, though. What if the length of UCASE is not the same as the length of STRING? To illustrate the problem, consider the effect of the statements

```
      DO 10, I = 1, LEN(STRING)
          UCASE (I:I) = UC(STRING(I:I))
10        CONTINUE
```

If UCASE is longer than STRING, then some characters of UCASE are never defined. Even worse, if STRING is longer than UCASE, then the DO loop stores characters in nonexistent locations in UCASE—a practice which will very likely cause an execution error, as we mentioned in Chapter 5.

One way to solve the problem is to use the DO statement:

```
DO 10, I = 1, MIN(LEN(UCASE), LEN(STRING))
```

This assures that I is always a legal index for both STRING and UCASE.

An even simpler method is to set UCASE equal to STRING to begin with, then convert just the characters of UCASE. Here is the code.

```
* UCASE — CONVERT THE STRING TO UPPER CASE
*
      CHARACTER *(*) FUNCTION UCASE(STRING)
```

```
      CHARACTER STRING*(*), UC*1
      INTEGER I
      UCASE = STRING
      DO 10, I = 1, LEN(UCASE)
          UCASE(I:I) = UC(UCASE(I:I))
10        CONTINUE
      END
```

CHANGING THE VALUE OF AN ARGUMENT

Besides just returning a value, a function subprogram can have **side effects**. For example, a function subprogram can change the value of one or more of its arguments. This kind of side effect can be useful, but you must use it with caution.

Consider an example.

```
INTEGER FUNCTION PLUS1(N)
INTEGER N
N = N + 1
PLUS1 = N
END
```

The value of the function is 1 plus the value of the argument. The value of the argument N is changed by the statement

```
N = N + 1
```

An argument whose value is redefined by a subprogram in this manner is sometimes called an **output argument**.

The following program uses the PLUS1 function to control a loop which prints the values 1 through 10.

```
      INTEGER I
      I = 0
10    IF (PLUS1(I) .LE. 10) THEN
          PRINT *, I
          GO TO 10
      END IF
      END
```

This use of side effects is perfectly legal in FORTRAN. It has the disadvantage, though, of being somewhat obscure. From looking at the main program you cannot tell that the value of I is being altered.

What do you think would happen if a program executed the following statement?

```
N = PLUS1(5)
```

The value of N would be set to 6. But the subprogram also redefines the value of the *constant* 5! If the program went on to execute the statement

    I = 5

it might assign I the value 6. This is clearly a bug. Unfortunately, on many systems the bug would be undetected by FORTRAN and you would have to discover it yourself by laboriously analyzing the program. The rule governing the use of side effects is as follows:

Rule for Side Effects
If a subprogram changes the value of a dummy argument, then the corresponding actual argument in the subprogram must be a variable—*not* a constant or an expression.

The penalty for violating this rule is that you will introduce a bug into your program that is usually obscure and difficult to detect.

EXAMPLE 7.7 Random Numbers
If you roll a die, it comes up showing a number from 1 to 6. The number is "random" in the sense that all six numbers are equally probable, and there is no way of knowing in advance which number will come up.

The very nature of programming makes it practically impossible to generate genuinely "random" numbers with a computer. It is, however quite easy to generate what we call **pseudorandom numbers**.

The RANDOM function in this example generates a sequence of such numbers. Each execution of the statement

    X = RANDOM(SEED)

will set X equal to a number in the range

$$0 < X < 1$$

The number X is random in the sense that all values between 0 and 1 are equally probable, and there is no obvious pattern to them. For most practical purposes, the numbers appear to be random.

The RANDOM function works by changing the value of its argument. Each time the subprogram is executed, the value of the argument is some "random" integer. This value is used to generate a new "random" integer, which becomes the new value of the argument, to be used for the next execution as in Figure 7.3.

The technique for generating a sequence of pseudorandom integers is as follows.

Algorithm for Generating Random Integers
1. Suppose that j, k, and m are integer constants. Let I be an integer such that

$$0 \leq I \leq m - 1$$

FIGURE 7.3

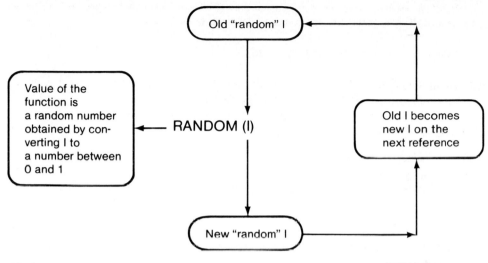

The RANDOM function changes the value of its argument to generate a sequence of random integers

$$I_0, I_1, I_2, I_3, \ldots, I_n, \ldots$$

2. Multiply I by j.
3. Add k to the result.
4. Divide by m and find the remainder.
5. Store the remainder as the new value of I. This is the next random value in the sequence.
6. To generate another pseudorandom integer I, go back to 2.

Mathematically speaking, this procedure generates sequence of integers

$$I_0, I_1, I_2, I_3, \ldots, I_n, \ldots$$

where each number in the sequence is computed from the previous one by the formula

$$I_{n+1} = (j\, I_n + k) \qquad \text{modulo } m$$

for some constants j, k and m. This method, called the **linear congruential** method of generating pseudorandom numbers, is one of the most widely used, and its mathematical properties have been studied extensively. We will not discuss the theory except to say that if you choose

$$
\begin{aligned}
j &= 5243 \\
k &= 55397 \\
m &= 262139
\end{aligned}
$$

then the algorithm just given above generates numbers that are apparently quite random.*

From the pseudorandom integers generated by the above method, it is an easy matter to compute a random number between 0 and 1. For each I, let

RANDOM = (REAL(I) + 0.5)/REAL(M)

You can easily check that RANDOM is greater than 0 and less than 1, since $0 \leq I \leq M$. A simple test program and the RANDOM function itself are shown below.

```
*  TEST PROGRAM FOR THE RANDOM
*  NUMBER GENERATOR
       INTEGER I, SEED
       REAL RANDOM
       PRINT *, 'TEN RANDOM NUMBERS'
       SEED = 0
       DO 10, I = 1, 10
            PRINT *, RANDOM(SEED)
10          CONTINUE
       END
*  RANDOM NUMBER GENERATOR
*  THE VALUE IS A RANDOM NUMBER
*  GREATER THAN 0.0 AND LESS THAN 1.0.
*  THIS FUNCTION CHANGES THE VALUE OF
*  ITS ARGUMENT, WHICH MUST BE A VARIABLE.
*  THE INITIAL VALUE OF THE ARGUMENT
*  CAN BE ANY INTEGER GREATER THAN
*  OR EQUAL TO 0, AND LESS THAN 262139.
       REAL FUNCTION RANDOM(I)
       INTEGER I, J, K, M
       PARAMETER (J  =  5243,
     $            K  =  55397,
     $            M  =  262139)

       I = MOD(I *J + K, M)
       RANDOM = (REAL(I) + 0.5)/REAL(M)
       END
```

SUBROUTINES

There are two kinds of subprograms in FORTRAN. One kind is the function subprogram you have seen in the examples this far. The other kind is a **subroutine**.

A subroutine subprogram begins with a SUBROUTINE statement of the form

SUBROUTINE name (arg₁, arg₂ , . . . , argₙ)

---

*These values were chosen so that there should be no overflow problems in machines with a 32-bit word size. For a complete discussion of this method, see the *Art of Computer Programming*, Vol. 2, 2nd ed., by Donald E. Knuth (Reading, Mass.: Addison-Wesley, 1973).

where *name* is the subroutine name and arg_1, arg_2, arg_n are the **dummy arguments.**

Like a function, a subroutine is an independent program unit which consists of all the statements from the SUBROUTINE statement through the following END statement. Like a function, a subroutine is compiled separately, so statement numbers and variables in the subroutine are distinct from those in other program units. In fact, there are really only two differences between functions and subroutines:

1. A subroutine does not return a value—so the subroutine name is not a variable.
2. To execute a subroutine, you use a CALL statement.

The **CALL statement** has the form

CALL *name* (arg_1, arg_2, . . . , arg_n)

where *name* is a subroutine name, and arg_1, arg_2, . . . , and arg_n are the **actual arguments.** This statement says to execute the subroutine subprogram using the values of the actual arguments in place of the dummy arguments in the subroutine. For example, if a subroutine begins with the statement

SUBROUTINE SUB(X, Y)

then in a main program you might cause the subroutine to execute with the statement

CALL SUB(1.0, 3*A+1)

The subroutine named SUM would execute, using the values of the actual arguments 1.0 and 3*A+1 in place of the dummy arguments X and Y. When the subroutine executes a RETURN or an END statement, control will resume with the next statement after the CALL statement (Figure 7.4). Thus, *calling* a subroutine is analoguous to *referencing* a function. (In fact, many programmers will speak of "calling" a function, even though no CALL statement is used for function subprograms.)

EXAMPLE 7.8 Interchanging the Values of Two Variables
We will write a subroutine SWAP(A,B) that interchanges the values of its two arguments. That is, it sets A equal to the old value of B, and sets B equal to the old value of A. The principle is the same for any type of variable. For this example we assume that A and B are both character variables of length 1. Here is the subroutine.

```
*
* SWAP(A,B)
* A AND B ARE CHARACTER *1 VARIABLES.
* THIS SUBROUTINE INTERCHANGES THEIR VALUES
*
      SUBROUTINE SWAP (A,B)
      CHARACTER A, B, TEMP
      TEMP = A
      A = B
      B = TEMP
      END
```

FIGURE 7.4
THE CALL STATEMENT IN THE MAIN PROGRAM TRANSFERS CONTROL TO THE
FIRST EXECUTABLE STATEMENT IN THE SUBROUTINE

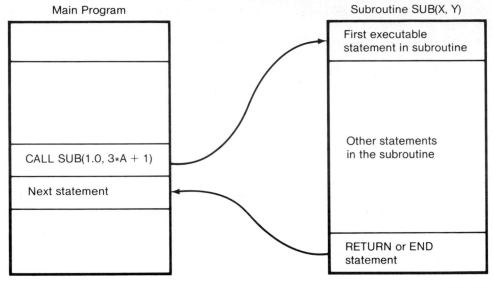

Within the subroutine, the value of the actual arguments in the CALL are used in place of the dummy arguments. When the subroutine executes a RETURN or END statement, control returns to the statement following the CALL in the main program.

In a main program (or in another subprogram), you could cause the SWAP subroutine to be executed with a statement such as

    CALL SWAP(X,Y)

where X and Y are character variables. Note that X and Y must be *variables*, not constants, since SWAP changes the values of its arguments. The rule for subroutines is analogous to the corresponding rule for functions:

Rule for Side Effects in a Subroutine
If a subroutine changes the value of a dummy argument, the corresponding actual argument must be a *variable*—that is, not a constant or an expression.

EXAMPLE 7.9 Reversing a String
We will now write a subroutine that reverses all the characters in a character variable, so that the first becomes the last and the last becomes the first, and so on. The subroutine REVERS(STRING), shown below, uses the SWAP subroutine from Example 7.8 to interchange the values of STRING(I:I) and STRING(J:J). The vaue of I starts at 1 and increases, and the value of J starts at LEN(STRING) and decreases. The process is repeated while I < J.

```
* REVERS — REVERSE A STRING
*
      SUBROUTNE REVERS(STRING)
      CHARACTER *(*) STRING
      INTEGER I, J
      I = 1
      J = LEN(STRING)
10    IF (I .LT. J) THEN
          CALL SWAP(STRING(I:I), STRING(J:J))
          I = I + 1
          J = J - 1
          GO TO 10
      END IF
      END
```

EXAMPLE 7.10 Palindromes

A *palindrome* is a word, sentence, or number that reads the same forward or backward. For example:

```
1881
DAD
ABLE WAS I ERE I SAW ELBA
```

You can use the REVERS subroutine to write a program that tests a character string to see if it is a palindrome.

The following program reads a character string as input and stores it in the variable FRONT. It then reverses the string, storing the result in the variable BACK. If FRONT equals BACK, the input line is a palindrome.

There is one tricky part in this program. In reversing the string, we don't want to include any blank spaces at the end. We want to reverse just the front part:

```
BACK(:I)
```

where I is the index of the last nonblank character (or where I is 1 if the whole string is blank). This value of I is easily computed by the function LTRIM, from Example 7.4. Thus, using the subprograms from Examples 7.4, 7.8, and 7.9, the palindrome program can be written as follows.

```
* PROGRAM TO TEST FOR PALINDROMES
* (STRINGS THAT READ THE SAME FORWARD OR BACKWARD)

      CHARACTER FRONT*80, BACK*80, ANSWER*25, QUOTE*1
      PARAMETER (QUOTE = '''')
      INTEGER I, LTRIM

* WHILE THERE IS MORE INPUT, READ A LINE AND REVERSE
* THE CHARACTERS (EXCEPT THE TRAILING BLANKS).
```

```
10      READ (*, *, END = 100) FRONT
        I = MAX(1, LTRIM(FRONT))
        BACK = FRONT
        CALL REVERS(BACK(:I))

* NOW COMPARE THE ORIGINAL STRING WITH THE REVERSED STRING,
* AND PRINT THE RESULT.

        IF (FRONT .EQ. BACK) THEN
            ANSWER = ' IS A PALINDROME.'
        ELSE
            ANSWER = ' IS NOT A PALINDROME.'
        END IF
        PRINT *, QUOTE // FRONT(:I) // QUOTE // ANSWER
        GO TO 10
100     END
```

ARRAYS IN SUBPROGRAMS

You can use arrays in a subprogram in the same way as you use them in a main program. For example, you can use a DIMENSION statement in a subprogram to set up an array for use within the subprogram. In subprograms, however, arrays have a very useful added capability: an array name can be a dummy argument. Furthermore, an array name that is a dummy argument can have adjustable dimensions, which means that the dimension bounds of the array can be variable expressions so that the actual size of the array is determined when the subprogram is called.

Let us consider an example. We will write a real function SUM that adds up the values of the elements in a real array. The function will have one argument, which is an array name. For the moment, let us assume that the array has exactly 100 elements. Here is a main program that uses the SUM function to compute the value

$$1^2 + 2^2 + 3^2 + 4^2 + \cdots + 99^2 + 100^2$$

```
* TEST PROGRAM FOR THE SUM FUNCTION
    REAL SQUARE(100), SUM
    INTEGER I
    DO 10, I = 1, 100
        SQUARE(I) = I**2
10      CONTINUE
    PRINT *, 'SUM OF SQUARES =' , SUM(SQUARE)
    END
```

The expression

SUM(SQUARE)

in the PRINT statement is a function reference, in which the argument is an array name. The following FORTRAN statements show how to correctly write the SUM function.

```
* FUNCTION TO SUM THE ELEMENT OF A REAL
* ARRAY OF 100 ELEMENTS.
      REAL FUNCTION SUM(X)
      REAL X(100)
      INTEGER I
      SUM = 0
      DO 10, I = 1, 100
          SUM - SUM ı X(I)
10        CONTINUE
      END
```

Notice that the dummy argument X is declared to be a real array in the statement

REAL X(100)

This means that the array X in the function will be replaced by the actual argument given when the function is referenced. In the example, the array SQUARE is the actual argument in the main program, so the elements of SQUARE are the ones that are actually added up by the function.

The type of an array argument in a function reference or subroutine call must be the same as the type of the array in the subprogram. Thus, it would be incorrect to use the expression

S = SUM(NPOINT)

if NPOINT is an integer array, since the SUM function subprogram declared the argument to be a real array.

The main drawback of the SUM function, as given above, is that it works only for arrays with exactly 100 elements. Of course, it would be much more useful if it would work with arrays of different sizes. We can make it do so by giving the array an **adjustable array declaration**.

An **adjustable array declaration** is an array declaration that contains one or more variables in the dimension bound expression. For example, if N is a variable, then

REAL X(N)

is an adjustable array declaration. This kind of array declaration is allowed *only* in a subprogram. Both the array name and the variable or variables in the dimension bound expression must be dummy arguments of the subprogram.

The following example shows how to rewrite the SUM function using an adjustable array declaration.

```
* FUNCTION TO SUM THE ELEMENTS OF A REAL ARRAY.
      REAL FUNCTION SUM(X, N)
      INTEGER I, N
      REAL X(N)
      SUM = 0
      DO 10, I = 1, N
          SUM = SUM + X(I)
10        CONTINUE
      END
```

To use this function in a main program you could supply, as arguments, the name of an array and its actual size. For example, in the sum program given before, you could change the PRINT statement to

```
PRINT *, 'SUM OF SQUARES = ', SUM(SQUARE, 100)
```

There is one other option you can use to declare an array in a subprogram. You can use an **assumed-size array declaration**. In this case, you write an asterisk in place of the upper dimension bound. For example, a subprogram in which LIST is a dummy argument could declare LIST to be an array with the statement

```
INTEGER LIST(*)
```

The asterisk in parentheses makes this an assumed-size declaration, which means simply that LIST is an array whose size is not given explicitly in the subprogram. The idea of an assumed-size dimension for an array is similar to the idea, which you saw in Chapter 5, of using an asterisk for the length specification of a character variable in a subprogram as in the statement

```
CHARACTER C *(*)
```

Using an assumed-size array declaration, you could rewrite the SUM function as follows.

```
* FUNCTION TO SUM THE FIRST N ELEMENTS OF
* A REAL ARRAY
      REAL FUNCTION SUM(X, N)
      INTEGER I, N
      REAL X(*)
      SUM = 0
      DO 10, I = 1, N
          SUM = SUM + X(I)
10        CONTINUE
      END
```

This is almost identical to the previous version, except for the declaration

```
REAL X(*)
```

which says that X is a real array whose size is determined by the program unit that references the function.

EXAMPLE 7.11 A Shell Sort
In Chapter 6 you saw an example of a sorting algorithm known as linear selection with exchange. The problem of efficiently sorting an array has been studied extensively, and many ingenious algorithms are known. In this example we demonstrate a technique called the **Shell Sort**, named after its inventor, D. L. Shell.

Suppose that N is an integer value and X is a real array having N or more elements. We will write a subroutine SORT that can be called with the statement

CALL SORT(X, N)

to rearrange the values of X(1) through X(N) in ascending order.

Figure 7.5 shows the Shell Sort algorithm. To convince yourself that this algorithm works, note that the value of NDELTA is divided by 2 on each iteration of the outer loop. In the last iteration of the outer loop, NDELTA is set to 1. With NDELTA equal to 1, the fact that the repeat loop terminates with INORDR being .TRUE. means that the decision always took the "else" branch in the innermost loop. This implies that X(I) is less than or equal to X(I+1) for each I from 1 to N 1. In other words, when the algorithm terminates, the array X is sorted in ascending order. A rigorous proof that the algorithm is valid would also have to show that the algorithm does, in fact, terminate eventually. The details are beyond the scope of this book, but

FIGURE 7.5
SHELL SORT ALGORITHM

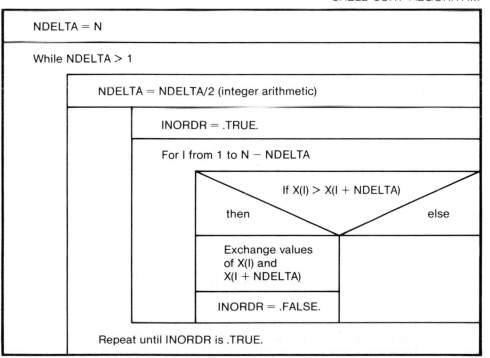

you can develop a good understanding of the method by working through a few examples with paper and pencil. Write down a sequence of 20 numbers and follow the steps of the algorithm to sort them in ascending order.

The following FORTRAN subroutine carries out the Shell Sort.

```
* SHELL SORT.
* SORT THE REAL ARRAY ELEMENTS X(1) TO X(N) IN
* ASCENDING ORDER.
*
      SUBROUTINE SORT(X, N)
      REAL X(*), TEMP
      INTEGER I, N, NDELTA
      LOGICAL INORDR
*
      NDELTA = N
10    IF (NDELTA .GT. 1) THEN
          NDELTA = NDELTA/2
20        INORDR = .TRUE.
          DO 30, I = 1, N - NDELTA
              IF (X(I) .GT. X(I + NDELTA)) THEN
                  TEMP = X(I)
                  X(I) = X(I + NDELTA)
                  X(I + NDELTA) = TEMP
                  INORDR = .FALSE.
              END IF
30        CONTINUE
          IF (.NOT. INORDR) GO TO 20
      GO TO 10
      END IF
      END
```

EXAMPLE 7.12 An Application of the SORT Subroutine
A class of college freshman took a placement test in English. Students who score above the median grade are permitted to enroll for the advanced class if they choose. Grades on the test have been keypunched on data cards for list-directed input. The first data card gives the number of students who took the test. Write a program that computes the median grade.

The **median** of a set of values is defined to be the number such that half of the values lie above it and half below it. If N students took the test and the grades are stored in array elements G(1) through G(N), then you can find the median by sorting the array G. The median grade is then the value of the "middle" element of the sorted array. If N is an even number, the median is the average of the two "middle" elements of the sorted array. For example, if N = 7, the median is the value of G(4). If N = 8, the median is the average of G(4) and G(5) (Figure 7.6).

The following program reads the grades and prints the value of the median.

```
* PROGRAM TO COMPUTE THE MEDIAN OF A SET OF GRADES.
*
      INTEGER NMAX
      PARAMETER (NMAX = 300)
      REAL G(NMAX), MEDIAN
      INTEGER I, N
```

FIGURE 7.6

TO COMPUTE THE MEDIAN OF A SET OF VALUES, SORT THEM

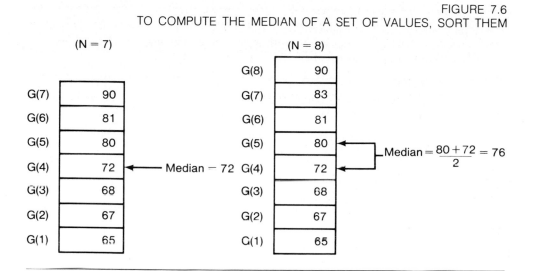

For an odd number of values, the median is then the middle value. For an even number of values, the median is the average of the two middle values.

```
*
* READ THE NUMBER OF GRADES, N, THEN READ THE GRADES
* INTO THE ARRAY G.
*
      READ *, N
      IF (N .GT. NMAX) STOP 'TOO MANY GRADES — INCREASE NMAX'
      READ *, (G(I), I = 1, N)
*
*     SORT THE GRADES.
*
      CALL SORT(G, N)
*
* PRINT THE VALUE OF THE MEDIAN.
*
      IF (MOD(N, 2) .EQ. 1) THEN
          MEDIAN = G((N + 1)/2)
      ELSE
          MEDIAN = (G((N + 1)/2) + G((N + 2)/2))/2
      END IF
      PRINT *, 'THE MEDIAN IS: ', MEDIAN
      END
```

STYLE MODULE—SUBSCRIPT ERRORS IN SUBPROGRAMS

All of the warnings about subscript errors given in Chapter 6 apply to subprograms as well as programs. There is an additional important rule to observe:

Rule for Subscripts in Subprograms
When using an array as an argument to a subprogram, make sure that the calling program specifies valid dimension bounds.

The size of an array in a subprogram must not exceed the size of an array in the calling program. If it does, a subscript error will result.

Consider the following subroutine, which sets all the elements of a real array ARRAY, of size SIZE, equal to some real number VALUE.

```
      SUBROUTINE SET (ARRAY, SIZE, VALUE)
      INTEGER SIZE, I
      REAL ARRAY(SIZE), VALUE
      DO 10, I = 1, SIZE
          ARRAY(I) = VALUE
10        CONTINUE
      END
```

Suppose that a main program uses an array X which is declared with the statement

```
   REAL X(100)
```

If this program calls the SET subroutine with the statement

```
   CALL SET(X, 200, 0.0)
```

then the subprogram will store values in $X(101)$, $X(102)$, . . . , $X(200)$, which is an error, since X has only 100 elements.

The error illustrated by this example is one of the most common sources of subscript errors. It is also one of the most difficult errors to locate when debugging a large program. You can guard against it by using symbolic constants and by including statements to check for valid dimension bounds, as in the following subroutine call:

```
   IF (N .LE. NSIZE) THEN
       CALL SET (X, N, V)
   ELSE
       PRINT *, 'ARRAY BOUND ERROR, N = ', N
   END IF
```

When you use a two-dimensional array in a subprogram, you can provide a two-dimensional adjustable array declarator, as in the following example:

```
   SUBROUTINE SOLVE (A, N, M)
   REAL A(N, M)
```

The array name and the dimension bound expressions in the REAL statement are dummy arguments to the subprogram.

There is a very important rule to observe when using such two-dimensional adjustable arrays.

Rule for Two-Dimensional Arrays in Subprograms
When the subprogram is called, the value of the first dimension bound expression *must be equal to* the actual size of the array, as specified in the calling program.

For example, suppose that a main program uses an array defined by:

    REAL SCORES (7, 20)

This main program could call subroutine SOLVE, that begins as in the above statements, with the statement:

    CALL SOLVE (SCORES, 7, 20)

It would be incorrect, however, to call the subprogram with the statement

    CALL SOLVE (SCORES, 5, 20)

because the first adjustable dimension, 5, is not equal to the first actual dimension, 7. The result would be that the subscripts would be incorrectly calculated in the subroutine. For instance, when the subroutine referred to array element

    SCORES (2, 1)

it would use a different memory location than the main program used for this same array element.

STYLE MODULE—SUBPROGRAM STYLE

Good programmers use subprograms as building blocks to put a large program together. Good programming style thus depends heavily on good style in writing subprograms. All the comments on style in the previous chapters apply to subprograms as well as to programs. In addition, the following guidelines will help you to write clear, effective subprograms. These guidelines are not inflexible rules, of course, but you should at least consider them before you decide to break them.

Keep the subprograms short.

It is usually better to write ten subroutines of 20 lines each, for example, than to write a single 200 line program that does the same thing. You can always break up a long subprogram into a series of CALL statements. Some programmers advocate limiting the length of each subprogram to one page—50 or 60 FORTRAN statements, including comments. That way, you can read the subprogram easily, without having to flip back and forth between pages to understand it.

The longer a subprogram is, the harder it is to read an understand. And readability is crucial for debugging. If you cannot understand it, you will never figure out what is wrong with it.

Make sure that each subprogram has a clearly defined purpose.

When you begin your top-level program design, you may have only a vague understanding of what really needs to be done at each step. Your success in applying the top-down method, however, will depend on your being able to sharpen your initial concepts into a precise algorithm. Before you begin writing FORTRAN statements, you should be able to state the exact effect of each subprogram in your planned solution.

Do not try to crowd too many tasks into a subprogram. Each subprogram should have one specific purpose. If you have two logically separate computations to carry out, it is best to write two separate subprograms.

By keeping subprograms short and logically independent, you will facilitate debugging. If you have a 2000 line program that does not work, you will have to search out the bug among 2000 FORTRAN statements. But if you can immediately isolate the problem to a 30 line subroutine, you might find the bug quickly.

Use subprograms to avoid redundancy.

If a procedure seems to involve repetitious programming steps, consider whether you can rewrite it as a series of calls to a general purpose subprogram. For example, if a program needs to compute the factorials of two numbers, you could write statements that compute the first factorial, then write almost duplicate statements that compute the second factorial. It is much more efficient, however, to write two references to a function subprogram that computes factorials.

Within reason, try to make each subprogram as general as possible. A subprogram that calculates the square root of 3 is obviously not as useful as a subprogram that calculates the square root of any number. By writing subprograms of general use, you can built up a library of routines that you can use in other programs, as well as the one you are working on at the moment.

Build on the work of others.

You can use not only your own subprograms, but those of other programmers. Almost all computer centers maintain a library of subprograms, and computer journals often publish FORTRAN subprograms of general interest. So before you spend a week writing a program that solves equations, for example, check to see if you can build your program from existing pieces.

Use subprograms to hide decisions.

You have to make many decisions when writing a program. Try to anticipate those that might change, and organize your subprograms so that a change will affect only one subprogram. For example, suppose you are writing a program that reads data from cards, but you know that a future version of the program will read data from a terminal. You might want to modify the second version so that it prompts the user by asking questions. Making such a change could be time-consuming if READ statements are spread throughout a large program. But if you perform input operations by calling a subroutine, you can just rewrite the subroutine as needed.

STYLE MODULE—SUBPROGRAMS AND DATA STRUCTURES

As you saw in Chapter 6, a crucial part of structured programming is defining the data structures used by the program. It is generally the case that there will be a set of basic operations you will want to perform to manipulate the data structure. You should identify these operations in your top-level design and then write a separate subprogram to carry out each one.

In designing the data structure and associated subprograms in this manner, you can achieve all of the stylistic goals listed in the previous section. You create a set of short subprograms, each with a clearly defined purpose, for working with the data structure. You avoid redundancy by making each commonly used operation into a subprogram. You hide decisions about the particular choice of the data structure from the program that uses it; the main program knows what the subprograms do, but it does not need to know how they do it. Thus, you design a set of general-purpose routines out of which you can construct a well-structured program.

The following example illustrates this technique for a data structure called a *stack*. An application is given in Exercise 16.

EXAMPLE 7.13 Stacks
A **stack** is a data structure for storing values and removing them in reverse order: like stacking plates in a cupboard—the last one you put away after dinner is the first one you take out for breakfast. To **push** a value onto a stack means to add it to the top of the stack. To **pop** a value from a stack means to remove the top value from the stack.

Suppose you want to represent a stack of integer values in FORTRAN. A convenient method is to use an integer array for storing the values. There are two other components of this data structure. You need some variable to indicate where the top of the stack is—that is, how many values have been pushed onto the stack. You also need to be able to detect and prevent a stack overflow condition. That is, you need to know the maximum number of values that can be pushed onto the stack in order to prevent the subscript errors in the stack array. It is convenient to incorporate these two variables into the integer array itself. You declare a stack with the statement

    INTEGER STACK(−1: LIMIT)

Values pushed onto the stack are stored in

    STACK(1), STACK(2), . . . , STACK(LIMIT)

The other two elements of the array are used to store the maximum size of the stack and the pointer to the top element, as follows:

    STACK(−1) = LIMIT
    STACK(0)   = subscript of the top element; equal to zero if
                 the stack is empty.

Figure 7.7 gives an illustration.
    There are four basic operations involved in using a stack.

1. *Clearing the stack.* This operation initializes the stack to be empty and defines the maximum stack size. It is accomplished with the statement

        CALL CLEAR(STACK, LIMIT)

    where STACK is the stack array, an integer array whose lower dimension bound is −1, and LIMIT is the stack size, an integer value not greater than the upper dimension bound of the array STACK.
2. *Determining if the stack is empty.* One could just as easily determine how many items are on the stack, but in practice it is usually sufficient to know whether or not the stack contains any items. The answer is given by the value of the logical function

        EMPTY(STACK)

    which is true if the stack is empty, and false otherwise.
3. Pushing a value onto the stack. The statement

        CALL PUSH(VALUE, STACK)

    stores the integer VALUE as the top item on STACK. If a stack overflow condition occurs, the subroutine will print an error message and stop the program.
4. Popping the top value. A reference to the integer function

        POP(STACK)

    will remove the top item from STACK and return it as the value of the function. If the stack is empty when the function is referenced, it will print an error message and stop the program.

FIGURE 7.7
FORTRAN DATA STRUCTURE FOR A STACK

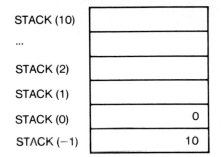

STACK (10)

...

STACK (2)

STACK (1)

STACK (0)   0

STACK (−1)   10

A stack initialized to indicate that it is empty
and can contain a maximum of 10 values

STACK (10)

...

STACK (2)

STACK (1)   1234

STACK (0)   1

STACK (−1)   10

State of the stack after pushing the value of 1234

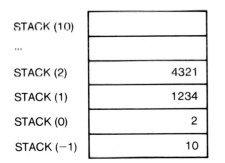

STACK (10)

...

STACK (2)   4321

STACK (1)   1234

STACK (0)   2

STACK (−1)   10

State of the stack after pushing the value of 4321

FORTRAN subprograms to carry out these operations can be written as follows.

```
      SUBROUTINE CLEAR(STACK, LIMIT)
* INITIALIZE THE STACK TO BE EMPTY.
      INTEGER STACK(-1: *), LIMIT
      STACK(-1) = LIMIT
      STACK(0) = 0
      END

      LOGICAL FUNCTION EMPTY(STACK)
```

```
* TRUE IF THE STACK IS EMPTY, FALSE OTHERWISE.
    INTEGER STACK(-1: *)
    EMPTY = STACK(0) .EQ. 0
    END


    SUBROUTINE PUSH(VALUE, STACK)
* PUSH THE INTEGER VALUE ONTO THE STACK.
    INTEGER VALUE, STACK(-1: *)
    IF (STACK(0) .GE. STACK(-1)) STOP 'STACK OVERFLOW'
    STACK(0) = STACK(0) + 1
    STACK(STACK(0)) = VALUE
    END


    INTEGER FUNCTION POP(STACK)
* POP THE TOP ITEM FROM THE STACK AND RETURN IT AS THE VALUE OF
* POP.
    INTEGER STACK(-1: *)
    IF (STACK(0) .LE. 0) STOP 'STACK UNDERFLOW'
    POP = STACK(STACK(0))
    STACK(0) = STACK(0) - 1
    END
```

STYLE MODULE—SUBPROGRAMS AND TOP-DOWN DESIGN

Subprograms are ideally suited to top-down program design. You begin by making an outline of your program. Each step in this top-level design is, in fact, a subprogram. If you can write precise specifications for a FORTRAN function or subroutine that carries out the step, then you can go ahead and write your main program, which will consist largely of CALL statements or function references.

The same method applies to writing each subprogram. If the subprogram involves many steps, approach it in a top-down fashion by specifying lower-level subprograms to carry out the steps. Eventually you reach a point where each step is so simple that you can easily write FORTRAN statements to carry it out. These are your bottom level subprograms.

Beginning programmers are sometimes reluctant to nest subprograms more than one level deep. That is, they will write a main program that calls several subroutines, but they hesitate to write subprograms that call other subprograms that call other subprograms. Of course, for a simple programming job, it is often unnecessary to nest subprograms more than one or two levels deep. But if you undertake a larger program, use as many levels of subroutines as necessary to carry out top-down design in a convenient manner. As a rule, it is better to write a large collection of short subprograms, nested several levels deep, than it is to write a small collection of large subprograms.

The following example illustrates this method in a program of moderate complexity.

EXAMPLE 7.14 Loan Payment Program
Suppose that amount of money A is borrowed at an interest rate R percent, to be paid back in N years. Let P be the annual payment. These quantities are related by the formula:

$$A = P \left(\frac{1 - \left(1 + \frac{R}{100}\right)^{-N}}{\frac{R}{100}} \right)$$

There are four variables in this formula. Write a program that reads values for any three of them and computes the value of the other one.

The input to this program will consist of four numbers, representing values of the four variables. For the unknown variable, you enter a value of zero. The other three values must be positive. The program should repeat the computation for as many data sets as you provide.

You can write a top-level design at once by observing that there are three logically independent steps in this program: reading the data, solving for the unknown value, and writing the results. The top-level outline, then, is as shown in Figure 7.8.

Without going any further in the program design, you can now write the FORTRAN main program, as shown below. In this program, we called the variables AMT, PMT, RATE, and YEARS, all of which are real variables. (By making YEARS a real variable, we allow for the possibility of a fractional number of years.)

```
* LOAN PAYMENT PROGRAM.
*
* THIS PROGRAM READS FOUR VALUES, CORRESPONDING TO THE VARI-
* ABLES:
*
* AMT      THE AMOUNT OF A LOAN (DOLLARS)
* PMT      THE ANNUAL PAYMENT (DOLLARS)
* RATE     THE ANNUAL INTEREST RATE (PERCENT — E.G.,
*          FOR 8 PERCENT, RATE = 8.0)
* YEARS    NUMBER OF YEARS OVER WHICH LOAN IS TO BE
*          REPAID
*
      REAL AMT, PMT, RATE, YEARS
* INPUT AND VERIFY THE DATA — STOP IF THERE IS NO MORE DATA.
10    CALL INPUT(AMT, PMT, RATE, YEARS)
* SOLVE FOR THE MISSING VARIABLE.
      CALL SOLVE(AMT, PMT, RATE, YEARS)
* OUTPUT THE RESULTS
      CALL OUTPUT(AMT, PMT, RATE, YEARS)
      GO TO 10
      END
```

To write the INPUT subroutine, you must decide on the form in which the data will be read. To keep this example simple, we will assume that the data is read from cards, so we can just use a READ statement. If the program were to run on a timesharing system, however, you might want a fancier version that asks questions to the user of the program and reads the responses to the questions. This is a major decision in writing this program. Because of the

FIGURE 7.8
LOAN PAYMENT PROGRAM—TOP-LEVEL DESIGN

Repeat:	
	Read values for the four variables. If the values, read are not legal values, write an error message and repeat this step. If there are no more data values, stop the program.
	Solve for the value of the unknown variable (the one for which a zero value was read).
	Output the results.

subroutine structure, the decision affects only the INPUT subroutine—the others would be the same in either case. This illustrates the principle of using subprograms to "hide" decisions, so that they can be changed later with the least effort.

Besides reading the data, the INPUT subroutine is supposed to check the data to make sure it is valid. The validity checking is really a separate task, and we can put it in a separate subprogram. We will use a logical function VALID which is true if its four arguments constitute a valid data set for the loan program. Figure 7.9 shows a top-level design for these subprograms.

FIGURE 7.9
INPUT AND VALID SUBPROGRAMS—TOP-LEVEL DESIGN

Subroutine: INPUT (AMT, PMT, RATE, YEARS)

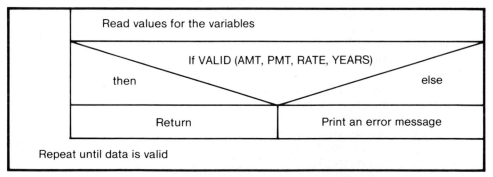

Logical funtion: VALID (AMT, PMT, RATE, YEARS)

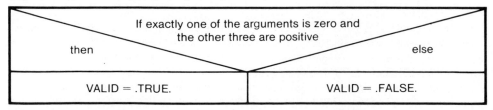

The INPUT subprogram can be written immediately.

```
* INPUT: READS THE DATA AND CHECKS FOR VALIDITY.
*
      SUBROUTINE INPUT(AMT, PMT, RATE, YEARS)
      REAL AMT, PMT, RATE, YEARS
      LOGICAL VALID
10    READ (*, *, END = 90) AMT, PMT, RATE, YEARS
      IF (.NOT. VALID(AMT, PMT, RATE, YEARS)) THEN
          PRINT *, 'INVALID DATA SET:', AMT, PMT, RATE, YEARS
          GO TO 10
      END IF
      RETURN
* AT THE END OF INPUT, STOP THE PROGRAM
90    STOP
      END
```

The VALID function is easy to write if you observe that the condition for validity is the same as the logical expression

(MIN(A,B,C,D) .GE. 0) .AND. (NZ .EQ. 1)

where A, B, C, and D are the four arguments, and NZ is the number of arguments that are equal to zero.

```
* VALID: THE VALUE OF THIS LOGICAL FUNCTION IS TRUE
* IF AND ONLY IF ONE OF THE FOUR ARGUMENTS IS
* ZERO AND THE OTHER THREE ARE POSITIVE
*
      LOGICAL FUNCTION (A, B, C, D)
      REAL A, B, C, D
      INTEGER NZ
* COUNT THE NUMBER OF ARGUMENTS THAT ARE ZERO.
      NZ = 0
      IF (A .EQ. 0) NZ = NZ + 1
      IF (B .EQ. 0) NZ = NZ + 1
      IF (C .EQ. 0) NZ = NZ + 1
      IF (D .EQ. 0) NZ = NZ + 1
* DATA IS VALID IF AND ONLY IF THE MINIMUM VALUE OF THE ARGUMENTS
* IS GREATER THAN OR EQUAL TO ZERO AND NZ = 1.
      VALID = (MIN(A, B, C, D) .GE. 0) .AND. (NZ .EQ. 1)
      END
```

The OUTPUT subroutine is quite simple. You can just write a series of PRINT statements to print the results, with titles.

```
* OUTPUT: OUTPUT THE RESULTS.
*
```

```
SUBROUTINE OUTPUT(AMT, PMT, RATE, YEARS)
REAL AMT, PMT, RATE, YEARS
PRINT *, 'AT AN INTEREST RATE OF ', RATE, ' PERCENT,'
PRINT *, 'A LOAN OF $', AMT
PRINT *, 'CAN BE PAID IN ', YEARS, ' YEARS'
PRINT *, 'WITH AN ANNUAL PAYMENT OF $', PMT
END
```

The subroutine SOLVE can assume that the data is valid, since that fact was checked in INPUT. Thus the value of exactly one argument to SOLVE is zero, and SOLVE must compute the value of that argument as a function of the other three. We will write SOLVE so that it simply references a function subprogram to carry out the small computation as in Figure 7.10.

```
* SOLVE: SOLVE FOR THE MISSING VARIABLE BY REFERENCING
* ONE OF FOUR FUNCTION SUBPROGRAMS.
*
      SUBROUTINE SOLVE(AMT, PMT, RATE, YEARS)
      REAL AMT, PMT, RATE, YEARS
      REAL FAMT, FPMT, FRATE, FYEARS
      IF (AMT .EQ. 0) THEN
          AMT = FAMT(PMT, RATE, YEARS)
      ELSE IF (PMT .EQ. 0) THEN
          PMT = FPMT(AMT, RATE, YEARS)
      ELSE IF (RATE .EQ. 0) THEN
          RATE = FRATE(AMT, PMT, YEARS)
      ELSE IF (YEARS .EQ. 0) THEN
          YEARS = FYEARS(AMT, PMT, RATE)
      ELSE
          PAUSE 'ERROR IN SOLVE SUBROUTINE'
      END IF
      END
```

FIGURE 7.10
SOLVE AND OUTPUT SUBPROGRAMS

Subroutine: SOLVE (AMT, PMT, RATE, YEARS)

If AMT = 0	Else If PMT = 0	Else If RATE = 0	Else If YEARS = 0	Else
AMT = FAMT (PMT, RATE, YEARS)	PMT = FPMT (AMT, RATE, YEARS)	RATE = FRATE (AMT, PMT, YEARS)	YEARS = FYEARS (AMT, PMT, RATE)	Error

Subroutine: OUTPUT (AMT, PMT, RATE, YEARS)

Print the values of the four arguments, with titles

Writing the functions FAMT, FPMT, FRATE, and FYEARS involves a little mathematics, since not all the required formulas were given as part of the problem. Deriving the formulas is not necessarily the programmer's job. On a large programming project, that sort of work might be done by a systems analyst. The important point to note is that by using subprograms, we have separated the mathematical analysis from the rest of the program. All we needed to know was that each of the four variables could be written as a function of the other three.

The formulas for the amount and the payment both involve an expression known as the *present worth factor*, which we can write as a function of the interest rate and the number of years:

$$\text{Amount} = \text{Payment} \times \text{Present Worth Factor}$$

and

$$\text{Payment} = \frac{\text{Amount}}{\text{Present Worth Factor}}$$

where

$$\textit{Present Worth Factor} = \frac{1 - \left(1 + \dfrac{Rate}{100}\right)^{-N}}{\dfrac{Rate}{100}}$$

In FORTRAN, we can write these functions as follows.

```
* FAMT: SOLVE FOR AMOUNT.
*
      REAL FUNCTION FAMT(PMT, RATE, YEARS)
      REAL PMT, RATE, YEARS, PWF
      FAMT = PMT *PWF(RATE, YEARS)
      END
* FPMT: SOLVE FOR PAYMENT.
*
      REAL FUNCTION FPMT(AMT, RATE, YEARS)
      REAL AMT, RATE, YEARS, PWF
      FPMT = AMT / PWF(RATE, YEARS)
      END
* PWF: COMPUTE THE PRESENT WORTH FACTOR AS A FUNCTION
* OF THE INTEREST RATE (IN PERCENT) AND NUMBER OF YEARS.
      REAL FUNCTION PWF (RATE, N)
      REAL RATE, N, R
      R = RATE/100
      PWF = (1 - (1 + R)**(-N))/R
      END
```

The formula for the number of years is:

$$\text{Number of Years} = \frac{\log\left(\dfrac{\text{Payment}}{\text{Payment} - \dfrac{\text{Amount} \times \text{Rate}}{100}}\right)}{\log\left(1 + \dfrac{\text{Rate}}{100}\right)}$$

In FORTRAN, we can write the FYEARS function as follows.

```
* FYEARS: SOLVE FOR THE NUMBER OF YEARS.
*
      REAL FUNCTION FYEARS(AMT, PMT, RATE)
      REAL AMT, PMT, RATE
      FYEARS = LOG(PMT/(PMT - AMT*RATE/100)) /
     $            LOG(1 + RATE/100)
      END
```

That leaves one more subprogram: FRATE. It turns out that solving for the interest rate is substantially more difficult than solving for the other three quantities. There is no simple formula you can use. In fact, the problem is essentially one of finding the root of a polynomial. A simple way to deal with this is to have the subprogram just print a message, assign the value zero to FRATE, then return.

```
* FRATE: SOLVE FOR THE INTEREST RATE.
* NOTE—THIS FUNCTION HAS NOT BEEN FULLY IMPLEMENTED
* IN THIS VERSION.
      REAL FUNCTION FRATE(AMT, PMT, YEARS)
      REAL AMT, PMT, YEARS
      PRINT *, 'SOLVING FOR THE INTEREST RATE IS NOT YET'
     $    //' SUPPORTED BY THIS PROGRAM.'
      FRATE = 0
      END
```

TOP-DOWN TESTING

A subprogram like FRATE in Example 7.14, which simply pretends to do its job, is sometimes called a **stub**. You can use stubs as we did in Example 7.14 to write a program in stages: a method called **top-down testing**.

The idea of top-down testing is to check your program as you write it. You begin by writing your main program, and perhaps your top-level subprograms, in FOR-TRAN. Instead of completing the lower-level subprograms, however, you just write them as stubs. Perhaps each such stub will just contain a PRINT statement to print out a message saying that it has been called. Then you can run the program, with the stubs, to check out the top level of your work. When the top level is debugged, you replace each stub with the completed subprogram.

The advantage of top-down testing is that once you have debugged the top levels of your program, you can forget about them and concentrate your attention on writing the lower level subprograms. In filling in the stubs, you never have to change any of the subprograms that call them. Thus, you check out and debug your program in the same top-down order in which you write it.

SUBPROGRAM STRUCTURE DIAGRAMS

It is often useful to supplement structured flowcharts with a diagram showing the relationships of the subprograms. The common method is to represent each program or subprogram by a rectangular box and to draw a line between boxes to represent a subroutine call or a function reference. Thus, if a main program calls subroutine A, the relation is shown as in Figure 7.11. If a main program calls subroutines A and B, and if subroutine A calls subroutines C and D, the diagram would look like Figure 7.12. Figure 7.13 shows a diagram for the program of Example 7.14.

FIGURE 7.11
SUBPROGRAM STRUCTURE DIAGRAM

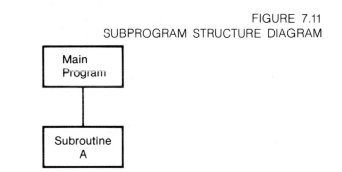

In subprogram structure diagram, individual program units are represented by boxes. Lines connect the boxes to show subroutine calls or function references.

FIGURE 7.12

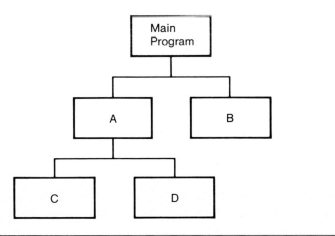

This diagram indicates that the main program calls subprogram A and B, while subprogram A calls subprograms C and D.

FIGURE 7.13
SUBPROGRAM STRUCTURE OF THE LOAN PAYMENT PROGRAM

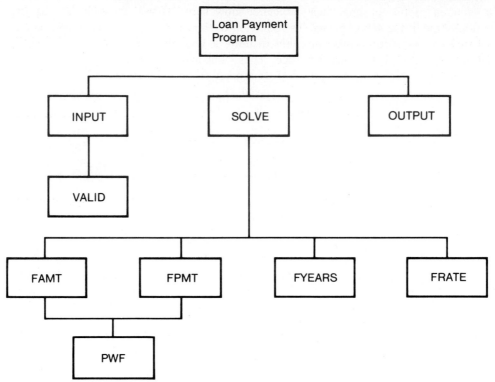

This kind of **subprogram structure diagram** does not show anything about the logic of the subprograms, but it clearly illustrates their relationship to each other. When beginning a large or a moderately large program, you should make a subprogram structure diagram and a top-level structured flowchart for each subprogram before doing anything else. When this overall design is done, you will be on the road to a well-structured program.

SUMMARY

Intrinsic functions are provided in FORTRAN for many common mathematical calculations such as square root and trigonometric sine. To use an intrinsic function, you write a function reference as part of an expression. The function reference consists of the function name and one or more arguments, enclosed in parentheses. You must supply the correct number of arguments, and they must be of the correct type. Intrinsic functions have specific names and generic names. When you reference an intrinsic function with the generic name, the FORTRAN compiler will determine the type of the function from the type of the arguments.

A function subprogram is an independent program unit—that is, it is compiled separately from the main program and other program units. Statement labels in the subprogram are independent of statement labels in any other program unit, as are the variables—except for the dummy arguments. You reference a programmer-defined function the same way you reference an intrinsic function. The actual arguments in the function reference replace the dummy arguments when the subprogram is executed. As with intrinsic functions, the number and types of the actual arguments must agree with the number and types of the dummy arguments. A function may change the value of an argument, in which case the actual argument must be a variable.

In a main program, an END statement acts like a STOP statement, but in a subprogram, an END statement acts like a RETURN, causing control to return to the calling program unit. In a function subprogram, the value of the function must be defined before the function returns.

A subroutine subprogram is like a function, except that it returns no value and is invoked by a CALL statement.

Subprograms are a valuable tool in top-down structured programming. Often, each step in a top-level program design can be written as a separate subprogram. By writing short subprograms, each having a well-defined purpose, you can break a large problem into small, manageable parts. You can also use subprograms to hide decisions that might change, thus making the program easier to modify. By implementing the subprograms in stages, using stubs where necessary, you can carry out top-down testing to check out a program in a structured way.

VOCABULARY

actual argument
agreement of argument types
arithmetic overflow
CALL statement
dummy argument
function
function name
function reference
FUNCTION statement
generic function name
intrinsic function
main program
output argument
program unit

pseudorandom number
recursive function
RETURN statement
side effect
specific function name
stub
subprogram
subprogram structure diagram
subroutine
SUBROUTINE statement
top-down testing
type of a function
value of a function

|||||||||||||||||||||||||||||||||||||||||||||||||||||||||||||||||||||||||||||||||||||||||||||||||||||||||

EXERCISES

1. Some of the following intrinsic function references are legal, and some are not. Which are which? If illegal, give the reason.
   - (a)   SQRT(100)
   - (b)   MIN(2,3,4)
   - (c)   ABS(−0)
   - (d)   ABS(1.0, 2.0)
   - (e)   SIN(1)
   - (f)   EXP(2.0, 2.0)
   - (g)   MIN(1.2, 2)
   - (h)   REAL(5)

2. What is the value of each of the following intrinsic function references? Give the type of the value.
   - (a)   ABS(−1.2)
   - (b)   SQRT(9.0)
   - (c)   MIN(2.0, 3.0, −1.0)
   - (d)   MAX(0, −1, −2)
   - (e)   INT(11.11)
   - (f)   REAL(10)
   - (g)   MOD(7, 3)
   - (h)   LEN('RULER')

3. Write a single FORTRAN assignment statement to perform each of the following instructions.
   - (a)   Let X equal the smallest of the numbers A, B, and C.
   - (b)   Let N equal the smallest integer greater than the square root of A.
   - (c)   Let X equal the fractional part of the number A (therefore, if A = 3.1416, let X = 0.1416).
   - (d)   Let N = 0 if M is an even integer, or N = 1 if M is an odd integer.
   - (e)   Let X equal the square root of A, if A is positive; otherwise, let X equal zero.
   - (f)   If the length of the character variable C is less than 5, let N equal 5; if the length of C is greater than 20, let N equal 20; otherwise, let N equal the length of C.
   - (g)   Let PI equal the value of π (using an intrinsic function reference).

Note: Exercises 4 to 8 require some familiarity with basic trigonometry.

4. If X and Y are the coordinates of a point in the plane, then the **polar coordinates**, r and θ, are equal to the distance of the point from the origin and the angle from the positive x-axis to the line from the origin to the point as in the figure at the top of page 281. Write function subprograms

   RADIUS(X, Y)

   and

   ANGLE(X, Y)

   to compute these polar coordinates.

5. Write a function subprogram DMS of three arguments, that converts an angle in degrees, minutes, and seconds to degrees. For example, 32° 40m 12s = 32.67°, so DMS (32., 40., 12.) should equal 32.67.

6. Write a function RADIAN(ANGLE) that converts an angle in degrees to radian measure and a function DEGREE(ANGLE) that converts an angle from radians to degrees.

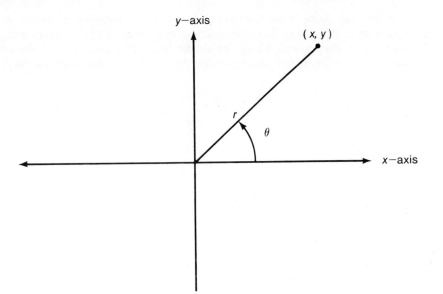

7. In the triangle shown below, if you know the values of angles A and B and the length of side C, you can find the other quantities using the formulas

$$A + B + C = 180°$$

and

$$\frac{\sin A}{a} = \frac{\sin B}{b} = \frac{\sin C}{c} \qquad \text{Law of Sines}$$

Write a subroutine ASA (for Angle Side Angle) such that the subroutine call

CALL ASA(SIDE A, SIDE B, SIDE C, ANGLE A, ANGLE B, ANGLE C)

will use the values of SIDE C, ANGLE A, and ANGLE B to store the correct values in the other three arguments. All angles should be in degrees.

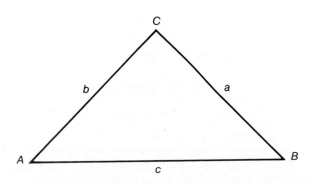

8. Use the subroutine from Exercise 7 to solve the following problem. A surveyor measured a distance of 50 meters along a line 2 meters from a river bank. A tree, 2 meters from the opposite shore, formed angles of 48° and 67.5° with the ends of the measured line as in the accompanying figure. What is the width of the river?

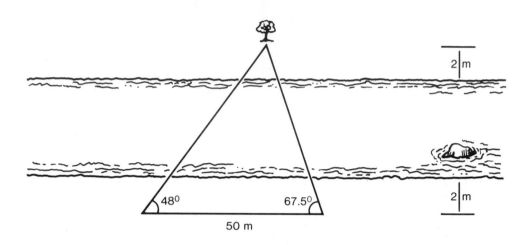

9. The **greatest common divisor** of two positive integers M and N is the largest number that divides both of them. For example, the greatest common divisor of 15 and 25 is 5, because 5 divides both 15 and 25, but no larger number does. **Euclid's algorithm**, one of the oldest algorithms in mathematics, is a famous method for computing the greatest common divisor. The procedure is shown in the accompanying structured flowchart. Write an integer function GCD of two integer arguments that computes their greatest common divisor by Euclid's algorithm. Write the function in such a way that it does *not* alter the values of its arguments. Write a test program and run it.

Euclid's Algorithm for Finding the GCD of M and N

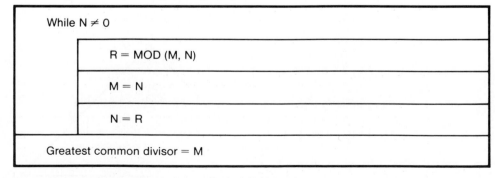

10. The **binary** (base 2) **number system** is a system of counting that uses only the digits 0 and 1. For example, the numbers 1 through 10 in binary notation are as follows:

```
 1 =    1 (binary)
 2 =   10 (binary)
 3 =   11 (binary)
 4 =  100 (binary)
 5 =  101 (binary)
 6 =  110 (binary)
 7 =  111 (binary)
 8 = 1000 (binary)
 9 = 1001 (binary)
10 = 1010 (binary)
```

Write a character-valued function

BINARY(N)

that returns a character string containing the binary representation of the integer N. The basic algorithm is shown in the accompanying structured flowchart.

Algorithm to set BINARY equal to a character string
giving the binary representation of N

Write the function subprogram to return a value of type CHARACTER*(*). The subprogram should not change the value of its argument. Also, include instructions to make sure that the substring expression for binary is never out of range. Finally, add instructions so that if N is negative, the function will return the correct value, preceded by a minus sign. Test the subprogram by running a main program that prints the binary representation of the numbers −10 through 129.

11. To **right-justify** a string means to insert blank spaces on the left so that the nonblank part of the string is flush with a right margin. For example, the string 'FORTRAN 77,' right-justified in a variable of 15 characters, would appear as shown below:

Write a CHARACTER*(*) function

RJUST(STRING, N)

where STRING is a character value, and N is an integer value, that returns the value of STRING right-justified so that the last nonblank character of STRING is in character number N. Include checks to insure that no substring expression is out of range.

12. To **center** a string means to insert blank spaces on the left and right so that the nonblank part is in the center of a sequence of character storage units. For example, the string 'FORTRAN 77,' centered in a variable of 15 characters, would appear as shown below:

Write a CHARACTER*(*) function

CENTER(STRING, N)

where STRING is a character value and N is an integer value, that returns the value of STRING centered in a sequence of N character storage units. Include checks so that no substring expression is out of range. Write a test program that reads input lines and prints them centered on the output page.

13. Write an integer function subprogram

COMBIN(N, K)

that computes the number of combinations of N things taken K at a time (see Exercise 13, Chapter 4). The formula is

$$\frac{N!}{K!(N - K)!}$$

Include statements to check that the arguments are valid. Write a test program that prints values of the function for N = 0 to 10 and K = 0 to N.

14. Using the RANDOM function from Example 6.7, write an integer function

NRAND(I, J, SEED)

that returns an integer value between I and J, inclusive, using SEED as in Example 7.7. For example,

NRAND(1, 6, SEED)

represents an integer number randomly chosen from 1 to 6. This could simulate the roll of a single die. The function should not modify the integer arguments I and J. Use the NRAND function to simulate 100 tosses of a coin by printing 100 random 0's and 1's. Is there any obvious pattern of the results? Have the program count the total number of 0's and 1's.

15. Suppose that someone made the following claim? "When you flip a coin and it comes up heads twice in a row, the chances are that it will come up heads the next time too." You can test this hypothesis with a computer simulation, as follows. Using the NRAND function from Exercise 14, simulate 1000 coin tosses. Count the number of times the "coin" comes up heads twice in a row. Each time it does, count the number of times the following coin toss is heads. Do the results support the claim?

16. The **octal** (base 8) **number system** uses the digits 0 through 7 to represent numbers. The following list shows decimal and octal equivalents of the numbers 1 to 18.

Decimal Number	Octal Number	Decimal Number	Octal Number
1	1	10	12
2	2	11	13
3	3	12	14
4	4	13	15
5	5	14	16
6	6	15	17
7	7	16	20
8	10	17	21
9	11	18	22

Write an integer function OCTAL(N) that returns an integer whose digits give the octal representation of the decimal integer N. For example, the value of OCTAL(17) is 21. The algorithm shown in the figure on page 286 uses a *stack* to store values. Use the subroutines and functions from Example 7.13. Write a test program for the OCTAL function by printing a decimal to octal conversion table for the numbers 1 through 200.

Function OCTAL (N)

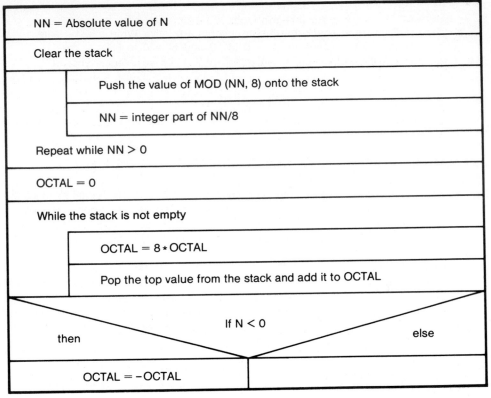

17. A **buffer** is a data structure for storing values in first-in-first-out (FIFO) order. It is called a buffer because it is an intermediate storage area where data is kept prior to being used by some other routine. In FORTRAN, a buffer of integer values can be represented by an array declared by

INTEGER BUFFER (−2:LIMIT)

Array elements

BUFFER(1), BUFFER(2), . . . , BUFFER(LIMIT)

provide storage for the values. Let

BUFFER(0) = LIMIT

to indicate the maximum amount of available buffer space. The other two elements are pointers, used as follows.

BUFFER(−2) = output pointer—this is the subscript of the first value to remove from the buffer

BUFFER(−1) = input pointer—this is the subscript of the first location available for putting a value into the buffer

The output pointer and the input pointer are always greater than or equal to 1 and less than or equal to LIMIT. When the output pointer is equal to the input pointer, it indicates that the buffer is empty. In the accompanying figure, OUT and IN represent the output and input pointers, and the shaded area represents data stored in the buffer.

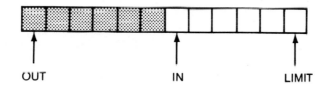

Write a subroutine

RESET(BUFFER, LIMIT)

that initializes a buffer, as described above, by setting the limit pointer to LIMIT and setting output and input pointers to 1, indicating an empty buffer.

18. Write a subroutine PUT(VALUE, BUFFER) that stores the integer value VALUE in BUFFER, which is a buffer as described in Exercise 17. The algorithm is shown in the accompanying figure.

ALGORITHM TO STORE A VALUE IN A BUFFER,
WHERE IN IS THE INPUT POINTER

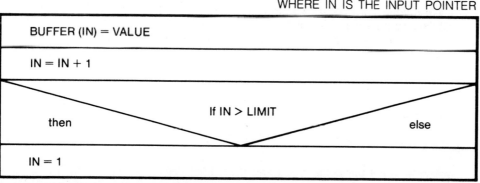

19. Write an integer function TAKE(BUFFER) that removes the next value from BUFFER, and returns it as the value of the function. BUFFER is a buffer as described in Exercise 17. The algorithm is shown in the figure on page 288.

ALGORITHM TO TAKE A VALUE FROM A BUFFER,
WHERE OUT AND IN ARE THE OUTPUT AND INPUT POINTERS

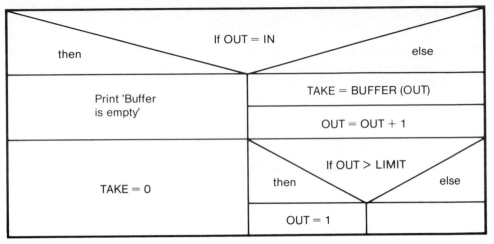

20. It is often convenient to treat character values as integers. The intrinsic function ICHAR(C) returns an integer code for the character C. Write an integer function

    GET(BUFFER)

    that does the following. Let BUFFER be a buffer as described in Exercise 17. If the buffer is empty, read a line of input as a character variable. Convert each character to an integer value, using the ICHAR function, and put each integer value in BUFFER, using the PUT subroutine from Exercise 18. If an end-of-file condition was encountered in the read, put the value -1 in the buffer, indicating an end of file. Now use the TAKE function from Exercise 19 to remove one value from the buffer and return it as the value of the GET function.

21. Write an integer function

    NBUF(BUFFER)

    whose value is the number of items currently stored in BUFFER, which is a buffer data structure as described in Exercise 17. Write a logical function

    FULL(BUFFER)

    which is true if the buffer is full and false otherwise.

22. Exercise 15 in Chapter 6 showed an algorithm for computing prime numbers. A modified version of this algorithm will print all the prime numbers that are less than $P(MAXLEN)**2$, where MAXLEN is the size of the array P that stores the primes. In this algorithm, LIMIT is the value of the greatest number to be tested for primeness by the program. The algorithm is shown in the structured flowchart on page 289. Use the subprograms you wrote in Exercises 17 to 20 for the buffer operations. Run the program with MAXLEN $= 25$ and LIMIT $= 10,000$.

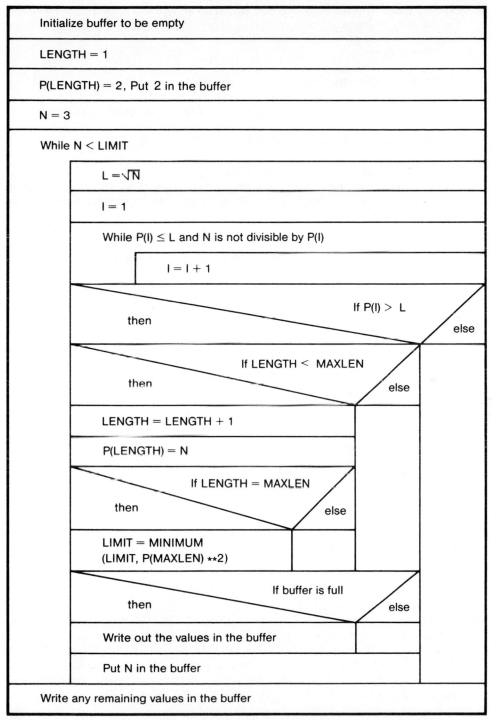

Initialize buffer to be empty

LENGTH = 1

P(LENGTH) = 2, Put 2 in the buffer

N = 3

While N < LIMIT

L = √N̄

I = 1

While P(I) ≤ L and N is not divisible by P(I)

I = I + 1

If P(I) > L

then   else

If LENGTH < MAXLEN

then   else

LENGTH = LENGTH + 1

P(LENGTH) = N

If LENGTH = MAXLEN

then   else

LIMIT = MINIMUM
(LIMIT, P(MAXLEN) **2)

If buffer is full

then   else

Write out the values in the buffer

Put N in the buffer

Write any remaining values in the buffer

23. Example 6.3 of Chapter 6 showed how to sort an array using pointers. Suppose that A is an array of character data containing N or more elements. Let POINTR be an integer array of N or more elements.

    Write a subroutine

    SORTP(A, N, POINTR)

    that stores the integers 1 to N in the array POINTR in an order such that

    A(POINTR(1)), A(POINTR(2)), A(POINTR(3)), . . . , A(POINTR(N))

    are in alphabetical order. Use the Shell Sort algorithm described in Example 7.11. Use the intrinsic function LLT for comparing the character array elements. Test your subroutine by writing a program that reads up to 200 input cards and prints them in alphabetical order.

FORMATTED
INPUT AND OUTPUT

INTRODUCTION In previous chapters we have been using **list-directed** READ and PRINT statements, so called because they simply read or print a list of values. These forms have the advantage of being easy to use, but they have a major limitation: They give the programmer no control over the format of the input or output line. For example, how can you print a real number so that it has exactly one decimal place? Or, how can you read an integer number from columns 5–10 of a card? To specify these details of input and output you must use a **format specification**.

The **formatted READ statement** and the **formatted PRINT statement** are used in conjuncton with a **FORMAT statement** which contains a list of **edit descriptors**. The edit descriptors specify how each variable is read or written. The main hurdle in understanding formatted input and output is understanding the function of each of the various types of edit descriptors.

THE FORMATTED PRINT AND READ STATEMENTS

In a list-directed PRINT statement such as

        PRINT *, 'THE ANSWER IS' , X

the asterisk after the word PRINT is a **format identifier** that specifies list-directed editing. The **formatted PRINT statement** has the same form, except that in place of the asterisk, you write the statement label of a **FORMAT statement**. An example is

        PRINT 75, N, A
    75 FORMAT(I4, F16.2)

The format identifier in this case is the number 75, which is the statement label of the following FORMAT statement. It is the FORMAT statement that describes how the variables N and A are to be printed.

293

The symbol

(I4, F16.2)

in the FORMAT statement is the **format specification** for the print lines. The symbol

I4

is an **edit descriptor** which says that the value of N will be printed as a four-digit integer. The second edit descriptor,

F16.2

says that the value of A will be printed in a field of 16 characters with 2 digits to the right of the decimal point. The **output list** of the formatted PRINT is a list of variables or expressions, separated by commas, just as for the list-directed PRINT. In the statement

PRINT 1000, A, B, (A + B)/2

the output list consists of two variables and an expression. Figure 8.1 shows the parts of the PRINT and FORMAT statements.

An example of a **formatted READ statement** is

```
        READ 10, SPEED
10      FORMAT(20X, F5.2)
```

FIGURE 8.1

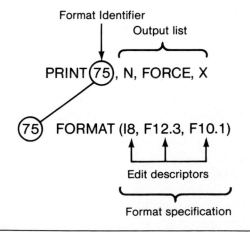

The variables in the output list will be printed according to the format specification. The statement number after the word "PRINT" tells which FORMAT statement to use.

This says to read the variable SPEED using FORMAT statement number 10. The edit descriptor

   20X

means to skip 20 spaces in the input line. The edit descriptor

   F5.2

means to read a five-digit real number with two decimal places. Thus the statements read the value of SPEED from columns 21–25 of the input line.

   Another form of formatted READ is illustrated by the statements

```
        READ(*, 10, END = 900) SPEED
   10   FORMAT(20X, F5.2)
```

There are three items within the parentheses of the READ. The asterisk is the **unit identifier**, which says to read from the default input unit—usually the card reader or the terminal. The number 10 is the format identifier, which says to use FORMAT statement number 10. The symbol END = 900 is the **end-of-file specifier** that says to go to statement 900 if there is no more input data. Both forms of the formatted READ are illustrated in Figure 8.2.

THE FORMAT STATEMENT

The FORMAT statement is nonexecutable. That is, like the INTEGER and REAL statements, it does not cause any machine action by itself. The READ and PRINT statements are executable, but the FORMAT statement just supplies information about how the reading or printing is to be done. You can put the FORMAT statements anywhere in your program or subprogram, except in front of IMPLICIT statements. Some programmers put all the FORMAT statements at the end of the program, just before the END line. Others prefer to put each FORMAT statement right after the READ or PRINT statement that uses it. We will follow the latter style.

   It is legal to use the same FORMAT statement for several READ or PRINT instructions. Thus, you could write

   PRINT 1000, APPLE

and

   PRINT 1000, BAKER

in the same program to print two variables using the same output format. As a matter of style, it is generally preferable to use a different FORMAT statement for each READ or PRINT, even if the format specifications happen to be the same.

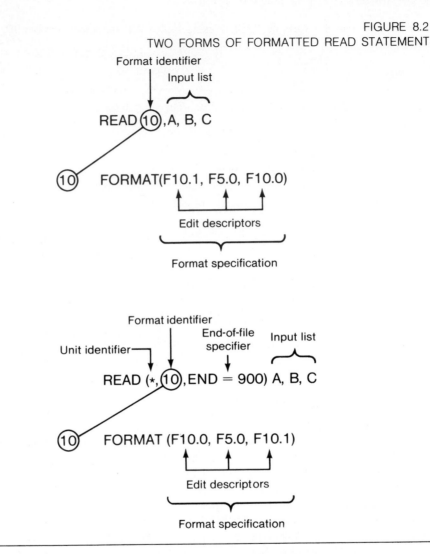

FIGURE 8.2
TWO FORMS OF FORMATTED READ STATEMENT

These two forms of the formatted READ statement are equivalent, except that the second form contains an end-of-file specifier that transfers control to statement 900 when there is no more input data.

INPUT AND OUTPUT FIELDS

You can think of each print line as being composed of a sequence of **output fields**. An output field is just a consecutive sequence of print columns. Figure 8.3 shows the number 37.0 printed in an output field of seven columns.

When describing output fields, blank spaces count as characters. Thus, we would say that the output field in Figure 8.3 consists of seven characters: three blank spaces, three digits, and a decimal point.

FIGURE 8.3
A FIELD IS A GROUP OF COLUMNS

Output field

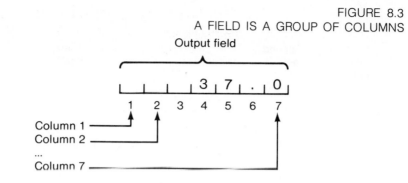

Column 1
Column 2
...
Column 7

Figure 8.4 shows a print line with three output fields: a field of eight characers (columns 1–8), followed by a field of 12 characters (columns 9–20), followed by a field of 10 characters (columns 21–30).

Similarly, you can think of an input line as a sequence of **input fields**, each field being a sequence of consecutive columns as read from the punch card or computer terminals. Figure 8.5 shows a punch card divided into three input fields.

When you prepare data to be input by a formatted read, you usually prepare each line in the same format so that each input value is always in the same field. Thus in Figure 8.5, the third item to be read would always be keypunched in columns 51–60 of the card. On punch cards, the columns are labeled so that you can see by looking at the card what columns a value is keypunched in. On a computer terminal, the columns generally are not labeled, but the principle is the same. Some terminals can be set up to tab to certain columns automatically, making it easy to align data in input fields.

The following sections explain the basic edit descriptors used in a FORMAT statement. There are two kinds: *repeatable* and *nonrepeatable*. The reason for these

FIGURE 8.4
A PRINT LINE WITH THREE OUTPUT FIELDS

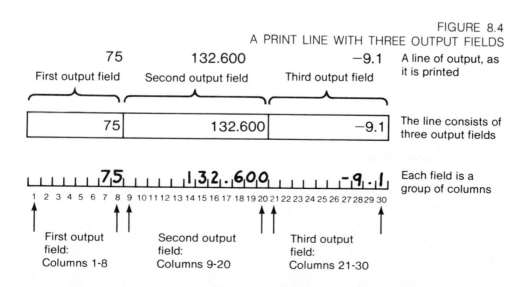

75   132.600   −9.1   A line of output, as
First output field   Second output field   Third output field   it is printed

75 | 132.600 | −9.1   The line consists of
                         three output fields

75   132.600   −9.1   Each field is a
                          group of columns
1 2 3 4 5 6 7 8 9 10 11 12 13 14 15 16 17 18 19 20 21 22 23 24 25 26 27 28 29 30

First output   Second output   Third output
field: field: field:
Columns 1-8   Columns 9-20   Columns 21-30

FIGURE 8.5
AN INPUT CARD

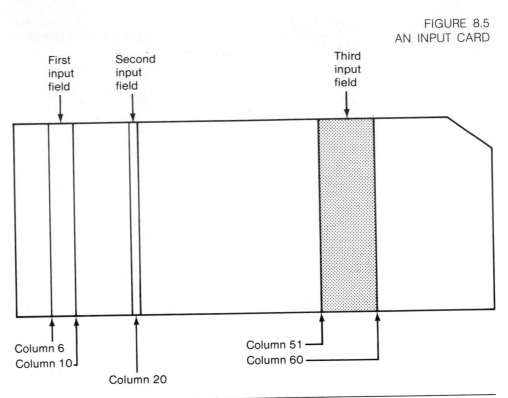

For formatted input, each input card is considered a sequence of input fields; each field is a certain group of columns from which a number is to be read. In this figure, the first field is columns 6–10; the second field is column 20; and the third field is columns 51–60.

names will become clear later, when we discuss repeat factors. The basic **repeatable edit descriptors** are:

I for integer data
F for real data
E for real data in exponential form
A for character data
L for logical data

The basic **nonrepeatable edit descriptors** are:

'string' for writing character constants
X for skipping spaces

Each edit descriptor specifies the form of one input or output field. A repeatable edit descriptor describes a field corresponding to some item in the input or output list

FIGURE 8.6

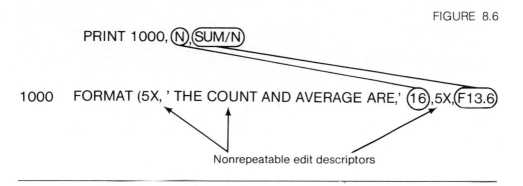

Nonrepeatable edit descriptors

The first item in the output list, N, will be printed according to the first repeatable edit descriptor, I6; the second item in the output list will be printed according to the second repeatable edit descriptor. The other edit descriptors in the format specification are nonrepeatable, and do not correspond to items in the output list.

of the READ or PRINT statement. A nonrepeatable edit descriptor does not correspond to any item in the input or output list. For example, Figure 8.6 shows a PRINT statement with two items in the output list and a FORMAT statement with five edit descriptors. The first value, N, is printed according to the first repeatable edit descriptor, I6; the second value, SUM/N, is printed according to the second repeatable edit descriptor, F13.6.

We will cover this topic in more detail after explaining the basic edit descriptors.

THE I EDIT DESCRIPTOR

To describe an integer field you use an **I edit descriptor**. For example

I6

means an integer field of six characters. To print a variable K in an I6 field, you could use the statements

```
      PRINT 75, K
75    FORMAT(I6)
```

On output, the number is always written in the rightmost characters of the field. A negative number is preceded by a minus sign which is printed immediately before the first digit (Figure 8.7).

Table 8.1 gives some examples.

TABLE 8.1
AN I6 EDIT DESCRIPTOR PRODUCES AN OUTPUT FIELD
OF SIX CHARACTERS, INCLUDING BLANK SPACES

PRINT 75, K
75   FORMAT(I6)

Values of Variable	Number Printed						
	Column	1	2	3	4	5	6
123					1	2	3
−123				−	1	2	3
−12					−	1	2
0							0
23444			2	3	4	4	4
−7650			−	7	6	5	0
9							9

On input, the I edit descriptor means to read an integer value. For example,

I4

means an integer field of four characters. The statements

        READ 1000, ITEM
1000 FORMAT(I4)

mean to read the value of the integer variable ITEM from the first four columns of the input data line.

An integer input value must not have a decimal point. A positive value can optionally be preceded by a plus sign. A negative value must be preceded by a minus sign. The number should be right-justified in the field. Thus, to read the number 12

FIGURE 8.7

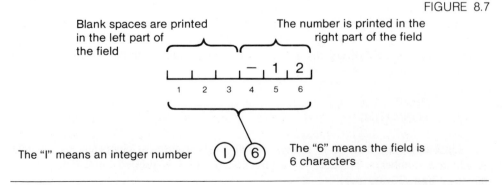

An I6 edit descriptor means to print an integer number right-justified in a field of 6 characters.

TABLE 8.2
AN I6 EDIT DESCRIPTOR MEANS TO READ
AN INTEGER NUMBER FROM SIX COLUMNS

Input Field						Value Read
Column 1	2	3	4	5	6	
			1	0	0	100
0	0	0	1	0	0	100
−	0	5	4	3	2	−5432
−					8	−8
	+		1	0	0	100
						0

TABLE 8.3
BLANK SPACES ARE TREATED AS ZEROS EVERYWHERE
IN THE INPUT FIELD—EVEN TO THE RIGHT OF THE NUMBER

Input Field						Value Read
Column 1	2	3	4	5	6	
			5			500
			5	0	0	500
	5					500000
		−	1	1		−110
	1		1		1	10101

from an I4 field, you should type two blank spaces followed by the digits 12. If you type the digits 12 followed by two blank spaces, the value would be read as 1200, since blank spaces are interpreted as zeros in an input field.* Tables 8.2 and 8.3 give some more examples.

Another form of the I edit descriptor is I$w.m$, where w and m are integer numbers. The first number gives the field width, and the second number gives the minimum number of digits to be printed. An example is

I9.4

On input, this is equivalent to an I9 edit descriptor. On output, the function is nearly the same, except that the number written will always have four digits, not counting any possible minus sign. Leading zeros would be added if necessary to make the output four digits long. Table 8.4 gives some further examples.

*Unless you use the BN edit descriptor, see page 317.

TABLE 8.4
THE I w.m DESCRIPTOR PRODUCES OUTPUT OF AT
LEAST m DIGITS IN A FIELD OF WIDTH w

Value	Edit Descriptor	Column 1	2	3	4	5
12	I5.3			0	1	2
−12	I5.3		−	0	1	2
0	I5.3			0	0	0
−1234	I5.3	−	1	2	3	4
1234	I5.3		1	2	3	4
1234	I5.5	0	1	2	3	4
0	I5.5	0	0	0	0	0
123	I5.2			1	2	3
0	I5.0					

THE F EDIT DESCRIPTOR

You use an **F edit descriptor** for printing real numbrs. (Think of the "F" as standing for "floating-point.") The F descriptor uses two numbers: one to tell how many characters in the field, and one to tell how many decimal places to print. The form is

Fw.m

where w and m are numbers: w is the width of the field, and m is the number of decimal places.

For example,

F9.4

means a nine-character field with four digits to the right of the decimal point. The statements

```
        X = −273.160
        PRINT 100, X
100  FORMAT(F10.2)
```

will produce the output shown in Figure 8.8.

In the computer memory, real numbers are stored as accurately as possible for the machine—typically with seven-place accuracy. When you print a real number, it is *rounded* to the correct number of digits. For instance, if you print the number 0.37 with an F6.1 edit descriptor, the output is

bbb0.4

FIGURE 8.8

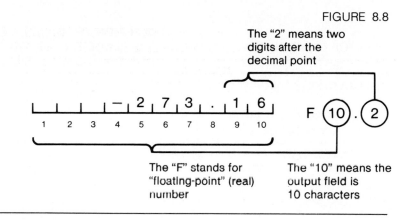

The "2" means two digits after the decimal point

The "F" stands for "floating-point" (real) number

The "10" means the output field is 10 characters

An F10.2 edit descriptor means to print a real number right-justified in a field of 10 characters, with two decimal places.

(where "b" stands for blank). Since the F6.1 says to print one digit to the right of the decimal point, the number 0.37 is rounded to 0.4. This is also illustrated by the following program, which prints the same number four ways.

```
        REAL W
11      FORMAT(F9.4)
        PRINT 11, W
        PRINT 22, W
        PRINT 33, W
        PRINT 44, W
22      FORMAT(F8.3)
33      FORMAT(F7.2)
        STOP
44      FORMAT(F6.1)
        END
```

This produces the following output:

```
0.3535
0.354
0.35
0.4
```

which is the value 0.3535 rounded to 4, 3, 2, and 1 places. This program illustrates again the fact that FORMAT statements are nonexecutable. For example, FORMAT 11 is *not* the first statement executed in the above program; the FORMAT is not executed at all. Likewise, after the statement

```
    PRINT 44, W
```

TABLE 8.5
AN F8.3 EDIT DESCRIPTOR PRODUCES AN OUTPUT FIELD
OF EIGHT CHARACTERS, INCLUDING BLANK SPACES, WITH THREE DIGITS
TO THE RIGHT OF THE DECIMAL POINT

FORTRAN Statements:

```
      PRINT 30, DELTA
30    FORMAT (F8.3)
```

Value of DELTA	*Number Printed*							
Column	1	2	3	4	5	6	7	8
21.3			2	1	.	3	0	0
5.0				5	.	0	0	0
−2.34567			−	2	.	3	4	6
−0.01			−	0	.	0	1	0
−50.0		−	5	0	.	0	0	0
−1234.0	*	*	*	*	*	*	*	*
0.0005				0	.	0	0	1
0.00005				0	.	0	0	0
0.				0	.	0	0	0

the next statement to be executed is

STOP

The intervening FORMAT statements have no effect on the flow of control.

Table 8.5 shows some examples of output printed in an F8.3 field.

As you saw before, several values can be printed on one line. The statements in the following example print four values on a line.

```
      INTEGER I
      REAL X, Y
      I = −10
      X = 2.0
      Y = 2.0/3.0
      PRINT 105, X, I, Y, I
105   FORMAT(F10.4, I10, F10.4, I10)
```

The output is shown in Figure 8.9.

When used for input, the F edit descriptor has the same form: F$w.m$. The number w tells the size of the input field. The number m tells where to *assume* a decimal point if one is not present in the input field.

You can keypunch a real number as a sequence of digits with a decimal point,

FIGURE 8.9
A LINE OF OUTPUT CONSISTING OF FOUR FIELDS

FORTRAN Statements:

PRINT 105, X,I,Y,I
105   **FORMAT (F10.4, I10, F10.4, I10)**

Output:

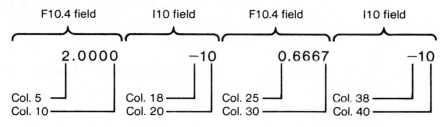

| F10.4 field | I10 field | F10.4 field | I10 field |

2.0000   −10   0.6667   −10

Col. 5   Col. 18   Col. 25   Col. 38
Col. 10   Col. 20   Col. 30   Col. 40

just as you would ordinarily write a real number in FORTRAN. In this case, the number m in the $Fw.m$ descriptor has no effect.

Frequently, it is convenient to omit decimal points from input data. For example, a billing program might read a five-digit number representing an amount in dollars and cents. Instead of writing a decimal point in each input line, you can omit the decimal point from the input data and have the program supply the decimal point automatically. You can do this by reading the number with an F5.2 edit descriptor. In general, the edit descriptor $Fw.m$ means to read w columns, and, if there is no decimal point in the input, to place a decimal point in front of the mth digit from the right. Table 8.6 gives some examples of the effect of the statements

        READ 6, T
6   FORMAT(F8.2)

TABLE 8.6
AN F8.2 EDIT DESCRIPTOR MEANS TO READ
EIGHT COLUMNS AND ASSUME A DECIMAL POINT
BEFORE THE SECOND-TO-LAST DIGIT IF NO
DECIMAL POINT IS PRESENT IN THE INPUT

Input Field									Value Read
Column	1	2	3	4	5	6	7	8	
			4	4	.	6	0	0	44.6
				−	1	2	3	1	−12.31
					2	.	2		−2.2
		−			2	2	2		−2.22
				1					1.0
						1			0.1
				−	1	0	1		−10.1

As this table indicates, the same rules apply for leading and trailing blank spaces with the F edit descriptor as with the I edit descriptor: blanks are treated as zeros. If the decimal point is written in the data to be read, trailing blanks do not make any difference since, for example, 3.2 = 3.20000. If no decimal point is written in the data, trailing blanks *will* make a difference since they are counted in determining where the assumed decimal point is to be placed.

The assumed decimal point may go anywhere in the input field. Reading under an F3.0 edit descriptor will cause the decimal point to be placed to the right of the last digit, if it is not already present in the input. An F3.3 edit descriptor assumes a decimal point at the very left of the field.

Real numbers can also be read in exponential form. You can type an input value in exponential form the same way you type a real constant in exponential form. For example, the statements

```
        READ 2000, X
2000 FORMAT(F7.0)
```

would read the input

```
   3.2E−3
```

then store the value 0.00321 in X. The nonexponent part of an input value in E form follows the rules for ordinary real numbers. The exponent part begins with the letter E, or with a plus or minus sign—for input values, the letter E is optional. If the input value contains a decimal point, the number m in an F$w.m$ edit descriptor has no effect. If the decimal point is omitted, however, one is assumed m places from the right of the nonexponent part. For example, the input value

```
   1234+5
```

would be read by an F6.3 edit descriptor as $1.234 \times 10^5 = 123400$. Table 8.7 gives some further examples.

TABLE 8.7
EDITING OF EXPONENTIAL INPUT DATA

Input Data	Edit Descriptor	Resulting Value
4.2E02	F6.2	420.0
1234E−10	F8.0	0.1234×10^{-6}
.3E5	F4.0	30000.0
12300	F5.4	1.23
−0123	F5.4	−0.0123
−765E−1	F7.4	−0.00765
34+5	F4.1	340000
34−5	F4.1	0.000034

EXAMPLE 8.1

Write a program to print a table of squares and square roots of numbers 1 through 100. The first few lines of output will look like this:

```
1    1     1.000000
2    4     1.414214
3    9     1.732051
4   16     2.000000
```

The numbers in the first column are the numbers 1 through 100; the second column contains the squares: 1^2, 2^2, 3^2, . . . ; the third column contains the square roots.

The numbers in the first two columns are all integers, so you can use an integer variable N for the number and the integer expression N**2 for the square. The third column contains real numbers between 1.0 and 10.0. These are real values, which can be computed with the expression

SQRT(REAL(N))

Remember that the SQRT function requires a real argument, so you can use the REAL function to convert N to a real value.

The last line of output will be

```
100       10000       10.000000
```

These are the largest numbers the program will print. Thus, the first output field must be at least three characters and the second output field at last five characters. If you want to print the square root with six decimal places, you must make the output field at least nine characters. In order to allow at least five blank spaces between the columns, you can use the format specification

(I8, I10, F14.6)

Here is the complete program.

```
* PROGRAM TO PRINT A TABLE OF SQUARES
* AND SQUARE ROOTS.
*
      INTEGER N, LIMIT
      PARAMETER (LIMIT = 100)
      DO 10, N = 1, LIMIT
          PRINT 100, N, N**2, SQRT(REAL(N))
10        CONTINUE
100   FORMAT(I18, I10, F14.6)
      END
```

THE APOSTROPHE EDIT DESCRIPTOR

The **apostrophe edit descriptor** has the form of a character constant. In the format specification, any text that is enclosed in single quotes (') is printed on the output just as it appears in the FORMAT statement. Here is an example:

```
        X = 12.566
        PRINT 55, X
55      FORMAT(' THE ANSWER IS', F7.3)
```

The output from this is

```
THE ANSWER IS 12.566
```

The apostrophe edit descriptor, being nonrepeatable, does not correspond to any variable in the output list. The variable X in this example is printed according to the F7.3 field descriptor. The characters between the quote marks are simply copied to the print line.

You may want to use an apostrophe edit descriptor to put titles at the beginning of the output. If there are no variables to be printed, you can omit the output list of the PRINT statement and the comma following the format identifier, as shown by:

```
        PRINT 60
        PRINT 70
60      FORMAT( ' ACME MFG. COMPANY')
70      FORMAT( ' QUARTERLY SALES REPORT')
```

Apostrophe editing is not legal in formats used for input.

THE X EDIT DESCRIPTOR

You can insert blank spaces in the print line with an **X edit descriptor**. The form is

nX

where n is a number that tells how many spaces to insert. For example

10X

means to leave ten blank spaces. To print a five-character integer field in columns 61 through 65 of the print line, you can use the format specification (60X, I5) as in the statements

```
        PRINT 200, KILOGM
200     FORMAT(60X, I5)
```

Like the apostrophe edit descriptor, the X edit descriptor does not correspond to any variable in the output list of the PRINT statement. Thus, the variable KILOGM in this example is printed according to the I5 field descriptor. The 60X means to print 60 blank spaces. So, the I5 field begins in column 61 of the print line.

As we will explain later in this chapter, the first character of a print line is used for *carriage control*. Unless you intend to use carriage control, you should begin each output format specification with a blank space, preferably by using a 1X edit descriptor.

When used with a READ statement, the X edit descriptor means to skip spaces on the input line. For example, the statements

```
      READ 200, KILOGM
  200 FORMAT(60X, I5)
```

mean to read the value of KILOGM from columns 61–65 of the input line. The 60X means to skip over 60 columns, so that the I5 field begins in column 61.

EXAMPLE 8.2

A program for a customer billing application uses two variables: NORDER, the customer's order number, and AMOUNT, the dollar amount of the order. The output line is to look like the following sample:

    ORDER NO. 1234   AMOUNT $ 304.75

Write the FORTRAN statements to print this line.

When designing an output format specification, you should begin with the field descriptors for the variables. You need to consider the size of the largest number the program might print. Suppose that the order number is always four or fewer digits, and is always a positive number (so we do not need to allow an extra column for a minus sign). You can use an I5 edit descriptor for NORDER. If the amount of the order is always less than or equal to $9999.99, you can print it with an F7.2 field descriptor. You can use apostrophe editing for the titles (and for the dollar sign), and X edit descriptors to provide a left margin of five spaces and to skip five spaces between the order number and the word "AMOUNT." Thus, the PRINT and FORMAT statements can be written as follows.

```
      PRINT 200, NORDER, AMOUNT
  200 FORMAT(5X, 'ORDER NO.', I5, 5X, 'AMOUNT $', F7.2)
```

Figure 8.10 shows the output fields produced by these statements.

THE E EDIT DESCRIPTOR

As you learned in Chapter 3, real constants can be written in an exponential form, similar to scientific notation. For instance, the constant

    3.0E8

FIGURE 8.10

FORTRAN Statements:

        PRINT 200, NORDER, AMOUNT
200   FORMAT (5X, 'ORDER NO.', I5, 5X, ' AMOUNT $', F7.2)

Output:

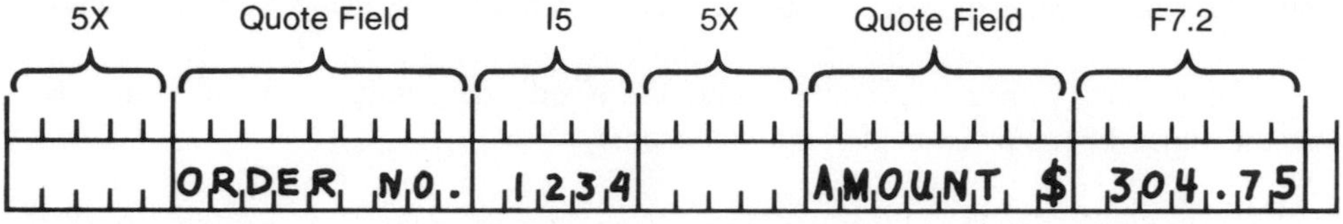

The output fields on the print line correspond to the field descriptors in the FORMAT statement.

means $3.0 \times 10^8 = 300{,}000{,}000$. You can output real numbers in E form by using the **E edit descriptor**. The form is

    Ew.m

where w is a number giving the width of the field, and m is a number telling how many decimal places to write. For example, when used with a PRINT statement, the edit descriptor

    E12.5

means to write a real number in exponential form in a field of 12 columns, with five-place accuracy. Table 8.8 shows some examples of E output editing.

When using an E$w.m$ edit descriptor for output, the numbers w and m should satisfy the inequality:

$$w \geq m + 7$$

TABLE 8.8
Ew.m EDITING

Value	Edit Descriptor	Output
−10.4	E8.1	−0.1E+02
−10.4	E9.2	−0.10E+02
−10.4	E12.4	b−0.1040E+02
0.0102	E8.2	0.10E−01
−0.0001	E10.2	b−0.10E−03
500000.0	E10.3	b0.500E+06
−14.37	E10.3	−0.144E+0.2

The reason is that one space is required for the possible minus sign, one space for the leading zero, one space for the decimal point, one space for the letter E, and three spaces for the exponent, including its sign. Thus, the edit descriptor E5.2 would not have a large enough field width to print any number.

Used for input, the E$w.m$ edit descriptor has exactly the same effect as F$w.m$. Either can be used to read real numbers in normal form or in exponential form.

THE A EDIT DESCRIPTOR

To read or write character values you use an **A edit descriptor**. (Think of the A as standing for "alphanumeric.") There are two forms. The first is

Aw

where w is a number specifying the field width. For instance,

A20

means a 20-character field. The second form is simply

A

which means a character field of unspecified size. For this form, the actual size of the field is equal to the length of the character item being read or written, as illustrated by the following statements.

```
      CHARACTER TITLE*23
      TITLE = 'THE SQUARE ROOT OF 2 IS'
      PRINT 10, TITLE, SQRT(2.0)
10    FORMAT(1X, A23, F9.6)
      END
```

The output from this program is:

THE SQUARE ROOT OF 2 IS 1.414214

The same effect could be accomplished with the FORMAT statement

```
10    FORMAT(1X, A23, F9.6)
```

The former method is easier, however, because the size of the character output field is determined by the size of TITLE, so it is not necessary to count characters in writing the FORMAT statement. For that reason, you will find that the A form is generally more convenient than the Aw form.

Another way of writing this program is to use an A edit descriptor for a character constant in the output list of the PRINT.

```
       PRINT 10, 'THE SQUARE ROOT OF 2 IS', SQRT(2.0)
10     FORMAT(1X, A, F9.2)
       END
```

This method is usually the most convenient way of providing titles in formatted output.

When using the Aw edit descriptor for output, if the size of the character item being printed is different than the field size, w, the effect is similar to that of a character assignment statement. If the field is larger than the value, blank spaces are added on the right. If the field is smaller than the value, the rightmost characters of the value are truncated. For input, the situation is similar, except that if the size of the Aw input field is greater than the size of the character item being read, then only the rightmost characters in the field are stored.

THE L EDIT DESCRIPTOR

Logical values are read and written using the **L edit descriptor**.

Lw

where w is a number giving the field width. On output, a logical value is represented by a letter T or F, right-justified in the field. On input, if the first nonblank character in the field is a T or F, the value will be read as the logical value .TRUE. or .FALSE.. The T or F in the input field may be preceded by a period. Thus, the strings .TRUE. and .FALSE. are legal logical input data.

CARRIAGE CONTROL

Carriage control is a way to control the vertical spacing of output. The name means that the program can control the movement of the print carriage of the line printer or terminal. For example, if you want your output to start at the top of a page, a PRINT statement can use carriage control to make the printer skip to the first line of a page before printing.

The first character on a line written by a formatted PRINT statement is the **carriage control character**. This carriage control character is not actually printed; it is used only to control the printer spacing, according to the codes listed in Table 8.9. As indicated in the table, other carriage control codes may be implemented on your system, but the four codes listed in the table are standard in all versions of FOR-TRAN.

TABLE 8.9

COLUMN 1 IS ALWAYS USED TO CONTROL THE PRINTER SPACING, ACCORDING TO THE FOLLOWING CODES

Character Printed in Column 1	Result
Blank	Single space before printing (normal spacing)
0 (zero)	Double space before printing
1 (one)	Skip to the beginning of next page before printing
+ (plus)	Do not space before printing
Other characters	Other special actions may be defined on particular systems

As an example, consider the following statements.

```
      PRINT 5
5     FORMAT('1THIS IS THE FIRST LINE')
      PRINT 6, 'THIS IS LINE 3'
6     FORMAT('0', A)
      END
```

The carriage control character 1 in FORMAT statement 5 causes the output:

THIS IS THE FIRST LINE

to be printed on the first line of a new page of output. The carriage control character 0 in FORMAT statement 6 causes the output:

THIS IS LINE 3

to be printed after skipping a line. Notice that the carriage control characters are not printed.

When using carriage control for output to a terminal, the exact function depends on the type of terminal. On a CRT terminal, the carriage control character 1 may clear the screen, for instance.

EXAMPLE 8.3 Printed Listings with Titles

In this example we will write a program to read a set of input lines and print them, double spaced, with a title and page number at the top of each page. The first input line will be the title.

The only difficult part of the algorithm is determining when to print the title line. You can use a variable to keep track of the line number of the last line that was printed. When the value of the line number is zero, you print the title line before copying the input line to output. Figure 8.11 shows the details of the procedure. The complete program is as follows.

```
* PROGRAM TO LIST A SET OF INPUT CARDS, DOUBLE SPACED,
* WITH A TITLE LINE ON EACH PAGE. THE FIRST INPUT
* CARD IS THE PAGE TITLE.
* VARIABLES AND SYMBOLIC CONSTANTS:
* LINENO   LINE NUMBER OF THE LAST LINE PRINTED.
*          WHEN LINENO IS ZERO, THE TITLE MUST BE PRINTED.
* LINSIZ   SIZE OF THE INPUT LINE AND TITLE LINE.
* MARGIN   CHARACTER VARIABLE SET TO BLANK SPACES FOR
*          DEFINING THE SIZE OF THE LEFT MARGIN.
* MAXLN    MAXIMUM NUMBER OF LINES PER PAGE (INCLUDING BLANK
*          LINES AND THE TITLE LINE).
* PAGENO   PAGE NUMBER.
* STRING   CHARACTER VARIABLE TO STORE THE INPUT LINE.
* TITLE    CHARACTER VARIABLE TO STORE THE PAGE TITLE.
*
      INTEGER LINSIZ
      PARAMETER (LINSIZ = 80)
      CHARACTER *(LINSIZ) TITLE, STRING, MARGIN*10
      INTEGER LINENO, MAXLN, PAGENO
      PARAMETER (MAXLN = 60)
*
* READ THE TITLE AND INITIALIZE VARIABLES.
*
      READ (*, 10, END = 900) TITLE
10    FORMAT(A)
      LINENO = 0
      PAGENO = 0
      MARGIN = ' '
*
* WHILE THERE IS MORE INPUT DATA, READ ONE LINE.
*
100   READ(*, 10, END = 900) STRING
*
*         IF LINE NUMBER IS ZERO, PRINT THE TITLE LINE.
*
          IF (LINENO .EQ. 0) THEN
              PAGENO = PAGENO + 1
              PRINT 105, MARGIN, TITLE, 'PAGE', PAGENO
105           FORMAT('1', A, A, 10X, A, I4)
              LINENO = 1
          END IF
*
*         PRINT THE LINE AND UPDATE THE LINE NUMBER.
*
          PRINT 115, MARGIN, STRING
115       FORMAT('0', A, A)
          LINENO = LINENO + 2
          IF (LINENO .GE. MAXLN) LINENO = 0
      GO TO 100
900   END
```

FIGURE 8.11
PROCEDURE TO LIST LINES, WITH TITLES

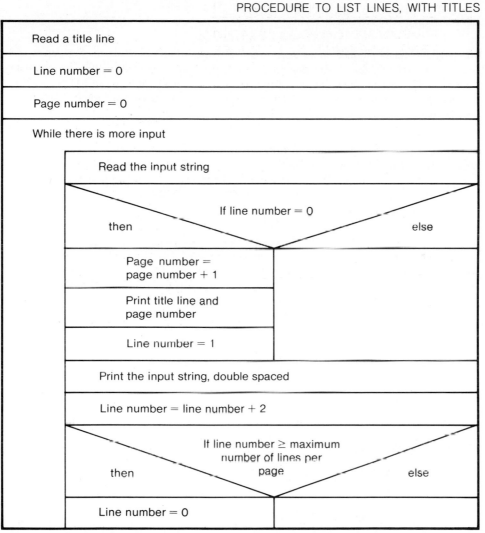

SOME COMMON MISTAKES

The five examples in this section illustrate common problems to avoid when using formatted input and output.

EXAMPLE 8.4 Incorrect Carriage Control
The following program is supposed to print the square roots of the numbers 1 through 199.

```
INTEGER N
DO 10, N = 1, 199
    PRINT 200, N, 'SQUARE ROOT = ', SQRT(REAL(N))
```

```
10      CONTINUE
200   FORMAT(I3, 5X, A, 5X, F12.6)
      END
```

This program should produce about three pages of output, right? Look again. For values of N between 100 and 199, the I3 edit descriptor causes the 1 to be printed in the carriage control column, so each line of output begins a new page. The output would be about 102 pages. Many a student has discovered carriage control only after receiving an embarrassingly large pile of program output.

EXAMPLE 8.5 Another Problem with Carriage Control
What is the output from this program?

```
      PRINT 5, 'THE SQUARE ROOT OF 2 IS', SQRT(2.0)
5     FORMAT(A, F12.6)
      END
```

The answer depends on your particular computer system. The letter T in the word THE is printed in the carriage control column. Since T is not one of the standard carriage control characters, the result is undefined. On one system, T as a carriage control character causes the printer to shift into printing eight lines per inch, and, as a side effect, ignores the rest of the output line. On that system, the program produces no output at all.

EXAMPLE 8.6 Wrong Type of Edit Descriptor
What output would be produced by the following program?

```
      REAL X
      INTEGER I
      I = 1
      X = 1
      PRINT 10, I, X
10    FORMAT(10X, F10.2, I10)
      END
```

The answer depends on your particular computer system, but the result would almost certainly not be what the programmer intended. The reason is that the wrong edit descriptors are used in the FORMAT statement: an F type edit descriptor for an integer value and an I type for a real value. Remember that real numbers and integers are stored differently in memory. When the computer tries to edit an integer value with an F descriptor, it will probably produce a value of zero, since on many systems, integers are stored in a form that is like a very small real number. Likewise, editing a real number with an I descriptor will likely cause a very large number to be printed.

The point to remember is this: Make sure that the edit descriptor is the correct type for the data being read or printed: I for integer data, A for character data, and so on.

EXAMPLE 8.7 Field Width Too Small
What is the output from the following program?

```
          PRINT 7, −1234.0
    7     FORMAT(1X, F8.3)
          END
```

The output is eight asterisks:

****

This is FORTRAN's way of diagnosing a field width too small to contain an output value. The F8.3 edit descriptor specifies three digits to the right of the decimal point. The decimal point occupies one position itself, and so does a minus sign, for a negative value. Thus, values printed in an F8.3 field must be in the range:

−999.999 to 9999.999

In general, if an output field is too small to edit a value as specified, the entire field is filled with asterisks.

EXAMPLE 8.8 Blanks as Zeros.
Suppose that an input card has a 1 keypunched in column 1 and blanks in all other columns. What value would be read by the following statements?

```
          REAL X
          READ 10, X
    10    FORMAT(F10.0)
```

The value stored in X would be 1.0E9, a large number. The reason is that blank spaces are interpreted as zeros in an input field. To read the value 1 with these statements, the value should either be right-justified in the input field, or else keypunched with a decimal point. Another option is to use a BN edit descriptor, as explained in the following section.

Suppose that the above statements were used to read the input value

1.0E2

keypunched beginning in column 1. This looks like it should represent the value $1.0 \times 10^2 = 100$; however, blanks are treated as zeros in exponents, too, so the value would be interpreted as 1.0E200000, which is much too large a number to be stored in memory.

THE BN AND BZ EDIT DESCRIPTORS

The **BN edit descriptor** lets you specify that blanks in a numeric input field are *not* to be interpreted as zeros. (You can think of BN as standing for Blanks are Null.) This edit descriptor itself does not correspond to an input field. It applies to all succeeding numeric edit descriptors in a format specification. For example, in the FORMAT statement

```
100   FORMAT(I4, BN, I5, F10.0)
```

the BN means that in the I5 and the F10.0 fields that follow, blank spaces are not to be treated as zeros. The BN does not affect the I4 field, which comes before it.

To take a specific example, suppose that a card is keypunched with a 1 in column 1, and blanks in all other columns. The statements

```
      READ 10, N
10    FORMAT(I6)
```

would read the value 100,000 for N, since the trailing blank spaces are read as zeros. But the statements

```
      READ 10, N
10    FORMAT(BN, I10)
```

would read the value 1 for N, because the BN specifies that blank spaces in the following I10 field are to be ignored.

The exact effect of BN editing on a numeric input field is to treat the input value as though all blank spaces were removed and the remaining characters right-justified in the field. The BN specification has no effect on output editing.

The **BZ edit descriptor** is the reverse of BN. It specifies that blanks be treated as zeros in remaining numeric input fields. Thus, in the FORMAT statement

```
10    FORMAT(F10.9, BN, F10.0, BZ, F9.2)
```

blanks are treated as null only in the F10.0 field.

THE SLASH IN THE FORMAT STATEMENT

Each READ statement begins a new line of input, and each PRINT statement begins a new line of output. It is possible to use a single READ statement to read more than one line of input. Likewise, a single PRINT statement can produce more than one line of output. This can be done with a slash character (/) in the FORMAT statement. For example

```
      X = 1.0
      N = 2
      PRINT 5, X, N
5     FORMAT(F10.0/I10)
```

will produce the output

```
1.
 2
```

The variable X is printed with the F10.0 edit descriptor. The slash in the FORMAT means to begin a new line. The variable N is printed with the I10 field beginning on the new line.

In general, whenever a slash is encountered in the FORMAT statement, a new line of input or output begins. It is not necessary to use commas in addition to the slash to separate edit descriptors.

On input, a slash will cause the remainder of the input line to be ignored; the following edit descriptor applies to the beginning of the following line of input. For example

```
        READ 10, A, B
10      FORMAT(F5.4/F5.4)
```

would read the input

```
1.    2.    3.
4.    5.    6.
```

and assign the values A = 1 and B = 4. The numbers 2 and 3 on the first input line are ignored because of the slash in the FORMAT. The numbers 5 and 6 on the second input line are ignored because only two variables were read.

It is important to allow for carriage control when a slash is used to begin a new line of output. Consider the statements

```
        I = 9
        J = 10
        PRINT 11, I, J
11      FORMAT(1X, I2/I2)
```

This will print a 9 on the next line of output and then skip to the top of a new page and print a zero. The reason is that when the slash begins a new line, column 1 of the new line is a carriage control character and the 1 from the number 10 causes a page eject. To avoid this problem, the FORMAT statement above could be changed to

```
11      FORMAT(1X, I2/1X, I2)
```

The slash can also be used at the beginning or end of the FORMAT specification. The statements

```
        A = 1.0
        PRINT 55, A
        PRINT 66, A
55      FORMAT(10X, F10.2)
66      FORMAT(/// 10X, F10.2)
```

produce the output

1.00

    (three blank lines)

1.00

The three slashes at the beginning of Statement 66 produce the three blank lines.

THE T, TL, AND TR EDIT DESCRIPTORS

The **T edit descriptor** is used in a FORMAT statement to indicate tabbing. Being nonrepeatable, the T edit descriptor does not correspond to a variable in the input or output list; it only controls spacing. Instead of specifying how many spaces to skip, as the X edit descriptor does, the T edit descriptor is used to *tab* to a certain column. The form is

    T*n*

where *n* is a number. This means to "tab to column *n*." In other words, it causes the next field descriptor to begin in column *n* of the input or output line.

    For example, consider the statements

```
      PRINT 100, A, B
100   FORMAT(T20, F10.4, T50, F10.4)
```

The T20 field descriptor causes the F10.4 field for the variable A to begin in column 20. The T50 field descriptor causes the F10.4 field for the variable B to begin in column 50. An equivalent FORMAT statement is

```
10    FORMAT(19X, F10.4, 20X, F10.4)
```

Note that the 19X field is in columns 1–19, and the first F10.4 is in columns 20–29; the 20X spaces over 30–49; then the last F10.4 is in columns 50–59.

    Used for input, the effect is similar. The FORMAT statement below reads A, B, and C from the beginning of a card and then tabs to column 80 to read the variable K.

```
      READ 10, A, B, C, K
10    FORMAT(3F6.0, T80, I1)
```

    The T edit descriptor can be very useful in aligning headings on output fields. Suppose a program needs to print the headings

```
QUANTITY    AMOUNT
SOLD        RECEIVED
```

where the first heading starts in column 20 and the second heading starts in column 40. This can easily be done as follows:

```
      PRINT 505
505   FORMAT('1', T20, 'QUANTITY', T40, 'AMOUNT'/
   $      T20, 'SOLD', T40, 'RECEIVED')
```

It is legal to read or write the same columns more than once by using the T edit descriptor to tab backward. For example, the statements

```
      READ 100, I, J, K
100   FORMAT(I1, T1, I2, T1, I3)
```

read the value of I from column 1, the value of J from columns 1–2, and the value of K from columns 1–3.

The **TR edit descriptor** has the form

TR*n*

where *n* is a number. It means to tab right *n* spaces. For instance, TR5 means to tab 5 spaces to the right. The **TL edit descriptor** is similar, but tabs to the left:

TL*n*

means to tab *n* spaces to the left of the current position.

REPEAT FACTORS

As you learned earlier, the I, F, E, A, and L edit descriptors are called **repeatable edit descriptors**. Each of these types may be preceded by a **repeat count** to indicate a number of repetitions. For example, the FORMAT statement

```
500   FORMAT(I10, I10, I10)
```

could be written as

```
500   FORMAT(3I10)
```

The number 3 is the repeat count. It means that the I3 field is repeated three times.

A repeat count may not be used directly with nonrepeatable edit descriptors. However, any edit descriptor or any sequence of edit descriptors may be repeated by enclosing it in parentheses and preceding it with a repeat count. For example, the FORMAT statement

```
10    FORMAT(I3, 2X, F6.0, I3, 2X, F6.0)
```

can be written as

```
10    FORMAT(2(I3, 2X, F6.0))
```

The repeat factor 2 indicates two repetitions of the entire format specification following in parentheses.

EXAMPLE 8.9
The subroutine BOX(STRING) shown below prints the value of the character variable STRING enclosed in a box formed from asterisks, as shown in Figure 8.12. The box begins on line 11 of a new page. This is accomplished by the edit descriptors

```
'1', 10(/)
```

The 10(/) repeats the slash edit descriptor 10 times, skipping to line 11. The line of asterisks is printed by the repeated edit descriptor

```
41('*')
```

Note that the slash and quote edit descriptors must be enclosed in parentheses to be repeated. The subroutine, along with the test program that produced Figure 8.12, are as follows.

```
            CALL BOX('SAMPLE OUTPUT FROM BOX')
            END
            SUBROUTINE BOX(STRING)
            CHARACTER*(*) STRING
            PRINT 1, STRING
   1        FORMAT('1', 10(/), T11, 41('*')/
       $            2(T11, '*', T51, '*'/)
       $            T11, '*', T18, A, T51, '*'/
       $            2(T11, '*', T51, '*'/),
       $            T11, 41('*'))
            END
```

INTERACTION OF THE INPUT-OUTPUT LIST WITH THE FORMAT

One question we have not yet considered is what happens when the number of items in the input or output list is different than the number of items in the format specification. There are two cases to consider.

   If there are fewer items in the input or output list than there are repeatable edit descriptors in the format specification, then remaining repeatable edit descriptors are simply ignored. For example, the statements

```
      PRINT 60, 1234
60    FORMAT(1X, I4, F10.0)
```

simply print the value 1234 according to the I4 edit descriptor. The F10.0 edit descriptor has no effect. If there are any nonrepeatable edit descriptors after the last repeatable edit descriptor used, they are processed as usual, up to the first repeatable edit descriptor for which there is no corresponding item in the input or output list. For example, the statements

```
      PRINT 60, 1234
60    FORMAT(1X, I4, 1X, 'IS THE ANSWER'/1X, 'NEW LINE',
$          F10.0, 'EXTRA CHARACTERS')
```

produce the output

```
123 IS THE ANSWER
NEW LINE
```

In this case, format processing continues up to the F10.0 edit descriptor, where it stops, since there are no remaining items in the output list.

If there are more items in the input or output list than there are repeatable edit descriptors, the format specification will be reused. To be precise, when the end of a format specification is reached while there are more items remaining in the input or output list, the following actions occur:

1. A new line of input or output is begun.
2. If there are no parenthesized groups within the format specification, the format specification is repeated from the beginning.
3. If there is a parenthesized group within the format specification, format control goes back to the beginning of the group that is terminated by the last right parenthesis.

Some examples will clarify this algorithm. The implied DO loop in the following statement says to print the values 1 through 10.

```
      PRINT 20, (K, K = 1, 10)
20    FORMAT (1X, 2I3)
```

The output is

```
1  2
3  4
5  6
7  8
9  10
```

FIGURE 8.12
SAMPLE OUTPUT FROM THE BOX SUBROUTINE IN EXAMPLE 8.9

```
*********************************************
*                                           *
*                                           *
*      SAMPLE OUTPUT FROM BOX      *
*                                           *
*                                           *
*********************************************
```

After the second number is printed, the end of the format specificaton is reached, so a new line of output is begun and the format begins again with the 1X edit descriptor. After the fourth number is printed, the same thing happens again. In all, there are five lines of output, with two numbers per line.

The effect of the third rule above is illustrated by the following statements:

```
      PRINT 100, (M, M = 1, 10)
100   FORMAT('1', 'VALUES OF M'/3(1X, I5))
```

The output is

```
VALUES OF M
   1    2    3
   4    5    6
   7    8    9
  10
```

In this case, the end of the format specification is reached after the number 3 is printed. Instead of going back to the beginning, however, control reverts to the beginning of the last repeated group in the format specification: that is, the

```
3(1X, I5)
```

group. Each new line of output is printed according to this group of edit descriptors.

AN ALTERNATIVE WAY OF WRITING FORMAT SPECIFICATIONS

All the READ and PRINT statements in this chapter used a FORMAT statement to supply the list of edit descriptors. Alternatively, you can include the format specification in the READ or PRINT statement itself. You can write the format specification as a character constant in place of the format identifier. This method is especially useful when the format specification is concise. As an example, the statements

```
    PRINT 7, X
7   FORMAT(1X, F12.4)
```

can be combined in the single statement

```
PRINT '(1X, F12.4)', X
```

The statements

```
    READ 100, LINE
100 FORMAT(A)
```

could be written as

```
READ '(A)', LINE
```

The statements

```
    READ(*, 200, END = 900) A, B, C
200 FORMAT(5X, BN, 3F10.2)
```

could be written as

```
READ(*, '(5X, BN, 3F10.2)', END = 900) A, B, C
```

Instead of a character constant, you can use a character variable or a character expression for a format identifier. The following statements use a character variable FMT to store the format specification.

```
CHARACTER FMT*50
REAL X
FMT = '(10X, BN, F10.0)'
READ(*, FMT, END = 1000) X
```

EXAMPLE 8.10

The following program reads 12 numbers, one per card, corresponding to monthly sales figures and prints them in two columns. Some sample output is shown in Figure 8.13.

```
* READ AND PRINT MONTHLY SALES FIGURES
*
      CHARACTER MONTH(12) *9
      REAL AMOUNT (12)
      INTEGER I
      READ '(BN, F10.2)', (A(I), I = 1, 12)

      MONTH(1)  = 'JANUARY'
      MONTH(2)  = 'FEBRUARY'
      MONTH(3)  = 'MARCH'
      MONTH(4)  = 'APRIL'
      MONTH(5)  = 'MAY'
```

```
        MONTH(6)  = 'JUNE'
        MONTH(7)  = 'JULY'
        MONTH(8)  = 'AUGUST'
        MONTH(9)  = 'SEPTEMBER'
        MONTH(10) = 'OCTOBER'
        MONTH(11) = 'NOVEMBER'
        MONTH(12) = 'DECEMBER'

        PRINT 100, (MONTH(I), AMOUNT(I),
     $         MONTH(I + 6), AMOUNT(I + 6), I = 1,6)

100  FORMAT('1' T20, 'MONTHLY SALES FIGURES'///
     $        (1X, T10, A, '$', 'F10.2', T40, A, '$', F10.2))

        END
```

FIGURE 8.13

MONTHLY SALES FIGURES

JANUARY	$999.99	JULY	$999.99
FEBRUARY	$999.99	AUGUST	$999.99
MARCH	$999.99	SEPTEMBER	$999.99
APRIL	$999.99	OCTOBER	$999.99
MAY	$999.99	NOVEMBER	$999.99
JUNE	$999.99	DECEMBER	$999.99

SUMMARY

Formatted input and output give the programmer control over the details of the appearance of the input or output line. The format specification contains a list of edit descriptors which describe the input or output fields. Repeatable edit descriptors describe fields corresponding to input or output list items. Nonrepeatable edit descriptors describe other fields in the input output line or give additional information about the way the editing is to be done.

The repeatable edit descriptors are

I   for integer editing
F   for real editing
E   for real editing in exponential form
A   for character editing
L   for logical editing

Nonrepeatable edit descriptors are

'string'	for writing character constants
X	for skipping spaces
/	for skipping to a new line
BN	for causing blank spaces to be treated as nulls
BZ	for causing blank spaces to be treated as zeros
T	for tabbing to a particular column
TL	for tabbing left
TR	for tabbing right

A repeat factor can be used before a repeatable edit descriptor to specify several occurrences of the same field. Groups of edit descriptors enclosed in parentheses can also be repeated.

Column 1 of a print line is not printed. Instead, it is used for a carriage control character that controls vertical spacing of output.

VOCABULARY

A edit descriptor
apostrophe edit descriptor
BN edit descriptor
BZ edit descriptor
carriage control
carriage control character
E edit descriptor
edit descriptor
end-of-file specifier
F edit descriptor
format identifier
format specification
FORMAT statement
formatted PRINT statement
formatted READ statement

I edit descriptor
input fields
L edit descriptor
list-directed
nonrepeatable edit descriptors
output fields
output list
repeat count
repeatable edit descriptors
T edit descriptor
TL edit descriptor
TR edit descriptor
unit identifier
X edit descriptor

EXERCISES

1. Each of the following FORMAT statements describes a sequence of integer input fields. Write the input columns that comprise each field. Example:

    100 FORMAT(I5, 1X, I5)

the input fields are columns 1–5 and 7–11.

(a) 100   FORMAT (1X, I4, 1X, I4)
(b) 100   FORMAT (I10, 10X, I10)
(c) 100   FORMAT (5X, I5, 5X, I5, I10)
(d) 100   FORMAT (20X, I6, I4, 10X, I5)
(e) 100   FORMAT (I2, I6, 3X, I6, 3X, I5)
(f) 100   FORMAT (I3, I2, I4, I10)
(g) 100   FORMAT (15X, I5)
(h) 100   FORMAT (20X, 10X, I10)

2. For each of the following lists of input fields, write a FORMAT statement to read an integer number from each field. Example:

   columns 1–5
   columns 6–10
   columns 15–19

A FORMAT statement is

  10   FORMAT (I5, I5, 4X, I5)

(a) columns 2–5
     column 9
     columns 11–14
(b) columns 5–9
     columns 11–14
     columns 16–19
(c) columns 1–9
     columns 20–29
     columns 40–49
(d) column 5
     columns 10–13
     columns 15–16
     columns 20–25
     columns 40–45

(e) column 80
(f) columns 1–5
     columns 6–10
     columns 11–15
(g) columns 1–2
     columns 3–4
     columns 10–12
     column 15
(h) columns 1–20
     columns 31–40

3. For each FORMAT statement, show what output would be printed by the statement

   PRINT 7, −123.45678

(a) 7   FORMAT (1X, F10.5)
(b) 7   FORMAT (1X, F12.5)
(c) 7   FORMAT (1X, F12.4)
(d) 7   FORMAT (1X, F10.2)

(e) 7   FORMAT (1X, F6.0)
(f) 7   FORMAT (1X, F10.9)
(g) 7   FORMAT (1X, F5.1)

4. An input line contains the following data, starting in column 1:

   12345−1234+123456789

The line is read by the statement

   READ (∗, 5, END = 100) X, Y, Z

For each of the following FORMAT statements, what values are stored in the real variables X, Y, and Z?

(a) 5   FORMAT (F5.0, F5.0, F10.4)
(b) 5   FORMAT (F5.2, F5.0, F10.3)
(c) 5   FORMAT (F5.5, F5.1, F10.9)
(d) 5   FORMAT (F5.4, 1X, F4.2, 2X, F5.1)
(e) 5   FORMAT (F2.0, F3.0, 2X, F3.0)
(f) 5   FORMAT (F5.0, F7.1, F4.3)
(g) 5   FORMAT (F8.4, F5.0, F6.3)

5. For each PRINT statement, show what output would be printed using the format statement

   25   FORMAT (1X, E12.5)

(a) PRINT 25, 1.0   (d) PRINT 25, 123.456
(b) PRINT 25, −123.0   (e) PRINT 25, 123.0E−2
(c) PRINT 25, 100.0   (f) PRINT 25, 5.0E2

6. X, Y, and Z are real variables. Write FORTRAN statements that will print each of them in an F12.3 field, skipping five spaces between the fields. Write FORTRAN statements that print the titles 'X VALUE', 'Y VALUE', 'Z VALUE' above the corresponding columns.

7. Write a program that prints a table of square roots of numbers 2 through 99. Each line of output should start in column 10 and have the form:

   THE SQUARE ROOT OF xx IS y.yyyyyy

   where xx is an integer and y.yyyyyy is a real value with six decimal places.

8. Write a subroutine

   PAGE(TITLE, PAGENO)

   that will skip to the top of a new page, print the character string TITLE starting in column 10, print the characters 'PAGE' starting in column 125, and print the integer value PAGENO in a four-place integer field starting in column 129.

9. An input line contains the following data, starting in column 1:

   123bbbb456bbb-789

   where 'b' represents a blank space. What values are assigned to the variables by each of the following statements? (I is an integer variable; X, Y, and Z are real.)

(a)   READ 10, I, X, Y
      10   FORMAT (I6, F6.0, F6.0)
(b)   READ 10, I, X, Y
      10   FORMAT (BN, I6, F6.0, F6.0)
(c)   READ 10, I, X, Y
      10   FORMAT (I6, BN, F6.0, F6.0)
(d)   READ 10, X, Y, Z
      10   FORMAT (F7.4, F6.3, F5.0)
(e)   READ 10, X, Y, Z
      10   FORMAT (BN, F7.4, F6.3, F5.0)

(f)   READ 10, X, Y, Z
    10   FORMAT (F7.4, BN, F6.3, BZ, F5.0)
(g)   READ 10, X, I
    10   FORMAT (F10.3, I6)
(h)   READ 10, X, I
    10   FORMAT (BN, F10.3, I6)

10. Using a slash edit descriptor, write a single FORMAT statement to produce the output described in Exercise 6.

11. Write a FORMAT statement to be used for printing the output line described below.

Columns	Item	Type
10–15	Part number	Integer
21–40	Description	Character
45–51	Unit price	Real, 2 decimal places
55–59	Quantity ordered	Integer
65–52	Total price	Real, 2 decimal places

12. Write a FORMAT statement to print a title line at the top of a page for the output described in Exercise 11. For example, beginning in column 10 of the top two lines on a page, write the title

    PART
    NUMBER

13. Write a FORMAT statement to be used for reading the input line described below.

Columns	Item	Type
1–2	Year	Integer
3–4	Month	Integer
5–6	Day	Integer
8–27	Location	Character
30–36	Latitude (degrees)	Real, with 3 assumed decimal places
37–42	Longitude (degrees)	Real, with 3 assumed decimal places
43–50	Elevation (meters)	Real, with 2 assumed decimal places
51–54	Surveyor identification	Integer

14. Two input lines contain the following data, starting in column 1.

    0123456789
    9876543210

    What values are assigned to the variables by each of the following statements?

```
(a)              READ 10, X, Y
       10    FORMAT (F5.2/F5.2)
(b)              READ 10, I, X, Y, Z
       10    FORMAT (F5.1, F2.0/I4)
(c)              READ 10, I, J, K, L,
       10    FORMAT (2I3/2I3)
(d)              READ 10, I, J, K, L
       10    FORMAT (2(I2, I3/))
(e)              READ 10, X
       10    FORMAT (/5X, F5.2)
(f)              READ 10, I, J, K, L, M, N, X
       10    FORMAT (4(I2, 1X)/2I2, F3.1)
```

15. Exercise 16 in Chapter 5 showed a histogram produced by storing values in a character variable. Another way to generate this kind of output is with an implied DO loop. For example, the following statements produce the output in the accompanying figure.

```
    P = 10.2
    TITLE = 'BRAND A'
    PRINT 10, TITLE, ('*', I = 1, NINT(P))
    PRINT 15, P, 'PERCENT', ('*', I = 1, NINT(P))
10  FORMAT (/1X, A, T30, 100A)
15  FORMAT (1X, F5.1, 1X, A, T30, 100A)
```

BRAND A   **********

10.2 PERCENT   **********

Write a subroutine

HISTO(LABELS, COUNT, N)

to print a histogram using this technique. LABELS is a character array giving a label (e.g., 'BRAND A') for each bar on the histograph. COUNT is a real array, giving the number of items in each category to be plotted. You should convert each element of COUNT to a percentage. N is the number of elements in the array COUNT.

16. Using an implied DO loop, write statements to print the following output:

```
.............................................
     1         2         3         4         5
12345678901234567890123456789012345678901234567890
.............................................
```

Modify the listing program of Example 8.3 to print similar output at the top and bottom of each page so that you can use a ruler to determine what columns a certain data field is in.

17. Rewrite the subroutine BOX of Example 8.9 to print a character array enclosed in a box made of asterisks. If LINE is a character array of N elements

CALL BOX(LINE, N)

should write each element on a separate line.
18. Write a program consisting of a single FORTRAN statement plus an END line, that produces the following output:

```
TABLE OF CUBES AND CUBE ROOTS
     N        CUBE      CUBE
                        ROOT
     1           1      1.00000
     2           8      1.25992
     3          27      1.44225
   . . .       . . .      . . .
    50       125000     3.68403
```

19. On a timesharing system, a program may be designed to ask the user to enter a *command*. For example the program might type:

COMMAND:

and the user might respond with some command such as

DISPLAY DATA

Suppose that a program is designed so that all legal commands have two parts: a verb and a noun. The verb always comes first and is separated from the noun by one or more blanks. Thus, in the command DISPLAY DATA, the verb is DISPLAY and the noun is DATA. Suppose that all the legal command verbs for the program are stored in a character array CVERB having NVERB elements. Write a subroutine.

GETCMD(NCMD, NOUN, CVERB, NVERB)

that asks the user to enter a command and reads the user's response. If the command verb is legal, the subroutine stores the command number in the integer variable NCMD. Thus, CVERB(NCMD) is the verb typed by the user. The subroutine stores the noun in the character variable NOUN. If the command typed by the user does not have a legal verb, the subroutine types the message

WHAT?

and prompts the user to reenter the command.
20. Modify the GETCMD subroutine of Exercise 19 so that the user can abbreviate the command verb. For example, instead of typing the words

DISPLAY DATA

the user could type

DISPL DATA

or

DISP DATA

or

DIS DATA

The user should be allowed to type only as many characters of the verb as are necessary to uniquely identify the command.

21. Write a program to help you balance your checkbook. The first input card for this program gives the previous balance of the account, from the last time your account was balanced. It has the following form:

Columns	Item
1–8	Date checkbook was balanced
1–2	Month (integer)
3	/
4–5	Day (integer)
6	/
7–8	Last two digits of year (integer)
9	Blank
10–12	BAL
13	Blank
14–20	Balance forward (real number, two assumed decimal places)

In this input card and all others used for this program, blanks should be ignored in each numeric field. For each check written during the month, prepare an input card in the following format.

Columns	Item
1–8	Date of check (same form as above)
9	Blank
10–12	CHE
13	Blank
14–20	Amount of check (real number, two assumed decimal places)

For each deposit to the account, prepare an input card in the following format.

Columns	Item
1–8	Date of deposit (same form as above)
9	Blank
10–12	DEP
13	Blank
14–20	Amount of deposit (real number, two assumed decimal places)

For each service charge to the account, prepare an input card in the following format.

Columns	Item
1–8	Date of service charge (same form as above)
9	Blank
10–12	SER
13	Blank
14–20	Amount of service charge

Arrange the input cards in the following order: BALANCE card first, other cards arranged by increasing date. The program should print a list of all transactions to the account and a running balance, similar to the sample output shown below.

PREVIOUS ACCOUNT BALANCE			$203.10
CHECK	$10.00	BALANCE	$193.10
CHECK	$85.00	BALANCE	$108.10
DEPOSIT	$75.50	BALANCE	$183.60
CHECK	$15.00	BALANCE	$168.60
SVC CHG	$ 1.00	BALANCE	$167.60
CHECK	$ 8.75	BALANCE	$158.85
CHECK	$20.00	BALANCE	$138.85
DEPOSIT	$25.00	BALANCE	$163.85

22. The checkbook program in Exercise 21 does not provide any detailed information about the checks written. Modify the input data format to include the check number and the name of the payee for each check. Modify the program to list this data on the output.

23. Modify the checkbook program so that the input data may be read in any order. The output should be sorted in chronological order by date of transaction. If more than one check is written on the same day, they should be sorted by check number.

24. The checkbook program in the previous exercises keeps track of the account balance, but it does not reconcile the balance with the statement the bank sends at the end of the month. In order to carry out such a reconciliation you need a way to determine which checks, deposits, and charges have been

posted according to the bank's statement. Modify the data formats and the algorithm to have the program balance the checkbook. Have the program list, on a separate page, all outstanding checks and deposits.

25. If you have a checking account of your own, what modifications would you make to the checkbook program for use with your own account? Can service charges on checks be computed automatically? Are there other types of transactions allowed (credit card purchases, automatic loans)? Does the monthly charge depend on the minimum balance? Is interest paid on balances over a certain amount? What other data could usefully be incorporated into this system (a list of tax-deductible expenses, or subtotals by categories such as medical expenses, clothing expenses, etc.)? Redesign the checkbook system for convenient management of your own account.

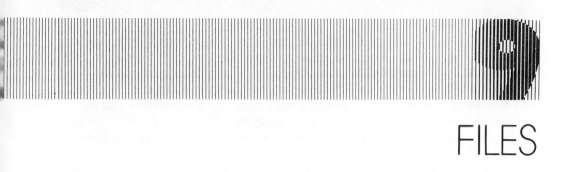

FILES

INTRODUCTION   Until now, our discussion of input and output has assumed that input was being read from a terminal or from cards and that output was sent to the terminal or line printer. There are several other devices commonly used for input and output.

A **magnetic tape** can be used to store data for a computer in much the same way that magnetic tape is used for record music or other audio signals. In the case of an audio tape, sound vibrations are transformed by an electromagnet into variations in a magnetic field. As the tape moves past the electromagnet (the recording head), the ferromagnetic surface of the tape records the variations in the field. To play back the tape, the process is carried out in reverse. Magnetic field variations on the tape are sensed by the electromagnet and transformed into sound. Computer tapes use the same principle. Instead of storing sound waves, however, computer tapes store numbers or characters. Any data that can be printed on a line printer can just as well be written on a tape. A person cannot read the tape directly, of course, but the tape can be read back by the tape drive and the data can be processed by a program.

Tape storage is very compact. A typical tape drive can record 1600 characters on a single inch of tape. This means that a standard 2100-foot reel of tape can store over 40 million characters, which is equal to about 500,000 punch cards. Furthermore, data on tape can be read faster and more reliably than data on cards.

A **magnetic disk** unit provides the most convenient way to store data on a computer system. Like a tape, a disk is coated with a thin layer of a substance that can be magnetized by an electromagnet to record and play back data. The difference is in the geometry. A disk is a flat platter, like a phonograph record. Data is recorded on any one of the tracks of the disk, which are like the groves on a phonograph record, except that they are concentric circles, rather than a spiral. To read data from a particular track, the disk unit positions the read head at the proper distance from the center, then reads the data as the disk revolves under the read head. A large disk unit can store the equivalent of many tapes.

In a FORTRAN program, you can use disk units, tape drives, or any other input-output device in almost the same way you use the card reader or printer. The general form of the FORTRAN READ and WRITE statements is the same,

337

regardless of the type of device being used. Thus, you need not be concerned with the physical characteristics of the different input-output devices. All you need to know are the general concepts of how data is organized into **files** and **records**. Auxiliary input-output statements such as **OPEN, CLOSE, REWIND**, and **ENDFILE** provide control over the files used by a FORTRAN program.

It is often useful to reformat data using READ and WRITE statements without transferring the data to any external device at all. This capability is provided in FORTRAN through **internal files**.

Two special kinds of input and output are covered in this chapter. **Unformatted input and output** is an efficient way to store data for later use by a program. **Direct access input and output** allows records in a file to be created or read in random sequence.

RECORDS, FILES, AND UNITS

A **record** is the smallest entity that can be created or read by a FORTRAN input or output statement. When using cards, each card is a record. For a printer, each print line is a record. On a terminal, each line of input or output is a record. On other devices, a record is generally whatever the programmer wants it to be. If you write several values to a magnetic tape, instead of to a print line, the data becomes a record on the tape. The computer's operating system marks the end of each record on the tape, so that it will know one record from the next when the data is read back. A record is a sequence of characters. Cards have 80 columns, so for card input, a record consists of 80 characters. On tape or disk, you can create records of any size. A record can consist of one character or of 1000 characters. In fact, a record can consist of zero characters.

A **file** is a sequence of records. A deck of punch cards is a file in which each card is a record. When writing to tape or disk, a program can output a sequence of records of various lengths to create a file.

The end of a file is marked by an **endfile record**, which is a special record to indicate that no more data follows. For example, when writing to a tape, a program might use only the first few feet of the tape. An endfile record following the data on tape tells the computer that the remainder of the tape is not part of the file.

Figure 9.1 shows a schematic representation of a tape file. You need not be concerned about the exact method the machine uses to record the data on the tape. The particular format may, in fact, vary from one computer system to the next. A FORTRAN program creates a file by writing a sequence of records. It reads the records of a file in the same manner as it reads cards from a file of input cards. The details are taken care of by the operating system.

When using cards, you generally think of an input deck as a single file. Similarly, a magnetic tape usually contains a single file, which may contain any number of records, from zero up to the maximum number of records that will fit on the tape (which is a large number). A disk unit is different in that a single disk can contain

FIGURE 9.1

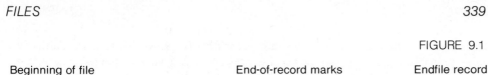

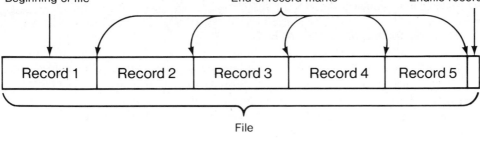

A file consists of a sequence of records, which may be different sizes. An endfile record marks the end of information.

many files. A single program might write two or more files onto a disk at the same time. The operating system has to know which tracks on the disk are used for which data. It is a complicated procedure, but one that need not be of concern to the FORTRAN programmer, since a disk file is used in the same way as a tape file or any other file in FORTRAN.

You use **unit numbers** in FORTRAN to distinguish one file from another. A unit number is an integer number that designates some file or some device. For example, a certain computer might use unit number 5 to mean your terminal. Unit number 2 might be the card reader, and unit number 3 the line printer. Unit numbers 7 through 20 might be disk files. The particular choice of unit numbers depends on the computer system. Generally speaking, there are three ways in which unit numbers become associated with a particular file.

1. Certain unit numbers may be predefined by the operating system. Thus, unit number 5 may be your terminal by default.
2. You may be able to use control cards or operating system commands outside of your FORTRAN program to define the meaning of unit numbers.
3. The OPEN statement, covered later in this chapter, can establish the connection between a unit number and a particular file.

In the following section you will see how unit numbers are used in READ and WRITE statements.

READ AND WRITE STATEMENTS

You have seen examples of formatted READ statements like the following:

```
READ(*, 1000, END = 900) A, B, C
```

The asterisk in this statement is the **unit identifier**. It means to use a standard input unit—probably the card reader or terminal, depending on your computer. The following statement is similar:

```
READ(8, 1000, END = 900) A, B, C
```

In place of the asterisk, however, is the number 8. This means to read from *unit number 8*, which might be a disk file. In general, you can use any integer expression in a similar fashion within a READ statement to identify a unit.

Since unit numbers depend on the computer being used, it is a good practice to represent them by means of a variable or a symbolic constant. For example, if unit 5 is a terminal on your system, you might begin a program with the statements

```
INTEGER TTY
PARAMETER (TTY = 5)
```

Any time you wanted to read from a terminal in your program, you could use a statement such as

```
READ (TTY, 50, END = 100) LINE
```

Corresponding to this form of the READ statement, there is a **WRITE statement** used for output to a particular unit. The form is

```
WRITE (unit, format) list
```

where *unit* is the unit identifier, *format* is a format identifier, and *list* is the output list. For example,

```
        WRITE(*, 100) 'RESULT IS ', X + Y
100   FORMAT(1X, A, F10.4)
```

The unit identifier in this case is an asterisk, meaning the standard output unit—generally a printer or terminal. This WRITE statement has exactly the same effect as the statement

```
PRINT 100, 'RESULT IS ', X + Y
```

In both cases, data is written to the standard output unit according to FORMAT statement 100. Using the general form of the WRITE statement, you can specify any unit for output. For example

```
WRITE (8, 100) 'RESULT IS ', X + Y
```

would create the same record on unit number 8, which might be a disk or tape unit. As with the READ, it is good programming practice to use a variable or symbolic constant for a unit identifier. For instance, if the printer is unit 6 on a certain system, you might define the symbolic constant PRNTR by

```
INTEGER PRNTR
PARAMETER (PRNTR = 6)
```

then use output statements such as

```
WRITE (PRNTR, 100) 'RESULT IS ', X + Y
```

THE OPEN AND CLOSE STATEMENTS

To **open** a file means to initialize the file so that input or output operations may be performed. It is not necessary to open the standard input and output units; they are initialized automatically when a FORTRAN program begins execution. When using other devices, such as disk or tape, you generally open a file explicitly by executing an **OPEN statement** prior to any input or output operations.

An example of an OPEN statement is

```
OPEN (UNIT = 1, FILE = 'DISK:MYDATA', STATUS = 'OLD')
```

Within the parentheses is a list of specifiers that give information about the file and determine how the file is to be opened.

The **unit specifier** tells which FORTRAN unit is to be associated with the file. In the example above,

```
UNIT = 1
```

means that FORTRAN unit number 1 will be used for the file being opened. This is the only way in FORTRAN of associating a unit number with a particular file or device. The OPEN statement causes the unit to be **connected** to the file, meaning that all subsequent operations on unit 1 refer to the file being opened.

The **file specifier** gives the name of the file. It may also specify the device on which the file resides. In the example above,

```
FILE = 'DISK:MYDATA'
```

means that the file being opened on unit 1 is a disk file called MYDATA. There is no standard form for file names or for device specifications. It depends on your particular computer system. Thus, programs should use a character variable or symbolic constant to specify file names.

The **status specifier** is a character expression whose value is one of four strings:

OLD   Meaning that the file already exists on the system. For example, the file might be a disk file created by a previous program.

NEW   Meaning that the file does not yet exist—it will be created by this program. For example, a tape that has not yet been written on is a new file.

SCRATCH   Meaning that the file will be created by this program, but will be deleted from the system when the program completes execution.

UNKNOWN   Meaning that none of the above statuses apply, in which case the status of the file depends on the operating system you are using.

The opposite of opening a file is **closing** a file, which is the operation used to finish processing on a file and return it to the operating system. When you close a tape file, for instance, the tape is usually rewound and dismounted from the tape drive by the operator. When you close a disk file, the operator usually does not physically dismount the disk, but the disk file is retained as a permanent member of the system's file set (unless you specified STATUS = SCRATCH in the OPEN statement, in which case the file is deleted when closed).

The FORTRAN statement to close a file is

CLOSE(UNIT = *n*)

or

CLOSE(*n*)

where *n* is an integer expression giving the unit number of the file. After the **CLOSE statement** is executed, the unit is **disconnected** from the file, meaning that the unit number can be used for a different file.

If you do not close a file yourself by using a CLOSE statement, FORTRAN will close the file for you when your program executes a STOP or END statement. Thus, use of the CLOSE statement is optional.

THE INPUT-OUTPUT STATUS SPECIFIER

It is often important for a program to determine whether an operation on a file has worked correctly or not. This information can be obtained by using an **input-output status specifier** in an OPEN, CLOSE, READ, or WRITE statement. The form of the input-output status specifier is

IOSTAT = *var*

where *var* is an integer variable or an integer array element.

Some examples of its use are:

OPEN(UNIT = 1, FILE = FNAME, STATUS = 'OLD', IOSTAT = K)
CLOSE(UNIT = NUNIT, IOSTAT = K)
READ(TTY, 100, IOSTAT = K) X, Y, Z
WRITE(6, '(A)', IOSTAT = K) (A(I), I = 1, N)

Each of these statements, when executed, causes the input-output specification variable K to become defined with a value that tells what happened when the statement executed. For example, if K = 0, that means the statement executed successfully.

In general, the specifier

IOSTAT = *var*

causes *var* to be defined as follows:

> *var* = 0   operation was successful
> *var* < 0   an error condition occurred
> *var* > 0   an end-of-file was detected on an input operation

If *var* ≠ 0, the exact value assigned depends on the system you are using. Different values can represent different error conditions. When a program detects an error, it is a good programming practice to have it print the error number, so that you can look it up in a system reference manual to determine the cause.

If an error is detected in executing an OPEN, CLOSE, READ, or WRITE statement that does not contain an input-output status specifier, program execution will be terminated immediately, and most systems will print a diagnostic message.

For example, the statement

READ(INUNIT, '(A)') LINE

will cause the program to terminate if an end-of-file condition or an error condition is detected on the file connected to INUNIT. To recover from either condition and continue execution, you could use an input-output status specifier, as follows.

```
READ(INUNIT, '(A)', IOSTAT = NSTAT) LINE
IF(NSTAT .LT. 0) THEN
      PRINT *, 'END OF FILE ON UNIT', INUNIT
      STOP
ELSE IF (NSTAT .GT. 0) THEN
      PRINT *, 'ERROR NUMBER', NSTAT, 'ON UNIT', INUNIT
      GO TO 1000
END IF
```

If an error is detected on a unit, the position of the file connected to the unit becomes undefined. If an error is detected while executing a READ statement, the values of variables in the input list are undefined. As usual, "undefined," in this sense, means that the exact effect depends on factors over which you have no control in standard FORTRAN.

Another way of detecting an error condition on a file is with an error specifier of the form

ERR = *n*

where *n* is a statement label. For example, in the statement:

    READ (7, 25, END = 100, ERR = 200) A, B

the error specifier

    ERR = 200

means to go to statement number 200 if there is an error. This is similar to the end-of-file specifier

    END = 100

which means to go to statement 100 if there is no more data.

EXAMPLE 9.1 Interactive File Control

On a timesharing system, it is often convenient to have a program ask you for the names of the files it will use, so that you can enter them at your terminal. The subroutine OPENIO in this example uses the units TTYIN and TTYOUT for input and output to a terminal. These units are assumed to be open. It asks the user to enter names for input and output files and opens them. If it is unsuccessful, it reports the error to the user and tries again. To stop execution of the program, the user can type END when asked for a file name. Figure 9.2 shows the procedure design.

```
*  OPENIO (INPUT, OUTPUT)
*  THIS SUBROUTINE ASKS THE USER TO ENTER
*  NAMES FOR THE INPUT AND OUTPUT FILES,
*  WHICH IT THEN OPENS ON UNITS INPUT AND OUTPUT.
*  THE SUBROUTINE DOES NOT RETURN UNLESS THE
*  FILES ARE OPENED SUCCESSFULLY. THE USER CAN
*  STOP THE PROGRAM BY TYPING 'END'
*
       SUBROUTINE OPENIO (INPUT, OUTPUT)
       INTEGER INPUT, OUTPUT
       INTEGER TTYIN, TTYOUT
       PARAMETER (TTYIN = 5, TTYOUT = TTYIN)
       INTEGER STAT
       CHARACTER FILENM*20
*
1      FORMAT(A)
2      FORMAT(1X, A)
3      FORMAT(1X, 'ERROR NUMBER', I5, 1X, 'OPENING FILE',
      $    1X, A, 1X, 'PLEASE TRY AGAIN.')
*
*  INPUT FILE.
*
100    WRITE(TTYOUT, 2) 'ENTER INPUT FILE NAME'
       READ(TTYIN, 1) FILENM
       IF (FILENM .EQ. 'END') STOP
```

FIGURE 9.2

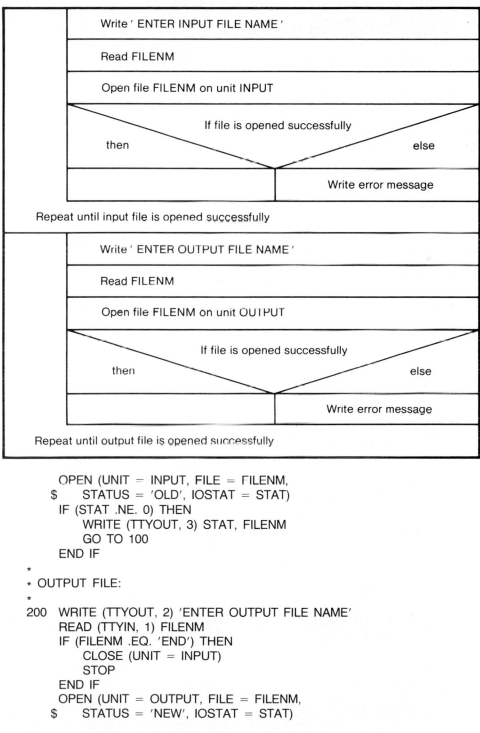

```
      OPEN (UNIT = INPUT, FILE = FILENM,
   $     STATUS = 'OLD', IOSTAT = STAT)
      IF (STAT .NE. 0) THEN
          WRITE (TTYOUT, 3) STAT, FILENM
          GO TO 100
      END IF
*
* OUTPUT FILE:
*
200   WRITE (TTYOUT, 2) 'ENTER OUTPUT FILE NAME'
      READ (TTYIN, 1) FILENM
      IF (FILENM .EQ. 'END') THEN
          CLOSE (UNIT = INPUT)
          STOP
      END IF
      OPEN (UNIT = OUTPUT, FILE = FILENM,
   $     STATUS = 'NEW', IOSTAT = STAT)
```

```
IF (STAT .NE. 0) THEN
    WRITE (TTYOUT, 3) STAT, FILENM
    GO TO 200
END IF
END
```

REWIND, BACKSPACE, AND ENDFILE STATEMENTS

Rewinding a computer tape is just like rewinding an audio reel-to-reel tape. The computer tape is not unloaded from the tape drive however. It is positioned at the beginning of information so that a READ statement will start reading with the first record.

The FORTRAN statement to rewind a file is

```
REWIND (UNIT = unit)
```

or

```
REWIND unit
```

where *unit* is the unit identifier, an integer expression. For example

```
REWIND 3
```

rewinds the file connected to unit 3.

If the unit is connected to a disk file, the effect is the same as for a tape: The file is positioned at the beginning of information, although, for a disk, this does not cause any physical movement on the disk unit. If the unit is a terminal, a printer, or some other device for which a rewind is not applicable, the REWIND statement causes no action (and no error). The REWIND statement also causes no action if the file is already positioned at the beginning.

The **BACKSPACE statement** is similar to REWIND. The form is

```
BACKSPACE (UNIT = unit)
```

or

```
BACKSPACE unit
```

where *unit* is the unit identifier. This statement simply positions a file before the preceding record. For example,

```
REWIND 7
READ(7, '(A)') AAA
BACKSPACE 7
READ(7, '(A)') BBB
```

These statements read the first record from unit 7 into both AAA and BBB. Backspacing a file is inefficient and should be avoided if possible.

The **ENDFILE statement** writes an end-of-file mark, which is a special record that indicates the end of a file. The form is

ENDFILE (UNIT = *unit*)

or

ENDFILE *unit*

where *unit* is the unit identifier.
For example,

ENDFILE 1

Write an end-of-file mark on unit 1. It is a good programming practice to use an ENDFILE statement prior to closing an output file. However, on most systems, an end-of-file mark will be written automatically when you rewind or close an output file.

Each of these statements may include an input-output status specifier to detect any error condition, such as trying to rewind a tape drive which has no tape mounted. Examples:

```
REWIND(UNIT = 2, IOSTAT = K)
BACKSPACE(UNIT = 2, IOSTAT = K)
ENDFILE(UNIT = 2, IOSTAT = K)
```

EXAMPLE 9.2 File Copying

The following program copies one file to another. This program uses the OPENIO routine from Example 9.1 to open the files. It reads character values into a character variable RECORD, and copies them to the output file. The maximum record size, MAXREC, is a symbolic constant. If an error condition is detected, the program reports it and closes the files.

```
* PROGRAM TO COPY A FILE.
* MAXIMUM RECORD SIZE IS MAXREC.
*
      INTEGER INPUT, OUTPUT, MAXREC, STAT
      PARAMETER (INPUT = 1, OUTPUT = 2, MAXREC = 132)
      CHARACTER RECORD*(MAXREC)
*
      CALL OPENIO(INPUT, OUTPUT)
*
100   READ (INPUT, '(A)', IOSTAT = STAT) RECORD
      IF (STAT .LT. 0) THEN
          PRINT *, 'SUCCESSFUL COPY'
          GO TO 200
      ELSE IF (STAT .GT. 0) THEN
          PRINT *, 'ERROR', STAT, 'ON UNIT', INPUT
```

```
            GO TO 200
        END IF
        WRITE (OUTPUT, '(A)', IOSTAT = STAT) RECORD
        IF (STAT .NE. 0) THEN
            PRINT *, 'ERROR', STAT, 'ON UNIT', OUTPUT
            GO TO 200
        END IF
        GO TO 100
*
* AT END OF FILE OR IF ERROR OCCURS:
*
200   ENDFILE(UNIT = OUTPUT, IOSTAT = STAT)
        CLOSE (UNIT = OUTPUT, IOSTAT = STAT)
        CLOSE (UNIT = INPUT, IOSTAT = STAT)
        END
```

EXAMPLE 9.3 Merging Files

Imagine that you have two decks of index cards, each sorted in alphabetical order. To **merge** these files means to combine them so that the resulting file is also in alphabetical order. Now imagine that you have two files, which might be tape or disk files, sorted in alphabetical order, according to the characters comprised in the entire record. The program in this example shows how to merge these files to create a single output file containing the combined input files. The program uses list directed input to read the names of the three files from the standard input unit.

The algorithm is basically the same as you would use to merge two card decks. Set both decks in front of you. Choose the card that comes first in alphabetical order and transfer it to the end of a third pile. Continue until all cards in one pile have been transferred, then transfer the remaining cards. A more formal explanation of this algorithm is shown in Figure 9.3.

To determine which record to copy, you can compare the two records as character strings. If either unit is at the end of file, however, you need to copy any remaining records from the other unit. The detailed procedure for deciding on the unit is shown in Figure 9.4.

```
* PROGRAM TO MERGE FILES.
* THE NAMES OF THE TWO INPUT FILES AND THE OUTPUT
* FILE ARE READ FROM THE STANDARD INPUT UNIT
* USING LIST-DIRECTED INPUT. THE THREE FILES
* ARE READ USING FORMATTED INPUT, AND ARE ASSUMED
* TO HAVE A RECORD SIZE OF AT MOST RECSIZ
* CHARACTERS. THE ENTIRE RECORD IS USED
* AS A MERGE KEY.
*
        INTEGER UNIT, STATUS(3), I, RECSIZ
        PARAMETER (RECSIZ = 132)
        CHARACTER FILE(3)*20, S(3)*3, RECORD(3)*(RECSIZ)
20      FORMAT(A)
*
* READ FILE NAMES AND OPEN FILES.
*
        READ(*, *) (FILE(I), I = 1, 3)
        S(1) = 'OLD'
        S(2) = 'OLD'
```

FIGURE 9.3
ALGORITHM FOR MERGING FILE 1 AND FILE 2 TO GIVE FILE 3

Open units 1 and 2 for input
Open unit 3 for output
Read a record from unit 1
Read a record from unit 2
While end of file has not been reached on both units 1 and 2

Decide whether the next output record should be the record from unit 1 or 2. Let UNIT equal the chosen unit.
Write an output record from the input record read from unit number UNIT.
Read a new record from unit number UNIT.

Close all three files

```
        S(3) = 'NEW'
        DO 30, I = 1, 3
            OPEN (UNIT = I, FILE = FILE(I),
     $          STATUS = S(I), IOSTAT = STATUS(I))
            IF (STATUS(I) .LT. 0)THEN
            WRITE (*, *) 'COULD NOT OPEN FILE',
     $          FILE(I) , ' - ERROR', STATUS(I)
                STOP 'PROGRAM TERMINATED'
            END IF
30          CONTINUE
*
*  START BY READING FROM EACH FILE.
*
        DO 50, UNIT = 1, 2
            READ (UNIT, 20, IOSTAT = STATUS(UNIT)) RECORD(UNIT)
```

FIGURE 9.4
PROCEDURE TO DECIDE WHETHER THE NEXT RECORD IN THE MERGE SHOULD
COME FROM UNIT 1 OR 2

If end of file on unit 1	Else If end of file on unit 2	Else If record 1 $\leq$ record 2	Else
UNIT = 2	UNIT = 1	UNIT = 1	UNIT = 2

```
50        CONTINUE
*
* WHILE THERE IS MORE DATA ON EITHER FILE, SELECT
* THE UNIT NUMBER OF THE NEXT RECORD.
*
100   IF (MIN(STATUS(1), STATUS(2)) .NE. 0) THEN
          IF (STATUS(1) .NE. 0) THEN
              UNIT = 2
          ELSE IF (STATUS(2) .NE. 0) THEN
              UNIT = 1
          ELSE IF (RECORD(1) .LE. RECORD(2)) THEN
              UNIT = 1
          ELSE
              UNIT = 2
          END IF
*
* COPY THE RECORD FROM THE SELECTED UNIT AND
* READ ANOTHER RECORD FROM THAT UNIT.
*
          WRITE(3, 20) RECORD(UNIT)
          READ(UNIT, 20, IOSTAT = STATUS (UNIT)) RECORD(UNIT)
          IF (STATUS(UNIT) .LT. 0) THEN
              PRINT *, 'INPUT ERROR NUMBER', STATUS(UNIT)
     $              'ON UNIT', UNIT
              STOP
          END IF
          GO TO 100
      END IF
*
* AT END OF INPUT ON BOTH INPUT FILES—
*
      ENDFILE 3
      DO 200, I = 1, 3
          CLOSE (UNIT = I)
200       CONTINUE
      END
```

INTERNAL FILES

Consider the following problem. A character variable CHAR contains a string representing a real number. For example,

CHAR = '1234.56'

How can you set a real variable X equal to the numeric value of CHAR?

If the value of CHAR were written on a file, you could simply read it with a formatted READ statement. Thus, one possible solution is to write CHAR to a file, rewind the file, and reread it with a numeric edit descriptor. You can achieve the same effect by regarding CHAR as an *internal file* and reading it directly as follows:

    READ(CHAR, '(F7.2)') X

In this READ statement, the unit identifier is the character variable CHAR. The statement says to read the value of X from the string CHAR using an F7.2 edit descriptor. Thus, the effect is the same as

$$X = 1234.56$$

Similarly, you can write to an internal file, as in this example:

    CHARACTER C*10
    REAL X
    X = 1.0/3.0
    WRITE(C, 100) X
100 FORMAT(F10.8)

This is equivalent to the statement

$$C = '0.33333333'$$

In general, an **internal file** is a character variable, a character array, a character array element, or a character substring that is used in place of a unit specifier in a formatted READ or WRITE statement. The character storage units are then read or written as though they were on an external file.

An internal file is not repositioned by a READ or WRITE. Data transfer always begins at the first character storage unit. List-directed input and output are not permitted with internal files, nor are auxiliary input-output statements such as REWIND, BACKSPACE, ENDFILE, or OPEN.

If the internal file is a character variable, character array element, or a substring name, it is considered to be a single record. If the internal file is a character array, then each array element is a record. For example, if C is a character array defined by

    CHARACTER C(5)*10

then the following statements define each element of C.

    WRITE(C, 90) (I, I = 1, 10)
90 FORMAT(10(I5/))

These statements have the same effect as

    C(1) = '   1'
    C(2) = '   2'
    C(3) = '   3'
    ....
    C(10) = '   10'

The slash in the format specification causes writing to begin in a new record, which for the internal file C means a new array element. As another example, the array C could be read as follows

        READ(C, '(F5.0)') (X(I), I = 1, 10)

This would have the same effect as

        X(1) = 1.0
        X(2) = 2.0
        X(3) = 3.0
        ....
        X(10) = 10.0

EXAMPLE 9.4 Error Checking of Input Data
A set of data cards has been prepared with eight real numbers per card, keypunched in an 8F10.2 format. As a first step in processing the data, the programmer decides to perform a simple validity check on the data. Valid data is to be copied to a file named DATA, with one value per record. Any invalid value is to be listed on the printer. To be acceptable, a value must be a real number in the range −100 to +100, inclusive. Zero is an acceptable value, but a blank input field is not. Because of possible keypunching errors, an input field might contain alphabetic data or other invalid numeric output.

To solve this problem you might try reading each card with the statement

        READ(*, '(8F10.2)', END = 900) (X(I), I = 1, 8)

Suppose, however, that some field had a nonnumeric value. The READ would cause an execution error which would halt the program. You could use an IOSTAT specifier to detect such errors, but then if an error were encountered, the remaining X values would be undefined, so the program could not reliably continue after finding the first error.

A solution is to read each card into a character array. Then you can reread each array element as an internal file, using an IOSTAT specifier, and perform the necessary error checking. In order to distinguish blank fields from fields with a zero value, you can use both the character and numeric representations of the data. Figure 9.5 shows a top-level design for the program.

An enhanced FORTRAN version is as follows.

```
* THIS PROGRAM READS A SET OF INPUT CARDS. IT CHECKS EACH
* VALUE FOR VALIDITY. ACCEPTABLE VALUES ARE COPIED TO A FILE.
* UNACCEPTABLE VALUES ARE DIAGNOSED ON A LISTING.
*
* TO BE VALID, AN INPUT FIELD MUST BE NONBLANK AND CONTAIN
* A REAL NUMBER GREATER THAN OR EQUAL TO XMIN AND LESS THAN
* OR EQUAL TO XMAX.
*
* CRDNUM = CARD NUMBER OF INPUT CARDS
* ERRCNT = NUMBER OF ERRORS
* I       = COUNTER FOR DO LOOPS
```

FIGURE 9.5
VALIDITY CHECKING OF INPUT DATA — TOP-LEVEL DESIGN

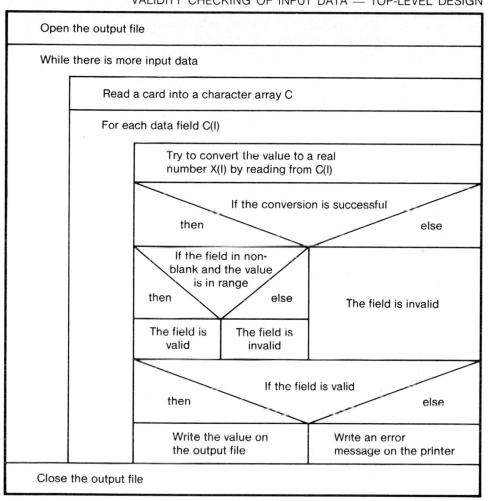

* NGOOD   = NUMBER OF GOOD DATA VALUES
* NPC   = NUMBER OF DATA VALUES PER INPUT CARD
* OUTPUT = UNIT NUMBER OF OUTPUT FILE
* STAT   = INPUT-OUTPUT STATUS
*
     INTEGER CRDNUM, ERRCNT, I, NGOOD, NPC, OUTPUT, STAT
     PARAMETER (NPC = 8, OUTPUT = 7)
*
* C(I)   = INPUT VALUE I, AS A CHARACTER STRING
* FNAME = FILE NAME OF OUTPUT FILE
* SPACE = BLANK SPACE
*

```
      CHARACTER C(NPC)*10, FNAME*(*), SPACE
      PARAMETER (FNAME = 'DATA', SPACE = ' ')
*
* X(I)   = INPUT VALUE I, AS A REAL NUMBER
* XMIN  = MINIMUM ACCEPTABLE INPUT VALUE
* XMAX  = MAXIMUM ACCEPTABLE INPUT VALUE
*
      REAL X(NPC), XMIN, XMAX
      PARAMETER (XMIN = -100, XMAX = 100)
*
* VALID = TRUE IF INPUT FIELD IS VALID
*
      LOGICAL VALID
*
* OPEN OUTPUT FILE
      OPEN (UNIT = OUTPUT, FILE = FNAME, STATUS = 'NEW', IOSTAT =
     $        STAT
      IF (STAT .NE. 0) THEN
          WRITE (*, *) 'ERROR NUMBER ', STAT, ' OPENING FILE',
     $        FNAME
          STOP 'RUN TERMINATED'
      END IF
* INITIALIZE COUNTERS
      CRDNUM = 0
      ERRCNT = 0
      NGOOD = 0
*
* FOR EACH INPUT CARD:
*
100   READ (*, '(8A)', END = 900) (C(I), I = 1, NPC)
      CRDNUM = CRDNUM + 1
* CHECK FOR VALIDITY
      DO 110, I = 1, NPC
      READ (C(I), '(F10.2)', IOSTAT = STAT) X(I)
      IF (STAT .EQ. 0) THEN
          IF (XMIN .LE. X(I) .AND. X(I) .LE. XMAX
     $        .AND. C(I) .NE. SPACE) THEN
              VALID = .TRUE.
          ELSE
              VALID = .FALSE.
          END IF
      IF (VALID) THEN
          NGOOD = NGOOD + 1
          WRITE (OUTPUT, '(A)') C(I)
      ELSE
          ERRCNT = ERRCNT + 1
          WRITE (*, *) '** ERROR IN CARD ', CRDNUM, ' VALUE NUMBER ',
     $        I, ' DATA IS: ', C(I)
```

```
        END IF
110   CONTINUE
      GO TO 100
*
* AT END OF INPUT DATA
*
900   WRITE (*, *) 'TOTAL OF ', CRDNUM, ' INPUT CARDS, WITH ',
     $   ERRCNT, ' DATA ERRORS.'
      CLOSE (UNIT = OUTPUT, IOSTAT = STAT)
      IF (STAT .NE. 0) THEN
          WRITE (*, *) 'OUTPUT FILE', FNAME, 'NOT CLOSED'
      ELSE
          WRITE (*, *) 'TOTAL OF ', NGOOD, ' VALUES WRITTEN TO FILE',
     $       FNAME
      END IF
      END
```

EXAMPLE 9.5 Computing a Format Specification
In a certain program, it is required to print values with statements similar to the following

```
      WRITE(*, 100) (Y(I), I = 1, N)
100   FORMAT(1X, 6F12.3)
```

Instead of using a fixed format specification, however, the programmer wants the repeat count, the field width, and the precision to be variables or symbolic constants given by the integer names RPT, WID, and PRECIS. In other words, the format specification must be equivalent to

```
100   FORMAT(1X, RPT F WID . PRECIS)
```

where RPT, WID, and PRECIS might vary. This use of variables in a format specification is not allowed in FORTRAN. The same effect can, however, be achieved by writing the format specification to an internal file, as in the following example.

```
      INTEGER RPT, WID, PRECIS
      PARAMETER (RPT = 6, WID = 12, PRECIS = 3)
      CHARACTER FMT *30
      WRITE (FMT, 7) RPT, WID, PRECIS
7     FORMAT ('(1X,', I3, 'F', I3, '.', I3, ')')
```

The WRITE statement stores the desired format specification in the character variable FMT. The effect is equivalent to the statement

```
      FMT = '(1X, 6F12. 3)'
```

The program could perform the required output using the statement

```
      WRITE(*, FMT) (Y(I), I = 1, N)
```

THE UNFORMATTED READ AND WRITE STATEMENTS

In executing the statement

    WRITE (*, '(1X, F12.3)') X

two main actions have to be carried out by the computer. First, the value of the variable X has to be formatted as a character string according to the format specification. Second, the character string has to be written to the output device. Converting the internal representation of X to a character string is necessary if the output is to be read by a person. Sometimes, however, the only purpose of writing data to a file is so that the file can be read by another program. In this case, converting numbers to character strings on output and converting character strings to numbers on input are simply extra steps which serve no real purpose. To avoid these extra steps, you can use the more efficient **unformatted READ and WRITE statements**.

The unformatted READ and WRITE statements have one main difference from their formatted counterparts: the format identifier is omitted. An example of an unformatted WRITE statement is

    WRITE (7) N, (X(J), J = 1, N)

The number 7 is the unit number. This statement means to write one unformatted record on unit 7 consisting of the values given in the output list. You could read this record with the unformatted READ statement.

    READ (7) N, (X(J), J = 1, N)

Do not confuse unformatted input and output with list-directed input and output. In list-directed input or output, the formatting is done for you automatically, but the records are formatted nonetheless. With unformatted output, no formatting occurs. The output record is a copy of the data in the same form in which it appears in computer memory. An unformatted READ simply copies data back into memory in its original form.

A record produced by an unformatted WRITE consists of a sequence of *values*, rather than a sequence of characters. Each unformatted WRITE creates one record on the output file, and each unformatted READ reads one record into memory. If the number of variables in the input list is smaller than the number of values in the record, the remaining values are ignored. The number of variables in the input list must not be greater than the number of values in the record. You can read and write variables of any type using unformatted input and output. The type of each variable in the input list of an unformatted READ should be the same as the type of the corresponding variable in the output list of the unformatted WRITE that produced the record.

There are some restrictions on the use of unformatted READ and WRITE statements. You cannot use both formatted and unformatted input or output on the same file. Thus, if you create the first record of a file using an unformatted WRITE, you must create all the records with unformatted WRITE statements. To read the records, you must use unformatted READ statements. Unformatted input and output should be used only with tapes, disks, or similar devices. There would be no point, for instance, in using unformatted output to a printer, since the result would be unintelligible.

Unformatted output should not be used to create files that are to be read on a different computer system. If you want to write a tape to send to someone who has a different type of system, use formatted output. You should also consult with someone in your computer center before attempting this to make sure that the output tape you are creating will comply with ANSI standards.

An example of unformatted input and output is given following the next section.

DIRECT ACCESS FILES

All of the files we have been using up to this point have been **sequential files**: files in which the records are written one after another, in sequence. For example, input from a card reader or a terminal is always sequential. If you want to read the 50th card in a set of input cards, the only way to do it is first to read all of the preceding 49 cards. A magnetic tape is also an inherently sequential device. If you write 100 records to a tape, then rewind the tape, you must read the records back in the same sequence in which they were written.

On a disk unit, there are two possible ways to organize data: as a sequential file, or as a direct access file. In a **direct access file** (sometimes called a **random access file**), you can write and read records in any sequence you like. For example, to read a direct access file with 50 records, you would not necessarily have to read the records in the order 1, 2, 3, . . . , 50. You could read the records in the order 1, 50, 2, 49, 3, 4, 17, ... In other words, you can access each record *directly*, without reading the rest of the file. The difference between sequential and direct access files is something like the difference between an audio tape and a phonograph record. A tape is sequential. If you want to play the second song recorded on the tape, you have to wind the tape forward to skip over the first song. On a phonograph record, you could play the second song by lifting the tone arm directly to the beginning of the song. Similarly, a disk unit can position its read or write head directly to begin with any data record in a direct access file.

To create a direct access file, you must open the file using an OPEN statement similar to the following:

```
OPEN (UNIT = 7, FILE = FNAME, ACCESS = 'DIRECT', RECL = N)
```

There are two specifiers in this statement that you have not seen before. The **access specifier**:

```
ACCESS = 'DIRECT'
```

says that this is a direct access file. For a sequential file you could specify ACCESS = 'SEQUENTIAL', but it is not necessary to do so, since sequential organization is the default. The **record length specifier**:

RECL = N

defines the length of each record on a direct access file. This specifier must be given for direct access files, and it must not be given for sequential files. On a direct access file, all records must be the same length. If the file is created using formatted WRITE statements, the record length is the number of characters in each record. If the file is written using unformatted WRITE statements, the record length is equal to the number of words of memory that comprise each record, which may depend on your particular computer system.

To read or write a record of a direct access file, you include a **record specifier** in the READ or WRITE statement. For example,

READ (7, 100, REC = K) A, B, C

This is equivalent to an ordinary formatted READ statement

READ (7, 100) A, B, C

except that instead of reading the next record on a sequential file, the record specifier:

REC = K

says to read *record number K* from the direct access file, where K may be any integer expression. A WRITE statement for a direct access file has a similar form. The statement

WRITE (1, '(A)', REC = 47) X

means to write the value of X into record number 47 on the direct access file connected to unit 1.

A direct access file may have any number of records, and you can write and read the records in any sequence, subject to the restriction that you must write a record before you can read it. One other restriction for direct access files is that you cannot use list-directed input and output to read and write records.

EXAMPLE 9.6 Creating a Direct Access File and an Index File
A business firm with approximately 300 employees maintains a sequential payroll file with one record per employee. Each record contains 250 characters. The first six characters of each record are a character field containing an employee identification code, which is unique to each employee. The payroll department wants a system to update payroll records from a terminal. They would like to be able to type in an employee identification code and see a display of selected information from the corresponding employee record. Write a program that reads the sequential input file and creates the direct access payroll file.

In addition to the direct access file, the program will require some way of determining the record number, given an identification code. A simple way is to set up an array INDEX to store the identification codes. The subscript of the array will give the record number of the employee record (Figure 9.6). At the end of the program, the INDEX array will be written to a sequential file so that it can be reread for subsequent processing of the direct access file. The index file can be a single record created by an unformatted WRITE statement:

WRITE(IDUNIT)ILEN, (INDEX(I), I = 1, ILEN)

where ILEN is the number of elements used in the INDEX array.

The procedure to create the direct access file is to read each sequential input record, store the employee identification code in the INDEX array, and write the record on a direct access file, using the array subscript as the record number (Figure 9.7).

```
* PROGRAM TO CREATE THE DIRECT ACCESS EMPLOYEE
* PAYROLL FILE.
*
* INUNIT, DAUNIT, IDUNIT ARE THE UNIT NUMBERS
* OF THE INPUT FILE, THE DIRECT ACCESS FILE,
* AND THE INDEX FILE.
* INNAME, DANAME, IDNAME ARE THE CORRESPONDING
* FILE NAMES.
* MAXLEN IS THE MAXIMUM SIZE OF THE INDEX.
* RECSIZ IS THE SIZE OF THE INPUT RECORD.
```

FIGURE 9.6
DATA STRUCTURE FOR EMPLOYEE PAYROLL FILE

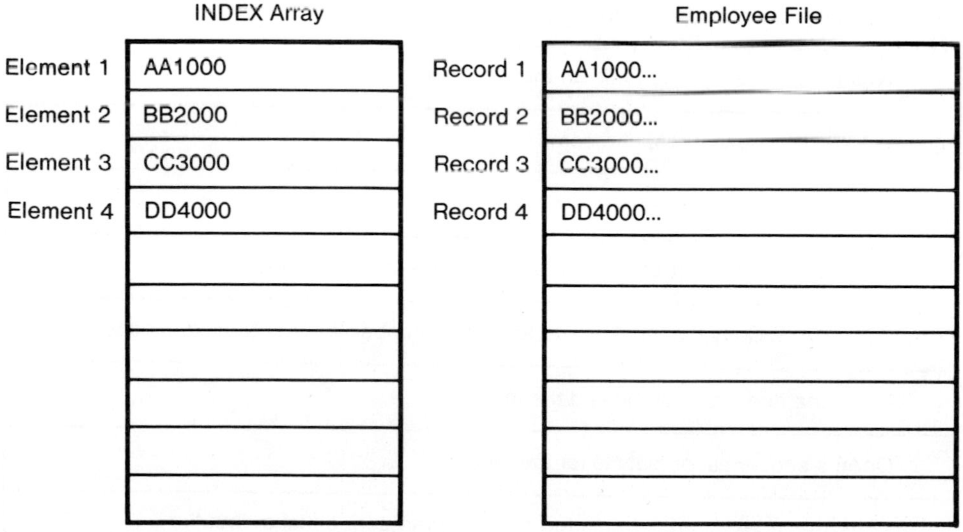

INDEX Array			Employee File	
Element 1	AA1000		Record 1	AA1000...
Element 2	BB2000		Record 2	BB2000...
Element 3	CC3000		Record 3	CC3000...
Element 4	DD4000		Record 4	DD4000...

If INDEX (I) = CODE, then record number I on the direct access file in the record for the employee with identification code, CODE.

```
* IDSIZE IS THE SIZE OF THE EMPLOYEE ID.
      INTEGER INUNIT, DAUNIT, IDUNIT
      PARAMETER (INUNIT = 1, DAUNIT = 2, IDUNIT = 3)
      CHARACTER *(*) INNAME, DANAME, IDNAME
      PARAMETER (INNAME = 'INFILE', DANAME = 'MASTER',
   $     IDNAME = 'INDEX')
      INTEGER MAXLEN, RECSIZ, IDSIZE
      PARAMETER (MAXLEN = 300, RECSIZ = 250,
   $     IDSIZE = 6
      INTEGER I, ILEN
      CHARACTER RECORD*(RECSIZ), INDEX(MAXLEN)*(IDSIZE)
*
* INITIALIZATION.
*
      ILEN = 0
      OPEN (UNIT = INUNIT, FILE = INNAME,
   $     ACCESS = 'SEQUENTIAL', STATUS = 'OLD')
      OPEN (UNIT = DAUNIT, FILE = DANAME,
```

FIGURE 9.7

PROCEDURE TO CREATE THE DIRECT ACCESS EMPLOYEE PAYROLL FILE
FROM A SEQUENTIAL INPUT FILE

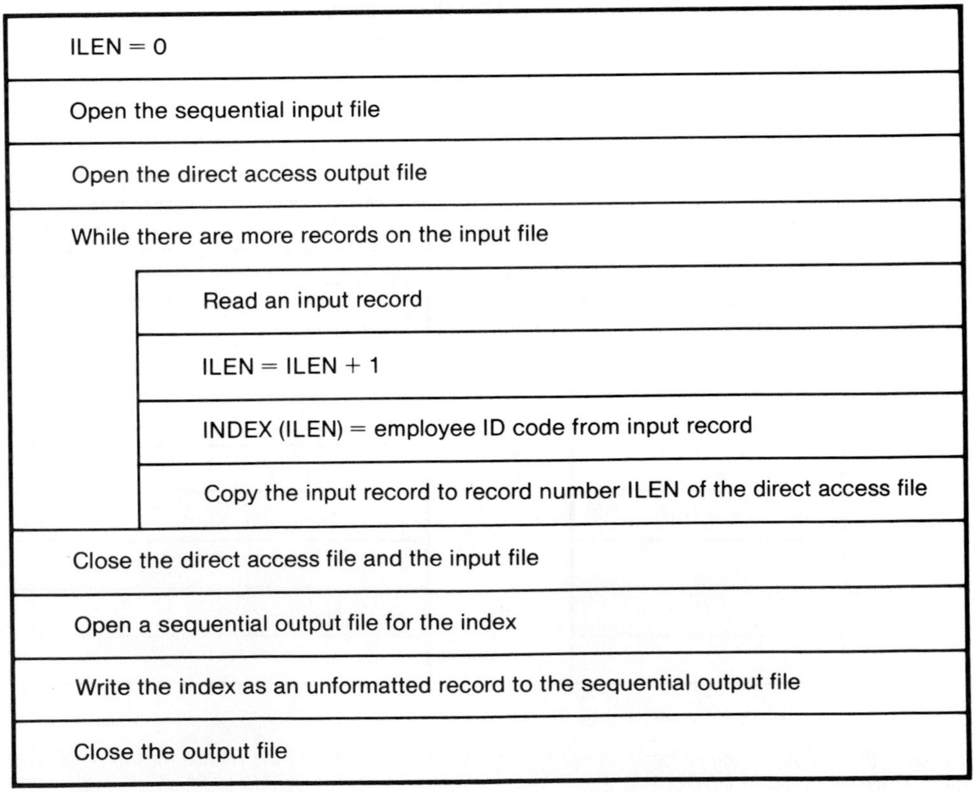

ILEN = 0
Open the sequential input file
Open the direct access output file
While there are more records on the input file

	Read an input record
	ILEN = ILEN + 1
	INDEX (ILEN) = employee ID code from input record
	Copy the input record to record number ILEN of the direct access file

Close the direct access file and the input file
Open a sequential output file for the index
Write the index as an unformatted record to the sequential output file
Close the output file

```
      $     ACCESS = 'DIRECT', RECL = RECSIZ, STATUS = 'NEW')
   *
   * READ EACH INPUT RECORD, ADD THE ID CODE TO THE
   * INDEX ARRAY AND COPY THE RECORD TO THE CORRESPON-
   * DING RECORD ON THE DIRECT ACCESS FILE.
   *
   100   READ (INUNIT, '(A)', END = 200) RECORD
         ILEN = ILEN + 1
         IF (ILEN .GT. MAXLEN) THEN
             PAUSE 'INDEX SIZE EXCEEDED'
             ILEN = MAXLEN
             GO TO 200
         END IF
         INDEX (ILEN) = RECORD(:IDSIZE)
         WRITE (DAFILE, '(A)', REC = ILEN) RECORD
         GO TO 100
   *
   * AT END, CLOSE FILES AND WRITE INDEX FILE.
   *
   200   CLOSE (UNIT = INFILE)
         CLOSE (UNIT = DAFILE)
         OPEN (UNIT = IDUNIT, NAME = IDNAME, STATUS = 'NEW')
         WRITE (IDUNIT) ILEN, (INDEX(I), I = 1, ILEN)
         CLOSE (UNIT = IDUNIT)
   *
         END
```

EXAMPLE 9.7 Retrieving Records from a Direct Access File

The payroll department manager wants to inspect records from the direct access file created in Example 9.6. The program in this example assumes that a terminal is available for input and output on unit number TTY. The program asks for an employee identification code. It searches the index, read from the index file created in Example 9.6. If the code is found in the INDEX array, the program types columns 7 through 75 of the corresponding employee record at the terminal. If the code is not found in the INDEX array, the program types an error message. The process is repeated until the user types the word END when asked for an employee identification code.

Figure 9.8 shows the general outline of the program. The FORTRAN statements are as follows.

```
   * PROGRAM TO DISPLAY INFORMATION FROM THE EMPLOYEE
   * PAYROLL FILE.
   *
   * TTY, DAUNIT, IDUNIT ARE THE UNIT NUMBERS OF THE
   * TERMINAL, THE DIRECT ACCESS FILE, AND THE
   * INDEX FILE.
   * DANAME AND IDNAME ARE THE FILE NAMES.
   * MAXLEN IS THE MAXIMUM SIZE OF THE INDEX.
   * RECSIZE IS THE SIZE OF THE INDEX RECORD.
   * IDSIZE IS THE SIZE OF THE EMPLOYEE ID.
```

```
      INTEGER TTY, DAUNIT, IDUNIT
      PARAMETER (TTY = 5, DAUNIT = 1, IDUNIT = 2)
      CHARACTER *(*) DANAME, IDNAME
      PARAMETER (DANAME = 'MASTER', IDNAME = 'INDEX')
      INTEGER MAXLEN, RECSIZ, IDSIZE
      PARAMETER (MAXLEN = 300, RECSIZ = 250, IDSIZE = 6)
      INTEGER I, ILEN
      CHARACTER RECORD*(RECSIZE), ID*(IDSIZE), INDEX(MAXLEN)*(IDSIZE)
*
* INITIALIZATION.
*
      OPEN (UNIT = IDUNIT, FILE = IDFILE,
```

FIGURE 9.8

PROCEDURE TO RETRIEVE RECORDS FROM THE DIRECT ACCESS EMPLOYEE FILE
FOR DISPLAY ON A TERMINAL

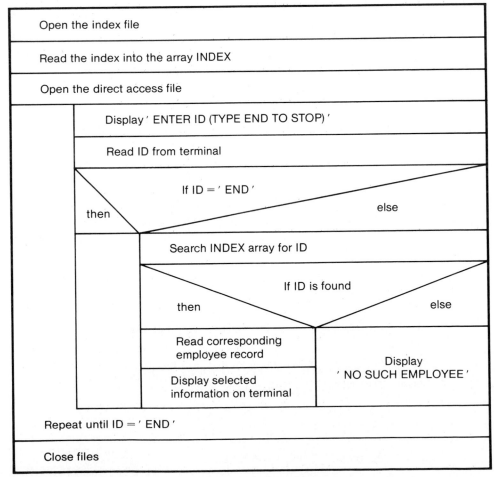

```
      $     ACCESS = 'SEQUENTIAL', STATUS = 'OLD')
            OPEN (UNIT = DAUNIT, FILE = DANAME,
      $     ACCESS = 'DIRECT', STATUS = 'OLD')
            READ (IDUNIT) ILEN, (INDEX(I), I = 1, ILEN)
*
* REPEAT UNTIL USER TYPES 'END'
*
100   WRITE (TTY, '(1X, A)') 'ENTER ID (TYPE END TO STOP)'
            READ (TTY, '(A)') ID
            IF (ID .NE. 'END') THEN
                DO 120, I = 1, ILEN
                    IF (ID .EQ. INDEX(I)) GO TO 125
120             CONTINUE
125         CONTINUE
            IF (I .LE. ILEN) THEN
                READ (DAUNIT, '(A)', REC = I) RECORD
                WRITE (TTY, '(1X, A)') RECORD(7:75)
            ELSE
                WRITE (TTY, '1X, A)') 'NO SUCH EMPLOYEE'
            END IF
            GO TO 100
        END IF
*
* CLOSE FILES AND STOP
*
        CLOSE (UNIT = IDUNIT)
        CLOSE (UNIT = DAUNIT)
        END
```

SUMMARY

Data can be stored on a file, which consists of a sequence of records. Each record has a certain length. An endfile record marks the end of a file.

The general form of the READ and WRITE statements use a unit number to identify the file being read or written.

A unit number is connected to a file by means of an OPEN statement. The OPEN statement also initializes the file for processing, and it may define certain properties of the file, such as the status. An OPEN statement is generally executed prior to any processing on a file, although certain files (such as the card reader) may not need to be explicitly opened in this manner.

To terminate processing on a file, a CLOSE statement may be executed. All open files are closed automatically when a program executes a STOP or END statement.

The REWIND statement positions a file at its beginning. The BACKSPACE statement backspaces over the record just read. The ENDFILE statement writes an endfile record.

An internal file is a character variable, character array, or character array element. You can use an internal file name in place of a unit identifier in a READ or WRITE statement. The character storage units of an internal file can be read or written as though they were part of an external file.

The unformatted READ and WRITE statements transfer data between computer memory and an external device without formatting. Data on an unformatted record is a sequence of values, in the same form in which it is stored in memory. Unformatted output is an efficient way of creating a file whose only purpose is to be read by another program.

A direct access file is organized on a disk unit so that records may be read or written in any sequence. To establish a direct access file, you use an access specifier and a record length specifier in the OPEN statement. In a READ or WRITE statement for a direct access file, you use a record specifier to tell which record of the file to read or write.

VOCABULARY

access specifier
BACKSPACE statement
close a file
CLOSE statement
connect a file
direct access file
disconnect a file
endfile record
ENDFILE statement
file specifier
input-output status specifier
internal file
merge

open a file
OPEN statement
random access file
record
record length specifier
record specifier
REWIND statement
status specifier
unformatted input and output
unit identifier
unit number
unit specifier

EXERCISES

1. It is often useful to "include" one or more copies of one file at certain points within another file. For example, suppose that a main program and several subroutines each use identical PARAMETER statements to define constants. Rather than copy the statements in each subprogram, you can write the PARAMETER statements on a separate file and "include" copies of the file into the program. Write a program that opens an input and output file, using the OPENIO subroutine from Example 9.1.

Copy each line of the input file to the output file, with one exception: If a line in the input file has the form

*INCLUDE filename

then open the file "filename" on an alternate input unit, copy the alternate input file to the output file, then close the alternate input file and continue reading from the main input file.

2. The program in Example 9.3 merges two input files. Rewrite this program to merge up to 10 input files into a single output file.

3. Write a program that reads a file containing a FORTRAN program and lists it on the printer. Read the name of the input file from the card reader or terminal. Start listing each program unit (main program or subprogram) on a new page of output. Number the lines of each subprogram in the left margin. List a maximum of 55 lines per page. At the top of each page, print a title giving the name of the subprogram and a page number.

4. Two common ways of writing a date such as July 4, 1976 are

$$7/4/76$$

and

$$4 \text{ JUL } 76$$

Using internal files, write a character-valued function

DAMOYR(DATE)

that converts a character string DATE in the first form to an equivalent date in the second form. For example, the value of

DAMOYR('7/4/76') is '4 JUL 76'

5. Write a character-valued function

MODAYR(DATE)

that performs the inverse of the function in Exercise 4. For example,

MODAYR('4 JUL 76') is '7/4/76'

6. Suppose that SECOND represents the time since midnight, in seconds, as an integer quantity. Write a character-valued function

TIME(SECOND)

that returns the time as a character string such as

'11:45 AM'   or   '1:13 PM'

7. *Pascal's Triangle* is the following array of numbers

$$1$$
$$1\ 1$$
$$1\ 2\ 1$$
$$1\ 3\ 3\ 1$$
$$1\ 4\ 6\ 4\ 1$$
$$1\ 5\ 10\ 10\ 5\ 1$$
$$\cdot\ \cdot\ \cdot$$

These numbers are the coefficients given by the binomial theorem in algebra. Each row begins and ends with a 1. Each other number in the triangle is the sum of the two numbers above it. Write a program that prints the first 11 rows of Pascal's Triangle. (*Hint*: For each row of the output, compute a format specification by writing to an internal file.)

8. Exercise 13 in Chapter 5 (page 175) called for a program to read lines of text and print each word on a separate line of output. Modify that program to read from any file and write to any file.

9. Modify the program in Exercise 8 to read a file containing a FORTRAN program and list each variable or statement name on a separate line. For example, for the input line

IF ((A + B) .LE. 10) GOTO 100

the output would be

IF
A
B
LE
10
GOTO
100

You may assume that variable names and statement parts contain no embedded blanks and that they are separated from other parts of the statement by a space or a special character. Also assume that statements are not continued on more than one line.

10. Modify the program of Exercise 9 so that it lists the variables and statement parts in alphabetical order, each one being followed by a list of all line numbers in which it appears. For example:

```
GOTO       LINES:  5   7
IF         LINES:  6
INTEGER    LINES:  1   2
J          LINES:  1   11   14
K          LINES:  2   11   14   15
```

| LT | LINES: | 6 |
| THEN | LINES: | 6 |

This program can be useful for producing a *cross-reference list* of statements and variables in a FORTRAN program.

11. Example 6.4 in Chapter 6 showed how to sort a set of input cards and list them on a printer. Use this technique to write a program that reads any file, sorts the records in alphabetical order, and writes them on a file. The names of the files should be input to the program.

12. Modify the program in Exercise 11 to sort on any *key field* in the input file. For example, if the key field is columns 15–20, the records should be sorted according to the data in columns 15–20 of the input record. The location of the key field should be input to the program.

13. The file sorting method used in Exercises 11 and 12 assumes that the entire file can be stored in memory. For "larger" files, that is not the case. The usual method of sorting a large file is to combine sort and merge operations. Read the first part of the input file, sort it, and write it to a scratch file. Then read the next part of the input file, sort it, and write it to another scratch file. When the entire input file has been read, rewind all the scratch files and merge them into the sorted output file. Write a sort/merge program using this method. Use unformatted input and output for the scratch files.

14. A certain university library maintains a direct access file with one record for each book in their collection. A book record has the format shown in Table 9.1.

TABLE 9.1

Columns	Item
1–15	Call number of book (Library of Congress system)
16–35	Author's last name
36–45	Author's first name
46–71	Name of joint author, if any
76–120	Title
121–135	Publisher
136–141	Date the book was acquired
142–147	If book is checked out, this field is the library card number of the person to whom it is on loan; otherwise, this field is blank
148–153	If book is checked out, this is the date due; otherwise, this field is blank
154–159	If book is no longer in the collection, this field is the date the book left the collection; otherwise, this field is blank
160	A code indicating the status of the book:
	blank = in the library
	1 = checked out
	2 = missing or stolen
	3 = out of circulation (for instance, at the binder)
	4 = on permanent loan

Each of the date fields in this record is in the form MMDDYY where MM is an integer representing the month, DD is the day, and YY is the last two digits of the year. All other fields are left-justified character items. An index file is also maintained as an unformatted sequential file. Each record on the index file was created by a statement of the form

WRITE (UNIT) N, (CALL(I), I = 1, N), (REC(I), I = 1, N)

where N is the number of elements in the arrays CALL and REC, CALL is a CHARACTER*15 array of call numbers, and REC is an integer array of record numbers. REC(I) is the record number on the direct access file of the book with call number CALL(I). The index file is sorted so that the CALL numbers are in alphabetical order. Write a program that lists the call number, author, title, and date due of all books that are checked out.

15. Each time a book is checked out of the library in Exercise 14, a card is prepared in the following format.

Columns	Item
1–6	Library card number of person to whom book is on loan
8–22	Call number of book
24–29	Date due
31	Blank

Each time a book is returned, a similar card is prepared, but with the letter 'R' in column 31. Suppose that all these cards are copied to a file and sorted in call number order. Write a program to read the file and update the book file to reflect the status of each book checked out or returned.

16. In a certain data-processing department, each program, or set of programs, is stored on magnetic tape, each 80-character record being one line of the program. Columns 73–80 of each record contain a sequence number, which may be any real number. The records are numbered in increasing order. To update a program on tape, a programmer prepares a set of correction cards, each of which has a sequence number in columns 73–80. For example, to insert a new line between lines 100 and 101, the programmer would make a correction card with sequence number 101.5. To replace the line 200 on the tape, a correction card with sequence number 200 would be prepared. To delete line 250, a correction card would have a sequence number 250 in columns 73–80 and the other columns blank. Write a program to read the correction cards, sort them by sequence number, and write a new tape by making the appropriate corrections to the old tape.

ADDITIONAL
TOPICS

INTRODUCTION If you have mastered the previous nine chapters, which present the main body of the FORTRAN language, you can consider yourself a well-educated FORTRAN programmer. The additional topics covered in this chapter can be very useful for certain applications, but they are features of the language which even professional programmers are likely to use only rarely.

You can read this chapter separately, or you can read individual sections in conjunction with other chapters. For instance, students who are familiar with the mathematical concept of complex numbers may wish to read that section after completing Chapter 3.

The following list shows which chapters are most closely related to the sections in this chapter:

Complex Numbers	
Double-Precision Numbers	Chapters 3 and 4
The DATA Statement	
The Computed GO TO	
The Assigned GO TO	Chapter 4
The Arithmetic IF Statement	
Common Storage	
Block Data Subprograms	Chapters 6 and 7
Statement Functions	
The SAVE Statement	
Alternate Returns from a Subroutine	Chapter 7
The EXTERNAL Statement	
The EQUIVALENCE Statement	Chapter 3

COMPLEX NUMBERS*

In mathematics, a **complex number** is a number of the form

$$a + bi$$

*Optional section. This section is intended for students who are familiar with the mathematical concept of complex numbers. It may be omitted by those who are not.

371

where i is the square root of negative 1 ($\sqrt{-1}$), the base of the imaginary numbers. A complex number has two parts: a **real** part, a, and an **imaginary** part, bi.

You can use complex numbers in FORTRAN. A FORTRAN **complex constant** is a pair of real constants separated by a comma and enclosed in parentheses. The first number is the real part of the complex constant. The second number is the imaginary part. Thus the FORTRAN constant

(1.0, 2.0)

represents the complex number

$1 + 2i$

Table 10.1 gives some other examples of complex constants.

TABLE 10.1
EXAMPLES OF COMPLEX CONSTANTS

Complex Number	FORTRAN Complex Constant
$1 + i$	(1.0, 0.0)
i	(0.0, 1.0)
$3 + 4i$	(3.0, 4.0)
5	(5.0, 0.0)
$-1/2 - 3.5i$	(−0.5, −3.5)
$-2\pi i$	(0.0, −6.283185)

You can declare **complex variables** in a program with a **COMPLEX statement** such as

COMPLEX C, W, Z

which says that C, W, and Z are complex variables. This statement is a type statement (like INTEGER and REAL) which must come before the first executable statement in your program.

You can also declare complex variables with an IMPLICIT statement such as

IMPLICIT COMPLEX (W − Z)

which says that variables beginning with W, X, Y, or Z are complex variables.

Complex arithmetic in FORTRAN is like complex arithmetic in algebra. The mathematical definitions of addition, subtraction, multiplication, and division of complex numbers are given by the formulas in Table 10.2. For example, according to the formula for division, the quotient

$$\frac{-7 \; - \; 4i}{2 \; + \; 3i}$$

is equal to $-2 \; + \;$ i. In FORTRAN, the complex expression

   (−7.0, −4.0)/(2.0, 3.0)

has the complex value (−2.0, 1.0).

TABLE 10.2
ARITHMETIC OPERATIONS FOR COMPLEX NUMBERS

Addition:

$$(a \; + \; bi) \; + \; (c \; + \; di) \; = \; (a \; + \; c) \; + \; (b \; + \; d)i$$

Subtraction:

$$(a \; + \; bi) \; (c \; + \; di) \; - \; (a \; - \; c) \; + \; (b \; - \; d)i$$

Multiplication:

$$(a \; + \; bi) \; (c \; + \; di) \; - \; (ac \; - \; bd) \; | \; (ad \; + \; bc)i$$

Division:

$$(a \; + \; bi)/(c \; + \; di) \; = \; \frac{ac \; + \; bd}{c^2 \; + \; d^2} \; + \; \frac{bc \; - \; ad}{c^2 \; + \; d^2} \; i$$

You learned before that you can mix integer and real data in an arithmetic expression. Mixed mode arithmetic extends to complex expressions as well.

> *Rule for Mixed Mode in Complex Expressions*
> You may combine a real (or integer) expression with a complex expression using the operators $+$, $-$, $*$, or $/$ to form a complex expression. The value of such an expression is a complex number computed using complex arithmetic after converting the value of the real (or integer) expression to a complex number with zero for the imaginary part.

For example, the value of the expression

   2*(1.1, 3.3) + 1

is the complex number (3.2, 6.6).

Notice that the rule does not say anything about the exponentiation operator (**). The rule governing exponentiation of complex expressions is this:

Rule for Complex Exponentiation
A complex expression may have an integer exponent. That is, if Z is a complex expression and N is an integer expression, then

  Z**N

is a valid complex expression. A complex expression may *not* have a real or a complex exponent.

This rule implies that the following expression is not allowed.

  (1.0, 1.0) ** 0.5

The reason for this restriction is that there is no unique definition of Z^x, when Z is a complex number, unless x is an integer.

You can store a value in a complex variable with an assignment statement. If Z is a complex variable, then

  Z = (1.0, 2.0)

simply stores the value of the complex constant in the variable Z.

If the right side of a complex assignment statement is an integer or real expression, then the value stored is a complex number with an imaginary part of zero. For example, if Z is complex,

$$Z = 2 + 2$$

stores the complex value (4.0, 0.0) in Z.

If you store the value of a complex expression in a real variable, only the real part is stored. Thus if X is real, then

  X = (2.2, 3.3)

stores the real value 2.2 in X.

If you store the value of a complex expression in an integer variable, only the real part is stored, and it is converted to an integer by truncating any decimal fraction. Thus if N is an integer variable, then

  N = (2.2, 3.3)

stores the value 2 in N.

There are several intrinsic functions which are useful for complex arithmetic: If Z is a complex expression, then

REAL(Z)

is a real number equal to the real part of Z. The function

AIMAG(Z)

is a real number equal to the imaginary part of Z. Thus

REAL((1.0, 2.0))

has the value 1.0, and

AIMAG((1.0, 2.0))

has the value 2.0.

The function CMPLX makes a complex number out of one or two integer or real numbers.

CMPLX(1.0 + 2.0, 3.0 + 4.0)

is equal to the complex number (3.0, 7.0).

CMPLX(5)

and

CMPLX(5.0)

both give the complex value (5.0, 0.0).

The **conjugate** of a complex number $a + bi$ is the complex number $a - bi$. The intrinsic function CONJG computes the conjugate of a complex expression. The value of

CONJG((1.0, 2.0))

is the complex number (1.0, −2.0).

The **absolute value** of a complex number $a + bi$ is the real number $\sqrt{a^2 + b^2}$. The intrinsic function ABS computes the absolute value of a complex expression. The value of

ABS((5.0, 12.0))

is the real number 13.0.

For more information about intrinsic functions, refer to Appendix A.

You can read and write complex numbers using the list-directed READ and PRINT statements. In input data, enclose a complex number in parentheses, just as you would write a complex constant. In output data, too, a complex number is enclosed in parentheses.

For formatted input and output, a complex number is treated as a pair of real numbers. Thus, each complex value in an input or output list corresponds to two edit descriptors in a format specification. For example,

```
        COMPLEX Z
        READ 10, Z
10      FORMAT (F10.0, F5.0)
```

The real part of Z is read according to the F10.0 edit descriptor, and the imaginary part is read according to the F5.0 edit descriptor.

EXAMPLE 10.1 Complex Roots
The number 1 has two square roots: +1 and −1. It has three cube roots:

$$1 \qquad -\frac{1}{2} + \frac{\sqrt{3}}{2}i \qquad -\frac{1}{2} - \frac{\sqrt{3}}{2}i$$

One of these roots is a real number, and the other two are complex numbers (Figure 10.1).

FIGURE 10.1
THE NUMBER 1 HAS THREE CUBE ROOTS, TWO OF WHICH ARE
COMPLEX NUMBERS

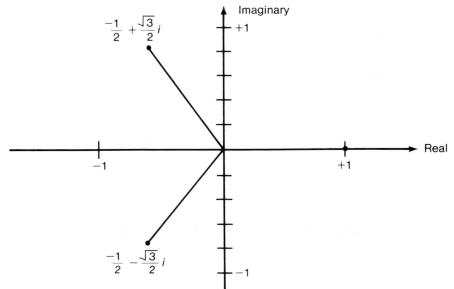

In general, if n is a positive integer, there are n nth roots of 1, given by

$$\cos \frac{2\pi k}{n} + \sin \frac{2\pi k}{n} \, i$$

where $k = 0, 1, 2, \ldots, n - 1$. These complex numbers are called the nth *roots of unity*. Write a program that reads an integer n and prints the nth roots of unity.

You can use the CMPLX function to form the sine and cosine parts of the above formula. A program loop computes the root for each value of k. Here is a complete program.

```
* COMPUTE THE NTH ROOTS OF UNITY.
      REAL TWOPI
      PARAMETER (TWOPI = 2 * 3.14159265)
      INTEGER K, N
      COMPLEX Z
      READ *, N
      DO 10, K = 0, N - 1
          Z = CMPLX(COS(TWOPI*K/N), SIN(TWOPI*K/N))
          PRINT *, Z
10        CONTINUE
      END
```

EXAMPLE 10.2 Center of Gravity and Area of a Triangle

You can use complex numbers to represent points in a plane. A point has an x-coordinate and a y-coordinate which you can store as the real and imaginary parts of a complex number.

Figure 10.2 shows a triangle. The three vertices, Z_a, Z_b, and Z_c correspond to the complex numbers (1.0, 1.0), (8.0, 3.0), and (6.0, 8.0). The **center of gravity** of this triangle is the point M. If you cut the triangle out of cardboard, you could balance it on a pin at point M. To compute the coordinates of M, add the three vertices, as complex numbers, and divide the result by 3.

If you subtract one vertex from another, as complex numbers, the result is a complex number whose magnitude (absolute value) equals the length of the line joining the vertices. Thus the length of side a in the figure is equal to

ABS((6.0, 8.0) − (8.0, 3.0))

Similarly you can find the lengths of sides b and c.

When you know the lengths of the sides of a triangle you can find the area of the triangle from the formula

$$\text{Area} = \frac{\sqrt{(s - a)\,(s - b)\,(s - c)}}{s}$$

where a, b, and c are the lengths of the sides, and s is the semiperimeter.

$$s = (1/2)\,(a + b + c)$$

(This is called *Heron's formula*.)

FIGURE 10.2
A TRIANGLE CAN BE REPRESENTED BY THREE COMPLEX NUMBERS, z_a, z_b, and z_c.

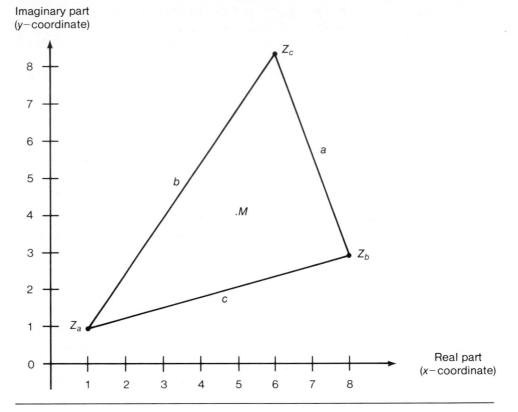

The real and imaginary parts of each number give the X and Y coordinates of the vertices. You can use complex arithmetic to find the location of M, the center of gravity, and the lengths of the three sides, a, b, and c.

The following program reads three complex numbers, ZA, ZB, and ZC, representing the coordinates of the vertices of a triangle. It prints the coordinates and the coordinates of the center of gravity of the triangle. It then prints the lengths of the sides and the area of the triangle.

```
* CENTER OF GRAVITY AND AREA OF A TRIANGLE,
* USING COMPLEX NUMBERS.
*
      REAL A, B, C, S
      COMPLEX ZA, ZB, ZC
      READ *, ZA, ZB, ZC
      PRINT *, 'VERTICES:', ZA, ZB, ZC
      PRINT *, 'CENTER OF GRAVITY:', (ZA + ZB + ZC)/3
```

```
A = ABS(ZB - ZC)
B = ABS(ZA - ZC)
C = ABS(ZA - ZB)
PRINT *, 'LENGTH OF SIDE JOINING ', ZA, ZB, '=', C
PRINT *, 'LENGTH OF SIDE JOINING ', ZB, ZC, '=', A
PRINT *, 'LENGTH OF SIDE JOINING ', ZA, ZC, '=', B
S = (A + B + C)/2
IF (S .NE. 0) THEN
    PRINT *, 'AREA =', SQRT((S-A)*(S-B)*(S-C)/S)
END IF
END
```

DOUBLE-PRECISION NUMBERS

All real arithmetic is subject to an inherent error because of the limited precision of computer storage locations. Often this error is not significant. Most machines provide at least seven-place accuracy for real numbers. Sometimes, however, you may need more precision than that. In that case, you can use **double-precision arithmetic**.

A double-precision constant or variable is like a real constant or variable, but it is stored in two memory locations.* The additional memory location provides storage for extra digits. If your computer gives seven-place precision for real numbers, it might give fourteen-place precision for double-precision numbers.

A **double-precision constant** in FORTRAN is like a real constant in exponential form, but you use the letter D instead of the letter E before the exponent. For example,

−6.2D4

is a double-precision constant representing the number -6.2×10^4.

You use a **DOUBLE PRECISION** type statement to declare variables to be double precision. For example,

DOUBLE PRECISION X, Y

means that X and Y will be double-precision variables in the program. Like the other type statements you have studied, this statement is nonexecutable and must come before the first executable statement in the program.

You can also declare double-precision variables with an IMPLICIT statement such as

IMPLICIT DOUBLE PRECISION (A, X − Z)

*Details about the way in which real and double-precision numbers are stored will depend on the particular machine you use. Some machines use two memory locations for real numbers and four memory locations for double-precision numbers.

Mixed-mode arithmetic using double-precision numbers follows a rule similar to the one for complex numbers.

Rules for Mixed-Mode in Double-Precision Expressions
You may combine a real (or integer) expression with a double-precision expression using the operators $+$, $-$, $*$, $/$, or $**$ to form a double-precision expression. The value of such an expression is a double-precision number computed using double-precision arithmetic after converting the real (or integer) expression to a double-precision number.

You cannot mix double precision and complex data in the same expression.

For example, the mixed-mode expression

```
2 * 3.131492654D0 + 1
```

is evaluated as though it were written

```
2.0D0 * 3.131592654D0 + 1.0D0
```

When you use an assignment statement to store a value in a double-precision variable, the value is converted to double-precision form by simply extending its precision. For example:

```
DOUBLE PRECISION X
X = 2
```

The assignment statement stores the double-precision value 2.0D0 in X.

When you store a double-precision value in a real variable, the value is converted to a real number by dropping the least significant digits. For example,

```
REAL E
E = 2.718281828459
```

If the computer you use provides seven-place accuracy for real numbers, the value stored in E would be the real number 2.718282.

The intrinsic functions REAL and DBLE can convert double-precision values to real and vice versa. The functions SQRT, SIN, COS, and so on can all take double-precision arguments and compute double-precision values. Refer to Appendix A for details.

EXAMPLE 10.3 Computation of π
The number π can be computed using the intrinsic function ATAN2, since inverse trigonometric functions use radian measures. The following program computes the value of π using both real and double-precision arithmetic. It also prints the difference of the two results as a double-precision number. This number indicates the limit of precision for a real number on your computer.

```
* COMPUTE THE VALUE OF PI
      REAL PI
      DOUBLE PRECISION DPI
      PI = ATAN2(-1.0, 0.0)
      DPI = ATAN2(-1.0D0, 0.0D0)
      PRINT *, 'PI = ', DPI
      PRINT *, 'PI (SINGLE PRECISION) = ', PI
      PRINT *, 'DIFFERENCE = ', DPI - PI
      END
```

THE DATA STATEMENT

The **DATA statement** is a nonexecutable statement that defines the *initial value* of a variable. An example is:

```
REAL PI
DATA PI / 3.1416 /
```

These statements declare PI to be a real variable whose initial value is 3.1416. To understand the significance of the DATA statement, consider some alternative ways of initializing PI. The statements:

```
REAL PI
PARAMETER (PI = 3.1416)
```

declare PI to be a real symbolic constant with the value 3.1416. The DATA statement serves a similar purpose, but defines PI to be a *variable*, not a symbolic constant. The statements

```
REAL PI
PI = 3.1416
```

define PI to be a real variable with the value 3.1416, but the value is assigned after the program begins execution, whereas the DATA statement assigns the initial value 3.1416 to PI when the program is compiled.

The form of the DATA statement is

$$\text{DATA } name_1, \ldots, name_n/value_1, \ldots, value_n/$$

where $name_i$ is a variable name, and $value_i$ is a constant of a symbolic constant of the same type as $name_i$. For example,

```
REAL A, B
CHARACTER C * 10
INTEGER N
DATA A, B, C, N / 0.0, 1.0, 'TITLE', 100 /
```

has the same effect as the statements

```
A = 0.0
B = 1.0
C = 'TITLE'
N = 100
```

except that the values are stored in the variables during compilation of the program, rather than during execution.

In the value list of a DATA statement, you can use a **repetition factor**, consisting of a constant followed by an asterisk, to specify a sequence of identical values. Thus, the following two statements are equivalent.

```
DATA A, B, C / 1.0, 1.0, 1.0 /
DATA A, B, C / 3*1.0 /
```

The symbol 3*1.0 means three consecutive values of 1.0. A repetition factor may be an integer constant or a symbolic integer constant.

You can use an implied DO loop in the variable list of a DATA statement, just as for a READ statement, except that only constants or constant expressions are allowed for the DO parameters. The following statements declare a real array X with initial values of zero in all elements.

```
INTEGER I, MAXX
PARAMETER (MAXX = 50)
REAL X(MAXX)
DATA (X(I), I = 1, MAXX) / MAXX * 0.0 /
```

EXAMPLE 10.4 Factorial Function
The function NFACT(N) computes the factorial of N (see Example 7.3). If $0 \le N \le 10$, then NFACT is computed directly by assigning a value from the array NF, which is initialized by a DATA statement.

```
      INTEGER FUNCTION NFACT(N)
* NFACT(N) = FACTORIAL OF N
      INTEGER N, LIM, I
      PARAMETER (LIM = 10)
      INTEGER NF(0:LIM)
      DATA (NF(I), I = 0, LIM) / 1, 1, 2, 6, 24, 120, 720,
     $    5040, 40320, 362880, 3628800 /
*
      IF (0 .LE. N .AND. N .LE. LIM) THEN
          NFACT = NF(N)
          RETURN
      ELSE IF (N .GT. LIM) THEN
          NFACT = NF(LIM)
          DO 10, I = LIM + 1, N
              NFACT = NFACT*I
```

```
10              CONTINUE
        RETURN
    ELSE
        PRINT *, 'ERROR – NEGATIVE ARGUMENT IN NFACT'
        STOP
    END IF
    END
```

THE COMPUTED GO TO

The computed GO TO is a form of GO TO statement which selects one of a number of statements to be executed, depending on the value of an integer variable. The form is

$$\text{GO TO } (s_1, s_2, s_3, \ldots, s_n), \text{ I}$$

where $s_1, s_2, s_3, \ldots, s_n$ is a list of statement labels. They must be integer constants. I is an integer expression. The comma in front of the integer expression is optional (you can leave it off).

This statement means the same as

```
IF (I .EQ. 1) THEN
        GO TO s1
ELSE IF (I .EQ. 2) THEN
        GO TO s2
ELSE IF (I .EQ. 3) THEN
        GO TO s3
. . . . . . . . . . . . . . . . . . . .
ELSE IF (I .EQ. n) THEN
        GO TO sn
END IF
```

If the value of I is less than 1 or greater than n, the computed GO TO does not branch, and the program continues with the next statement.

As a specific example, the statement

```
GO TO (10, 10, 20, 99) NVAR + 1
```

means GO TO 10 if NVAR + 1 equals 1 or 2, GO TO 20 if NVAR + 1 equals 3, GO TO 99 if NVAR + 1 equals 4.

EXAMPLE 10.5 A Dispatch Table
A program on a timesharing system asks the user to enter a command. If the user types:

INSERT   the program should branch to statement 1000
DELETE   the program should branch to statement 2000

REPLACE   the program should branch to statement 3000
PRINT   the program should branch to statement 4000
END   the program should branch to statement 9000

Any other response is illegal. Suppose that CMDTBL is a character array that has been initialized as follows.

```
      INTEGER CSIZ, CLEN, JUMP
      PARAMETER (CSIZ = 7, CLEN = 5)
      CHARACTER CMDTBL(CLEN)*(CSIZ), ANSWER*(CSIZ)
      DATA (CMDTBL(I), I = 1, CLEN) /
     $    'INSERT',
     $    'DELETE',
     $    'REPLACE',
     $    'PRINT',
     $    'END' /
```

The following statements will accept a command and dispatch the program to the appropriate section.

```
100   WRITE(TTY, ' (1X,A) ' ) 'ENTER YOUR COMMAND – '
      READ(TTY, ' (A) ' ) ANSWER
      DO 110, JUMP = 1, CLEN
          IF (ANSWER .EQ. CMDTBL(JUMP)) GO TO 115
110       CONTINUE
115   CONTINUE
      GO TO (1000, 2000, 3000, 4000, 9000) JUMP
      WRITE(TTY, ' (1X, A) ' ) 'INVALID COMMAND'
      GO TO 100
```

THE ASSIGNED GO TO

The **assigned GO TO** is a GO TO statement with a variable statement number. The form is

$$\text{GO TO I, } (s_1, s_2, \ldots, s_n)$$

where I is an integer variable and $s_1, s_2, \ldots, s_n$ is a list of statement labels, which must be integer numbers; this list gives all the possible statement numbers to which the statement might branch.

This statement means GO TO statement I, where I is one of the statement numbers in the list. Before executing this statement, some value must be assigned to I. This is *not* done by the usual assignment statement; that is, the following is incorrect:

```
* INCORRECT USE OF ASSIGNED GO TO.
      IWRONG = 10
      GO TO IWRONG, (10, 20, 25)
```

You must use a special **ASSIGN statement** to give a value to a variable in an assigned GO TO. The ASSIGN statement has the form:

ASSIGN *n* TO I

where *n* is an integer constant representing a statement number and I is an integer variable.

After this assignment has taken place, the variable I may be used in an assigned GO TO. Thus,

ASSIGN 122 to JUMP
GO TO JUMP, (100, 5, 122, 99)

will transfer to statement 122.

The reason the ASSIGN statement is required is that the value stored in JUMP is not really the integer value 122, but some address representing the location of statement 122. For this reason, the value of JUMP should not be modified in the program except by assigning a different value through another ASSIGN statement.

THE ARITHMETIC IF STATEMENT

There is another type of IF statement in FORTRAN, called the arithmetic IF statement because it tests the value of an arithmetic expression.

The general form of the arithmetic IF is

$$\text{IF } (E) \; n, \, z, \, p$$

where E is any arithmetic expression, and n, z, and p are statement labels. This statement means to evaluate the expression E and, if it is negative, go to statement n; if it is zero, go to statement z; if it is positive, go to statement p. In terms of the logical IF, the arithmetic IF is equivalent to the three statements:

IF (E .LT. 0) GO TO *n*
if (E .EQ. 0) GO TO *z*
GO TO *p*

For example:

IF (X − 5.0) 10, 10, 20

means if X − 5.0 is negative or zero, go to statement 10; otherwise, go to statement 20. This is equivalent to

IF (X .LE. 5.0) GO TO 10
GO TO 20

The statement

    IF((5.0∗X∗Y + 14.0)∗Z)20, 10, 10

means if the expression (5.0∗X∗Y + 14.0)∗Z is negative, go to statement 20; otherwise, go to 10.

Use of the arithmetic IF statement is not recommended, since it generally leads to poorly structured programs that are difficult to understand. You may see arithmetic IF statements in older FORTRAN programs, but such programming style is now considered obsolete by advocates of structured programming.

COMMON STORAGE

As you have seen, subroutines and function subprograms are independent program units, compiled separately from the main program. This means, for instance, that a variable named K may be used in a main program for one purpose and in a subroutine for an entirely different purpose. Until now, the arguments of the subroutine or function have provided the only method of passing values between program units. There is another way by which program units can communicate with each other: This is **common storage** (or blank common), which is used by means of the COMMON statement.

Common storage may be thought of as a sequence of memory locations in the computer. The **COMMON statement** lets you specify that particular variables be kept in a certain area of common storage. For example, normally when a variable named XXX is used in a program, the programmer has no control over where in the computer memory the variable is located. With the COMMON statement, the programmer can specify that XXX is to be in the first location of common storage. Now suppose a subroutine says a variable named ABC is to be in the first word of common storage. Then ABC and XXX are in the same place; that is, they are really the same variable. If the main program sets XXX = 1.0, then when the subroutine is called, ABC will have the value 1.0, since ABC is the same memory location as XXX. This is how common storage is used to pass values among program units. The following program gives an example.

```
        COMMON XXX
        XXX = 3.1416
        PRINT 10, XXX
        CALL SUB
        STOP
10      FORMAT(F20.5)
        END
        SUBROUTINE SUB
        COMMON ABC
        PRINT 10, ABC
* THE VALUE PRINTED IS THE VALUE STORED
* IN THE FIRST WORD OF THE COMMON STORAGE
* AREA. THIS VALUE IS 3.1416, WHICH WAS
```

```
* STORED BY THE MAIN PROGRAM
10    FORMAT(F20.5)
      RETURN
      END
```

This program will print:

```
3.14160
3.14160
```

In general, the COMMON statement has the form

COMMON $name_1$, $name_2$, ..., $name_n$

where $name_1$, $name_2$, and so on, are variable names or array names. Like the DIMENSION statement, the COMMON statement is a nonexecutable declaration which must come at the beginning of the program unit, before the first executable statement. This statement means that the variables or arrays named are to be stored in common storage in the order in which they are listed. If the names are real or integer variable names (not arrays), then each name occupies one memory location in common storage. For example,

```
COMMON I, V, M
```

means to store I in the first location of common, V in the second location, and M in the third.

The names in the COMMON statement may also be array names. When this is done, the COMMON statement may give dimension information. For example,

```
DIMENSION W(10)
COMMON I, W, X
```

is the same as the shorter form

```
COMMON I, W(10), X
```

This statement means that the first location of common storage is occupied by I, the second through eleventh locations are occupied by the array W, and the twelfth location by X.

The list of variable names in a COMMON statement can be different program units. The main program might include the statement

```
COMMON X(3), Y, Z(2)
```

and a subroutine might contain the statement

```
COMMON A, B, C, D, E, F
```

Then the variable A and X(1) are both stored in the same location, X(2) and B are stored in the same location, and so on. This is illustrated in Figure 10.3. Each variable should be of the same type as the corresponding variable.

Although the COMMON statements can be different in different program units, in practice they are frequently identical. This has the effect of making the variables in common **globally defined**. That is, the variables in common can be used by any program unit. This is an efficient way to pass information among subprograms, especially when much information has to be shared.

An extension of the ordinary COMMON statement is the **labeled COMMON statement**, which is similar, except that it allows a label for the common storage area. For example,

COMMON/BLOK/A, B, C

says to store A, B, and C in the common storage area called BLOK. The idea of this is simply to allow more than one common storage area. The general form of the labeled common statement is

COMMON/*block*/*name*$_1$, *name*$_2$, . . . , *name*$_n$

where *block* is a one- to six-character block name, beginning with a letter, and *name*$_1$, etc., are variable or array names, just as for the unlabeled COMMON statement.

The effect of this statement is identical to that of the unlabeled common except that the variables are stored in the named common block.

Labeled common blocks with different names are separate from each other and from unlabeled common storage. This feature can be especially useful when writing a

FIGURE 10.3

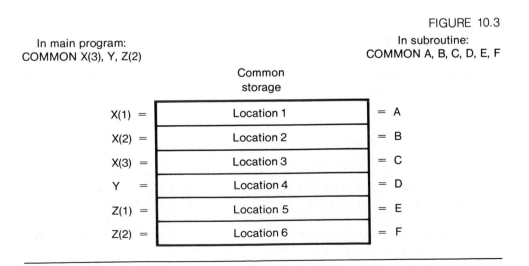

Example of common statement

system of subroutines that work together. If you want to use common storage to pass information among the subroutines, you can set up a labeled common block. Then these subroutines can be used with a main program or with another system of subroutines which also uses common storage. Since the common storage blocks are labeled differently, they will not interfere with each other. There is one other difference between labeled and unlabeled common storage. Labeled common storage can be initialized with a DATA statement; unlabeled common storage cannot be.

BLOCK DATA SUBPROGRAMS

A DATA statement may not be used to initialize a variable which is in common storage. Thus the following is not allowed

```
COMMON WRONG(3)
DATA WRONG / 1., 2., 3. /
```

It is allowable, however, to use a DATA statement to initialize a variable in *labeled* common storage. This is one important difference between labeled and unlabeled common. Variables in labeled common can be initialized by DATA statements only by using a special type of subprogram called a **BLOCK DATA subprogram**.

The BLOCK DATA subprogram contains no executable statements. Only declaration statements (such as INTEGER, COMMON/X/) and DATA statements may be used. The BLOCK DATA subprogram begins with the statement

```
BLOCK DATA
```

or

```
BLOCK DATA name
```

where *name* is any legal subprogram name. The declarations and DATA statements follow. Like other subprograms, it is terminated by an END line.

STATEMENT FUNCTIONS

Function subprograms, as you have seen, are a very useful feature of FORTRAN. A **statement function** is similar to a function subprogram, but it is not a subprogram. It is a function defined by a single statement. A statement function may be defined in any program unit. Within the program unit, you can reference the statement function just like a function subprogram. Unlike a subprogram, though, a statement function cannot be referenced outside of the program unit in which it is defined.

All statement function definitions must come at the beginning of a program before the first executable statement and after all other declarative statements. The **statement**

function definition is a declarative statement having the same form as an assignment statement:

$$f(x_1, x_2, \ldots, x_n) = expression$$

where f is the function name; $x_1, \ldots, x_n$ are variables specifying the dummy arguments of the statement function; and *expression* is any expression which may involve the dummy arguments.

For example, the statement function definition

    F(X) = X + SIN(X) + COS(X)

declares that the expression F(X) is equivalent to the expression

    X + SIN(X) + COS(X)

throughout the program unit. You could replace the dummy argument X with any actual argument, just as for function subprogram. Thus,

    PRINT *, F(A + B)

has the same effect as

    PRINT *, A + B + SIN(A + B) + COS(A + B)

EXAMPLE 10.6 Nth Roots
You have seen examples of the SQRT function, used to compute square roots. There is no intrinsic function to compute nth roots, but you can write such a function easily as a statement function. Mathematically, the nth root of a positive number x is written

$$\sqrt[n]{x}$$

which is the same as

$$x^{\frac{1}{n}}$$

This value is computed by the statement function ROOT defined by

    ROOT(X, N) = X**(1.0/REAL(N))

The following program prints a table of roots of numbers 2 through 100.

```
* ROOT TABLE.
      INTEGER N
      REAL X, ROOT
      ROOT(X, N) = X**(1.0/REAL(N))
```

```
      *
            PRINT 10, (N, N = 2, 10)
      10    FORMAT('1'//T20, 'TABLE OF NTH ROOTS OF X'/,
            $     T15, 'X', T20, 'N = ', T25, 9I10/)
      *
            DO 20, X = 2.0, 100.0
                  PRINT 15, X, (ROOT(X, N), N = 2, 10)
      15          FORMAT (T10, F10.0, 9F10.7)
      20          CONTINUE
            END
```

THE SAVE STATEMENT

The **SAVE statement** is a declarative statement used to specify that certain variables in a subprogram are to remain defined even after the subprogram executes a RETURN or END statement. Normally, when a subprogram returns, all variables in the subprogram become undefined except for the following.

1. Variables in blank common storage
2. Variables that were initially defined (for example, by a DATA statement) and have not been redefined
3. Variables appearing in a named common block that appears in the subprogram and in at least one other program unit that is referencing the subprogram

The statement

> SAVE var_1, var_2, . . . , var_n

means to save the values of the variables in the list when the subprogram returns. The listed variables must not be part of a labeled common block, but you can save the entire common block with a statement such as

> SAVE *block*

where *block* is the common block name. The statement

> SAVE

with no list of variables or block names means to save all variables and labeled common blocks used in the subprogram.

EXAMPLE 10.7 Random Numbers
In Chapter 7 you saw an example of a program to generate random numbers. The function RANDOM(I) worked by changing the value of its argument. The following version of the RANDOM function has no argument. Instead, it saves the value of the variable I between successive function references. The initial value of I is defined by a DATA statement.

```
* RANDOM NUMBER GENERATOR
    REAL FUNCTION RANDOM( )
    INTEGER I, J, K, M
    PARAMETER (J = 5243,
  $             K = 55397,
  $             M = 262139)
   SAVE I
   DATA I / 0 /
*
    I = MOD(I * J + K, M)
    RANDOM = (REAL(I) + 0.5)/REAL (M)
    END
```

The following test program will generate the same random numbers as the example in Chapter 7.

```
      INTEGER I
      REAL RANDOM
      DO 10, I = 1, 10
          PRINT *, RANDOM ( )
 10       CONTINUE
      END
```

ALTERNATE RETURNS FROM A SUBROUTINE

Normally, a SUBROUTINE subprogram returns to the calling program at the statement following the CALL. There is a method by which you can have it return to some other statement in the calling program. The following example illustrates the technique:

```
* TEST OF ALTERNATE RETURN.
      DO 10, I = 1, 10
          CALL SUB(I, *5, *100)
          PRINT *, 'NORMAL RETURN'
          GO TO 10
  5       PRINT *, 'ALTERNATE RETURN 1'
 10       CONTINUE
      STOP
100   PRINT *, 'ALTERNATE RETURN 2'
      END
      SUBROUTINE SUB(I, *, *)
      INTEGER I
      IF (I .LE. 5) RETURN
      IF (I .LE. 9) RETURN 1
      RETURN 2
      END
```

Notice that two of the dummy arguments in SUB are asterisks. The corresponding actual arguments in the CALL statement are statement labels of statements in the main program, preceded by asterisks. In the subroutine SUB, the statement

    RETURN 1

means to take the first **alternate return**, which means to return to the main program and GO TO statement 5. Likewise, the statement

    RETURN 2

in the subprogram means to take the second alternate return, which means to return to the main program and GO TO statement 100.

In general, if a subroutine has n dummy arguments which are asterisks, then the statement

    RETURN i

where i is an integer expression, means to take the ith alternate return. The corresponding actual argument must be an **alternate return specifier** of the form

    *S

where s is a statement label of a statement in the calling program. The effect is to return to the calling and go to statement s. If the value of i is less than 1 or greater than n, the subroutine returns in the usual manner.

THE EXTERNAL STATEMENT

A dummy argument of a function or subroutine subprogram may itself be a subprogram name. For example, the argument F in the following function is a function itself.

    REAL FUNCTION DELTA(F, X)
    DELTA = F(X + 1)
    END

Suppose that a main program contains the statement

    Z = DELTA(FUNC, Y)

where FUNC is some function subprogram name. The main program must have a way of informing the FORTRAN compiler that FUNC is a subprogram name, rather than a variable, so that the argument can be passed correctly. It does so by declaring FUNC in an **EXTERNAL statement** of the form

    EXTERNAL FUNC

In general, when an actual argument to a subprogram is a subprogram name, the *calling* program must declare the argument as an external reference by including an EXTERNAL statement. Note that the EXTERNAL statement goes in the program unit that does the calling, not in the program unit being called. Thus, in the example above, the EXTERNAL statement goes in the main program, not in DELTA.

The form of the EXTERNAL statement is

    EXTERNAL $name_1$, $name_2$, . . .

where $name_1$, $name_2$, . . . are the names of subprograms to be used as arguments. This statement is a declarative statement which goes at the beginning of the program unit.

Only external subprogram names may be used as arguments. A statement function name or a generic intrinsic function name may not be an argument.

EXAMPLE 10.8 Integration by the Trapezoidal Rule

If $f(x)$ is a real-valued function, the integral $\int_a^b f(x)dx$ may be approximated by the *trapezoidal rule*:

$$\int_a^b f(x)\ dx = \left[(1/2)(f(a) + f(b)) + \sum_{i=1}^{n-1} f\left(a + i\left(\frac{b-a}{n}\right)\right) \right]\frac{b-a}{n}$$

where n is some positive integer, giving the number of subintervals to use. The following subprogram carries out this computation.

```
*  COMPUTE THE INTEGRAL OF F FROM A TO B
*  USING THE TRAPEZOIDAL RULE WITH N SUBINTERVALS.
      REAL FUNCTION TRAP(F, A, B, N)
      REAL F, A, B
      INTEGER I, N
*
      TRAP = (F(A) + F(B))/2
      DO 5, I = 1, N - 1
         TRAP = TRAP + F(A + I*(B-A)/N)
5        CONTINUE
      TRAP = TRAP * (B-A)/N
      END
```

The following main program and function subprogram use the TRAP function to approximate the value of

$$\int_0^{2\pi} \sin^2(x)\ dx$$

Note that the EXTERNAL statement goes in the main program.

```
* MAIN PROGRAM TO TEST TRAP FUNCTION.
      REAL SINSQ, TRAP
      EXTERNAL SINSQ
      PRINT *, TRAP(SINSQ, 0.0, 2*3.14159, 1000)
      END
* FUNCTION TO COMPUTE SIN - SQUARED OF X.
      REAL FUNCTION SINSQ(X)
      REAL X
      SINSQ = SIN(X)**2
      END
```

THE EQUIVALENCE STATEMENT

The EQUIVALENCE statement permits the use of two or more names for the same variable. It is a declaration, which comes at the beginning of the program. The form of the EQUIVALENCE statement is

EQUIVALENCE ($name_1$, $name_2$, . . . , $name_n$), (. . .), . . .

All the names enclosed in each set of parentheses refer to the same memory location throughout the program. For example,

EQUIVALENCE (A, B), (I, J)

means that throughout the program unit, A and B refer to the same memory location, and I and J both refer to another memory location. Thus,

```
      EQUIVALENCE(A, B)
      B = 0.0
      A = 1.0
      PRINT 10, B
10    FORMAT(F10.1)
```

prints the value 1.0, not 0.0. The statement A = 1.0 assigns the value 1.0 to both A and B since they are the same variable.

Array names cannot be equivalenced by this statement, but array elements can be. The declarations

```
      DIMENSION X(10)
      EQUIVALENCE(X(1), XFIRST), (X(10), XLAST)
```

let XFIRST be used as an alternate name for X(1) and XLAST as an alternate name for X(10).

To equivalence two arrays, it is sufficient to equivalence any two corresponding elements. Thus,

```
DIMENSION A(10), B(20)
EQUIVALENCE(A(1), B(1))
```

will let the array be referred to by either the name A or B. The size of the array is effectively 20, since the last ten elements of B are available to A as well.

It is allowable to equivalence variables of different types. This may cause problems, however, due to the different internal representations of numbers.

SUMMARY

A complex number in FORTRAN is a pair of real numbers which corresponds to the mathematical concept of a complex number consisting of a real part and an imaginary part. Complex constants are enclosed in parentheses. Complex variables are declared in a COMPLEX statement. Complex arithmetic in FORTRAN follows the mathematical rules for arithmetic with complex numbers. There are several intrinsic functions for calculation with complex data.

Double-precision data is like real data, but it is stored with approximately twice the precision. Thus, if a real variable is stored with seven-place precision, a double-precision value will be stored with fourteen-place precision. Double-precision constants are like E-form constants, but use the letter D in place of E. Double-precision variables are declared in a DOUBLE PRECISION statement.

The DATA statement is a declaration that stores an initial value in a variable before execution begins.

The assigned and computed GO TO statements are control statements used to branch to one of several statement labels. For the computed GO TO, the choice depends on the value of an integer expression. For the assigned GO TO, the choice is determined by a value given to a variable with an ASSIGN statement. The arithmetic IF statement is an obsolete control statement for branching to one of three statements, based on the sign of a numeric value.

Common storage provides a method of sharing data among separate program units. Blank common or labeled common storage may be declared with a COMMON statement. To initialize values in labeled common with a DATA statement, a BLOCK DATA subprogram must be used.

A statement function is defined by a one-line declaration that makes a function reference equivalent to some expression. The definition applies only to the program unit in which it appears.

The SAVE statement declares that certain variables in a subprogram are to retain their values even after the subprogram returns.

Alternate returns allow a subroutine to return to any statement in the calling program—not just to the statement following the call.

An EXTERNAL statement must be used in the calling program if some subprogram's actual argument is a subprogram name.

The EQUIVALENCE statement permits different variable names to be used as synonyms within a program unit.

VOCABULARY

alternate returns
alternate return specifier
arithmetic IF statement
ASSIGN statement
assigned GO TO statement
blank common
BLOCK DATA subprogram
COMMON statement
common storage
complex number
COMPLEX statement
computed GO TO statement

conjugate
DATA statement
double-precision number
DOUBLE PRECISION statement
EQUIVALENCE statement
EXTERNAL statement
imaginary part of a complex number
labeled common
real part of a complex number
repetition factor in a DATA statement
SAVE statement
statement function

EXERCISES

1. Let W be a complex array of four elements with

$$W_1 = 1 + i$$
$$W_2 = -1 + i$$
$$W_3 = -1 - i$$
$$W_4 = 1 - i$$

   Write a program that prints a multiplication table of these complex numbers. The output will be an array that lists the products

   $$W_i * W_j$$

   for each choice of i and j.

2. Exercise 4 of Chapter 7 (page 280) showed that a point in the plane can be represented either as a pair of coordinates (x, y), or as a pair of polar coordinates (r, θ). A point in polar coordinate form can be represented as a single complex

number. The real part is the radius, and the imaginary part is the angle. For example,

```
COMPLEX ZP
ZP = CMPLX(RADIUS, ANGLE)
```

Write a complex-valued function of a complex variable

```
RECT(ZP)
```

that converts the polar coordinate form ZP to a complex number representing the same point in rectangular coordinate form. Write an inverse function

```
POLAR(Z)
```

that converts rectangular coordinates to polar form as complex numbers.

3. Modify the program in Example 10.1 to compute the sum and the product of all the roots of unity and print these numbers at the end of the output. Also, use the functions from Exercise 2 to print the roots in both rectangular and polar coordinates. Run the program for $n = 10$ and for $n = 11$.

4. Write a program that acts as a calculator on an interactive system. The program prompts the user by typing

```
READY (TYPE END WHEN FINISHED)
```

The user can then type an expression such as

```
12.3 * 14
```

The program types the result:

```
172.2
```

The user can then type another expression, or type END to stop the program. An expression can consist of two real numbers separated by an operator: $+$, $-$, $*$, or $/$. Use a character variable to store the line typed, then read from an internal file to decode the operator and the two operands. Use a computed GO TO to select the statements to be executed depending on the operator typed.

5. Modify the calculator program in Exercise 4 to do arithmetic with complex numbers.

6. If Z is a complex number and ANGLE is an angle, in radians, write a complex-valued statement function

```
ROTATE(Z, ANGLE)
```

that returns the coordinates of the point obtained by rotating Z about the origin through an angle of ANGLE.

7. Write a real-valued statement function

RAD(DEG, MIN, SEC)

that converts an angle in degrees, minutes, and seconds to radians.

8. Write a real-valued statement function

LOG(BASE, X)

that computes the logarithm of X in the base BASE.

9. Write a subroutine

QSOLV(A, B, C, X1, X2)

that solves the quadratic equation

$$Ax^2 + Bx + C = 0$$

where A, B, and C are complex numbers, and stores the two solutions in the complex variables X1 and X2. (See Example 4.3.)

10. A good method of solving an equation

$$f(x) = 0$$

is the technique of *interval halving*. Suppose that $a < b$, $f(a) < 0$, and $f(b) > 0$ (see figure on page 400). Then there must be some number X between a and b that solves the equation. Consider the midpoint of the interval

$$c = \frac{a + b}{2}$$

If $f(c) < 0$, then X must be between c and b. If $f(c) > 0$, then X must be between a and c. Thus, you have reduced the interval in which the unknown X lies to half of its original size. If the function is decreasing, that is if $f(a) > 0$ and $f(b) < 0$, you use a similar technique. Continuing in this method, you can pinpoint the location of X to any desired degree of accuracy. Write a function

ROOT (F, XA, XB, EPSILN)

that returns a value of X solving

F(X) = 0

in the interval XA to XB to an accuracy of EPSILN. Test your function by finding a solution of

$$1.3X^3 - 26.013X^2 + 0.975X - 19.50975 = 0$$

between 1.0 and 100.0. Remember to include an EXTERNAL statement in the program that calls ROOT.

ROOTS BY INTERVAL HALVING

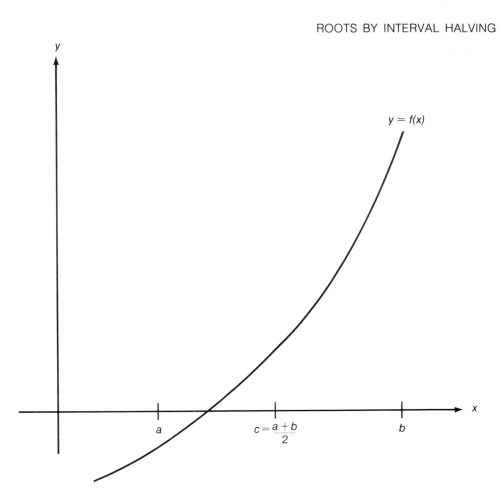

11. Rewrite the factorial function NFACT from Example 10.4 so that the values of the array NF are computed on the first call to the subprogram, rather than being initialized in the DATA statement. Use a variable FIRST which is declared in a SAVE statement and initialized in a DATA statement. The value of FIRST determines whether this is the first call to NFACT. If so, initialize the array NF; otherwise, proceed as in Example 10.4.

12. Exercises 22 to 24 in Chapter 7 (page 288) described subprograms for storing and fetching items in a buffer. Rewrite these routines so that the buffer is kept in a labeled common block declared by

```
INTEGER LIMIT, BUFFER
COMMON /BUFBLK/ LIMIT, BUFFER(-2:LIMIT)
EQUIVALENCE (BUFFER(-2), OUTPTR), (BUFFER(-1), INPTR)
```

13. Write a subroutine

    NEXTC (CHAR, * *)

that stores the next character from the standard input file in the character variable CHAR. At the end of a line of input, the routine takes the first alternate return. At the end of file, the routine takes the second alternate return.

INTRINSIC FUNCTIONS

TYPE CONVERSION FUNCTIONS

- INT(X)   Convert to integer type, truncating any fractional part.

If argument type is	Value type is
Integer	Integer
Real	Integer
Double	Integer
Complex	Integer

If the argument is negative, the value is negative. If the argument is complex, the value is obtained by converting the real part to integer. Examples:

```
INT(0.5) = 0
INT(1.9) = 1
INT(−1.5) = −1
INT(10) = 10
INT((1.5, 2.5)) = 1
```

- REAL(X)   Convert to real type.

If argument type is	Value type is
Integer	Real
Real	Real
Double	Real
Complex	Real

If the argument is complex the value is the real part of the complex number. Examples:

```
REAL(1) = 1.0
REAL(-5) = -5.0
REAL(3.2) = 3.2
REAL(1.234D0) = 1.234
REAL((1.0, 2.0)) = 1.0
```

* DBLE(X)   Convert to double precision type.

If argument type is	Value type is
Integer	Double
Real	Double
Double	Double
Complex	Double

If the argument is complex, the value is the same as DBLE(REAL(X)). Examples:

```
DBLE(1.0) = 1.0D0
DBLE(1) = 1.0D0
DBLE((1.0, 2.0)) = 1.0D0
```

* CMPLX(X) or CMPLX(X, Y)   Convert to complex type.

If type of argument (or arguments) is	Value type is
Integer	Complex
Real	Complex
Double	Complex
Complex	Complex

If two arguments are given, they must have the same type. Examples:

```
CMPLX(1) = (1.0, 0.0)
CMPLX(1.0) = (1.0, 0.0)
CMPLX(1, 2) = (1.0, 2.0)
CMPLX(1.0, 2.0) = (1.0, 2.0)
```

* NINT(X)   Round to nearest integer.

If argument type is	Value type is
Real	Integer
Double	Integer

The effect is similar to INT(X), but the value is rounded, rather than truncated. Examples:

```
NINT(0.1) = 0
NINT(0.6) = 1
NINT(0.5) = 1
NINT(−0.5) = −1
NINT(−1.1) = −1
```

- AINT(X) Truncate fractional part.

If argument type is	*Value type is*
Real	Real
Double	Real

Same as INT(X), but value is real. Examples:

```
AINT(0.1) = 0.0
AINT(0.6) = 0.0
AINT(−1.5) = −1.0
```

- ANINT(X) Round to nearest integer.

If argument type is	*Value type is*
Real	Real
Double	Real

Same as NINT(X), but value is real. Examples:

```
ANINT(0.1) = 0.0
ANINT(0.6) = 1.0
ANINT(−1.5) = −2.0
```

- CHAR(X) Convert integer to character.

If argument type is	*Value type is*
Integer	Character

Suppose that there are n characters in the computer's character set. If $0 \leq X \leq n - 1$, then CHAR(X) is the character corresponding to the integer X. The value of the function depends on the particular machine being used. Examples: (machine dependent):

```
CHAR(1) = 'A'
CHAR(2) = 'B'
```

- ICHAR(X)   Convert character to integer.

If argument type is	Value type is
Character∗1	Integer

This is the inverse function of CHAR. As with CHAR, the particular values are machine dependent. However, on any machine:

CHAR(ICHAR(X)) = X for any character X.

and ICHAR(CHAR(X)) = X for $0 \le X \le n - 1$

Examples (machine dependent):

ICHAR('A') = 1
ICHAR('B') = 2

ABSOLUTE VALUE

- ABS(X)   Absolute value of X.

If argument type is	Value type is
Integer	Integer
Real	Real
Double	Double
Complex	Real

Examples:

ABS(1.0) = 1.0
ABS(−1) = 1
ABS((3.0, 4.0)) = 5.0

MODULO FUNCTION

- MOD(X, Y) X modulo Y = the remainder when X is divided by Y.

If argument type is	Value type is
Integer	Integer
Real	Real
Double	Double

Examples:

```
MOD(17, 5) = 2
MOD(8, 2) = 0
MOD(-5, 3) = -2
MOD(3.123, 1.0) = 0.123
MOD(-7.5, 2.0) = -1.5
```

MAXIMUM AND MINIMUM

• MAX(A, B) or MAX(A, B, C) or MAX(A, B, C, D) etc. Find maximum value.

If argument type is	Value type is
Integer	Integer
Real	Real
Double	Double

Finds the maximum value of two or more arguments, all of which must have the same type. Examples:

```
MAX(2, 5) = 5
MAX(2, -5) = 2
MAX(2, 3, 4) = 4
MAX(2.1, 5.2) = 5.2
```

• MIN(A, B) or MIN(A, B, C) or MIN(A, B, C, D) etc. Find minimum value.

If argument type is	Value type is
Integer	Integer
Real	Real
Double	Double

Examples:

```
MIN(2, 5) = 2
MIN(2, -5) = -5
MIN(2, 3, 4) = 2
MIN(2.1, 5.2) = 2.1
```

LENGTH AND INDEX

• LEN(X) Length of a character expression:

If argument type is	Value type is
Character	Integer

Examples:

```
LEN('A') = 1
LEN('ABC') = 3
LEN('DON''T') = 5
```

- INDEX(A, B)   Location of substring B within string A.

If argument type is	Value type is
Character	Integer

If B is a substring of A, then INDEX(A, B) is the index of the first character of B. If B is not a substring, INDEX(A, B) = 0. Examples:

```
INDEX('ABCD', 'B') = 2
INDEX('ABCABC', 'BC') = 2
INDEX('ABCD', 'X') = 0
```

COMPLEX OPERATIONS

- AIMAG(X)   Imaginary part of a complex number.

If argument type is	Value type is
Complex	Real

Examples:

```
AIMAG((1.0, 2.0)) = 2.0
AIMAG((3.2, −1.0)) = −1.0
```

- CONJG(X)   Complex conjugate.

If argument type is	Value type is
Complex	Complex

The conjugate of $a + bi$ is $a - bi$. Examples:

```
CONJG((1.0, 2.0)) = (1.0, −2.0)
CONJG((0.0, −1.0)) = (0.0, 1.0)
```

SQUARE ROOT

- SQRT(X)   Square root.

If argument type is	Value type is
Real	Real
Double	Double
Complex	Complex

Examples:

```
SQRT(4.0) = 2.0
SQRT(2.0) = 1.4142
SQRT((3.0, 4.0)) = (2.0, 1.0)
```

EXPONENTIAL AND LOGARITHMIC

- EXP(X) Exponential function e^x, where $e = 2.71828.\ .\ .\ .\ .$

If argument type is	Value type is
Real	Real
Double	Double
Complex	Complex

Examples:

```
EXP(1.0) = 2.7182
EXP(2.0) = 7.3891
EXP((3.0, 3.14159)) = (−20.0855, 0.0)
```

- LOG(X) Natural logarithm, $\log_e x$.

If argument type is	Value type is
Real	Real
Double	Double
Complex	Complex

Examples:

```
LOG(2.7182) = 1.0
LOG(7.3891) = 2.0
```

- LOG10(X) Common logarithm, $\log X$.

If argument type is	Value type is
Real	Real
Double	Double

Examples:

```
LOG10(100.0) = 2.0
LOG10(1000.0) = 3.0
```

TRIGONOMETRIC AND INVERSE TRIGONOMETRIC

- SIN(X)   Trigonometric sine of X, where X is in radians.

If argument type is	*Value type is*
Real	Real
Double	Double
Complex	Complex

Example:

```
SIN(3.14159) = 0.0
```

- COS(X)   Trigonometric cosine of X, where X is in radians.

If argument type is	*Value type is*
Real	Real
Double	Double
Complex	Complex

Example:

```
COS(3.14159) = 1.0
```

- TAN(X)   Trigonometric tangent of X, where X is in radians.

If argument type is	*Value type is*
Real	Real
Double	Double

Example:

```
TAN(3.14159/4.0) = 1.0
```

- ASIN(X)   Inverse trigonometric sine, in radians.

If argument type is	*Value type is*
Real	Real
Double	Double

The value returned is in the range:

$$-\pi/2 \leq \text{ASIN(X)} \leq \pi/2$$

Example:

ASIN(0.0) = 0.0

- ACOS(X) Inverse trigonometric cosine, in radians.

If argument type is	Value type is
Real	Real
Double	Double

The value returned is in the range:

$$0 \leq \text{ACOS(X)} \leq \pi$$

Example:

ACOS(0.0) = 1.5708

- ATAN(X) Inverse trigonometric tangent in radians.

If argument type is	Value type is
Real	Real
Double	Double

The value returned is in the range:

$$-\pi/2 \leq \text{ATAN(X)} \leq \pi/2$$

Example:

ATAN(1.0) = 0.7854

- ATAN2(Y, X) Inverse trigonometric tangent of Y/X, in radians.

If argument type is	Value type is
Real	Real
Double	Double

Value returned is in the range:

$$-\pi < \text{ATAN2(Y, X)} \leq \pi$$

This function correctly handles the case where X = 0. Examples:

```
ATAN2(1.0, 1.0) = 0.7854
ATAN2(1.0, 0.0) = 5.5708
ATAN2(1.0, −1.0) = 2.3562
```

- SINH(X) Hyperbolic sine of X, $(e^x - e^{-x}) / 2$

If argument type is	Value type is
Real	Real
Double	Double

Example:

```
SINH(1.0) = 1.1752
```

- COSH(X) Hyperbolic cosine of X, $(e^x + e^{-x}) / 2$

If argument type is	Value type is
Real	Real
Double	Double

Example:

```
COSH(1.0) = 1.5431
```

- TANH(X) Hyperbolic tangent of X, $(e^x - e^{-x}) / (e^x + e^{-x})$

If argument type is	Value type is
Real	Real
Double	Double

Example:

```
TANH(1.0) = 0.7616
```

STRING COMPARISON

Each of the following four functions takes two character arguments and returns a logical value.

- LGE(A, B) Lexically greater or equal.

True if A is greater than or equal to B when compared according to the ASCII collating sequence; otherwise, false.

Similarly, the following functions compare A to B according to the ASCII collating sequence:

- LGT(A, B) Lexically greater than.
- LLE(A, B) Lexically less than or equal to.
- LLT(A, B) Lexically less than.

ANSWERS
AND HINTS
TO SELECTED
EXERCISES

CHAPTER 1

1. (a) Not an algorithm—Step 3 cannot be carried out, since the answer to the question is not known.
   (b) Not an algorithm—The instruction to be carried out after Step 3 is not precisely determined.
   (c) Not an algorithm—It never terminates, since N is never zero.
   (d) A valid algorithm.
3. If it is Monday, Wednesday, or Friday morning, and if it is not a holiday, then take the school books. If it is raining, or if it looks like it will rain, then take an umbrella. If the temperature is less than 60°, then wear a coat.
5. Driving a car requires a tremendous amount of judgment and intelligence. It is arguable whether it is possible in theory for a machine to carry out so complex a task. It is certainly impractical according to today's technology.
7. Draw a circular arc with center at point B which intersects line segments AB and BC. Let D be the point where the arc intersects AB. Let E be the point where the arc intersects BC. Draw a circle with center D and radius greater than or equal to DE. Draw another circle of the same radius with center E. The two circles intersect in two points. Draw a line segment through these two points and extend it to meet the point B. This line segment bisects the given angle.
9. Using the given set of weights, you can choose combinations that will give any total weight from 1 to 63 grams. Thus, one algorithm is as follows: Put the object on the left balance. Weigh it against a 1 gram weight. If it does not balance exactly, weigh it against 2 grams. If it does not balance exactly, weigh it against 3 grams, then 4 grams, then 5 grams, and so on. If the object weighs 63 grams or less, then at some point the weights will balance exactly or the weights will be heavier. The first

415

time this happens the sum of the weights is approximately equal to the weight of the object. The boundary condition is that an object heavier than 63 grams cannot be weighed.

11. Pick the first card and hold it in your left hand. With your right hand, turn over each of the other nine cards. If any card you turn over comes before the card you are holding in your left hand, put that new card in your left hand and put the old card from your left hand on the stack. When all the cards are turned over, the card in your left hand is the one that comes first in alphabetical order, so put it face down in a new pile. Now sort the remaining nine cards the same way. For 1000 cards, it might be faster to break them into 10 sets of 100 each. Sort each set, then arrange the 10 sets into a single sorted set.

13. See Example 6.3 in Chapter 6.

15. Let N = 1, S = 1, X = 0.
    While N ≤ 100, do the following
        X = X + S/N
        N = N + 1
        X = −S
    Print X

17. Let X = 1, F = 1.
    While X ≤ F, do the following
        F = F × X
        X = X + 1
    Print F

19. The variables A, B, and C represent the number of pennies in rows 1, 2, and 3. Repeat the following procedure:

    Read R, the row number, and N, the number of pennies taken.
    If R = 1, then
        If N > A, print "Illegal move,"
        Otherwise, let A = A − N.
    If R = 2, then
        If N > B, print "Illegal move."
        Otherwise, let B = B − N.
    If R = 3, then
        If N > C, print "Illegal move."
        Otherwise, let C = C − N.

    If A + B + C = 0, print "You win," then stop.
    If A + B + C = 1, print "I take the last penny, I win," then stop.
    If A > 0, print, "I take 1 from Row 1.", and let A = A − 1. Otherwise, if B > 0, print "I take 1 from Row 2." and let B = B − 1.
    Otherwise, print, "I take 1 from Row 3," and let C = C − 1.

21. Let V be the value of the hand, counting any aces as 11.
    If V ≥ 17, stand.
    If V > 21, do the following for each ace in the hand, if any.
        Let V = V − 10
        If V ≥ 17, stand.
    If V > 21, fold.
    If V < 17, take a card.

23. The numbers circled should be:
    2, 3, 5, 7, 11, 13, 17, 19, 23, 29, 31, 37, 41, 43, 47, 53, 59, 61, 67, 71, 73, 79, 83, 89, 97.

25.
```
         INTEGER X, Y
         X = 1
   10    IF (X .NE. 100) THEN
             Y = X *X
             PRINT *, X, Y
             X = X + 1
             GO TO 10
         END IF
         END
```

27.
```
         REAL X
         INTEGER N
         N = 1
         X = 0
   10    IF (N .NE. 100) THEN
             X = X + N
             N = N + 1
             GO TO 10
         END IF
         PRINT *, X
         END
```

29.
```
         INTEGER A, B
         A = 0
         B = 1
         N = 2
   10    IF (N .NE. 20) THEN
             PRINT *, A
             PRINT *, B
             A = A + B
             B = A + B
             N = N + 2
             GO TO 10
         END IF
         END
```

CHAPTER 2

1. This is a lab exercise. Have your instructor or computer center personnel assist you with this.
3. This is a lab exercise. Find out if there is a reference manual available for the particular terminal you are using. It might pay to practice typing on the terminal and to make sure that you are familiar with the function of each key on the keyboard.
5. This is a lab exercise.

7. This is a lab exercise. It will be well worth your while to take your time on this one and make sure you understand it. You will be going through a similar procedure for each program you run in this class. The correct answer for the program is: 15, 176, 352.50.

9. The first lines of output should be:

X = 50 SQUARE ROOT = 7.0711
X = 49 SQUARE ROOT = 7.0000
X = 48 SQUARE ROOT = 6.9282

The program will probably terminate with a message such as:

ERROR – NEGATIVE NUMBER TO A REAL POWER.

It may be difficult to determine the last value of X from the printout, since if the program terminates with an error, all the output may not be printed.

CHAPTER 3

1. (a) 0.5 (real)
   (b) 1000 (integer)
   (c) 3.1416 (real)
   (d) −1.5 (real)
   (e) 0.3333333 (real)
   (f) 0 (integer) or 0.0 (real)
   (g) 1000000 (integer)
   (h) 98.6 (real)

3. (a) legal
   (b) illegal (too many characters)
   (c) illegal (period not allowed)
   (d) legal
   (e) illegal (begins with a number)
   (f) legal
   (g) illegal (plus sign not allowed)
   (h) illegal (minus sign not allowed)
   (i) legal
   (j) illegal (too many characters)
   (k) legal
   (l) legal

5. (a) 6   (e) 3
   (b) 5   (f) 8
   (c) 30   (g) 6
   (d) 6   (h) 6
   (i) 5   (m) 0
   (j) 3   (n) 1
   (k) 0   (o) 3
   (l) 0.2   (p) 15

7. (a) R**2
   (b) (A − B) *X**3
   (c) 1.0/(1.0/R1 + 1.0/R2 + 1.0/R3)
   (d) B*H/3.0
   (e) 10.0/(MAX − MIN)
   (f) A/(B +C/D)
   (g) A/(B + C/(D + E/F))
   (h) (1.0 + 1.0/N)**N

9. (a) $RESULT = \dfrac{12a^2 - 2a + 31}{4a + 6}$

   (b) $y = \dfrac{2x + 3.5\,(1 - x)}{9}$

   (c) $z = a - 2b + 3c - 6$
   (d) $DET = ad - bc$
   (e) $w = x^2 - 5ax + 6a^2$
   (f) $y = x^2 + (1 - 2a^2)\,x + 2a^2$

11.   REAL TOTAL
         INTEGER ONEPR, TWOPR, THREE, STRAIG,
     $ FLUSH, FULL, FOUR, STFLSH, NADA

```
      PARAMETER (ONEPR = (52 *3 *48 *44 *40) / (2 *6) )
      PARAMETER (TWOPR = (52 *3 *48 *3 *44) / (2 *2 *2) )
      PARAMETER (THREE = (52 *3 *2 *48 *44) / (2 *2 *3) )
      PARAMETER (STRAIG = 10 *4 **5 − 10 *4)
      PARAMETER (FLUSH = (52 *12 *11 *10 *9) / (2 *3 *4 *5) − 4 *10)
      PARAMETER (FULL = (52 *3 *2 *48 *3) / (2 *6) )
      PARAMETER (FOUR = (52 *3 *2 *48) / (2 *3 *4) )
      PARAMETER (STFLSH = 4 *10)
      PARAMETER (TOTAL = (52 *51 *50 *49 *48) / (2 *3 *4 *5) )
      PARAMETER (NADA = TOTAL − ONEPR − TWOPR − THREE −
     $      STRAIG − FLUSH − FULL − FOUR − STFLSH)
      PRINT *, 'NUMBER OF HANDS, PROBABILITY'
      PRINT *, 'ONE PAIR', ONEPR, ONEPR / TOTAL
      PRINT *, 'TWO PAIRS', TWOPR, TWOPR / TOTAL
      PRINT *, 'THREE OF A KIND', THREE, THREE / TOTAL
      PRINT *, 'STRAIGHT', STRAIG, STRAIG / TOTAL
      PRINT *, 'FLUSH', FLUSH, FLUSH / TOTAL
      PRINT *, 'FULL HOUSE', FULL, FULL / TOTAL
      PRINT *, 'FOUR OF A KIND', FOUR, FOUR / TOTAL
      PRINT *, 'STRAIGHT FLUSH', STFLSH, STFLSH / TOTAL
      PRINT *, 'NOTHING', NADA, NADA / TOTAL
      PRINT *, 'TOTAL NUMBER OF HANDS', TOTAL
      END
```

13.
```
      INTEGER N
      REAL X
      X = 0
10    IF (X .LT. 5) THEN
         N = X + 0.5
         PRINT *, X, N
         X = X + 0.1
         GO TO 10
      END IF
      END
```
The value of N is the value of X rounded to the nearest integer.

15.
```
      INTEGER N
      REAL X, SUM, SIGN
      SUM = 0
      SIGN = 1
      X = 1
      READ *, N
10    IF (X .LE. N) THEN
         SUM = SUM + SIGN / X
         X = X + 1
         SIGN = − SIGN
         GO TO 10
      END IF
      PRINT *, SUM
      END
```

```
17.        REAL F
           INTEGER N, I
           N = 1
    10     IF (N .LE. 100) THEN
               F = 1
               I = 1
    20         IF (I .LE. N) THEN
                   F = F *I
                   I = I + 1
                   GO TO 20
               END IF
               PRINT *, N, F
               GO TO 10
           END IF
           END


19.        REAL SCALE, INCHES, FEET, CM
           READ *, INCHES, FEET
           SCALE = INCHES / FEET
    10     READ (*, *, END = 20) FEET
               PRINT *, 'BLDG DIMENSION =', FEET, 'FT'
               PRINT *, 'MODEL DIMENSION =', SCALE *FEET, 'FT=',
         $         2.54 *SCALE *FEET, 'CM'
               GO TO 10
    20     END
```

CHAPTER 4

1. (a) STOP
   (b) GO TO 20
   (c) PAUSE
   (d) IF (N .EQ. NTOP) STOP
   (e) IF (X .LE. X2) GO TO 1
3. (a) READ (*, *, END = 90) D
        IF (D .GT. 0) GO TO 90

   (b) 10 IF (N .LT. M) THEN
                N = N *2
                GO TO 10
            END IF

   (c) IF (0 .LT. X .AND. X .LT. 10) THEN
            N = 1
        ELSE
            N = 0
        END IF

(d) IF (0 .LT. X .AND. X .LT. 10) THEN
    N = 1
  ELSE IF (10 .LE. X .AND. X .LT. 100) THEN
    N = 2
  ELSE
    N = 3
  END IF

(e) IF (0.0001 .LE. X .AND. X .LT. 0.001) THEN
    N = −4
  ELSE IF (0.001 .LE. X .AND. X .LT. 0.01) THEN
    N = −3
  ELSE IF (0.01 .LE. X .AND. X .LT. 0.1) THEN
    N = −2
  ELSE IF (0.1 .LE. X .AND. X .LT. 1.0) THEN
    N = −1
  ELSE IF (1.0 .LE. X .AND. X .LT. 10.0) THEN
    N = 0
  ELSE IF (10.0 .LE. X .AND. X .LT. 100.0) THEN
    N = 1
  ELSE
    N = 1
  END IF

5. (a)

P	Q	P .NEQV. A
.TRUE.	.TRUE.	.FALSE.
.TRUE.	.FALSE.	.TRUE.
.FALSE.	.TRUE.	.TRUE.
.FALSE.	.FALSE.	.FALSE.

(b)

P	Q	.NOT. P .NEQV. Q
.TRUE.	.TRUE.	.TRUE.
.TRUE.	.FALSE.	.FALSE.
.FALSE.	.TRUE.	.FALSE.
.FALSE.	.FALSE.	.TRUE.

(c)

P	Q	.NOT. P .OR. Q
.TRUE.	.TRUE.	.TRUE.
.TRUE.	.FALSE.	.FALSE.
.FALSE.	.TRUE.	.TRUE.
.FALSE.	.FALSE.	.TRUE.

(d)

P	Q	.NOT. P .AND. .NOT. Q
.TRUE.	.TRUE.	.FALSE.
.TRUE.	.FALSE.	.FALSE.
.FALSE.	.TRUE.	.FALSE.
.FALSE.	.FALSE.	.TRUE.

(e)

P	Q	R	P .OR. Q .AND. R
.TRUE.	.TRUE.	.TRUE.	.TRUE.
.TRUE.	.TRUE.	.FALSE.	.FALSE.
.TRUE.	.FALSE.	.TRUE.	.FALSE.
.TRUE.	.FALSE.	.FALSE.	.FALSE.
.FALSE.	.TRUE.	.TRUE.	.TRUE.
.FALSE.	.TRUE.	.FALSE.	.FALSE.
.FALSE.	.FALSE.	.TRUE.	.FALSE.
.FALSE.	.FALSE.	.FALSE.	.FALSE.

```
7.      REAL OLD, NEW
        LOGICAL, INORDR
        INORDR = .TRUE.
        READ (*, *, END = 90) OLD
        PRINT *, OLD
10      READ (*, *, END = 90) NEW
        PRINT *, NEW
        IF (OLD .LE. NEW) THEN
        ELSE
            PRINT *, 'OUT OF ORDER'
            INORDR = .FALSE.
        END IF
        OLD = NEW
        GO TO 10
*
90      IF (INORDR) THEN
            PRINT *, 'NUMBERS ARE IN ORDER'
        ELSE
            PRINT *, 'SOME NUMBERS ARE OUT OF ORDER'
        END IF
        END


8.      INTEGER CUT 4, CUT 3, CUT 2, CUT 1
        INTEGER ID, SCORE, GRADE
        READ *, CUT 4, CUT 3, CUT 2, CUT 1
10      READ (*, *, END = 20) ID, SCORE
        IF (SCORE .GE. CUT 4) THEN
            GRADE = 4
        ELSE IF (SCORE .GE. CUT 3) THEN
```

```
               GRADE = 3
           ELSE IF (SCORE .GE. CUT 2) THEN
               GRADE = 2
           ELSE IF (SCORE .GE. CUT 1) THEN
               GRADE = 1
           ELSE
               GRADE = 0
           END IF
           PRINT *, 'STUDENT;', ID, 'SCORE:', SCORE,
      $       'GRADE:', GRADE
           GO TO 10
   20    END
```

11. (a) 3 times, final value 61
    (b) 21 times, final value −0.5
    (c) 0 times, final value 10
    (d) 21 times, final value 11
    (e) 7 times, final value N + 4
    (f) 7 times, final value 4 *N

```
13.        INTEGER N, K, TOP, BOTTOM, I
   10    READ (*, *, END = 50) N, K
           TOP = 1
           DO 20, I = N − K + 1, N
               TOP = TOP *I
   20        CONTINUE
           BOTTOM = 1
           DO 30, I = 1, K
               BOTTOM = BOTTOM *I
   30        CONTINUE
           PRINT *, 'N=', N, 'K=', K,
      $       'C(N,K) =', TOP / BOTTOM
           GO TO 10
   50    END
```

```
15.        N = 0
           SUMPOS = 0
           SUMNEG = 0
   10    READ (*, *, END = 90) A
           IF (A .LT. 0) THEN
               SUMNEG = SUMNEG + A
               N = N + 1
           ELSE IF (A .GT. 0) THEN
               SUMPOS = SUMPOS + A
               N = N + 1
           END IF
           IF (A .NE. 0) GO TO 10
   90    PRINT *, N, SUMPOS, SUMNEG
           END
```

17.

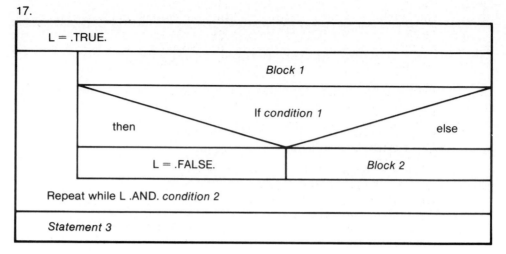

19.   INTEGER I, J, N, X, Y
           DO 30, I = 1, 7
               DO 20, J = 1, 7
                   X = I
                   N = J
                   Y = 1
     10   IF (N .GT. 0) THEN
                       IF (N .EQ. (N / 2) *2) THEN
                           N = N / 2
                           X = X *X
                       ELSE
                           N = N - 1
                           Y = Y *X
                       END IF
                       GO TO 10
                   END IF
                   PRINT *, I, J, Y
     20   CONTINUE
     30   CONTINUE
           END

This program sets Y = I**J where I and J each range from 1 to 7.

CHAPTER 5

1. (a)   'ABC'   (d)   'ABC'
   (b)   '14'   (e)   'ABC'
   (c)   'A'

3. (a) .FALSE.
   (b) .TRUE.
   (c) .TRUE.
   (d) .FALSE.
   (e) not determined
   (f) .FALSE.
   (g) not determined
   (h) .FALSE.
   (i) .TRUE.
   (j) .FALSE.

5.
```
      CHARACTER INPUT *39, OUTPUT *38, DASH
      PARAMETER (DASH = '—')
10    READ (*, '(A)', END = 20) INPUT
      OUTPUT = ' '
      OUTPUT (1:11) = INPUT (31:33) // DASH //
   $     INPUT (34:35) // DASH // INPUT (36:39)
      OUTPUT (14:25) = INPUT (14:25)
      OUTPUT (27:36) = INPUT (1:10)
      OUTPUT (38:38) = INPUT (12:12)
      PRINT *, OUTPUT
      GO TO 10
20    END
          I = I + 1
          GO TO 40
       END IF
*     FIND NEXT BLANK CHARACTER
          J = I
50     IF (LINE (J:J) .NE. BLANK) THEN
          J = J + 1
          GO TO 50
       END IF
*     PRINT THIS WORD
       PRINT *, LINE (I:J — 1)
       I = J
       GO TO 30
      END IF
      GO TO 10
90    END
```

7.
```
      CHARACTER LINE *50, STAR
      PARAMETER (STAR = '*')
      LINE = ' '
      DO 10, I = 1, 50
          LINE (I:I) = STAR
          PRINT *, LINE
10        CONTINUE
      END
```

9.
```
* CHECKERBOARD
      CHARACTER STAR*10, BLANK*10, P*20
      CHARACTER*80 LINE 1, LINE 2
```

```
            INTEGER I, J
            PARAMETER (STAR = '**********')
            PARAMETER (BLANK = '          ')
            P = STAR // BLANK
            LINE 1 = P // P // P // P
            P = BLANK // STAR
            LINE 2 = P // P // P // P
            DO 30, I = 1, 4
                DO 10, J = 1, 6
                    PRINT *, LINE 1
10                  CONTINUE
                DO 20, J = 1, 6
                    PRINT *, LINE 2
20                  CONTINUE
30              CONTINUE
            END
```

11. *Hint:* Special characters can be treated the same as blank characters were treated in Example 5.6. If the last nonblank character on a line is a hyphen, subtract 1 from the word count. The hyphenated word will be counted as the first word in the next line.

13.
```
* READ INPUT TEXT AND PRINT WORDS ON SEPARATE LINES.
      CHARACTER LINE*81, SPCHAR*10, BLANK*1
      PARAMETER (BLANK = ' ')
      INTEGER I, J
      SPCHAR = ',.+-*/()''$'
*
* WHILE THERE IS MORE INPUT, GET A LINE OF TEXT.
*
10    READ (*, '(A)', END = 90) LINE (1:80)
      LINE (81:81) = BLANK
* CONVERT SPECIAL CHARACTERS TO BLANKS
      DO 20, I = 1, 80
          DO 10, J = 1, 10
              IF (LINE (I:I) .EQ. SPCHAR (J:J)) THEN
                  LINE (I:I) = BLANK
                  GO TO 20
              END IF
10            CONTINUE
20        CONTINUE
      I = 1
* WHILE I IS LESS THAN 81:
30    IF (I .LT. 81) THEN
*     FIND NEXT NONBLANK CHARACTER
40        IF (LINE (I:I) .EQ. BLANK) THEN
```

15.
```
      * METRIC CONVERSION
            CHARACTER UNITS *6
            REAL X
10          READ (*, *, END = 90) X, UNITS
            IF (UNITS .EQ. 'INCHES') THEN
                  PRINT *, X, UNITS, '=', 2.54*X, 'CM.'
            ELSE IF (UNITS .EQ. 'FEET') THEN
                  PRINT *, X, UNITS, '=', 30.48*X, 'CM.'
            ELSE IF (UNITS .EQ. 'YARDS') THEN
                  PRINT *, X, UNITS, '=', 0.9144*X, 'METERS.'
            ELSE IF (UNITS .EQ. 'MILES') THEN
                  PRINT *, X, UNITS, '=', 1.609344*X, 'KM.'
            ELSE
                  PRINT *, X, UNITS, ' (UNKNOWN UNITS) '
            END IF
            GO TO 10
90          END
```

17.
```
      * REMOVE ALL BLANK SPACES
            CHARACTER LINE *80, BLANK
            PARAMETER (BLANK = ' ')
            INTEGER I, J
10          READ (*, '(A)', END = 90) LINE
            J = 1
            DO 20, I = 1, 80
                  IF (LINE (I:I) .NE. BLANK) THEN
                        LINE (J:J) = LINE (I:I)
                        J = J + 1
                  END IF
20          CONTINUE
            PRINT *, LINE(:J)
            GO TO 100
90          END
```

19.
```
      * PRINTER PLOT
            CHARACTER PLOT*101, BLANK, STAR
            PARAMETER (BLANK = ' ', STAR = '*')
            INTEGER I
            REAL X, Y
            PLOT = BLANK
            DO 10, X = -10.0, 10.0, 1.0 / 3.0
                  Y = X**2
                  I = Y + 1.5
                  PLOT (I:I) = STAR
                  PRINT *, PLOT
                  PLOT (I:I) = BLANK
10          CONTINUE
            END
```

CHAPTER 6

1. (a)   REAL VECTOR (100)
   (b)   INTEGER NUMBER (−10:10)
   (c)   CHARACTER LETTER (26)
   (d)   CHARACTER PAGE (MAXLIN) *(LINLEN)
   (e)   INTEGER BOARD (8, 8)
   (f)   REAL CUBE (0:3, 0:3, 0:3)

3. Because of the subscript error in the array X, this program will terminate abnormally. The particular error message depends on your computer system.

5. If the output says that no elements were nonzero, then your operating system probably initializes arrays to zeros. It is very poor programming practice to rely on this fact, however. You should always initialize arrays and variables explicitly.

7.
```
* COMPUTE THE MEAN AND STANDARD DEVIATION.
* LIST ALL MEASUREMENTS THAT DIFFER FROM THE MEAN BY MORE
* THAN ONE STANDARD DEVIATION.
      INTEGER MAXN
      PARAMETER (MAXN = 200)
      INTEGER I, N
      REAL X(MAXN), XBAR, SX, SSQ, S
      N = 0
      DO 10, N = 1, MAXN
          READ (*, *, END = 20) X(N)
10        CONTINUE
20    N = N − 1
      SX = 0
      SSQ = 0
      DO 30, I = 1, N
          SX = SX + X(I)
          SSQ = SSQ + X(I)**2
30        CONTINUE
      XBAR = 0
      S = 0
      IF (N .GT. 0) XBAR = SX/N
      IF (N .GT. 1) S =
     $    ((SSQ − SX**2/N) / (N − 1)) **0.5
      PRINT *, 'N=', N
      PRINT *, 'MEAN=', XBAR
      PRINT *, 'STD DEV=', S
      PRINT *, 'THE FOLLOWING VALUES DIFFER' //
     $    'FROM THE MEAN BY MORE THAN S'
      DO 40, I = 1, N
          IF (X(I) .GT. XBAR+S .OR.
     $        X(I) .LT. XBAR−S) PRINT *, X(I)
40        CONTINUE
      END
```

```
9.  * CHANGE MAKING
        REAL COIN(9), PURCH, AMT, CHANGE
        INTEGER NPENNY(9), NCHANG, N, I
        CHARACTER DENOM(9) *20
        COIN(1) = 20.00
        COIN(2) = 10.00
        COIN(3) = 5.00
        COIN(4) = 1.00
        COIN(5) = 0.50
        COIN(6) = 0.25
        COIN(7) = 0.10
        COIN(8) = 0.05
        COIN(9) = 0.01
    * LET NPENNY (I) = NUMBER OF PENNIES IN COIN (I).
        DO 10, I = 1, 9
            NPENNY(I) = 100 *COIN(I) + 0.5
10          CONTINUE
        DENOM(1) = 'TWENTY DOLLAR BILLS'
        DENOM(2) = 'TEN DOLLAR BILLS'
        DENOM(3) = 'FIVE DOLLAR BILLS'
        DENOM(4) = 'ONE DOLLAR BILLS'
        DENOM(5) = 'FIFTY CENT PIECE'
        DENOM(6) = 'QUARTERS'
        DENOM(7) = 'DIMES'
        DENOM(8) = 'NICKLES'
        DENOM(9) = 'PENNIES'
    * READ PURCHASE AMOUNT AND AMOUNT GIVEN
20      READ (*, *, END = 90) PURCH, AMT
    * COMPUTE AND PRINT CHANGE
        PRINT *, 'PURCHASES $', PURCH
        PRINT *, 'AMOUNT GIVEN $', AMT
        CHANGE = AMT - PURCH
        IF (CHANGE .LT. 0) THEN
            PRINT *, 'THAT'S NOT ENOUGH'
            GO TO 20
        ELSE IF (CHANGE .EQ. 0) THEN
            PRINT *, 'THANK YOU'
            GO TO 20
        END IF
    * COMPUTE EXACT CHANGE IN PENNIES
        NCHANG = 100 *CHANGE + 0.5
        DO 30, I = 1, 9
            N = NCHANG / NPENNY(I)
            IF (N .GT. 0) THEN
                PRINT *, N, DENOM(I)
            END IF
            NCHANG = NCHANG - N *NPENNY(I)
30          CONTINUE
```

```
            GO  TO  20
      90    END


11.   * ROMAN  NUMERALS
            CHARACTER INPUT*20, ROMAN(7)
            INTEGER I, J, NUMBER, V(20), VALUE(7)
            ROMAN(1)  =  'M'
            VALUE(1)  =  1000
            ROMAN(2)  =  'D'
            VALUE(2)  =  500
            ROMAN(3)  =  'C'
            VALUE(3)  =  100
            ROMAN(4)  =  'L'
            VALUE(4)  =  50
            ROMAN(5)  =  'X'
            VALUE(5)  =  10
            ROMAN(6)  =  'V'
            VALUE(6)  =  5
            ROMAN(7)  =  'I'
            VALUE(7)  =  1
      * READ  ROMAN  NUMERAL
      10    READ (*, *, END = 90) INPUT
      * STORE CORRESPONDING VALUES IN ARRAY V
            DO 30, I = 1, 20
               DO 20, J = 1, 7
                  IF (INPUT(I:I) .EQ. ROMAN(J)) THEN
                     V(I)  =  VALUE(J)
                     GO TO 30
                     END IF
      20       CONTINUE
            V(I)  =  0
      30    CONTINUE
      * EVALUATE THE ROMAN NUMERAL
            NUMBER = 0
            DO 40, I = 1, 19
               IF (V(I) .LT. V(I + 1)) THEN
                  NUMBER = NUMBER - V(I)
               ELSE
                  NUMBER = NUMBER + V(I)
               END IF
      40    CONTINUE
      *
            PRINT *, INPUT, '=', NUMBER
            GO TO 10
      90    END


13.   * PETER  THE  POSTMAN
            LOGICAL OPEN(200)
            INTEGER I, J
```

```
              DO 10, I = 1, 200
                  OPEN(I) = .TRUE.
      10        CONTINUE
              DO 30, J = 2, 200
                  DO 20, I = 1, 200, J
                      OPEN(I) = .NOT. OPEN(I)
      20            CONTINUE
      30        CONTINUE
              DO 40, I = 1, 200
                  IF (OPEN(I)) PRINT *, I
      40        CONTINUE
              END


15.   * PRINT PRIME NUMBERS
              INTEGER MAXLEN
              PARAMETER (MAXLEN = 200)
              INTEGER P(MAXLEN), I, L, LENGTH, N
              REAL AN
              LENGTH = 1
              P(LENGTH) = 2
              N = 3
      10    IF (LENGTH .LT. MAXLEN) THEN
                  I = 1
                  AN = N
                  L = AN**0.5
      20        IF (P(I) .LE. L .AND. N .NE. (N/P(I)) *P(I)) THEN
                      I = I + 1
                      GO TO 20
                  END IF
                  IF (P(I) .GT. L) THEN
                      LENGTH = LENGTH + 1
                      P(LENGTH) = N
                  END IF
                  GO TO 10
              END IF
              PRINT *, (P(I), I = 1, MAXLEN)
              END


17.   * MORSE CODE
              CHARACTER LETTER(37)*1, MORSE(37)*5
              CHARACTER INPUT*80, OUTPUT*130
              INTEGER I, J, OUTPTR
      * READ EACH LETTER AND CORRESPONDING CODE
              DO 5, I = 1, 37
                  READ (*, '(A)', END = 90) INPUT
                  LETTER(I) = INPUT(1:1)
                  MORSE(I) = INPUT(3:7)
      5         CONTINUE
      * OUTPTR = POINTER TO POSITION IN OUTPUT LINE
```

```
                        OUTPTR = 1
          * READ A LINE
          10    READ(*, '(A)', END = 90) INPUT
          * FOR EACH CHARACTER, FIND THE CORRESPONDING
          * CODE AND PUT IT IN THE OUTPUT LINE
                DO 30, I = 1, 80
                    DO 20, J = 1, 36
                        IF (INPUT(I:I) .EQ. LETTER(J)) GO TO 25
          20          CONTINUE
          25       CONTINUE
                   IF (OUTPTR .GT. 75) THEN
                       PRINT *, OUTPUT
                       OUTPTR = 1
                   END IF
                   OUTPUT (OUTPTR:OUTPTR + 4) = MORSE(J)
                   OUTPTR = OUTPTR + 5
          30       CONTINUE
                GO TO 10
          90    IF (OUTPTR .GT. 1) PRINT *, OUTPUT
                END
```

19. * SOLUTION OF LINEAR EQUATIONS

```
                REAL A(2,2), B(2), X, Y, DET
          10    READ (*, *, END = 90) A(1, 1), A(1, 2), B(1),
               $    A(2, 1), A(2, 2), B(2)
                PRINT *, A(1, 1), '*X+', A(1, 2), '*Y=', B(1)
                PRINT *, A(2, 1), '*X+', A(2, 2), '*Y=', B(2)
                DET = A(1, 1) *A(2,2) - A(1, 2) *A(2, 1)
                IF (DET .EQ. 0) THEN
                    PRINT *, 'DOES NOT HAVE A UNIQUE SOLUTION'
                ELSE
                    X = (A(2, 2)*B(1) - A(1, 2)*B(2))/DET
                    Y = (A(1, 1)*B(2) - A(2, 1)*B(1))/DET
                    PRINT *, 'HAS SOLUTIONS:'
                    PRINT *, 'X=', X
                    PRINT *, 'Y=', Y
                END IF
                GO TO 10
          90    END
```

CHAPTER 7

1. (a) illegal (requires real argument)
   (b) legal
   (c) legal
   (d) illegal (requires one argument)
   (e) illegal (requires real argument)
   (f) illegal (requires one argument)

    (g)   illegal (arguments must be of same type)

    (h)   legal

3. (a)   X = MIN(A, B, C)

    (b)   N = INT(SQRT(A)) + 1

    (c)   X = A − INT(A)

    (d)   N = MOD(M, 2)

    (e)   X = SQRT(MAX(A, 0.0))

    (f)   N = MIN(MAX(LEN(C), 5), 20)

    (g)   PI = 4.0 *ATAN2(1.0, 1.0)

5. DMS(HR, MIN, SEC) = HR + MIN/60.0 + SEC/3600.0

7. SUBROUTINE ASA(SIDE A, SIDE B, SIDE C, ANGLE A, ANGLE B, ANGLE C)

```
      REAL PI, RAD
      PARAMETER (PI = 3.14159265)
      RAD(X) = PI*X/180.0

      ANGLE C = 180 − ANGLE A − ANGLE B
      SIDE A = SIDE C *SIN(RAD(ANGLE A))/SIN(RAD(ANGLE C))
      SIDE B = SIDE C *SIN(RAD(ANGLE B))/SIN(RAD(ANGLE C))
          END
```

9. * TEST PROGRAM

```
          INTEGER I, J, GCD
   10     READ (*, *, END = 20) I, J
          PRINT *, I, J, 'GCD =', GCD(I, J)
          GO TO 10
   20     END
    * EUCLID'S ALGORITHM
          INTEGER FUNCTION GCD (MM, NN)
          INTEGER M, N, MM, NN, R
          M = MM
          N = NN
   10     IF (N .NE. 0) THEN
              R = MOD(M, N)
              M = N
              N = R
              GO TO 10
          END IF
          GCD = M
          END
```

11. * RIGHT JUSTIFY A STRING IN N COLUMNS

```
          CHARACTER *(*) FUNCTION RJUST (STRING, N)
          CHARACTER *(*) STRING
          INTEGER L, N
          RJUST = ' '
          DO 10, L = LEN(STRING), 1, −1
              IF (STRING(L:L) .NE. ' ') GO TO 15
```

```
10        CONTINUE
15     CONTINUE
       RJUST (MAX(1, N - L + 1):) = STRING(:MAX(1, L))
       END


13.  * TEST PROGRAM
       INTEGER N, K, COMBIN
       DO 10, N = 0, 10
          DO 10, K = 0, N
10                PRINT *, N, K, COMBIN(N, K)
       END
     * COMBINATIONS OF N THINGS, K AT A TIME
       INTEGER FUNCTION COMBIN(N, K)
       INTEGER N, K, I, KK, TOP, BOT
       IF (N .LT 0 .OR. K .LT. 0 .OR. K .GT. N) THEN
          PRINT *, 'ERROR - COMBIN', N, K
          COMBIN = 1
          RETURN
       END IF
       KK = MAX(K, N - K)
       TOP = 1
       DO 10, I = N - KK + 1, N
          TOP = TOP *I
10        CONTINUE
       BOT = 1
       DO 20, I = 1, N - KK
          BOT = BOT*I
20        CONTINUE
       COMBIN = TOP/BOT
       END


15.        INTEGER N, NRAND, NHEAD, NTAIL, SEED
       SEED = 0
       N = 0
       NHEAD = 0
       NTAIL = 0
     * SIMULATE 1000 TOSSES, 1 = HEAD, 2 = TAIL
10     IF (N .LT. 1000) THEN
          N = N + 1
          IF (NRAND(1, 2, SEED) .EQ. 1) THEN
             N = N + 1
             IF (NRAND(1, 2, SEED) .EQ. 1) THEN
                N = N + 1
                IF (NRAND(1, 2, SEED) .EQ. 1) THEN
                   NHEAD = NHEAD + 1
                ELSE
                   NTAIL = NTAIL + 1
                END
             END IF
```

```
            END IF
              GO TO 10
          END IF
          PRINT *, 'H, H, H', NHEAD
          PRINT *, 'H, H, T', NTAIL
          END
```

17.
```
          SUBROUTINE RESET(BUFFER, LIMIT)
          INTEGER LIMIT, BUFFER(-2:LIMIT)
          BUFFER(0) = LIMIT
          BUFFER(-2) = 1
          BUFFER(-1) = 1
          END
```

19.
```
          INTEGER FUNCTION TAKE(BUFFER)
          INTEGER BUFFER(-2:*)
          IF (BUFFER(-1) .EQ. BUFFER(-2)) THEN
              PRINT *, 'ERROR IN TAKE — EMPTY BUFFER'
              STOP
          END IF
          TAKE = BUFFER(BUFFER(-2))
          BUFFER( 2) = BUFFER(-2) + 1
          IF (BUFFER(-2) .GT. BUFFER(0))
     $        BUFFER( 2) = 1
          END
```

CHAPTER 8

1. (a) column 2–5, 7–10
    (b) column 1–10, 21–30
    (c) column 6–10, 16–20, 21–30
    (d) column 21–26, 27–30, 41–45
    (e) column 1–2, 3–8, 12–17, 21–25
    (f) column 1–3, 4–5, 6–9, 10–19
    (g) column 16–20
    (h) column 31–40

3. (b represents a blank space)
    (a) b–123.45678
    (b) bbb–123.45678
    (c) bbbb–123.4568
    (d) bbbb–123.46
    (e) bb–123.
    (f) b**********
    (g) b*****

5. (b represents a blank space)
    (a) bb0.10000E1
    (b) b–0.12300E3
    (c) bb0.10000E3
    (d) bb0.12346E3
    (e) bb0.12300E1
    (f) b–0.5000E3

7.
```
          INTEGER N
          DO 10, N = 2, 99
              PRINT 20, N, SQRT(REAL(N))
   10         CONTINUE
   20     FORMAT(10X, 'THE SQUARE ROOT OF', I3,
     $        1X, 'IS', F9.6)
          END
```

9. (a) I = 12300
          X = 45600.0
          Y = −7890.0
    (b) I = 123
          X = 456.0
          Y = −789.0
    (c) I = 123000
          X = 456.0
          Y = −789.0
    (d) X = 123.0
          Y = 456.0
          Z = −7890.0

    (e) X = 0.0123
          Y = 0.456
          Z = −789.0
    (f) X = 123.0
          Y = 0.456
          Z = −7890.0
    (g) X = 1230000.456
          I = −78
    (h) X = 123.456
          I = −78

11. FORMAT(11X, I6, 6X, A20, 4X, F7.2, 3X, I5, 7X, F8.2)

13. FORMAT(3I2, 1X, A20, 2X, F7.3, F6.3, F8.2, I4)

15.
```
        SUBROUTINE HISTO(LABELS, COUNT, N)
        CHARACTER LABELS (*)*(*)
        REAL COUNT(*), SUM, PCT
        INTEGER I, J, N
        SUM = 0.0
        DO 10, I = 1, N
            SUM = SUM + COUNT(I)
10      CONTINUE
        DO 20, I = 1, N
            PCT = 100 *COUNT(I)/SUM
            PRINT 30, LABELS(I), PCT, ('*', J = 1, NINT(PCT))
20      CONTINUE
        RETURN
30      FORMAT('0', T5, A, 5X, F5.1, 2X, 'PERCENT',
     $      5X, 100A)
        END
```

17.
```
        SUBROUTINE BOX(LINE, N)
        INTEGER I, J, L, N
        CHARACTER STAR, SPACE, LINE(N)*(*)
        PARAMETER (STAR = '*', SPACE = ' ')
        L = LEN(LINE(1))
        PRINT 100
        PRINT 101, (STAR, J = 1, L + 22)
        PRINT 101, STAR, (SPACE, J = 1, L + 20), STAR
        DO 10, I = 1, N
            PRINT 102, STAR, LINE(I), STAR
10      CONTINUE
        PRINT 101, STAR, (SPACE, J = 1, L + 20), STAR
        PRINT 101, (STAR, J = 1, L + 22)
        RETURN
100     FORMAT ('1', 10(/))
101     FORMAT (T11, 120A1)
102     FORMAT (T11, A1, 10X, A, 10X, A1)
        END
```

19.
```
         SUBROUTINE GETCMD( NCMD, NOUN, CVERB, NVERB)
         INTEGER I, J, NCMD, NVERB
         CHARACTER*(*) NOUN, CVERB(NVERB), CLINE*80, SPACE
         PARAMETER (SPACE = ' ')
*  READ A COMMAND
10       PRINT 15
15       FORMAT(1X, 'COMMAND—')
20       READ (*, 25, END = 90) CLINE
25       FORMAT(A)
*  FIND FIRST SPACE
         CLINE(80:80) = SPACE
         I = 1
30       IF (CLINE(I:I) .NE. SPACE) THEN
             I = I + 1
             GO TO 30
         END IF
         I = MIN(1, I − 1)
*  FIND COMMAND IN LIST
         DO 40, NCMD = 1, NVERB
             IF (CLINE(1:I) .EQ. CVERB(NCMD)) GO TO 50
40           CONTINUE
         PRINT 45
45       FORMAT(1X, 'WHAT?')
         GO TO 10
*  FIND THE NOUN
50       IF (CLINE(I:I) .EQ. SPACE .AND. I .LT. 80) THEN
             I = I + 1
             GO TO 50
         END IF
         J = I
60       IF (CLINE(J:J) .NE. SPACE) THEN
             J = J + 1
             GO TO 60
         END IF
         J = MIN(I:J − 1)
         NOUN = CLINE(I:J)
         END


21.  *  CHECKBOOK PROGRAM
         INTEGER MO, DA, YR
         REAL AMT, BAL
         CHARACTER CODE*3
         READ(*, 100, END = 90) MO, DA, YR, CODE, AMT
         IF (CODE .NE. 'BAL') THEN
             PRINT 105, 'FIRST INPUT MUST BE BALANCE'
             STOP
         END IF
         BAL = AMT
         PRINT 110, BAL
10       READ(*, 100, END = 90) MO, DA, YR, CODE, AMT
         IF (CODE .EQ. 'CHE') THEN
```

```
                    BAL = BAL − AMT
                    PRINT 115, 'CHECK', AMT, BAL
                 ELSE IF (CODE .EQ. 'DEP') THEN
                    BAL = BAL + AMT
                    PRINT 115, 'DEPOSIT', AMT, BAL
                 ELSE IF (CODE .EQ. 'SER') THEN
                    BAL = BAL − AMT
                    PRINT 115, 'SVC CHG', AMT, BAL
                 ELSE
                    PRINT 105, 'ILLEGAL CODE' // CODE // 'LINE IGNORED'
                 END IF
                 GO TO 10
        90    STOP
       100    FORMAT (3(I2, 1X), A3, 1X, F7.2)
       105    FORMAT (1X, A)
       110    FORMAT ('1', 'PREVIOUS ACCOUNT BALANCE', T35, '$', F7.2)
       115    FORMAT (1X, A10, 1X, '$', F7.2, T25, 'BALANCE', T35,
          $       '$', F7.2)
              END
```

23. *Hint:* Read the input data into arrays. Create an array of sort keys where the key for each input card is equal to 10000 ∗YR + 100 ∗MO + DA, where YR, MO, and DA are the parts of the date. Sort this array of sort keys using pointers, as in Example 6.7, then process the data in the arrays as in Exercise 21.

25. *Hint:* This is an exercise in program design. It will help you to discover some of the practical considerations involved in making a program usable. Discuss your proposed design with a classmate or teacher before writing the program.

CHAPTER 9

```
   1.  * FILE COPY PROGRAM WITH 'INCLUDE' FEATURE.
       * COPY INPUT FILE TO OUTPUT FILE.
       * IF ANY LINE IN THE INPUT FILE BEGINS WITH
       *    '*INCLUDE'
       * IN COLUMNS 1–8, THEN COLUMNS 10–LINSIZ OF THE
       * LINE ARE A FILE NAME OF A FILE WHICH
       * WILL BE INCLUDED IN THE OUTPUT FILE AT
       * THAT POINT.
       * AN INCLUDED FILE MAY CONTAIN AN INCLUDE
       * DIRECTIVE. THE MAXIMUM LEVEL OF INCLUSION IS
       * NFILES.
              INTEGER NFILES, LINSIZ
              PARAMETER (NFILES = 4, LINSIZ = 100)
              INTEGER INPUT, OUTPUT, STATUS
              CHARACTER LINE*(LINSIZ)
              INPUT = 1
              OUTPUT = NFILES + 1
              CALL OPENIO(INPUT, OUTPUT)
        10    READ (INPUT, '(A)', IOSTAT = STATUS) LINE
```

```
            IF (STATUS .LT. 0) THEN
                WRITE (*, *) 'ERROR READING FILE'
                STOP
            ELSE IF (STATUS .GT. 0) THEN
                CLOSE (INPUT)
                INPUT = INPUT - 1
                IF (INPUT .GT. 0) GO TO 10
                CLOSE (OUTPUT)
                STOP
            END IF
            IF (INPUT(:8) .EQ. '*INCLUDE') THEN
                INPUT = INPUT + 1
                IF (INPUT .GT. NFILES) THEN
                    WRITE (*, *) 'TOO MANY INCLUSION LEVELS'
                    STOP
                END IF
                OPEN (UNIT = INPUT, FILE = LINE(10:),
     $              STATUS = 'OLD', IOSTAT = STATUS)
                IF (STATUS .NE. 0) THEN
                    WRITE (*, *) 'COULD NOT OPEN FILE' // LINE(10:)
                    STOP
                END IF
                GO TO 10
            END IF
            WRITE (OUTPUT, '(A)') LINE
            GO TO 10
            END

    3.  * LIST FORTRAN PROGRAM.
        * LINEPP = MAX NO. OF LINES PER PAGE
        * LINENO = LINE NUMBER
        * PAGENO = PAGE NUMBER
        * TITLE = TITLE LINE
        * INPUT = INPUT UNIT, OUTPUT = OUTPUT UNIT
            INTEGER LINEPP, INPUT, OUTPUT
            PARAMETER (LINEPP = 55, INPUT = 1, OUTPUT = 2)
            INTEGER LINENO, PAGENO
            CHARACTER LINE*80, TITLE*72
            LINENO = 0
            PAGENO = 0
            TITLE = ' '
            CALL OPENIO (INPUT, OUTPUT)
    10      READ (INPUT, 1000, END = 100) LINE
        * IS THIS A FUNCTION OR SUBROUTINE STATEMENT:
            IF (LINE(1:1) .NE. 'C' .AND. LINE(1:1) .NE. '*'
     $          .AND. (INDEX(LINE, 'FUNCTION') .GT. 0 .OR.
     $              INDEX(LINE, 'SUBROUTINE') .GT. 0)) THEN
                TITLE = LINE
                LINENO = 0
            END IF
```

```
      * IS A NEW PAGE NEEDED:
            IF (MOD(LINENO, LPP) .EQ. 0) THEN
                  PAGENO = PAGENO + 1
                  WRITE (OUTPUT, 1000) TITLE, PAGENO
            END IF
      * WRITE THE OUTPUT LINE
            LINENO = LINENO + 1
            WRITE (OUTPUT, 1005) LINENO, LINE(1:72), LINE(73:)
            GO TO 10
1000  FORMAT ('1', 5X, A, 5X, 'PAGE', I3//)
1005  FORMAT (11X, I5, 5X, A, 5X, A)
100   END
```

5.
```
      * CONVERT DATE FROM FORM DD MMM YY TO FORM MM/DD/YY
            CHARACTER*(8) FUNCTION MODAYR(DATE)
            CHARACTER DATE*9
            CHARACTER MONTHS(12)*3, MO*3
            INTEGER DA,YR, I
            MONTHS(1) = 'JAN'
            MONTHS(2) = 'FEB'
            MONTHS(3) = 'MAR'
            MONTHS(4) = 'APR'
            MONTHS(5) = 'MAY'
            MONTHS(6) = 'JUN'
            MONTHS(7) = 'JUL'
            MONTHS(8) = 'AUG'
            MONTHS(9) = 'SEP'
            MONTHS(10) = 'OCT'
            MONTHS(11) = 'NOV'
            MONTHS(12) = 'DEC'
      * DATE MUST BE IN THE FORM DD MMM YY, WHERE
      * DD AND YY ARE 2-CHARACTER FIELDS
            READ (DATE, 10) DA, MO, YR
10          FORMAT (BN, I2, 1X, A3, 1X, I2)
            DO 20, I = 1, 12
                  IF (MO .EQ. MONTHS(I)) GO TO 25
20          CONTINUE
            I = 0
25          CONTINUE
            WRITE (MODAYR, 30) I, DA, YR
30          FORMAT (I2, '/', I2, '/', I2)
            END
```

7.
```
      * PASCAL'S TRIANGLE
      * MAXN = MAXIMUM VALUE OF N.
      * FSIZE = FIELD SIZE.
            INTEGER I, N, MAXN, FSIZE
            PARAMETER (MAXN = 7, FSIZE = 6)
            INTEGER P(0:MAXN)
```

```
              CHARACTER FMT*50
              FMT = ' '
              DO 5, I = 1, MAXN
                  P(I) = 0
    5         CONTINUE
              P(0) = 1
              DO 20, N = 0, MAXN
                  DO 10, I = N, 1 −1
                      P(I) = P(I) + P(I − 1)
    10            CONTINUE
                  WRITE (FMT, 15) FSIZE/2*(MAXN − N), N + 1, FSIZE
    15        FORMAT ('(T10, ', I3, 'X,', I3, 'I', I3, ')')
                  WRITE (*, FMT) (P(I), = 0, N)
    20        CONTINUE
              END


 9.  * PRINT INDIVIDUAL WORDS FROM A FORTRAN PROGRAM
              INTEGER I, J, INPUT, OUTPUT
              CHARACTER LINE *73
              LOGICAL SPCHAR
              INPUT = 1
              OUTPUT = 2
              CALL OPENIO(INPUT, OUTPUT)
    10    READ (INPUT, 15, END = 90) LINE
    15    FORMAT (A)
              LINE(73:) = ' '
              I = 1
        * SKIP OVER ANY BLANKS OR SPECIAL CHARACTERS
    20    IF (I .LE. 72 .AND. SPCHAR(LINE(I:I))) THEN
                      I = I + 1
                      GO TO 20
              END IF
              IF (I .LE. 72) THEN
    *             SKIP TO NEXT BLANK OR SPECIAL CHARACTER
                      J = I
    30            IF (.NOT. SPCHAR(LINE(J:J))) THEN
                          J = J + 1
                          GO TO 30
                      END IF
    *             WRITE THIS WORD
                      WRITE (OUTPUT, 15) LINE(I:J − 1)
                      I = J
                      GO TO 20
              END IF
    90    END
              LOGICAL FUNCTION SPCHAR(X)
        * FALSE IF X IS AN ALPHANUMERIC CHARACTER,
        * TRUE OTHERWISE
              CHARACTER ALPHA*(*), X*1
```

```
PARAMETER(ALPHA = 'ABCDEFGHIJKLMNOPQRSTUVWXYZ012345689')
IF (INDEX(ALPHA, X) .EQ. 0) THEN
    SPCHAR = .TRUE.
ELSE
    SPCHAR = .FALSE.
END IF
END
```

11. *Hint*: Follow the general organization of Example 6.4, but use the input and output techniques illustrated in Example 9.2.
13. *Hint*: This program can be written by combining the techniques from Exercise 2 and Exercise 11.

CHAPTER 10

1.
```
        INTEGER I, J
        COMPLEX W(4)
        W(1) = (1.0, 1.0)
        W(2) = (-1.0, 1.0)
        W(3) = (-1.0, -1.0)
        W(4) = (1.0, -1.0)
        PRINT 20, (W(J), J = 1,4)
        DO 10, I = 1, 4
            PRINT 30, W(I), (W(I)*W(J), J = 1, 4)
10          CONTINUE
20      FORMAT (T20, 4(F3.0, '+', F3.0, '*I', 5X)//)
30      FORMAT (T10, F3.0, '+', F3.0, '*I'),
    $       T20, 4(F3.0, '+', F3.0, '*I', 5X)//)
        END
```

3.
```
    * COMPUTE THE NTH ROOTS OF UNITY.
        REAL TWOPI
        PARAMETER (TWOPI = 2 *3.14159265)
        INTEGER K, N
        COMPLEX Z, SUM, PROD
        READ *, N
        SUM = 0
        PROD = 0
        DO 10, K = 0, N - 1
            Z = CMPLX(COS(TWOPI*K/N), SIN(TWOPI*K/N))
            PRINT *, Z
            SUM = SUM + Z
            PROD = PROD *Z
10          CONTINUE
        PRINT *, 'SUM=', SUM
        PRINT *, 'PRODUCT = ', PROD
        END
```

5. *Hint*: Assume that both operands are written as complex constants. The first operand consists of everything from the first left parenthesis to the first right parenthesis. Read from this substring into a complex variable.

```
7.        REAL RAD, DEG, MIN, SEC, PI
          PARAMETER (PI = 3.14159265)
          RAD(DEG, MIN, SEC) = PI/180*(DEG + MIN/60 + SEC/3600)


9.        SUBROUTINE QSOLV(A, B, C, X1, X2)
          COMPLEX A, B, C, X1, X2
          IF (A .EQ. 0) THEN
              IF (B .EQ. 0) THEN
                  IF (C .EQ. 0) THEN
*                     TRIVIAL CASE
                      X1 = 0
                      X2 = 0
                  ELSE
*                     IMPOSSIBLE CASE
                      X1 = 0
                      X2 = 0
                  END IF
              ELSE
*                 LINEAR CASE
                  X1 = -C/B
                  X2 = X1
              END IF
              X1 = (-B + SQRT(B**2 - 4*A*C))/(2*A)
              X2 = CONJG(X1)
          END IF
          END


11.       INTEGER FUNCTION NFACT(N)
*  NFACT(N) - FACTORIAL OF N
          INTEGER N, LIM, I
          PARAMETER (LIM = 10)
          INTEGER NF(0:LIM)
          LOGICAL FIRST
          SAVE NF, FIRST
          DATA FIRST / .TRUE. /
          IF (FIRST) THEN
              NF(0) = 1
              DO 5, I = 1, LIM
                  NF(I) = I*NF(I-1)
5             CONTINUE
              FIRST = .FALSE.
          END IF
```

(Other statements are the same as in Example 10.4.)

13.
```
* GET NEXT CHARACTER FROM INPUT.
* AT END OF LINE, TAKE FIRST RETURN.
* AT END OF FILE, TAKE SECOND RETURN
      SUBROUTINE NEXTC(CHAR, *, *)
      INTEGER PTR, LINSIZ
      PARAMETER (LINSIZ = 80)
      CHARACTER LINE *(LINSIZ), CHAR
      SAVE LINE, PTR
      DATA PTR / 0 /
*
      IF (PTR .EQ. 0) THEN
          READ (*, '(A)', END = 90) LINE
      END IF
      PTR = PTR + 1
      IF (PTR .GT. LINSIZ) THEN
          PTR = 0
          RETURN 1
      END IF
      CHAR = LINE(PTR:PTR)
      RETURN
90    RETURN 2
      END
```

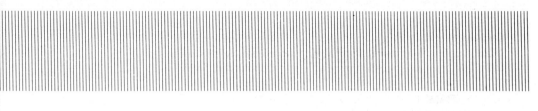

INDEX